D1617050

# General He Yingqin

A revisionist study of the career of General He Yingqin, one of the most prominent military officers in China's Nationalist period (1928–49), and one of the most misunderstood figures in twentieth-century China. Western scholars have dismissed He Yingqin as corrupt and incompetent, yet the Chinese archives reveal that he demonstrated considerable success as a combat commander and military administrator during civil conflicts and the Sino-Japanese War. His work in the Chinese Nationalist military served as the foundation of a close personal and professional relationship with Chiang Kai-shek that lasted for more than two decades. Against the backdrop of the Nationalist revolution of the 1920s through the 1940s, Peter Worthing analyzes He Yingqin's rise to power alongside Chiang Kai-shek, his work in building the Nationalist military, and his fundamental role in carrying out policies designed to overcome the regime's greatest obstacles during this turbulent period of Chinese history.

PETER WORTHING is Associate Professor of History at Texas Christian University. He is the author of *Occupation and Revolution: China and the Vietnamese August Revolution of 1945* and *A Military History of Modern China: From the Qing Conquest to Tian'anmen Square*.

# General He Yingqin

*The Rise and Fall of Nationalist China*

Peter Worthing

*Texas Christian University*

# CAMBRIDGE
## UNIVERSITY PRESS

University Printing House, Cambridge CB2 8BS, United Kingdom

Cambridge University Press is part of the University of Cambridge.

It furthers the University's mission by disseminating knowledge in the pursuit of education, learning and research at the highest international levels of excellence.

www.cambridge.org
Information on this title: www.cambridge.org/9781107144637

© Peter Worthing 2016

First published 2016

Printed in the United States of America by Sheridan Books, Inc.

*A catalogue record for this publication is available from the British Library*

*Library of Congress Cataloguing in Publication data*

ISBN 978-1-107-14463-7 Hardback
ISBN 978-1-316-50781-0 Paperback

# Contents

# Maps

(All maps created by Carol Zuber-Mallison of ZM Graphics, Inc.)

# Acknowledgments

This book is the result of more than ten years of research on He Yingqin and Nationalist China. Like all authors of such works, I have accumulated a number of debts to those who have helped along the way. At my home institution, Texas Christian University, I am grateful to my colleagues in the department of history who supported this project. Alan Gallay in particular provided valuable feedback and sound advice. Andy Schoolmaster, Dean of the AddRan College of Liberal Arts, supported this project in a number of ways. Beyond providing additional resources for research trips and a mid-career research grant, he arranged for me to take a one-semester sabbatical despite the fact that I was serving as department chair at the time. Jill Kendle, Kay Edmondson, and Clare Taylor of the interlibrary loan department of the Mary Coutts Burnett Library at TCU assisted with a steady stream of materials from libraries across the country. Without their help, I could not have completed this project. I would also like to acknowledge the help of two graduate students in our department, Jessica Webb and Shawn Devaney, who provided research support. Harold Tanner of the University of North Texas and Parks Coble of the University of Nebraska read portions of the manuscript and offered important suggestions and corrections. At Cambridge University Press, I must acknowledge the help of Asian studies editor Lucy Rhymer and two anonymous readers, who also made suggestions for strengthening the manuscript. Karen Anderson Howes provided first-rate copy-editing, improving the prose and saving me from a number of missteps.

I have benefited from institutional support from the Research and Creative Activities Fund at TCU, which funded early research trips to archives and libraries. In the United States, I am indebted to Hsiao-t'ing Lin, Curator of the East Asia Collection at the Hoover Institution, Stanford University, Xue Zhaohui and the staff of the Stanford East Asia Library, and Vicky Fu Doll, Chinese and Korean Studies Librarian at the University of Kansas Library. In Taipei, I relied on the help of director Lu Fangshang and the staff of the Guoshiguan (Academia Historica) and the staff of the Taiwan National Library. In the People's Republic of China, the staff of the Second Historical Archives in Nanjing provided help in locating materials.

I would be remiss if I did not acknowledge my friends and teammates on the Whalers Hockey Club, especially Vance Carter, who never tired of asking, "Hey, Professor, is the book done yet?" In the end, it is perhaps the people closest to us who provide the most important sources of support and inspiration during long periods of research and writing. My deepest gratitude and thanks go to my wife Mona Narain and daughter Tanushri. They made it all possible.

# Introduction

On October 22, 1987, the *New York Times* published a lengthy obituary of Chinese Nationalist general He Yingqin, who had passed away at the age of ninety-seven in Taipei, Taiwan. The article reviewed He Yingqin's long career as a prominent military officer under Nationalist leader Chiang Kai-shek, but did so with a curiously negative tone. It noted that he served as "minister of war" for fourteen years, but emphasized that he "was removed from the post, reportedly under strong urging of the United States Government." It pointed to his "sharp rivalry with Maj. Gen. Joseph Stilwell" and referred to General George C. Marshall's criticism of He Yingqin for adopting a "wait and watch" policy during the Pacific War. It then described He Yingqin as one of a number of Chinese generals who "fled mainland China for Taiwan in 1949 with Chiang Kai-shek after losing the civil war to the Communists."[1] Readers of the *New York Times* no doubt concluded from this rather unflattering summation that He Yingqin had amassed a dismal record as a soldier and administrator. One should not blame the author of the obituary, Edward Hudson, for its overall negative tone. As he prepared to write, he no doubt did some research in English-language popular and scholarly writings on Nationalist China and drew upon what he found, almost all of it critical of He Yingqin.

The obituary reflects a widely accepted yet fundamental misreading of He Yingqin's career and role in the Nationalist period of modern Chinese history. This book argues that He Yingqin had the best military education and training available in his day, spent decades working effectively at the highest levels of the Nationalist military and government, and played a central role in implementing policies designed to achieve the regime's most important objectives. From humble beginnings in southwestern China, He Yingqin rose to become one of the most important figures in the Nationalist military and a virtual right-hand man to

---

[1] "Gen. Ho Ying-chin Dies at 97; A Nationalist Chinese Leader," *New York Times*, October 22, 1987.

1

Chiang Kai-shek. Against the backdrop of the Nationalist revolution and state-building efforts of the 1920s through the 1940s, this book analyzes He Yingqin's rise to power alongside Chiang Kai-shek, his work as the top administrator of the Nationalist military, and his efforts to overcome the greatest challenges of the period. In doing so, it contributes to a more comprehensive and accurate understanding of one of the leading figures in the history of China during the twentieth century, as well as a general reassessment of the Nationalist government and military as a whole.

I first became interested in He Yingqin when working on another project that dealt with the Chinese Nationalist army in Vietnam at the end of the Pacific War.[2] His name popped up occasionally in the course of my research, since he served at the highest levels of the Nationalist military, but he did not occupy a prominent place in the resulting narrative. At one point, I came across an event in which He Yingqin played an important role in supporting the commanders of the Chinese occupation force in dealing with a difficult problem. His actions seemed to me quite rational and appropriate, and yet they ran counter to Nationalist government policy at the time. It then occurred to me that this man, who had such a strong influence on this particular issue, must have played important roles in other major issues of the Nationalist army and government. I therefore decided to take a closer look at him and his career.

Beginning with a review of the secondary sources in English, I examined the works of historians and journalists who wrote about the Nationalist period, the Sino-Japanese War, and the Chinese Civil War in search of information about He Yingqin. I quickly drew two conclusions about this body of literature. First, Western writers have paid little attention to He Yingqin and devoted precious few words to him in their works. Checking the indices of most books revealed no reference to him, or at best a few page numbers on which his name appeared in passing references. Western scholars of Nationalist China have made no serious attempt to understand his role in this period. Second, those writing in English who described him in any detail tended toward negative characterizations, typically describing him as incompetent and corrupt. These works, written between the 1940s and 1980s, set the parameters for most Western assessments of the Chinese Nationalist regime in general and He Yingqin in particular. For example, Theodore White and Annalee Jacoby's 1946 book *Thunder out of China* described He Yingqin as "responsible, more

---

[2] Peter Worthing, *Occupation and Revolution: China and the Vietnamese August Revolution of 1945* (Berkeley: University of California at Berkeley Center for Chinese Studies, 2001).

than any other man except Chiang Kai-shek, for the incompetent
direction and gradual rotting away of the Chinese armies in the field."[3]
In her Pulitzer Prize-winning book *Stilwell and the American Experience
in China*, Barbara Tuchman drew heavily on Joseph Stilwell's diaries and
attributed the "debility of the Chinese Army" largely to He Yingqin's
mismanagement.[4] Owen Lattimore, who served as personal advisor to
Chiang Kai-shek for several months in 1941–42, described He Yingqin
as "treacherous" and interested only in "building his personal power."[5]
Academic historians have likewise taken a dim view of He Yingqin's
career accomplishments. Lloyd Eastman, a prominent scholar of China's
Republican period, sometimes gently characterized him as "pompous
and modestly endowed"[6] while at other times pulling no punches in
declaring him "incompetent."[7] Moreover, there seemed to be no con-
sensus regarding He Yingqin's relationship to Chiang Kai-shek and the
Nationalist regime. Some described him as one of Chiang's most trusted
subordinates while others suggested that Chiang had a deep distrust
of He.[8] Some writers have repeated the accusation by Song Meiling
(Madame Chiang Kai-shek) that He Yingqin pushed for military action
during the 1936 Xi'an Incident, hoping that Chiang would die in the
fighting so He could take his place.[9] While many of these works are
dated, they continue to influence Western writing on He Yingqin's role
in the Nationalist regime to the present day, perpetuating these broadly
negative views. In his 2003 biography of Chiang Kai-shek, Jonathan
Fenby described He Yingqin as a "master of manipulation," and claimed
that He and his associates "made fortunes for themselves from their
positions," and that he "did all he could to block army reform."[10] In
her 2009 biography of Song Meiling, Hannah Pakula called He Yingqin

---

[3]  Theodore White and Annalee Jacoby, *Thunder out of China* (New York: William Sloane
     Associates, 1946), 105.
[4]  Barbara Tuchman, *Stilwell and the American Experience in China, 1911–1945* (New York:
     Macmillan, 1971), 483.
[5]  Owen Lattimore, *China Memoirs: Chiang Kai-shek and the War Against Japan*, compiled
     by Fujiko Isono (Tokyo: University of Tokyo Press, 1990), 115.
[6]  Lloyd Eastman, "Nationalist China During the Sino-Japanese War 1937–1945," in John
     K. Fairbank and Albert Feuerwerker, eds., *The Cambridge History of China*, vol. XIII,
     Republican China 1912–1949, Part 2 (Cambridge: Cambridge University Press, 1986),
     571.
[7]  Lloyd Eastman, *Seeds of Destruction: Nationalist China in War and Revolution, 1937–1949*
     (Stanford: Stanford University Press, 1984), 143.
[8]  See O. Edmund Clubb, *Twentieth-Century China*, 2nd edn. (New York: Columbia Uni-
     versity Press, 1972), 208.
[9]  Jay Taylor, *The Generalissimo: Chiang Kai-shek and the Struggle for Modern China* (Cam-
     bridge, MA: Harvard University Press, 2009), 130.
[10] Jonathan Fenby, *Generalissimo: Chiang Kai-shek and the China He Lost*
     (London: Free Press, 2003), 345–46.

"the personification of corruption."[11] With a clear reference to White and Jacoby's initial assessment of He more than six decades earlier, in 2011 Frank McLynn described him as "the man most responsible for the corruption and disarray in the Chinese army."[12] Indeed, whereas White and Jacoby placed He Yingqin second to Chiang Kai-shek in terms of his deleterious effect on the Nationalist army, sixty years later McLynn elevated him to the top position.

Clearly, the message one would inevitably take away from the existing English-language writing on He Yingqin is that he was at best of little consequence during the Nationalist period and at worst incompetent and of questionable loyalty to Chiang and the regime. It is no great stretch to suggest that, in this light, He Yingqin represents the problems that many believed caused the failure of the Nationalist regime on the mainland: incompetent leadership and widespread corruption. After reading these accounts, I asked myself how someone of such modest ability, even downright incompetence, managed to rise to the highest levels of the Nationalist military and remain there for decades. Moreover, the descriptions I read in the secondary English-language sources seemed to contradict my earlier research in which He Yingqin's actions with regard to the Nationalist occupation of Vietnam appeared appropriate and well thought out. As a result, I resolved to undertake a critical study of his career.

There were other reasons why I found He Yingqin intriguing. His entry in Howard Boorman's *Biographical Dictionary of Republican China* reveals that He had an impressive array of professional experiences and had been directly involved in many of the most important events in China in the first half of the twentieth century.[13] He attended new military schools established as a part of the late Qing reforms to China's educational and military systems, studied abroad in Japan, fought in the 1911 Revolution, participated in May Fourth-era activities in his home province, served as an instructor and administrator at the Whampoa Military Academy, commanded troops during the Northern Expedition, directed the early encirclement campaigns against the Chinese Communist Party's (CCP) Jiangxi Soviet, negotiated with the Japanese military in north China during the 1930s, commanded military forces attempting to rescue Chiang Kai-shek during the 1936 Xi'an Incident, served as minister of military

[11] Hannah Pakula, *The Last Empress: Madame Chiang Kai-shek and the Birth of Modern China* (New York: Simon & Schuster, 2009), 813.
[12] Frank McLynn, *The Burma Campaign: Disaster into Triumph, 1942–1945* (New Haven: Yale University Press, 2011), 168.
[13] Howard L. Boorman, *Biographical Dictionary of Republican China*, 3 vols. (New York: Columbia University Press, 1967–71), vol. I, 79–84.

administration, chief of staff to Chiang Kai-shek, and then commander of the Chinese army in the Sino-Japanese War, represented China as head of a military delegation to the United States and to the United Nations Military Staff Committee in 1946, returned to China in 1948 to serve as minister of national defense and premier, and then withdrew to Taiwan with Chiang and others in 1949. In short, He Yingqin's career followed the rise and fall of the Nationalist regime, and he had a front-row seat to the most important military and political events of the period. This makes him an excellent focal point for a study of the Nationalist military.

This book contributes to a body of scholarship that since the 1990s has shed new light on the Nationalists and Chiang Kai-shek. One of the most important works of this type is Hans van de Ven's *War and Nationalism in China, 1920–1945*, in which he argues that scholars must move beyond superficial assessments of Nationalist officials as inept and restore "rationality" to the people and policies of Nationalist China, especially with regard to the Sino-Japanese War.[14] With this in mind, this book addresses a series of questions designed to reassess He Yingqin's role in building and directing the Nationalist military. For example, are the existing English-language assessments of He accurate? Was he incompetent or corrupt? How did he rise to the highest ranks of the Chinese military and government? What was his record as a combat commander? As a military administrator? What was the nature of He Yingqin's relationship with Chiang Kai-shek? Did he aspire to replace Chiang as the dominant military and political figure in China? What does this mean for our understanding of the Nationalist government and military, in a defining period of modern Chinese history?

Fortunately, there are sufficient primary sources available to make a study of He Yingqin's career possible. In 1984 Taiwan's Ministry of National Defense (*guofangbu*) published a multivolume series of documentation, commemorating He Yingqin's ninety-fifth birthday. A team of researchers drew upon scattered materials at the ministry's archives to produce these volumes, which cover various aspects of his career. The centerpiece of this series is the two-volume *He Yingqin jiangjun jiuwu jishi changbian* (A Record of General He Yingqin's Ninety-Five Years), which amounts to a chronological record of his career. The series includes other volumes with detailed records of specific aspects of He Yingqin's career, such as his work as commander of the Eastern Route Army during the Northern Expedition (*donglujun beifa zuozhan jishi*) and his service as chair of the Beiping Branch of the Military Affairs Commission

[14] Hans van de Ven, *War and Nationalism in China, 1925–1945* (London: RoutledgeCurzon, 2003), 249.

(*Beiping junfenhui sannian*). Additional materials published under the auspices of the Ministry of National Defense provide information on his time as minister of military administration (*junzheng shiwu nian*). These sources reproduce texts of telegrams, speeches, committee and conference reports, and policies, all of which provide important insights into He Yingqin's life and career with supporting documentation. Other important sources include published collections of speeches, radio broadcasts, and newspaper opinion pieces that He Yingqin gave or penned over the course of his career. After 1928 he emerged as something of a spokesperson for the Nationalist military, giving numerous speeches and reports, which reveal his views on important issues. He left no diary or memoir, so it is difficult to ascertain his personal views, but through an examination of his public remarks one can gain a sense of what he valued and believed that China needed.

There are also many memoirs, reminiscences, and autobiographies of others who knew He Yingqin that include references to him and his work. Some have appeared as books while others are shorter pieces published in the *Wenshi ziliao* series in the People's Republic of China (PRC) or in popular periodicals in Taiwan, but collectively they offer glimpses into He Yingqin's life, career, and relationships with others. Scholars in both the PRC and Taiwan have produced secondary works about him, including a couple of book-length biographies, academic journal articles on specific aspects of his career, and shorter pieces in more general historical publications. These Chinese-language sources yield a picture of He Yingqin that differs significantly from that presented in the works of Western writers.

Using these Chinese-language source materials, this book makes three novel arguments relating to He Yingqin and the history of China's Nationalist military. First, it provides a corrective to the traditional negative characterizations of He Yingqin that have informed the English-language narratives. Hans van de Ven has attributed the tendency to describe Nationalist military officers in wholly negative terms to the influence of prominent critics of the Chinese war effort against the Japanese, such as Americans General Joseph Stilwell and journalist Theodore White. This "Stilwell–White paradigm," as van de Ven calls it, has profoundly influenced Western interpretations of Nationalist China and impeded accurate assessments of the Nationalist regime and its officials.[15] This book moves beyond this paradigm, utilizing

---

[15]  Van de Ven, *War and Nationalism*, 6–8; Mark Peattie, Edward J. Drea, and Hans van de Ven, eds., *The Battle for China: Essays on the Military History of the Sino-Japanese War of 1937–1945* (Stanford: Stanford University Press, 2011), 448–52.

Chinese-language source materials to challenge existing interpretations and shed new light on several important aspects of He Yingqin's career. This approach offers a more balanced and comprehensive evaluation of He Yingqin's work within the Nationalist military. For example, far from being incompetent, He Yingqin had an impressive record as a combat commander in the late 1920s. Rather than allow the Chinese armies to "rot in the field" during the Sino-Japanese War as some have claimed, as minister of military administration he devoted great effort to improving the conscription system in order to provide sufficient soldiers for frontline units. While most American officials regarded He Yingqin as a die-hard reactionary, during the Chinese Civil War he proposed progressive economic reforms as the most effective way to counter the appeal of the Chinese communists.

Second, it demonstrates that He Yingqin played a central role in building the Nationalist military and supporting Chiang Kai-shek's attempts to extend the authority of the Nanjing government. He Yingqin presided over instruction at the Whampoa Military Academy, commanded Chiang's best forces in the Eastern and Northern Expeditions, coerced regional militarists into cooperating with Chiang, negotiated unpopular but, from his perspective, necessary agreements with the Japanese military in north China, and coordinated military supplies, conscription, and training during the war against Japan. He Yingqin's work on these critical issues played a significant role in determining the major successes and failures of the Nationalist regime from the 1920s through the 1940s.

Third, it argues that He Yingqin and Chiang Kai-shek shared a personal and professional bond that led them to work closely for decades, although with occasional clashes. Their relationship rested on mutual respect and trust, but also on the understanding that they needed each other. On one occasion in 1928 when Chiang vented his displeasure with He Yingqin, the former angrily declared, "Without Chiang Kai-shek, there is no He Yingqin!" There is truth to this statement, but it is equally true that, without He Yingqin, Chiang would not have enjoyed the same success in dealing with his internal and external opponents. Understanding He's role in this period is essential for comprehending the manner in which Chiang developed and implemented his major policies. Of the core group of officers at the top level of the military and government, none worked as long or as closely with Chiang Kai-shek, nor had as much influence on the fate of the Nationalist regime, as did He Yingqin.

Born in remote Guizhou province, He Yingqin spent his childhood far from the national stage he would later occupy. After beginning his basic education in his home county, he developed into a strong student and won highly competitive scholarships to military schools, first in

Wuchang and then in Japan. This early training, particularly his experience in Japan, had a strong impact on He Yingqin and helped shape his character. Moreover, when he left Japan, he had achieved a position roughly equivalent to that of a lieutenant in the Japanese Imperial Army, with a total of nine years of elementary and advanced military training behind him. In the midst of his studies he briefly returned to China when the fighting broke out in Wuchang in October 1911, but resumed his studies in Japan shortly thereafter.

After his education in Japan, he returned to his home province where he became part of the provincial elite, serving as commandant of the Guizhou Military Academy. During this period, He Yingqin gained practical experience as an administrator, reorganizing the academy and implementing the training methods and pedagogy that he had learned in Japan. He also grew increasingly active in provincial politics, supporting Sun Yat-sen's Republican program along with progressive causes associated with the May Fourth and New Culture Movements. In 1920 he participated in an ill-fated coup attempt against the provincial governor and had to flee to neighboring Yunnan province. The trouble followed him and, in December 1921, an assassin shot He Yingqin in a Kunming teahouse, nearly killing him. He survived, but his career in Guizhou ended, forcing him to find another situation.

He traveled to Shanghai to avoid further attacks and to recuperate from his wounds. His family and school connections eventually brought him an opportunity that would change the course of his life and career. He obtained introductions to both Sun Yat-sen and Chiang Kai-shek, which resulted in a position as a faculty member, and ultimately head of instruction, at the Whampoa Military Academy. During this phase of his career he established a professional relationship with Chiang. The two men held common views on the development of China's military as a foundational part of its modernization, and shared a strong appreciation for the role of spirit and aggressive action in achieving victory in battle. At the same time, they differed in personality: Chiang more emotional, volatile, and expressive while He tended toward sober, serious, and quiet. They made an odd couple in some respects, but complemented each other as well.

During their work together at the Whampoa Military Academy and in the early campaigns of the National Revolutionary Army (NRA), He Yingqin demonstrated to Chiang his capabilities as a combat commander. As Chiang's star rose with the completion of the Northern Expedition and the establishment of the new government in Nanjing, He Yingqin rose along with him. He's military victories in the NRA's early campaigns led Chiang to regard He as a capable and reliable subordinate

and cemented He's position as Chiang's "right-hand man" for the next
two decades. After establishing the capital in Nanjing in 1928, the new
government faced a series of revolts as regional commanders such as
Feng Yuxiang, Li Zongren, Zhang Fakui, and Tang Shengzhi rose in
opposition, culminating in the Central Plains War of 1930. He Yingqin
played a central role in defeating each of these opponents and helped
Chiang survive the greatest challenge to the regime to date. He Yingqin
took over as minister of military administration in 1930, a position from
which he addressed the major tasks of the period, including building a
strong, centralized military force, suppressing the Chinese Communist
Party, and dealing with Japanese military aggression in Manchuria and
north China. This marked a turning point in He Yingqin's career as he
shifted from a role as a combat commander to a military administrator.
While his star rose rapidly as a result of the success he achieved in the first
stage of his career, after 1930 he faced a series of increasingly difficult
challenges that would tax his abilities and hurt his reputation in China
and abroad.

In the next several years of his career he confronted three difficult
issues: the military campaigns against the CCP, Japanese aggression in
north China, and the Xi'an Incident. In each case, He Yingqin worked
to extend central control against regional and political opponents and
fend off the predatory actions of the Japanese military. Following Chiang
Kai-shek's view that China needed time to unify the country and modernize the military before confronting the Japanese, He Yingqin served
as the principal negotiator with Japanese military officials and concluded
important agreements, including what many call the 1935 "He–Umezu
Agreement," which yielded Chinese authority to the Japanese military
and drew widespread criticism from the Chinese public. He Yingqin's
participation in the negotiations helped delay war with Japan to allow
for continued development of the Nationalist military, but his reputation suffered as the Chinese press and activists vented their frustration at
the government's refusal to take military action against Japan. In 1936,
He Yingqin's alleged eagerness to use military force to resolve the Xi'an
Incident led some, most notably Chiang's wife Song Meiling, to conclude that He had sought to kill Chiang and replace him as paramount
leader. There is good reason to doubt this accusation, as once the episode
came to a peaceful resolution He Yingqin continued to work closely with
Chiang with no sign of conflict or tension. Regardless, it led some to
question his loyalty to Chiang and further tarnished He's reputation.

With the outbreak of war with Japan in 1937, He Yingqin faced the
daunting task of mobilizing the state for a long and brutal war. As minister of military administration, he presided over the essential task of

recruiting and training new soldiers. From his perspective, the question that would determine victory or defeat was whether the Nationalists could continue to put enough men in the field until the Japanese had exhausted their resources. Nationalist conscription practices in the war drew sharp criticisms and came to represent the regime as a whole: corrupt, unfair, coercive, brutal, and ineffective. Reports circulated around the wartime capital Chongqing of unfortunate peasants taken from their fields and bound and roped together like beasts of burden, most of whom either deserted or died before ever reaching forward units of the Nationalist army. Painfully aware of these abusive practices, He Yingqin worked continuously to eliminate them. Despite repeated attempts to rectify the work style of conscription officials, it proved impossible to eliminate the abuses. Continuing problems in conscription contributed to He Yingqin's poor reputation in some circles and provided fodder for his critics.

A second major challenge He Yingqin faced during the war involved coordinating with Allied military officials who joined forces with the Chinese after 1941. In particular, He Yingqin had to work closely with Joseph Stilwell, who arrived in China as Chiang Kai-shek's American chief of staff in March 1942. As Chiang's Chinese chief of staff, He Yingqin found himself often at odds with Stilwell as the two men sometimes worked at cross-purposes. The blunt and acerbic Stilwell focused almost exclusively on operations in Burma, which he saw as the key to strengthening the Chinese war effort against Japan. The stoic and formal He saw value in the Burma campaign, but also had responsibility for operations on various fronts in China. The story of Stilwell's conflict with Chiang Kai-shek is well known, but Stilwell criticized He as the greatest obstacle to successful operations in Burma and the reform of the Chinese military. Stilwell's condemnations strongly influenced American views of He Yingqin and the Nationalist army.

When the Sino-Japanese War ended, He Yingqin represented China at the surrender ceremony in Nanjing, which may have been the high point of his career. Shortly thereafter, he took an assignment as the head of the Chinese delegation to the United Nations Military Staff Committee, which took him to New York for a two-year sojourn in the United States. As the civil war raged back in China, He Yingqin grew increasingly convinced that the Nationalists could not resolve the conflict with the CCP through military force alone. Contrary to his reputation among American observers as a die-hard reactionary who demanded military action against the communists, He advocated socioeconomic policies designed to address the problems that made the CCP platform attractive to many Chinese peasants, including land reform.

After He Yingqin's two years in the United States, Chiang called him back to China, where he served brief terms as both minister of national defense and premier. By this time, He's relationship with Chiang Kai-shek had reached a new stage in which, while still loyal to Chiang, He Yingqin concluded that no progress could take place with regard to either negotiations with the CCP or a military campaign against it unless Chiang stepped aside. Despite Chiang's January 1949 decision to "step down," he continued to issue orders to unit commanders as had long been his habit. As premier, He Yingqin failed to find acceptable means to limit Chiang's direct involvement in military preparations, which prevented a unified command of Nationalist forces. He concluded that under the circumstances he could not mount a realistic defense against the CCP, and resigned his position in May. This marked the end of his career on the mainland, and he withdrew to the island of Taiwan with Chiang Kai-shek and others as Mao Zedong and his colleagues established the new state of the PRC.

The conclusions of this book form part of a growing movement to revise our understanding of the Nationalist period and its leading officers. Neither incompetent, corrupt, nor irrational, He Yingqin rose to the highest levels of the Nationalist military and government and remained there for an extended period, primarily due to his capabilities as a combat commander and military administrator. During his career, he played a central role in the development of the Nationalist military and took responsibility for dealing with the most pressing problems the young Nanjing government faced as it sought to extend central authority over all of China. In simplest terms, this book amounts to a response to Hans van de Ven's earlier call for new studies of the Nationalist Chinese leadership with a detailed analysis of He Yingqin's career based on Chinese-language sources.

# 1    Life and death in a Kunming teahouse

One fine Sunday in December 1921, He Yingqin sat at a table on the third floor of the Fenghua Teahouse in Kunming, chatting with his friend Wang Yongyu and enjoying some refreshments. The teahouse did a brisk business on such afternoons, with customers coming, going, and occupying tables on all three floors. At one point, He Yingqin excused himself and went down to the first floor where the owner operated a bath house, particularly popular on crisp winter days. After about half an hour, He Yingqin emerged from the relaxing hot bath, dressed in his uniform, and prepared to rejoin his friend at their table. Suddenly shots rang out, as assassins fired several rounds at He Yingqin, setting off a panic among the teahouse patrons. He Yingqin drew his pistol and returned fire. Chaos ensued as smoke from the gunfire filled the room, and dozens of people shouted and screamed as they scurried toward the exit. He Yingqin staggered up the stairs and collapsed on a couch, where Wang Yongyu found him ashen-faced and bleeding from wounds in his chest and leg.[1]

He Yingqin survived the attack, but lost the position he had worked hard for years to achieve. The early years of his education and training had taken him to Guiyang, Wuchang, and Japan, and he had returned to his home province with a first-class military education and a desire to help modernize China. In attempting to do so, he found himself thrust into the complicated world of warlord politics and military conflict in Guizhou, which gave him additional experience, but also nearly ended his life in a Kunming teahouse. Ironically, though he almost died, the attack forced him to leave the relative backwater of Guizhou province and ended up launching his ascent to the highest levels of the Chinese military and government.

---

[1] This account of the attack comes from Zhu Guangting, an eyewitness. See Zhu Guangting, "He Yingqin zai Kunming beici jianwen" [An Account of the Shooting of He Yingqin in Kunming], in Tu Yueseng, ed., *Xingyi Liu, Wang, He sanda jiazu* (Guizhou: Zhongguo wenshi chubanshe, 1990), 152–53.

### Early education and training

Born in 1890, He Yingqin grew up in a family with strong Confucian values and a tradition of military service at the local level. He spent his youth in the village of Nidang, near the town of Xingyi in southwestern Guizhou province, where his family operated a successful cloth-weaving and -dyeing business. The family had left its ancestral home in Jiangxi several generations before He Yingqin's birth, first raising cattle and then engaging in farming and trade. As the He family prospered, it occasionally used its resources to carry out public works projects in the area, to support and lead the local defense forces against bandits, and to educate its sons, making it a rather prominent family in the area. The patriarch, He Qimin, favored frugality and simplicity and made sure that He Yingqin and his four brothers and six sisters learned the value of hard work, laboring alongside hired hands in the family's business.[2]

After beginning his education with a village teacher, studying the *Three Character Classic* and other Confucian texts, at age thirteen He Yingqin saw an advertisement for a newly reformed Xingyi county primary school, which included a Western curriculum. By the first decade of the twentieth century, this had become a common trend in China, and opportunities to attend such schools appeared even in remote Guizhou. During this early period of educational reform, many older people regarded these modern schools with a healthy dose of suspicion, but like many youngsters He Yingqin and his brothers eagerly sought admission. He Qimin initially hesitated, perhaps worrying about tuition fees and living expenses as much as the potential impact of the newfangled learning, but eventually agreed to enroll He Yingqin and two of his brothers in the new school.[3]

According to one story, He Yingqin found a unique way to convince his father to allow him to attend this new school. Finding himself alone and otherwise unoccupied, young He Yingqin crept into his father's private room to look at one of his most prized possessions, an old hunting rifle that hung on the wall. When He Yingqin took the weapon down to examine and play with it, he accidentally pulled the trigger and discharged the weapon, filling the room with smoke and blowing a small hole in

---

[2] He Yingqin shangjiang jiuwu shouyan congshu bianji weiyuanhui, *He Yingqin jiangjun jiuwu jishi changbian* [A Record of General He Yingqin's Ninety-Five Years] (hereafter *HYQJJ*), 2 vols. (Taipei: Liming wenhua shiye youxian gongsi, 1984), vol. I, 2; He Jiwu, *Guizhou zhengtan yiwang* [Recollections of Guizhou Politics] (Taipei: Zhongwai tushuguan chubanshe, 1982), 12.

[3] Li Yuan, *Jiang Jieshi he He Yingqin* [Chiang Kai-shek and He Yingqin] (Changchun: Jilin wenshi chubanshe, 1996), 9; Xiong Zongren, *He Yingqin: xuanwozhong de lishi* [He Yingqin: History in the Vortex], 2 vols. (Guiyang: Guizhou renmin chubanshe, 2001), vol. I, 16–17.

the ceiling. Too terrified to face his father's wrath, he raced out the back door of the house and fled the scene. His family searched for him for several days with no luck, until a letter arrived in which He Yingqin announced that he had gone to Xingyi, the nearby county seat, and sat for the entrance examination to the new Xingyi County Primary School. He had won admission to the new "Western-style" school and asked for his father's blessing and support to enroll. Angry at his son's actions but also relieved to learn he had come to no harm, He Yingqin's father concluded that his third son had shown considerable aptitude in passing the examination. He not only provided He Yingqin with tuition and funds to support him in the county seat, but also enrolled his two elder sons as well.[4]

He Yingqin had a certain academic ability, but his initiation to formal schooling proved difficult. As a village boy, albeit from a rather prosperous family, who had grown up outside the county seat, he lacked the polish of some of his more urbane and affluent classmates. His clothes, both made and dyed at home, his traditional peasant grass sandals, and his rural accent led others to call him *xiang balao* or "country bumpkin."[5] Moreover, the new subject matter at the school meant that He Yingqin lagged behind his classmates academically, forcing him to struggle to keep up. From an early age he displayed a stubborn willingness to work hard, perhaps drawing upon the lessons he had learned at home in the family business. In addition to his academic work, he also had a hard time with physical fitness and outdoor exercise, part of the new school's curriculum. As he was neither fluid nor natural in his physical movements, his classmates occasionally ridiculed him. He Yingqin accepted these challenges, practicing in his own time and patiently following the commands of his instructors. On one occasion, after correcting his movements several times, his physical education instructor criticized him in front of the other students and ordered him to stand at attention to the side. When the class period ended and the other students and the instructor had left, He Yingqin remained in place at rigid attention, as he had not been told to do otherwise.[6]

He Yingqin began his formal schooling at a time of transition in China's educational and military systems. In the first decade of the twentieth century, the Qing government attempted to centralize and regulate military education as a part of its general plan for strengthening China's armed

[4] Xiong Zongren, *He Yingqin: xuanwozhong de lishi*, I, 15–16; Li Yuan, *Jiang Jieshi he He Yingqin*, 9–10.
[5] Li Yuan, *Jiang Jieshi he He Yingqin*, 10.
[6] Xiong Zongren, *He Yingqin: xuanwozhong de lishi*, I, 18.

forces and ordered each province to establish a military primary school.[7] The larger plan called for a three-tiered system of military education with primary schools in each provincial capital, three army middle schools, and creation of a formal military university at Baoding.[8] Accordingly, in the fall of 1906 Guizhou provincial authorities established the Guiyang Army Primary School and organized entrance examinations for students from the surrounding area to form the first class.

A number of factors propelled He Yingqin toward a military education and career. First, the Qing government's abolition of the Confucian examination system in 1905 had removed the traditional route to power and prestige for ambitious and educated Chinese. This destroyed any hope that He Yingqin might become a traditional scholar-official. Second, Japan's military victory over Russia in 1905 stunned the world and caught the attention of countless young Chinese who now clearly saw Japan as a model for addressing China's own military weakness. Like others of his generation, He Yingqin came to believe that a revitalized China must begin with a strong and modern military, and Japan's military development deeply impressed those who sought to help China defend itself against foreign aggression. These two events lent new prestige to the military profession in China and attracted thousands of students to military schools. For He Yingqin, who had already showed both academic aptitude and a preference for discipline and hard work, the army primary school and a military career must have seemed a natural fit. In comparison to other options, such as returning home to work in the family business, he saw this as his most promising opportunity. Competition for admission, however, proved fierce as provincial army primary schools such as the one in Guiyang sometimes received thousands of applications for 200 to 300 openings. Regardless, He Yingqin passed the entrance examination and entered the first class of the Guiyang Army Primary School in February 1907, marking the beginning of his formal military education.[9]

Designed to strengthen the military forces of the Qing Dynasty, schools such as the Guiyang Army Primary School ironically produced many students who showed greater interest in changing China's traditional

---

[7]  Edward Dreyer, *China at War, 1901–1949* (New York: Longman, 1995), 21–22.
[8]  Chen-ya Tien, *Chinese Military Theory: Ancient and Modern* (Oakville, ON: Mosaic Press, 1992), 167. The first three army middle schools appeared in Qinghezhen (Hebei), Wuchang, and Nanjing. A fourth, in Xi'an, came later.
[9]  Anita O'Brien, "Military Academies in China, 1885–1915," in Joshua A. Fogel and William T. Rowe, eds., *Perspectives on a Changing China: Essays in Honor of Professor C. Martin Wilbur on the Occasion of His Retirement* (Boulder, CO: Westview Press, 1979), 171; *HYQJJ*, I, 7–8; Li Yuan, *Jiang Jieshi he He Yingqin*, 11.

political and social system, gravitating toward Sun Yat-sen's Tongmenghui (Revolutionary Alliance), a broad-based organization dedicated
to the overthrow of Manchu rule and the establishment of a republic.
Copies of the Tongmenghui periodical *Min Bao* circulated widely among
the students, spreading ideas of revolution and republic. Qing authorities
tried to squash this movement among cadets, and He Yingqin saw some
thirty classmates expelled for revolutionary activity during his time.[10]
Discussion of revolutionary ideas on campus had little influence on him
at this time as he did not see himself as a revolutionary, but simply as an
obedient and dedicated student.

While He Yingqin worked hard at his studies, he adapted naturally to
the discipline and order of the military school. Some who studied with
him in Guiyang described him as a model cadet.[11] He found that the
military environment suited his personality and temperament and reinforced his core values of traditional morality, hard work, and discipline.
He graduated at the top of his class and in the winter of 1908 he passed
the entrance exam for admission to the Wuchang Army Number Three
Middle School. This meant leaving his native province for neighboring
Hubei province, where he would meet students from all over China.
Although he had to adjust to life away from home, complaining that he
had to eat fish at every meal, the school was much larger, more prestigious, and well supported. In the fall of 1909, He Yingqin entered the
second class of cadets at Wuchang.[12]

The Wuchang Army Number Three Middle School based its curriculum on the Japanese military school model, which presented He Yingqin
with a new set of challenges such as an academic program that included
algebra and analytical geometry. While other students spent their free
time and vacations visiting some of Wuchang's historic and scenic locations, he preferred to stay on campus, studying for his classes and poring
over maps to sharpen his knowledge of geography and terrain.[13] Some no
doubt considered him a dry and colorless young man, but he excelled at
the Wuchang middle school, both academically and in terms of military
training, which the new school emphasized far more than the Guiyang
Army Primary School. In only his second semester in Wuchang, He
Yingqin learned of an opportunity to sit for a competitive examination
for a study-abroad program in Japan. Admission to a Japanese military

[10] Xiong Zongren, *He Yingqin: xuanwozhong de lishi*, I, 21–22.
[11] See reference to fellow student Wang Jian'an, in Xiong Zongren, *He Yingqin: xuanwozhong de lishi*, I, 22–23.
[12] *HYQJJ*, I, 9; Li Yuan, *Jiang Jieshi he He Yingqin*, 11–12. The Wuchang Army Middle
School had approximately 1,000 cadets. See O'Brien, "Military Academies in China,
1885–1915," 174.
[13] *HYQJJ*, I, 9; Li Yuan, *Jiang Jieshi he He Yingqin*, 12.

academy represented a valuable training opportunity for a Chinese cadet in the early twentieth century and would all but assure him of a prominent position as an instructor upon his return to China. In a testimony to his hard work and academic success, the next semester, when the school posted the list of names of successful candidates, He Yingqin's name appeared at the top of the list, first among all who took the examination. As a result, in 1910, he joined a group of twenty Chinese students bound for study in Japan.[14] Having succeeded in military schools in Guiyang and Wuchang and on his way to an elite Japanese military academy, He Yingqin had developed from a "country bumpkin" into a promising young military professional.[15] He had now begun to excel in the classroom, to travel beyond the confines of his home county, province, and country, all in pursuit of a professional military education. His decision to enter the military profession had opened up a new world to He Yingqin that he had never envisioned.

At that time, when Chinese students arrived in Japan to study at a military academy, they first attended a special school for Chinese students called the Shimbu Gakko. In the spirit of pan-Asianism, the Japanese government established this school in 1903 near Tokyo in order to instruct Chinese students in the Japanese language and to provide basic military training in preparation for advanced study in a Japanese military academy.[16] After preliminary study at the Shimbu Gakko, and a period of service and training in the Japanese Imperial Army, Chinese students took a test for admission to the elite Rikugun Shikan Gakko military academy.[17] Perhaps the most prestigious of Japan's military academies, the Shikan Gakko produced an entire generation of officers for the Japanese Imperial Army. In 1900 it began accepting Chinese cadets, though they suffered a high attrition rate. According to some estimates, as many as 1,000 Chinese students went to study there between 1900 and 1908, but as few as 229 completed their program and graduated from the Shikan Gakko. Those who did graduate could expect to return to China and work in the best military academies, including the Baoding Academy, where they would train Chinese cadets according to the Japanese military educational model.[18]

[14]  Xiong Zongren, *He Yingqin: xuanwozhong de lishi*, I, 24–25; Li Yuan, *Jiang Jieshi he He Yingqin*, 13.
[15]  Li Yuan, *Jiang Jieshi he He Yingqin*, 12.
[16]  Chen Ningsheng and Zhang Guangyu, *Jiang Jieshi he huangpu xi* [Chiang Kai-shek and the Whampoa Clique] (Zhengzhou: Henan renmin chubanshe, 1994), 2.
[17]  *HYQJJ*, I, 10.
[18]  Xu Ping, "Riben shiguan xuexiao he jiu zhongguo lujun 'shiguanxi'" [Japan's Shikan Gakko and the "Shikan Gakko Faction" in the Military of Old China], *Minguo chunqiu*, 4 (2001), 57–60.

He Yingqin's time in Japan played a critical role in his development as an officer and had a significant impact on his career trajectory. First, it reinforced his belief in the importance of discipline, duty, and obedience. He admired the manner in which Japanese soldiers immediately and unquestioningly obeyed the orders of their superiors, believing that only this same discipline and dedication could reinvigorate and strengthen China after decades of weakness and imperialist exploitation. This inspired him to export to his homeland the military spirit, loyalty to superiors, and dedication to duty that he saw all around him in Japan.[19] Second, he began to make important contacts that would have a decisive influence on his subsequent career. He made the acquaintance of Wang Boling, who would later recommend him for a position with Sun Yat-sen's revolutionary government in Guangzhou. He also met a young cadet one class ahead of him at the Shimbu Gakko who at the time used the name Jiang Zhiqing, later known in China and around the world as Chiang Kai-shek. Although the two had only a general acquaintance at the time, Chiang later offered He a position as a military instructor in part because of their common experience as cadets in Japan.[20] Third, his experience in Japan and contacts with other cadets from around China aroused a new type of nationalism in He Yingqin, leading to his first involvement in anti-Qing activities. Although the Japanese government had agreed to a Qing court request to restrict revolutionary activities among Chinese students in Japan, many Chinese cadets, including several from Xingyi county in Guizhou, had already joined Sun Yat-sen's Tongmenghui.[21] Prior to his arrival in Japan, He Yingqin had shown no interest in such activity, but perhaps his first-hand view of Meiji Japan led him to see the inherent weakness of the Manchu government and the promise of Sun's revolutionary program. In 1910, Japan had already emerged as a modern industrial state with a powerful military, and He Yingqin could not help but see the stark contrast between Tokyo and the areas of China in which he had lived and studied. The Meiji government and Imperial Army, which had not only presided over the defeat of Russia but more

[19] Xiong Zongren, *He Yingqin: xuanwozhong de lishi*, I, 26; Li Yuan, *Jiang Jieshi he He Yingqin*, 15. On Japanese military academies, see Theodore Failor Cook, "The Japanese Officer Corps: The Making of a Military Elite, 1872–1945" (Ph.D. dissertation, Princeton University, Princeton, NJ, 1987), 114.

[20] A list of Chinese students who graduated from the Shikan Gakko can be found in Shen Yunlong, ed., *Riben lujun shiguan xuexiao zhonghua minguo liuxuesheng mingbu* [Foreign Students from the Republic of China at Japan's Rikugun Shikan Gakko] (Taipei: Wenhai chubanshe, 1977). Chiang Kai-shek graduated from the Shimbu Gakko and served in a Japanese artillery regiment, but did not graduate from the Shikan Gakko and therefore is not listed.

[21] See Marius Jansen, *The Japanese and Sun Yat-sen* (Cambridge, MA: Harvard University Press, 1954), 121–24.

recently also annexed Korea, must have seemed light years ahead of their Chinese counterparts. Similar feats, He Yingqin and other cadets concluded, could not be accomplished under the Manchu government. He tended to view political issues from a military vantage point, and not until his experience in Japan did he embrace the idea that political revolution might be a necessary precursor to military modernization. For the first time in his life, He Yingqin began to gravitate toward the politics and the principles of Sun Yat-sen, joining the Tongmenghui on the eve of the 1911 Revolution.[22]

This new interest in revolutionary activity led him to return to China in the wake of the revolt in Wuchang in October 1911, which caused numerous provinces to secede and eventually toppled the Manchu government. Many Chinese students in Japan became so caught up in the excitement that they left school without authorization, Chiang Kai-shek among them.[23] He Yingqin now clearly saw himself as a supporter of Sun Yat-sen and wanted to return to China to fight with the revolutionaries, but his sense of discipline prevented him from doing so until the school authorities gave him official leave. The school granted him leave, perhaps realizing that denying authorization did not deter Chinese cadets from departing without authorization, but a shortage of funds delayed his return to China. He left for China only when a wealthy Japanese supporter of the Tongmenghui provided him with financial aid.[24]

He Yingqin went to Shanghai to serve under the command of Chen Qimei, who had also studied in Japan and who served as head of the general affairs department of the Tongmenghui.[25] Chen had sent telegrams to Japan to call all cadets from the Shimbu Gakko and Shikan Gakko to serve in the Shanghai Army, one of several military forces that opposed the Qing government after the initial revolt in October 1911. As fate would have it, He Yingqin and Chiang Kai-shek both responded to the invitation and soon found themselves officers in the first division, Chiang in command of the fifth regiment and He Yingqin commanding a company in the third regiment.[26] He Yingqin served as a drill instructor helping to train the Shanghai Army, but also took part in the fighting around the city and quickly rose to the rank of

---

[22] Li Yuan, *Jiang Jieshi he He Yingqin*, 15.
[23] Chiang applied for and received a 48-hour leave, but immediately left for China before receiving permission. The Japanese Ministry of Foreign Affairs expelled students who left without formal leave. See Li Yuan, *Jiang Jieshi he He Yingqin*, 16–17; Taylor, *Generalissimo*, 21.
[24] Xiong Zongren, *He Yingqin: xuanwozhong de lishi*, I, 27.
[25] Li Yuan, *Jiang Jieshi he He Yingqin*, 16.
[26] *HYQJJ*, I, 11; Xiong Zongren, *He Yingqin: xuanwozhong de lishi*, I, 28–29.

battalion commander. In the fall of 1912, he learned that his mother had passed away from illness. He took leave and rushed home to Xingyi county, but the funeral had already taken place and he could only visit her grave.[27]

He Yingqin's participation in the fighting did not last long. Following the abdication of the last Manchu emperor in February 1912, the new president of the Republic of China, Yuan Shikai, proved uninterested in parliamentary government. In the summer of 1913, several southern provinces including Jiangsu rose in opposition to the government in what is known as the Second Revolution. Yuan controlled the most powerful remnant of the Qing military, the Beiyang Army, which crushed the poorly organized southern forces. In the wake of this defeat, Sun Yat-sen and others fled to Japan to regroup and continue the revolutionary movement. Likewise, many Chinese students who had returned from Japan to participate in the revolution went back to finish their studies. In December 1913, He Yingqin returned to the Shimbu Gakko where he quickly finished the remainder of his program and took an assignment in the fifty-ninth regiment of the Japanese Imperial Army at Utsunomiya, north of Tokyo. All Japanese military cadets served for a period of time in an infantry unit in order to put the officer candidate in close contact with enlisted men like those he would one day command. The training and discipline of the Japanese army proved rigorous, but again He Yingqin excelled in this environment, earning a promotion after six months.[28]

Instruction and training in the Japanese military focused on the practical skills required of ordinary soldiers and squad leaders, with the aim of producing troops with a mastery of basic skills and exposure to all the things a soldier or lower-ranking officer might encounter in combat. It also emphasized the development of moral character, or what some call the *bushido* spirit, stressing absolute obedience, honor, courage, and loyalty to superiors.[29] Chinese cadets lived and trained exactly as Japanese soldiers, experiencing the same indoctrination in the "way of the warrior." When he completed his studies at the Shimbu Gakko and his term of service in the fifty-ninth regiment, He Yingqin had acquired a solid educational and practical foundation for his military career. In the fall of 1914, he and five other students from Guizhou entered the Shikan Gakko at Ichigaya in central Tokyo, where their instruction in tactics and

---

[27]  Li Yuan, *Jiang Jieshi he He Yingqin*, 17–18: *HYQJJ*, I, 11.
[28]  Li Yuan, *Jiang Jieshi he He Yingqin*, 18–21; Cook, "The Japanese Officer Corps," 113; *HYQJJ*, I, 15.
[29]  Cook, "The Japanese Officer Corps," 147, 159–60.

strategy continued, along with advanced training in swordsmanship and horsemanship.[30]

Over the course of their time in Japan, Chinese students had to confront the reality of Japanese imperialism in China, especially after 1915 and the Twenty-One Demands imposed on Yuan Shikai's government. He Yingqin no doubt had conflicted feelings and, while he admired Japan for its imperial system and military spirit, he could not fail to see that Japan had predatory designs on China and may have seen that future conflict between the two nations was inevitable. This harsh reality motivated He to learn his craft to the best of his abilities in order to return to China so he could contribute to its military strength and revival. There is no doubt that he disapproved of Japan's brazen pursuit of economic and political advantages in China, as in the years after his return to China he often and openly criticized Japan's aggressive foreign policy *vis à vis* China. Ironically, the Shikan Gakko produced a number of prominent Japanese officers He Yingqin would later meet in China, including Umezu Yoshijiro, who would represent the Japanese in negotiations with He over north China in 1935. He also encountered Okamura Yasuji, who would command the China Expeditionary Force and play an important role in Operation Ichigo in 1944.[31]

Despite the fact that He Yingqin had joined the Tongmenghui and participated in the 1911 Revolution, his personality changed little, and he remained a rather sober and serious person. A 1916 photograph of several classmates from Guizhou studying at the Shikan Gakko reveals the essence of He's personality and character. The others around him are dressed in Western-style suits or fashionable "Sun Yat-sen" jackets and trousers. He Yingqin sits front and center, the only person in the group wearing his cadet's uniform. His classmates lean against each other, place a hand on each other's shoulders, cross their legs, or lean back in their chairs, yet He Yingqin sits ramrod straight, hands on his thighs, sword prominently displayed in front of him, the very picture of military formality.[32]

As one might expect of young men far from home, many Chinese students went out with Japanese girls or visited brothels during their free time. He Yingqin, on the other hand, eschewed such activities and preferred to study or read newspapers from China. In the rare instance that he sought more frivolous entertainment, he might visit the theater. The rules at the Shikan Gakko prohibited cadets from "talking love"

[30] *HYQJJ*, I, 17–19.     [31] Xiong Zongren, *He Yingqin: xuanwozhong de lishi*, I, 30.
[32] The photograph is in Xiong Zongren, *He Yingqin zhuan* [Biography of He Yingqin] (Taiyuan: Shanxi renmin chubanshe, 1993).

with young women and barred entrance to those with "loose morals or dissolute character." He Yingqin had no intention of risking expulsion for such transgressions. This pattern of behavior may have contributed to his later nickname in military circles, "Grandma" or "old lady He."[33] Neither charismatic nor flamboyant, He was on the contrary reserved, formal, and even stoic. Indeed, he felt most comfortable and at home with the rigid discipline and order of the military. Given his personality and predilections, He Yingqin did not fit the bill of a dynamic leader or innovator, but rather that of a loyal subordinate and follower.

After graduating from the Shikan Gakko, He Yingqin returned to China with training equivalent to that of a second lieutenant in the Japanese army, a total of nine years of elementary and advanced military training behind him. At the time, such credentials almost guaranteed work opportunities, as Chinese graduates of Japanese military academies formed an elite group within the Chinese military, enjoying greater prestige than graduates of Chinese military academies. Accordingly, in 1916 He Yingqin had three different offers of employment waiting for him. He could return to serve in the Shanghai Army as he had in 1912; he could go to Yunnan and serve under provincial governor Tang Jiyao; or he could return to Guizhou as an officer in the Guizhou Army. Along with a few other Guizhou cadets, He Yingqin decided to return to his home province, and in the autumn of 1916 he began his career as a Guizhou Army officer.[34]

## The Guizhou Army and Military Academy

At the time he returned to his native province, two prominent figures dominated Guizhou's military and political landscape, the military governor Liu Xianshi and his nephew Wang Wenhua, commander of the Guizhou Army. Despite the family connection, the two had emerged as rivals, with Liu representing the old "warlord" style of politics and retaining ties to other regional commanders such as Tang Jiyao in Yunnan and Duan Qirui of the Beijing government. Liu showed little

---

[33] Cook, "The Japanese Officer Corps," 134. See also He's remarks to Okamura Yasuji in 1956 in He Yingqin shangjiang jiuwu shouyan congshu bianji weiyuanhui, *He Yingqin jiangjun jiangci xuanji* [General He Yingqin's Selected Speeches] (hereafter *HYQJJJCXJ*) (Taipei: Liming wenhua shiye youxian gongsi, 1984), 299; Xiong Zongren, *He Yingqin: xuanwozhong de lishi*, I, 30–31; Tsung-jen Li and Te-kong Tong, *The Memoirs of Li Tsung-jen* (Boulder, CO: Westview Press, 1979), 232.

[34] Ni Tuanjiu, *He Yingqin shangjiang zhuan* [Biography of General He Yingqin] (Taipei: Taibei yinhang, 1984), 3; *HYQJJ*, I, 29; Xiong Zongren, *He Yingqin: xuanwozhong de lishi*, I, 32–33.

Map 1: Southwestern China

interest in reform and concentrated on maintaining his position in Guizhou and preserving his relations with any regional force that might rise to national prominence. The younger Wang represented the more progressive and republican politics of Sun Yat-sen, having joined Sun's Gemingdang (Revolutionary Party) while in Nanjing and Shanghai in 1917, but kept quiet about his political views around his uncle.[35]

Wang Wenhua sought out talented officers whose political views matched his own, and he naturally viewed He Yingqin and other Japanese-trained Guizhou men as important to his efforts to reorganize the provincial army.[36] Wang Wenhua himself had graduated from a teachers' college, but he and his brother Wang Boqun had cultivated a group of young officers with training from the Shikan Gakko, the Yunnan Military Academy, and the Baoding Military Academy. He Yingqin quickly fell in with the Wang brothers, serving as commander of the fourth regiment of the first division and as commander of the cadet battalion at the Guizhou Military Academy. Wang Wenhua found He in particular an impressive addition to the force and took the young officer under his wing. Students who returned from Japan immediately occupied high-ranking positions, which tended to rankle those who had graduated from Chinese military academies. This created both a "Shikan faction" and an "academy faction" within the officer corps of the Guizhou Army.[37]

His prior training and new relationship with Wang Wenhua propelled He Yingqin into the center of Guizhou political and military affairs, providing him with a platform from which to reach new professional heights. It also meant personal changes, as in the spring of 1917 He Yingqin married Wang Wenhua's sister, Wang Wenxiang. While this marriage alliance no doubt improved He's standing in Guizhou's political and military networks, the couple seemed happy together. Wang Wenxiang remained with He Yingqin for her entire life.[38] Shortly thereafter, Wang Wenhua appointed He commandant of the newly reformed Guizhou Military

[35] Chen Xianqiu, "Xinhai yihou ershinian jian guizhou junzheng gaishu" [A Summary of Guizhou Political and Military Affairs in the Twenty-Five Years After the 1911 Revolution], *Wenshi ziliao xuanji*, 15 (n.d.), 149–51; Guizhou daxue lishixi, "Guizhou junfa Liu Xianshi fajiashi" [A History of the Rise of the Family of Guizhou Warlord Liu Xianshi], *Guizhou wenshi ziliao xuanji*, 3 (n.d.), 196; Gui Baizhu, "Liu Xianshi jituan neibu douzheng sanji" [Random Notes on the Internal Struggles of the Liu Xianshi Clique], *Guizhou wenshi ziliao xuanji*, 1 (n.d.), 102; Zhang Pengnian, "Xinhai yilai sishi nianjian Guizhou zhengju de yanbian" [The Evolution of Guizhou Politics in the Forty Years After the 1911 Revolution], *Guizhou wenshi ziliao xuanji*, 2 (n.d.), 53; *HYQJJ*, I, 34; Ni Tuanjiu, *He Yingqin shangjiang zhuan*, 5.

[36] *HYQJJ*, I, 29.

[37] Ni Tuanjiu, *He Yingqin shangjiang zhuan*, 3; Xiong Zongren, *He Yingqin: xuanwozhong de lishi*, I, 37–40.

[38] *HYQJJ*, I, 30; Xiong Zongren, *He Yingqin: xuanwozhong de lishi*, I, 38–40.

Academy. He Yingqin and Wang Wenhua placed great importance on the academy as a way to develop a group of young officers to support their own political and military vision for Guizhou. A natural fit for this position, He used the same instructional techniques he had experienced at the Shikan Gakko, organizing a curriculum that emphasized physical fitness, strategy, tactics, terrain, weapons, and communications. Most of the instructors working under He Yingqin's command had graduated from the Baoding Military Academy, which also used a Japanese military educational model and Wang even kept a Japanese advisor on staff.[39] The academy welcomed students who had completed high school and within one year provided them with basic military training. Applicants who hoped to attend the academy had to meet physical fitness requirements and pass eyesight and hearing exams before sitting for the entrance exam. In order to build the corps of cadets and to retain local talent, He Yingqin established a policy of granting immediate acceptance to the academy for any Guizhou student who tested into the Yunnan Military Academy. The first class enrolled 189 students and began in early July 1917.[40]

As He Yingqin's status in the Guizhou Army improved due to his close personal and professional relationship with Wang Wenhua, his work in building the Guizhou Military Academy became a source of tension between Wang Wenhua and Liu Xianshi. Wang and He hoped that their control over the academy and its graduates would strengthen the position of the "young Turks" who favored greater emphasis on republican politics and military reform. It would also lessen Guizhou's dependence on neighboring Yunnan, which had a powerful provincial army. Liu had come to the office of provincial governor with the help of Yunnan's military and political leader Tang Jiyao and continued to rely on Yunnan's military support. Liu could see rather clearly that He and Wang might develop their own power base at the academy, especially when relatives or applicants closely linked to Liu Xianshi did not get admission. In order to counter the influence of Wang and He, in August 1917 Liu set up a second military academy, called the Suiying xuexiao, under the command of his cousin Liu Xianqian.[41]

Liu Xianshi hoped that this new military academy would successfully compete with the Guizhou Military Academy under Wang's and He's control and that he would be able to attract and train young men who would become loyal officers. Unfortunately for Liu, the Suiying xuexiao

[39] *HYQJJ*, I, 31; Li Yuan, *Jiang Jieshi he He Yingqin*, 22.
[40] Xiong Zongren, *He Yingqin: xuanwozhong de lishi*, I, 56.
[41] Xiong Zongren, *He Yingqin: xuanwozhong de lishi*, I, 52–53.

could not match the standards of its rival. He Yingqin used the model of training that he had experienced in Japan with a period of preparatory training, as he had had at the Shimbu Gakko, and then formal instruction in advanced subjects. By contrast, instructors who had never attended a military academy themselves and had little battlefield experience staffed Liu Xianqian's academy. It lasted only long enough to produce two classes of graduates before closing its doors. By contrast, the reorganization and resuscitation of the Guizhou Military Academy proved so successful that He Yingqin began to accept applications from students from several neighboring provinces. He and Wang remained ever vigilant against spies and informants from Liu Xianqian's Suiying xuexiao, and subjected all candidates from other provinces to careful scrutiny before making a judgment on their admission. In fact, when He Yingqin found that two cadets had passed on information about how the academy was run to Liu Xianqian, he expelled them immediately. In five years as commandant of the academy He graduated 495 students, many of whom went on to serve in various positions in the Guizhou Army, reinforcing He's growing influence within that force.[42] Local observers of this conflict noted that, while remaining outwardly loyal to Liu Xianshi, Wang Wenhua and He Yingqin gradually strengthened the forces favoring change and prepared to oust Liu from power.[43]

The developing rivalry between Liu and Wang soon spilled over into unexpected areas of Guizhou society, as Wang Wenhua realized that he might take advantage of a burgeoning student movement to weaken his uncle's position. Moving the struggle into this new arena, Wang and his supporters stepped in to play a critical role in organizing and directing student activism in Guiyang. This created a curious situation in which Guizhou military authorities directed student organizations and linked the student movement to the militarist power struggle between Liu and Wang.[44] Student activism in Guizhou developed as the influence of the New Culture Movement spread from Beijing, Shanghai, and other major cities to the more remote areas of China. Reacting in part to Japanese imperialism and the Twenty-One Demands of 1915, popular periodicals such as *New Youth* and *Weekly Critic* published essays that inspired young, educated Chinese to consider new ideas, practices, and institutions. In 1917, Guizhou newspapers began printing articles on topics such as Western-style democracy, the Bolshevik Revolution, literary reform, and other "modern" ideas and practices that might help revive and strengthen

---

[42] Xiong Zongren, *He Yingqin: xuanwozhong de lishi*, I, 52–53, 57.

[43] Zhang Pengnian, "Xinhai yilai sishi nianjian guizhou zhengju de yanbian," 53.

[44] On this topic, see Peter Worthing, "Toward the Minjiu Incident: Militarist Conflict in Guizhou, 1911–1921," *Modern China*, 33, 2 (April 2007), 258–83.

China. Schools and groups of students in Guiyang began active discussion of the "isms" of the day, such as nationalism, materialism, and socialism. Others began to demand educational reform, adding foreign languages, science, and mathematics to the school curricula.[45]

Wang Wenhua and He Yingqin came to see that they might take advantage of the changing conditions in Guizhou and that the New Culture Movement that criticized traditional authority could be useful in their struggle with Liu Xianshi. In order to capitalize on this growing movement, in late 1918 Wang and He discussed creating a new youth organization. Their inspiration undoubtedly came from progressive student organizations sprouting elsewhere in China at the time, such as Beijing, where students had created a Young China Students Association in June.[46] Calling their organization the Young Guizhou Association (YGA), they modeled it on the nineteenth-century Italian nationalist Giuseppe Mazzini's Young Italy Movement. The new organization encouraged the young people of Guizhou to join together in an effort to modernize the province.[47] Wang and He believed that, if it were properly developed, they could use this organization as an effective tool to advocate their republican program, to strengthen their own political base, and to undermine the authority of Liu Xianshi, who represented the old style of warlord politics that New Culture-era intellectuals criticized. The creation of the YGA marked the beginning of the expansion of the power struggle from the military academies into the larger realm of students and educators in Guizhou.

He Yingqin took the nominal lead in organizing and directing the YGA while Wang operated behind the scenes. Beginning with a core group of cadets from the Guizhou Military Academy, He Yingqin then invited representatives from other schools and organizations to join the YGA, and membership quickly expanded to seventy individuals. The guiding principles of the YGA reflected the prominent themes of intellectuals and young people elsewhere in China engaged in the New Culture Movement. Advocating patriotism and humanitarianism, the YGA urged its members to "sacrifice themselves for the country, to unite with the masses to protect the country, to advance learning and knowledge, and to exercise and develop their bodies."[48] At YGA functions, He used language typical of the period, describing Guizhou as a sick old man that needed

---

[45] Xiong Zongren, *Wusi yundong zai guizhou* [The May Fourth Movement in Guizhou] (Guiyang: Guizhou renmin chubanshe, 1986), 22–23.

[46] Xiong Zongren, *Wusi yundong zai guizhou*, 26.

[47] *HYQJJ*, I, 35; Ni Tuanjiu, *He Yingqin shangjiang zhuan*, 6; Xiong Zongren, *He Yingqin: xuanwozhong de lishi*, I, 59–60.

[48] Xiong Zongren, *He Yingqin: xuanwozhong de lishi*, I, 60–61.

revitalization through the actions of young people to make it a militarily strong and politically progressive province. The YGA consistently pushed a reform agenda, which contrasted with Liu Xianshi's conservative rule. The rhetoric of this new organization spread rapidly through local newspapers and wall posters, leading its membership to swell to more than 2,000 by the end of 1918.[49] Within a month of its establishment, members cast votes to elect He Yingqin as chair of the YGA with an overwhelming majority.[50] The YGA emerged as the first real force for progressive change in Guizhou since 1911, with He as its recognized leader. With some eighty-one YGA county branch offices opening across the province, He Yingqin's reputation and influence spread rapidly.[51]

As the YGA attracted more attention to political issues in Guizhou, the power struggle between Liu Xianshi and Wang Wenhua grew more intense. Liu undoubtedly recognized the danger of allowing Wang and He to control the student movement, as they might use it to incite criticism of his rule. Yet he refrained from taking action to curb its activities or expansion. Instead, he attempted to offset the impact of Wang's new organization by once again creating a rival to counteract the influence of this new organization. Liu formed a separate student organization called the Republic of China Patriotic Students Association (PSA), hoping to attract capable young people away from the YGA. The guiding principles of the PSA resembled those of the YGA and its members sometimes even criticized provincial authorities. Although a number of young men held memberships in both, the two organizations clearly marked the division of supporters of Liu Xianshi from those of Wang Wenhua and He Yingqin. Guizhou proved a curious example of militarist cooperation with students when military officials took leading roles in directing the student activism of the New Culture and May Fourth Movements.[52]

As had been the case when Liu Xianshi established a rival military academy, the PSA proved no match for the superior organizational skills of He Yingqin and Wang Wenhua. In early March 1919, the YGA stepped up its activities and began publishing a newspaper in Guiyang, the *Young Guizhou Association Daily*, which served as the mouthpiece for the organization and helped spread its message across the province. Articles dealt with typical issues of the New Culture Movement, such as opium suppression, opposition to Japanese imperialism, and encouraging women

[49] Xiong Zongren, *Wusi yundong zai guizhou*, 25–26; Li Yuan, *Jiang Jieshi he He Yingqin*, 23; Xiong Zongren, *He Yingqin: xuanwozhong de lishi*, I, 61.
[50] Xiong Zongren, *He Yingqin: xuanwozhong de lishi*, I, 64.
[51] *HYQJJ*, I, 35; Ni Tuanjiu, *He Yingqin shangjiang zhuan*, 6; Xiong Zongren, *He Yingqin: xuanwozhong de lishi*, I, 77.
[52] Xiong Zongren, *He Yingqin: xuanwozhong de lishi*, I, 67.

to cut their hair short in modern fashion. Guizhou students and military cadets who had emerged as a base of support for Wang's faction in Guizhou politics penned a stream of articles in the *YGA Daily* advocating political and social change, making it the leading voice of activism and helping spread ideas about reform and revolution in Guizhou province.[53]

YGA members did not specifically attack Liu Xianshi, yet they did not necessarily need to in order to make their point. For example, in March 1919, Liu and other local dignitaries attended a rally of both the YGA and PSA at which a student speaker addressed an enthusiastic crowd on the virtues of modernization, democracy, and freedom. "Old people think about the past," he told the audience, "while young people think about the future. Old people are conservative, while young people are aggressive." "The past belongs to the old people," he concluded, "but the future belongs to the young people!"[54] Almost fifty years old at the time, Liu Xianshi likely interpreted these remarks as directed at himself. The rhetoric may have reflected that of other youth organizations of the time, but the specific goal of the YGA under He Yingqin's control remained the purely local objective of weakening Liu's political standing. By the spring of 1919, the YGA clearly dominated the student movement in Guizhou.

The dramatic political protests that took place in Beijing in May 1919 added intensity to the student movement across China. The Versailles Peace Conference, at which the victorious powers of World War I decided to award control of Germany's former territorial concessions in Shandong to Japan, changed the nature of the student movement in China in general and in Guizhou in particular. In Beijing, students launched the famous demonstration on May 4, 1919, resulting in the arrest of students and outrage among young people around China. Word of these events reached Guiyang slowly, initially through the letters of Guizhou students studying in Beijing addressed to friends and family. For example, Xu Tingdong learned of these events through a letter from a former classmate who had gone to study in Beijing. The author of the letter had been arrested and described the ordeal of the students in police custody.[55] As word spread through such letters, Guizhou newspapers began printing detailed stories on the Versailles Conference and the activities of students in other cities. *Guizhou Gongbao* reported on the activities of Guizhou students in Beijing for three straight days.[56]

---

[53]  *HYQJJ*, I, 35.    [54]  Xiong Zongren, *Wusi yundong zai Guizhou*, 29–30.

[55]  Xu Tingdong, "Guizhou 'wusi' yundong de huiyi" [Recollections of the "May Fourth" Movement in Guizhou], *Guizhou wenshi ziliao xuanji*, 3 (n.d.), 64–65.

[56]  Xiong Zongren, *Wusi yundong zai Guizhou*, 37–38.

News from Beijing generated increased student activity in Guizhou. The numbers remained small, but student organization in Guiyang improved in part through the work of Guizhou students studying in other provinces. For example, Guizhou students from Hunan organized a National Salvation Association with some 600 members. Representatives from national student organizations began to filter into Guiyang with the goal of uniting various regional student organizations into a national alliance. Taking inspiration from the actions of students elsewhere in China and seeking to unite with other student organizations, students at the Institute of Law and Politics in Guiyang called a meeting to discuss the creation of a Guizhou branch of the National Student Alliance (NSA). As the leader of the YGA, He Yingqin welcomed these connections and helped establish the Guizhou branch of the NSA.[57]

He Yingqin and the YGA increased their political activities and demands for reform in the wake of the May 4, 1919, demonstrations, pushing their reform agenda in Guizhou. In late May, YGA leaders met with representatives from eighty-one counties in order to begin preparations for the creation of a new representative body called the Guizhou National People's Assembly. Wall posters throughout Guiyang described the assembly and its purpose, calling on the people of Guizhou to fight for the return of Shandong province, for the abolition of the Twenty-One Demands, and against Japanese imperialism. More than one thousand people attended the opening session of the assembly in June at Meng Cao Park. He Yingqin gave the keynote address, describing the events at Versailles, reviewing the history of Japanese imperialism in China, and detailing the suffering of colonial people in Korea and Vietnam. He urged the audience to send telegrams to the Chinese delegates at Versailles and to the Beijing government demanding that they refuse to sign the treaty as well as the abolition of the "unequal treaties" between China and foreign powers. He also insisted on the release of the imprisoned Beijing students and the removal of six "pro-Japanese" ministers from the cabinet. Afterwards, He Yingqin led the students into the streets for a demonstration march. During the summer of 1919, Guizhou students and military cadets continued to engage in the unfolding patriotic, anti-imperialist movement, with Wang Wenhua and He Yingqin exercising control.

The growing influence of the YGA and connections with students beyond Guizhou's borders, combined with the fact that Wang and He controlled it, exacerbated Liu Xianshi's concerns that the student

---

[57] Xiong Zongren, *Wusi yundong zai Guizhou*, 45–46; Xiong Zongren, *He Yingqin: xuanwozhong de lishi*, I, 74–78; Zhang Ming, "Xinhai geming qianhou de He Yingqin" [He Yingqin Before and After the 1911 Revolution], *Dangdai guizhou*, 30 (October 2011), 65.

movement could pose a serious political threat. Since the PSA showed none of the vitality or popularity of the YGA, Liu made several attempts to curtail the activities of Guiyang students and to weaken YGA influence, none of which succeeded. Meanwhile Wang Wenhua and He Yingqin continued to push for political change in Guizhou. As a first step they organized a committee that advocated a "renovation" (*shuaxin*) of the Guizhou provincial government through the separation of military and civilian affairs. They took advantage of the fact that others had grown discontented with Liu's rule and persuaded Ren Kecheng, a member of the Constitutional Preparation Society and Wang's former teacher, to chair the committee. The committee requested that Liu Xianshi resign his position as military governor (*dujun*) and appoint Wang Wenhua, already commander in chief of the Guizhou Army, as his replacement. This would leave civilian power in the hands of Liu, who would retain his position as provincial governor (*shengzhang*), and place complete provincial military authority in the hands of Wang Wenhua. Not surprisingly, the proposal enraged Liu Xianshi, who refused this direct challenge to his authority.[58]

### The Minjiu Incident

Now fully convinced that his nephew had turned against him, but still wary of Wang Wenhua's military strength, Liu began plotting to remove Wang as commander in chief, triggering a series of events that led to a violent clash known in Guizhou history as the Minjiu (1920) Incident. In early 1920, troops from Guizhou allied with those from Yunnan under the combined command of Tang Jiyao and marched into Sichuan province in order to meet a challenge from its military governor, Xiong Kewu, who rejected the influence of Yunnan and Guizhou and asserted Sichuan's independence from its neighbors. Wang Wenhua led the Guizhou troops and spent the next several months in Sichuan, which gave Liu Xianshi an opportunity to oust his nephew from power.[59] According to some sources, Tang Jiyao began the plot when he complained to Liu that Wang was unfit to command, pointing out that he had no formal military education and relied heavily on his Japanese-trained subordinates, such as He Yingqin and Gu Zhenglun.[60] According to others, Liu Xianshi initiated the plot, requesting that Tang use his authority as commander

---

[58] Gui Baizhu, "Liu Xianshi jituan neibu douzheng sanji," 105; Xiong Zongren, *He Yingqin: xuanwozhong de lishi*, I, 93.

[59] Donald Sutton, *Provincial Militarism and the Chinese Republic: The Yunnan Army, 1905–1925* (Ann Arbor: University of Michigan Press, 1980), 232–33.

[60] Chen Xianqiu, "Xinhai yihou ershinian jian guizhou junzheng gaishu," 153.

of the combined force to remove Wang from command of his troops, replacing him with another officer.[61] In any event, Wang Wenhua soon got wind of the plot and drew up his own plan to "sweep out the princes," meaning to remove Liu Xianshi's key supporters and force him to step down. To avoid suspicion and to distance himself from the plot against his uncle, Wang Wenhua did not return to Guiyang to take a direct role in the coup. Instead, he boarded a ship and traveled to Shanghai.[62] According to Zhang Pengnian, a member of Liu's circle and observer of the power struggle, Wang and his fellow plotters drew up two lists of names: one group for immediate assassination and another group to be observed, with ultimate decisions on whether or not to kill them put off to a later date.[63]

In October 1920, all Guizhou forces left Sichuan, returning to Guiyang via Zunyi, north of the capital. On November 10, He Yingqin and others involved in the plot met to go over the list of those targeted for assassination. According to Guizhou historian Xiong Zongren, He Yingqin argued in favor of a short list, while others advocated a longer list of ten or more names in order to completely eviscerate Liu's faction. Eventually they agreed that excess bloodshed might turn the people of Guiyang against them, so they trimmed the list to four names, all key supporters of Liu Xianshi. After the assassinations removed Liu's base of support, Wang planned to force him to resign.[64]

Shots rang out in Guiyang late in the night of November 10, indicating that the coup had begun. The plotters succeeded in assassinating two of the four targets, but the other two escaped. As Liu learned what had happened, he resigned his military and civil positions and fled to his home in Xingyi city, appealing to his sister, Wang Wenhua's mother,

---

[61] Guizhou daxue lishixi, "Guizhou junfa Liu Xianshi fajiashi," 196.

[62] Lin Yuxian, "Guizhou 'minjiu shibian' qinliji" [A Personal Record of the Guizhou "Minjiu Incident"], Guizhou wenshi ziliao xuanji, 1 (n.d.), 116; Chen Xianqiu, "Xinhai yihou ershinian jian guizhou junzheng gaishu," 152–53.

[63] Zhang Pengnian, "Xinhai yilai sishi nianjian guizhou zhengju de yanbian," 60. Gui Baizhu claimed that, according to what many people at the time believed, Wang wanted to arrest the men on the list and hold them for a short period rather than kill them. It is not clear if this is so, and if so when and how the plan changed to killing the men on the list. See Gui Baizhu, "Liu Xianshi jituan neibu douzheng sanji," 109.

[64] Zhang Pengnian, "Xinhai yilai sishi nianjian guizhou zhengju de yanbian," 61–62; Xiong Zongren, He Yingqin: xuanwozhong de lishi, I, 101. Ni Tuanji argues that He Yingqin had no role in the Minjiu Incident and knew nothing of it until afterwards. See Ni Tuanjiu, "Yunlong qihe shoujian qixun: He Yingqin zhuan zhi si" [A Perfect Occasion for Initial Outstanding Achievements: Biography of He Yingqin, Part IV], Zhongwai zazhi, 43, 5 (May 1988), 62. The four men targeted for assassination were Guo Chongguang, leader of the local Qilaohui secret society, which supported Liu, Xiong Fanyu, Liu's chief secretary, He Linshu, who replaced Chen Tingce as director of political affairs, and Ding Yizhong, head of military affairs.

for protection.[65] From the perspective of the plotters, success or fail-ure still lay in the balance. Rumors circulated throughout the city that Yunnan forces were approaching Guizhou together with Liu Xianqian's force to put down the coup and restore Liu Xianshi to power. He Yingqin quickly moved to implement the second part of the plan, which called for Ren Kecheng to serve as acting provincial governor until Wang Wen-hua returned to take that position. Though critical of Liu Xianshi, Ren wanted no part of the coup and fled to Anshun. A detachment of soldiers found him and escorted him back to Guiyang, but he quickly fled again and took refuge in a Catholic church. Unable to secure Ren's coopera-tion, the leaders of the coup turned to acting director of political affairs Zhou Hongbin, who agreed to serve as acting provincial governor.[66]

Liu Xianshi's resignation and departure from Guiyang did not end the power struggle in which He Yingqin had involved himself. Wang Wenhua had deliberately stayed away, hoping physical distance might mitigate public condemnation for overthrowing his uncle and the murder of prominent officials. Meanwhile, he had taken funds to Shanghai with which to buy weapons and equipment to strengthen the Guizhou Army.[67] The distance did little to protect him as Liu's supporters followed Wang to Shanghai, plotting revenge. In March 1921, as Wang stepped out of a hotel restaurant that he frequented and into a waiting car, assassins shot him dead.[68] As Liu Xianshi's supporters began returning to Guizhou, He Yingqin quickly left for Kunming, where an old classmate from the Shikan Gakko, Wang Boling, put him to work as an instructor at the Yunnan Military Academy.

His departure from Guizhou proved insufficient to protect him as Liu's men found him in Kunming and attempted to kill him at the Fenghua Teahouse in December 1921. Witnesses reported seeing Liu Xianshi's nephew Liu Yuanchang lurking around afterwards, and an investigation revealed that another relative, Liu Dunwu, had hired the assassins.[69] Wang Yongyu, He Yingqin's companion that day, went for help, and others rushed He Yingqin to a French hospital on Denghua Street, where

[65] Lin Yuxian, "Guizhou 'minjiu shibian' qinliji," 118–19; Xiong Zongren, *He Yingqin: xuanwozhong de lishi*, I, 104–05.

[66] Gui Baizhu, "Liu Xianshi jituan neibu douzheng sanji," 110–11; Xiong Zongren, *He Yingqin: xuanwozhong de lishi*, I, 103. Gui Baizhu claims that Lu Tao served as acting provincial governor. See Gui Baizhu, "Liu Xianshi jituan neibu douzheng sanji," 110.

[67] Chen Xianqiu, "Xinhai yihou ershinian jian guizhou junzheng gaishu," 153.

[68] Zhang Pengnian, "Xinhai yilai sishi nianjian guizhou zhengju de yanbian," 63–65; Guizhou daxue lishixi, "Guizhou junfa Liu Xianshi fajiashi," 197; Gui Baizhu, "Liu Xianshi jituan neibu douzheng sanji," 111.

[69] *HYQJJ*, I, 41; Li Yuan, *Jiang Jieshi he He Yingqin*, 24; Xiong Zongren, *He Yingqin: xuanwozhong de lishi*, I, 153.

a French-trained Vietnamese surgeon operated to remove the bullet from his chest. To forestall a second attempt on his life, He Yingqin let it be known that he intended to let bygones be bygones and would not pursue the perpetrators.[70] He Yingqin ended his career in Guizhou in failure, pain, and humiliation. He had relied on his relationship with Wang Wenhua to help him rise within the Guizhou Army, but his support base collapsed with the failure of the 1920 coup. After his wounds healed enough to allow him to travel, He went to Shanghai to stay with his brother-in-law Wang Boqun, with little idea of what the future held for him.

An examination of He Yingqin's education and early career indicates that his rise to prominence in Guizhou came through a combination of professional capability and personal connections. His early years reflect none of the incompetence or corruption that later critics claimed. Indeed, by the standards of the time, He Yingqin had a first-rate military education, acquired in both China and Japan, which prepared him well for a career as a military officer. At the Shimbu Gakko and the Shikan Gakko in particular, he learned his profession from one of the best sources available to Chinese cadets of his time. His period of service in the Japanese Imperial Army honed his practical skills and he gained valuable experience as commandant of the Guizhou Military Academy, all of which he would put to good use in the next stage of his career. His serious wounds and expulsion from his home province, which came about due to his participation in the ill-fated coup against Liu Xianshi, may have appeared as a significant setback at the time, but they proved temporary as his move to Shanghai presented a new opportunity that led him to prominence on the national stage.

---

[70] Zhu Guangting, "He Yingqin zai Kunming beici jianwen," 153; Xie Boyuan, "Wosuo liaojie de He Yingqin" [The He Yingqin I Knew], in Tu Yueseng, ed., *Xingyi Liu, Wang, He sanda jiazu*, 138. Xie identifies the doctor as Vietnamese.

## 2    "Like Bao Shuya and Guan Zhong"

As a part of his routine, the commandant of the Whampoa Military Academy liked to occasionally tour the grounds and observe the work of both cadets and the officers who trained them. On one particular day in early 1924 he came across two officers, He Yingqin and Wang Boling, in the midst of leading war exercises in which candidates for instructor positions at the academy had to make a frontal assault on an enemy position. Wang favored a more careful and circuitous approach to the target, which would take more time but result in fewer casualties. He Yingqin, on the other hand, suggested a direct frontal attack which would bring a swifter victory, but with potentially higher casualties. The commandant offered a critique of the exercise in which he praised He's decisive action and willingness to take risks to achieve victory. He's subsequent victory in the exercise no doubt improved his standing at the academy and in the commandant's estimation.[1]

Having survived the disastrous turn of events in Guizhou and Yunnan, He Yingqin had found a new situation in Guangdong that suited him well and brought him into close cooperation with an old classmate from Japan, the Whampoa Military Academy commandant Chiang Kai-shek. This marked the beginning of a long professional and personal relationship with Chiang and the start of He's rise within the ranks of the Chinese army. Beyond training cadets to serve in the revolutionary army, He Yingqin eventually commanded the academy's best forces in the Eastern Expeditions of 1925, where he delivered important battlefield victories and ensured the survival of the revolutionary government. His military success and support for Chiang during these early years of the Nationalist revolution paved the way for Chiang's rise as commander in chief of the National Revolutionary Army. Within a matter of a few years, He Yingqin rose from being a minor military administrator from a remote province to serving as one of the top officers in the Nationalist military. These early victories demonstrated He's reliability and skill as a commander,

---

[1]  Li Yuan, *Jiang Jieshi he He Yingqin*, 28; *HYQJJ*, I, 51.

and provided the foundation for his lasting relationship with Chiang Kai-shek.

## The Whampoa Military Academy

After recuperating in Shanghai from the attempted assassination, He Yingqin looked to his network of former classmates and colleagues for help in finding a suitable military position. Through his brother-in-law Wang Boqun, who now served as Sun Yat-sen's head of communications, He Yingqin heard of plans to establish a new military academy to train a national revolutionary army. Wang arranged for He to travel to Guangzhou to meet with Sun, who later appointed him as a military advisor to his supreme headquarters.[2] In 1923, Sun had agreed to work with Soviet advisors to build a revolutionary military force that could defeat the various "warlord" armies and unite China under a single government. As a part of this agreement, in February 1924, Sun's government established the Whampoa Military Academy, which required the services of a number of military instructors. Chiang Kai-shek chaired the academy's preparatory committee that began searching for qualified men to serve on the faculty. Wang Boling, who had studied in Japan with He Yingqin and now served on the preparatory committee, recommended He. Familiar with He from their days in Japan and common service under Chen Qimei at Shanghai, and undoubtedly aware that Sun had already appointed him as a military advisor, Chiang invited He to Guangzhou to discuss opportunities at the new military academy.[3]

On February 8, He Yingqin met with Chiang Kai-shek and visited the campus on Changzhou Island. Dismayed at the decrepit condition of the facility and the feeble gun emplacements, which dated back to the late Qing period, He Yingqin nonetheless deemed it a suitable place to begin training young men to be soldiers and officers, removed as it was from the city of Guangzhou and all of its distractions. Despite some initial doubts about the job and its low salary, he decided to accept the position.[4] After all, his training in Japan, his experience with the Guizhou Military Academy, and his progressive politics made him ideal for this kind of work. The next day, Chiang arranged for He to meet with Sun again, who then appointed him military advisor to the Whampoa

---

[2]  Xiong Zongren, *He Yingqin: xuanwozhong de lishi*, I, 135.

[3]  Li Yuan, *Jiang Jieshi he He Yingqin*, 26; Xiong Zongren, *He Yingqin: xuanwozhong de lishi*, I, 136; Xie Boyuan, "Wosuo liaojie de He Yingqin," 138.

[4]  Li Zhonggong, "Wosuo zhidao de He Yingqin" [The He Yingqin I Knew], *Wenshi ziliao xuanji*, 36 (n.d.), 205.

Military Academy and urged him to help build the school.[5] The personal
and professional relationships forged at the Whampoa Military Academy
would help promote the careers of a number of men who would later
assume important positions in Chiang's army. Chiang handpicked the
officers and faculty members for the academy, and this marked He's
emergence as one of Chiang's protégés.[6]

The academy got off to a rocky start as Chiang Kai-shek left only weeks
after its establishment, in part because of disagreements with Soviet advisors over the curriculum and management of the academy.[7] Sun Yat-sen
temporarily appointed Liao Zhongkai commandant of the academy in
Chiang's place, but after an absence of only a month Chiang returned
and the Soviet advisors limited their demands, allowing work to begin
in earnest.[8] He Yingqin, on the other hand, threw himself into his work
wholeheartedly from the start. The political struggles of the leading members of Sun's revolutionary government did not concern him, nor did the
presence of Soviet advisors. The academy featured a rigorous training
regimen, and He Yingqin worked hard at his duties, rising early and
retiring late. According to another Whampoa officer, He Yingqin "was
up every day working before the cadets rose and rested only after they
had retired."[9] Such hard work was necessary as the faculty expected the
cadets to complete a course of instruction in six months that cadets at
the Baoding Military Academy completed in two years.[10]

In early May, Sun made He Yingqin chief of instruction, overseeing
the training and instruction of the 50-odd young graduates of other military academies who would then instruct the 499 students of the first
official class.[11] In effect, this appointment not only put him in charge of

[5] Xiong Zongren, *He Yingqin: xuanwozhong de lishi*, I, 136.
[6] Richard E. Gillespie, "Whampoa and the Nanking Decade (1924–1936)" (Ph.D. dissertation, American University, Washington, DC, 1971), 88, 98.
[7] F. F. Liu, *A Military History of Modern China, 1924–1949* (Princeton: Princeton University Press, 1956), 9.
[8] Keiji Furuya, *Chiang Kai-shek: His Life and Times*, English edn. abridged by Chang
Chun-ming (New York: St. John's University Press, 1981), 121; Chen and Zhang,
*Jiang Jieshi he huangpu xi*, 28–29.
[9] Wu Xiangxiang, "He Yingqin dajiang caineng fujiang mingyun" [General He Yingqin's
Luck and Capability], in *Minguo bairen zhuan*, vol. IV (Taipei: Zhuanji wenxue chubanshe, 1971), 99; Xiong Zongren, *He Yingqin: xuanwozhong de lishi*, I, 143. According to
Richard Gillespie, sixteen-hour workdays were common for faculty and officers at the
Academy. See Gillespie, "Whampoa and the Nanking Decade (1924–1936)," 82; Chen
Yuquan, "He Yingqin yu huangpu junxiao" [He Yingqin and the Whampoa Military
Academy], Part I, *Huangpu*, 6 (2010), 21.
[10] Gillespie, "Whampoa and the Nanking Decade (1924–1936)," 102A. Beginning with
the third class the time was extended to one year.
[11] *HYQJJ*, I, 51; Wu Xiangxiang, "He Yingqin dajiang caineng fujiang mingyun," 98; Ni
Tuanjiu, "Yunlong qihe shoujian qixun: He Yingqin zhuan zhi si," 10.

all instructors and cadets at the academy but also placed him in a position to work closely with Chiang Kai-shek, a virtual number-two man in the Whampoa hierarchy.[12] As he had with Wang Wenhua, He Yingqin would emerge as a close subordinate and "right-hand man" of the commandant, a position he took to naturally. Instruction at the academy emphasized basic military drill and practical skills such as knowledge of weapons and tactics. Cadets attended classroom and field activities from Monday through Saturday, with political lectures on Sunday. Whampoa differed from other Chinese academies in that it sought to prepare cadets for immediate combat service and therefore devoted significant time to fieldwork and physical fitness.[13] He Yingqin and other instructors felt significant pressure, as the success of Sun's movement depended upon the academy's ability to produce a group of young officers superior to those of the "warlord" armies and to prepare them for immediate combat. The curriculum reflected the strong influence of Japanese concepts and techniques, with the faculty members and officers constantly stressing discipline and self-sacrifice, and criticizing the cadets for selfish or individualistic habits or actions. They believed that only through working together and showing what many called the aggressive "Whampoa spirit" could the revolutionary army overcome material disadvantages and achieve its goal of unifying China through armed force.[14]

His position at the academy brought He Yingqin into close collaboration with Chiang Kai-shek for the first time. As commandant, Chiang played an active role in the daily activities of the academy, delivering lectures, inspecting dormitories, and supervising the work of students and faculty members alike. As Ray Huang has noted, throughout his life Chiang enjoyed talking about his own experience as a military cadet in Japan, living the Spartan lifestyle of a disciplined soldier.[15] Chiang's speeches to the faculty and cadets typically emphasized personal attitude and behavior, subordination to the party, and sympathy for the common people. Chiang repeatedly told the cadets they should be disciplined, obedient, and prepared to sacrifice their lives for the good of the nation.[16]

[12]  Li Yuan, *Jiang Jieshi he He Yingqin*, 28.
[13]  Gillespie, "Whampoa and the Nanking Decade (1924–1936)," 103–07.
[14]  Tien, *Chinese Military Theory*, 167.
[15]  Ray Huang, "Chiang Kai-shek and His Diary as a Historical Source," *Chinese Studies in History*, 29, 1–2 (Fall–Winter 1995–96), 19.
[16]  Richard Landis, "Training and Indoctrination at the Whampoa Academy," in F. Gilbert Chan and Thomas Etzold, eds., *China in the 1920s: Nationalism and Revolution* (New York: New Viewpoints, 1996), 81–82; C. Martin Wilbur and Julie Lien-ying How, *Missionaries of Revolution: Soviet Advisors and Nationalist China, 1920–1927* (Cambridge, MA: Harvard University Press, 1989), 113; Gillespie, "Whampoa and the Nanking Decade (1924–1936)," 108–10; F. F. Liu, *Military History of Modern China*, 10.

In his analysis of Chiang Kai-shek's speeches to Whampoa cadets, Tien Chen-ya identifies consistent references to revolutionary spirit with three key points of emphasis. First, Chiang continuously stressed the importance of a willingness to take risks and of having the courage to sacrifice one's life in order to achieve victory in battle. If the revolution had any chance for success, Chiang believed, soldiers must be willing to lay down their own lives for the greater cause. This aggressive spirit of self-sacrifice played a prominent part in the training of cadets at Whampoa, as it did in Japanese military academies. Second, Chiang recognized the enormity of the task ahead as the revolutionary forces faced numerically superior opponents in China's regional "warlord" armies. In order to overcome this disadvantage, he believed in the need for unity of purpose, coordinated action, and proper strategy. If well led, motivated, and possessed of an appropriately aggressive strategy, the revolutionary forces could overcome any odds or obstacles. Third, Chiang demanded strict discipline as an essential component of a strong military force. Soldiers not only must obey orders and maintain discipline, but also must have complete confidence in their commanders in order to fight effectively. This belief is reflected in Chiang's 1924 implementation of the Law of Joint Responsibility (*lianzuo fa*), which called for the execution of those who retreated from battle without orders.[17] He Yingqin strongly identified with these themes, which helped bind the two men together. When Chiang gave speeches or lectured, sometimes for hours at a time, He Yingqin stood at rigid attention taking in every word.[18] Although in many ways an "odd couple," the emotional and charismatic Chiang Kai-shek and the serious and sober He Yingqin had a great deal in common when it came to the training and ideology of the modern Chinese soldier.

At Whampoa, Chiang sought to surround himself with men of outstanding ability and moral character, citing the example of nineteenth-century scholar-official Zeng Guofan, whose moral character, integrity, and leadership skills served as a model for Chiang.[19] Fastidious in his own personal habits, Chiang immediately took to He Yingqin in part because he did not drink or smoke opium and was known for his

---

[17] Tien, *Chinese Military Theory*, 170–74. Specifically, the Law of Joint Responsibility stated that any commander who gave up his position without orders to do so faced execution. If troops abandoned a commanding officer in the field, that officer's subordinates would be executed. Designed to ensure military discipline, it also served as a deterrent to bold action by officers in the field who might be held accountable if things went badly.

[18] Li Yuan, *Jiang Jieshi he He Yingqin*, 130–31.

[19] See Chiang's remarks on Zeng Guofan in Furuya, *Chiang Kai-shek*, 56.

dedication and hard work.[20] One American military officer who knew He in 1934 described him as a "man of excellent moral habits," noting specifically that he "does not smoke opium and drinks only a sip of wine when he believes the occasion requires it."[21] Such characteristics made him stand out among his colleagues as just the kind of officer Chiang had in mind. Other Chiang protégés, such as Wang Boling, had similar credentials to He Yingqin, including training at the Shikan Gakko and prior work as an instructor at the Yunnan Military Academy. Yet Wang smoked opium and gambled, sometimes neglecting his duty as a result. He Yingqin, in contrast, excelled at taking and executing orders.[22] He Yingqin later recalled that, when he led cadets on early morning marches, he often returned to find Chiang observing. As a result, Chiang placed more and more trust and responsibility with He, in some cases taking it away from Wang Boling. He Yingqin gratefully accepted this recognition and trust from Chiang Kai-shek.[23] The relationship rested on more than traditional military hierarchical relations, arising from common training experience and work habits.

Reports from Soviet and American officials familiar with He Yingqin confirm that he stood out as exactly the kind of disciplined and capable officer that Chiang sought. In his 1982 memoir, Alexander Cherepanov, a Soviet advisor at the Whampoa Academy, remarked on He's manner and character, noting that at their first meeting he sat rigidly with his back straight and his hands on his knees, displaying a very military bearing. He reminded Cherepanov of a "diligent pupil from the front row of a classroom."[24] Evidently, He Yingqin preferred to take the advice of Soviet advisors in private, which Cherepanov attributes to vanity and a reluctance to "lose face" in front of the cadets, but he also confirms that He Yingqin performed his duties at Whampoa efficiently and effectively.[25] Major John Magruder, an American military attaché stationed in China in the late 1920s and early 1930s, corroborated this assessment of He's personal character and capabilities, describing him as "conservative, not impulsive," "a man of good character," and "a very good

---

[20]  Li Zhonggong, "Wosuo zhidao de He Yingqin," 205; Li Yuan, *Jiang Jieshi he He Yingqin*, 130–31.

[21]  See Lieutenant Colonel W. Drysdale's remarks, G-2 Report, Military Intelligence Division, Record Group 165, National Archives, Washington, DC.

[22]  Li Zhonggong, "Wosuo zhidao de He Yingqin," 206.

[23]  Chen and Zhang, *Jiang Jieshi he huangpu xi*, 44; Li Zhonggong, "Wosuo zhidao de He Yingqin," 206.

[24]  Alexander I. Cherepanov, *As Military Advisor in China*, translated by Sergei Sosinsky (Moscow: Progress Publishers, 1982), 72.

[25]  Cherepanov, *As Military Advisor in China*, 72, 85.

soldier."[26] These characteristics helped He Yingqin establish a good working relationship with Chiang Kai-shek, and his job as chief of instruction at the Whampoa Academy offered him compensation for the situation he had lost in Guizhou. He found a new patron in Chiang, who in turn found a reliable and disciplined subordinate in He. The match proved favorable to both parties.

### The First Eastern Expedition: Danshui and Mianhu

While their common training, attitudes, and work styles brought He Yingqin to Chiang Kai-shek's side at the academy, tangible proof of He's value to Chiang and the revolutionary government came with his performance in the Eastern Expeditions of 1925. This confirmed Chiang's confidence in him and greatly strengthened their relationship. Commanding troops in two critical battles in the spring of 1925, He Yingqin demonstrated to Chiang Kai-shek that he possessed the very qualities Chiang spoke of so often: a willingness to take risks, the ability to overcome numerically superior forces, and strict discipline. This represented a turning point in He's career and marked the true start of his rapid rise under Chiang's command.

In November 1924, Sun Yat-sen traveled to Beijing at the invitation of northern power figures Duan Qirui, Zhang Zuolin, and Feng Yuxiang in order to discuss the problem of national unity.[27] With Sun making the journey north, Guangdong militarist Chen Jiongming began to prepare an attack on Guangzhou and Sun's revolutionary government. Chen commanded a collection of diverse military units numbering approximately 50,000 troops, spread across eastern Guangdong.[28] Aware that Chen posed a potential threat to his base at Guangzhou, Sun had already ordered the creation of the so-called Whampoa or Cadet army in the fall of 1924 to form the basis of a force that could defend against Chen Jiongming's threat.[29]

Since September, He Yingqin had been preparing to assemble a training regiment composed of Whampoa officers and cadets to undertake a campaign against Chen Jiongming. This unit combined soldiers recruited from neighboring areas and officers drawn from the ranks of the

---

[26] See Major John Magruder's written evaluations of He Yingqin from 1928 and 1934, Military Attaché, Military Intelligence Division, Record Group 165, National Archives, Washington, DC.

[27] Furuya, *Chiang Kai-shek*, 150; C. Martin Wilbur, *The Nationalist Revolution in China, 1923–1928* (Cambridge: Cambridge University Press, 1983), 20.

[28] Wilbur and How, *Missionaries of Revolution*, 143.

[29] *A Brief History of the Republic of China Armed Forces*, microfilm, Scholarly Resources (Taipei: Office of Military History, 1971), 14.

faculty and the first class of Whampoa cadets. Some company command-ers came from local military units, but most battalion and regimental commanders were Whampoa Academy faculty members. Platoon and squad leaders came from the ranks of the first class of graduates.[30] When the revolutionary government activated the First Training Regiment at a full strength of 1,835 (combat strength of approximately 1,200) in October 1924, Chiang Kai-shek appointed He Yingqin its commander. The government created a Second Training Regiment under the com-mand of Wang Boling in December 1924. These two Whampoa-based units would do much of the fighting in the First Eastern Expedition.[31]

The First Training Regiment as a whole performed well in the campaign against Chen Jiongming's troops, with key victories in two important battles at Danshui and Mianhu in February and March 1925 respectively. The Eastern Expedition began when the First and Second Training Regiments, both under the overall command of Chiang Kai-shek, combined with elements of the Guangdong Army under Xu Chongzhi to attack Chen Jiongming in eastern Guangdong.[32] As Edward Dreyer has pointed out, the fact that Sun Yat-sen and Chiang Kai-shek deployed two regiments of cadets immediately after their graduation indicates the critical nature of this campaign, upon which the very exis-tence of the revolutionary government depended.[33] In early February, the First Training Regiment moved east along the Guangzhou–Jiulong railroad, clearing it of enemy troops and advancing on the town of Danshui.[34]

Cadets serving in the training regiments had only been through a six-month training period at the Whampoa Academy, but they tended to display higher morale and better discipline than those of the armies they faced. According to Soviet advisors, the Whampoa troops were popular with the locals, in stark contrast to Chen Jiongming's troops.[35] Yet the two training regiments suffered from a shortage of supplies and equipment. Officers carried Mauser pistols and infantrymen either a 7.9 mm Mauser rifle or Japanese-made 6.5 mm rifle, but ammunition remained varied

[30] Gillespie, "Whampoa and the Nanking Decade (1924–1936)," 119–20.
[31] Li Yuan, *Jiang Jieshi he He Yingqin*, 36; Chen and Zhang, *Jiang Jieshi he huangpu xi*, 62–63. Others have translated *jiaodaotuan* as "indoctrinated regiment" or "instructional regiment." The term "training regiment" seems more appropriate as the cadets leading it had only had six months of preparation and were learning on the job. See also Harry H. Collier and Paul Chin-chih Lai, *Organizational Changes in the Chinese Army, 1895–1950* (Taipei: Office of the Military Historian, 1969), 72.
[32] Wilbur and How, *Missionaries of Revolution*, 143.    [33] Dreyer, *China at War*, 121.
[34] Wilbur and How, *Missionaries of Revolution*, 143–44.
[35] See Document Three in Wilbur and How, *Missionaries of Revolution*, 485.

and scarce. Some soldiers had only 200 to 250 rounds for the entire expedition.[36] Marching for two to three hours and then resting for 15 to 20 minutes, the troops ate only two meals of cooked rice balls and various vegetables per day, barely sufficient to sustain them. The lack of appropriate topographical maps and intelligence perhaps posed the greatest difficulty. He Yingqin had no choice but to rely on information from soldiers familiar with the area or to interview local inhabitants for intelligence. In most cases, the Whampoa units had no idea of enemy positions until they encountered them, and communication between the training regiments proved difficult.[37]

The second division of the Guangdong Army under the command of Zhang Mingda arrived at Danshui first, reaching the outskirts on the evening of February 12. It is unclear exactly how many enemy troops occupied Danshui, but they must have numbered at a minimum 1,000 under the command of Hong Zhaolin, one of Chen Jiongming's generals.[38] More importantly, a wall 4 to 6 meters high, with artillery emplacements and lookout posts, surrounded the city, posing a challenge for attacking forces. Lanterns hanging outside the walls illuminated the area to prevent a night attack.[39] Zhang initially tried to take Danshui with a frontal assault by one company, but heavy fire forced the soldiers to turn back with significant losses. Another assault on the morning of February 14 dislodged enemy troops from positions outside the town walls, but again failed to take the city.[40]

He Yingqin's First Training Regiment arrived at a point 5 to 6 kilometers south of Danshui on the afternoon of February 14, as did Wang Boling's Second Training Regiment. Once again, the lack of intelligence and communication between units led to confusion. According to Cherepanov, Wang initially mistook Zhang Mingda's forces for enemy troops and a 15-minute firefight ensued, but with few casualties. Likewise, He Yingqin and his Soviet advisors believed that friendly troops controlled Danshui and unexpectedly took fire as they approached.[41] Once the three units established contact, they surrounded the city and

---

[36] Gillespie, "Whampoa and the Nanking Decade (1924–1936)," 159; Cherepanov, *As Military Advisor in China*, 132; Collier and Lai, *Organizational Changes*, 72.

[37] Cherepanov, *As Military Advisor in China*, 119.

[38] Cherepanov claims that the two training regiments took 700 prisoners while 300 of Hong's troops escaped Danshui, leading to the estimate of 1,000 troops. See Cherepanov, *As Military Advisor in China*, 123–25. Hong Zhaolin had a total of 15,000 troops under his command in the area. See Collier and Lai, *Organizational Changes*, 83.

[39] He Yingqin, "Mianhu zhanyi zhi huiyi" [Reminiscences of the Battle of Mianhu], *Geming wenxian*, 11 (1977), 270.

[40] Cherepanov, *As Military Advisor in China*, 119–21.

[41] Cherepanov, *As Military Advisor in China*, 120–21.

began planning a coordinated attack. Agreeing that Danshui must be taken quickly before reinforcements could arrive, Wang Boling, Zhang Mingda, He Yingqin, and their Soviet advisors drew up a plan for an artillery barrage, followed by a frontal assault in which troops would use ladders to scale the city walls. Although he approved of the plan, He Yingqin refused to agree to such an assault until Chiang personally approved the plan. He had no objection to taking risks in battle or launching bold frontal assaults, but not without Chiang's authorization. Once Chiang arrived on the scene and gave his approval, preparation began for an attack on the morning of February 15, with elements of He Yingqin's First Training Regiment making the initial assault.[42]

The coordinated attack on Danshui began when the artillery of the training regiments, consisting of two cannons, opened fire in the early morning. After approximately 30 minutes, the infantry onslaught began with the first battalion of the First Training Regiment spearheading the attack on the city in three separate columns. Observing the battle from a small hill, He Yingqin could see that fierce gunfire from the city wall prevented attacking forces from moving forward more than a short distance. Despite the usual difficulty in communicating with his troops, He sent additional units forward, using a bugler to sound the advance. The artillery barrage proved moderately effective, driving defenders from the wall and opening up a small breach near the top of the wall at the southeast corner. Unfortunately, the engineers had prepared only a small number of ladders during the night, limiting the number of troops that could get through the breach into the city. Other soldiers used a human-ladder technique, boosting each other up the wall and into the breach. Once inside, they opened the town gates to allow troops from the First and Second Training Regiments to enter the town. Hong Zhaolin's forces gathered some 2,000 reinforcements from the north of Danshui and mounted a sudden counterattack, driving Wang Boling's Second Training Regiment out of the city, but He Yingqin's troops successfully repulsed the attack and preserved the victory.[43] The capture of Danshui meant the acquisition of much-needed weapons and ammunition, including 590 rifles, 5 machine guns, and 700 prisoners. The 2 training regiments suffered 10 killed and 40 wounded.[44] According to Cherepanov, Chiang initially believed that the battle had been lost, but

[42] Li Yuan, *Jiang Jieshi he He Yingqin*, 38; *HYQJJ*, I, 69; Xiong Zongren, *He Yingqin: xuanwozhong de lishi*, I, 160.
[43] Cherepanov, *As Military Advisor in China*, 123–25.
[44] Cherepanov, *As Military Advisor in China*, 122–23; Li Yuan, *Jiang Jieshi he He Yingqin*, 39; Xiong Zongren, *He Yingqin: xuanwozhong de lishi*, I, 160–61. Cherepanov claims that there were 1,000 rifles.

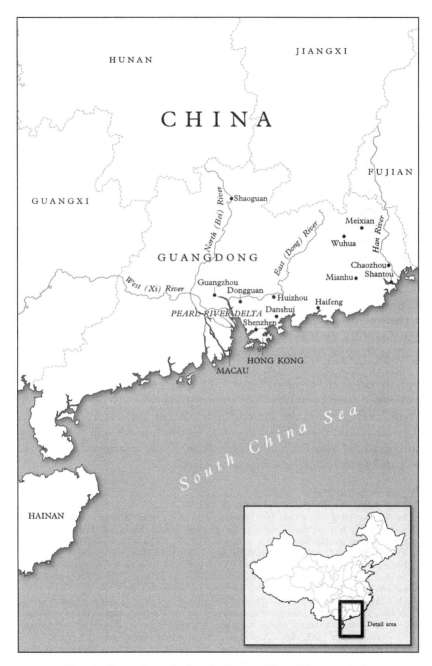

Map 2: Guangdong during the Eastern Expeditions

his disappointment turned to elation when He Yingqin informed him of the victory.[45]

In He Yingqin's first important action as a regimental commander, his troops won an important victory with an aggressive attack on a well-defended city. Even Cherepanov, whose memoirs tend to emphasize the role of Soviet advisors and disparage Chiang's officers, praises the Whampoa forces for having fought well.[46] As had been the case at the Whampoa Academy, Wang Boling's shortcomings highlighted He Yingqin's capabilities. After the Whampoa forces took Danshui, the First Training Regiment mopped up resistance and rounded up prisoners in and around the city while Zhang Mingda's troops acted as a security force. When Hong Zhaolin's troops mounted the unexpected counterattack, Wang Boling's force failed to take up proper positions, leaving He and Zhang to defend the city. After the battle, Chiang Kai-shek criticized Wang Boling and relieved him of command of the Second Training Regiment, replacing him with one of He Yingqin's battalion commanders, Shen Yingshi, the man who had led the initial assault on Danshui.[47]

Following the success at Danshui, He Yingqin and the First Training Regiment again played a critical role in the battle at Mianhu, the most decisive battle of the First Eastern Expedition. A small town to the west of Shantou, Mianhu is easily approachable from the east, which is flat, but there are hilly wooded areas to the north and west. At Chiang's order, He Yingqin's First Training Regiment moved west on March 9, approaching Mianhu late in the evening of March 12. Information from local villagers varied, suggesting that Chen Jiongming had between 10,000 and 30,000 troops in the area under the command of Lin Hu. He Yingqin's own estimate placed the number closer to 8,000, but this still heavily outnumbered his own force of roughly 1,200.[48] Nonetheless, He Yingqin prepared to attack the next morning, March 13.

[45] Cherepanov, *As Military Advisor in China*, 126.
[46] Cherepanov, *As Military Advisor in China*, 123.
[47] Li Yuan, *Jiang Jieshi he He Yingqin*, 41; Chen and Zhang, *Jiang Jieshi he huangpu xi*, 63; Xiong Zongren, *He Yingqin: xuanwozhong de lishi*, I, 159–61; Cherepanov, *As Military Advisor in China*, 127. In his recollection of the battle, He Yingqin incorrectly states that Shen Yingshi died in the fighting. Shen succeeded Wang Boling as commander of the Second Training Regiment and died of illness in 1926. See the editor's note in He Yingqin, "Mianhu zhanyi zhi huiyi," 270. When Shen later suffered a wound, Qian Dajun took command of the regiment.
[48] He Yingqin, "Mianhu zhanyi zhi huiyi," 272; Xiong Zongren, *He Yingqin: xuanwozhong de lishi*, I, 163. The true number of enemy forces at Mianhu is impossible to ascertain, but He's own assessment seems accurate. A captured Soviet document puts enemy troop strength at 7,000. See Chapter III, "The Revolutionary Army of Canton," Military Intelligence Division, Record Group 165, National Archives, Washington, DC. According to other Chinese Nationalist sources, Lin Hu had command of a total of 8,000 men. See Collier and Lai, *Organizational Changes*, 83.

With no solid intelligence regarding enemy positions, the battle plan called for the first battalion to move forward slowly until it encountered the forward enemy line and engaged in a firefight. The second battalion stood in reserve, and the third battalion, along with two machine-gun squads, moved to the right, attempting to find the end of the enemy line and roll up its flank.[49] As expected, the first battalion made contact but, due to the numerical superiority of the opposing force, it quickly suffered casualties. He Yingqin began sending units from the second battalion into battle to support the first battalion, to little effect. Meanwhile the third battalion encountered equally heavy resistance, suffering significant casualties. Unable to break through or to communicate with the other battalions, each unit continued to fight independently. On a few occasions, enemy troops threatened He's command post, wounding one of his bodyguards and killing another.[50] The arrival of reinforcements from the Second Training Regiment and the seventh division of the Guangdong Army at approximately two o'clock in the afternoon turned the tide of the battle. The First Training Regiment fought bravely against overwhelming odds, just as Chiang had so often urged the cadets to do at Whampoa, exhausting its artillery ammunition and sustaining approximately 30 percent casualties in each battalion.[51]

While the success of the First Training Regiment at Danshui and Mianhu is clear, not all observers approved of He Yingqin's individual performance as a regimental commander. Cherepanov praised his work at the Whampoa Academy, but criticized He's conduct in combat. For example, during a battle near the east station outside Pinghu on February 10, 1925, the First Training Regiment exchanged fire with 300 to 400 of Chen Jiongming's troops, routing them and occupying the station on February 12. He Yingqin's unit won the engagement, but Cherepanov states that in the midst of battle the former "grew blue in the face, rolled his eyes and his legs gave way under him." Only with the assistance of three soldiers did he slowly recover and begin giving orders based on Cherepanov's advice.[52] The author makes no attempt to explain the cause of this "spell," but clearly implies simple cowardice. Cherepanov's criticism is not surprising as almost all officers who remained loyal to Chiang Kai-shek and ended up opposing the Chinese Communist

---

[49] He Yingqin, "Mianhu zhanyi shihua," in *HYQJJJCXJ*, 151.

[50] He Yingqin, "Mianhu zhanyi shihua," 151; He Yingqin, "Mianhu zhanyi zhi huiyi," 273; Xiong Zongren, *He Yingqin: xuanwozhong de lishi*, I, 164–65.

[51] He Yingqin, "Mianhu zhanyi shihua," 152; He Yingqin, "Dongzheng beifa dao tongyi" [Eastern and Northern Expeditions to Unification], *Zhongwai zazhi*, 44, 2 (August 1988), 84; Ni Tuanjiu, "Yunlong qihe shoujian qixun: He Yingqin zhuan zhi si," 11.

[52] Cherepanov, *As Military Advisor in China*, 118.

Party receive the same derogatory treatment. Yet one cannot discount the possibility that He Yingqin indeed had difficulty in his first real combat experiences. The mistaken belief that friendly forces controlled Danshui may be a case in point; however, the Soviet advisors also made this error.

Nonetheless, the victory at Mianhu broke the back of Chen Jiongming's force, preserved the victory of the First Eastern Expedition, ensured the survival of the Guomindang (GMD) and its army, and confirmed Chiang Kai-shek's confidence in He Yingqin. The fighting at Danshui and Mianhu exhibited the power of the "Whampoa spirit" over numerical superiority, reflecting the key points of willingness to take risks, self-sacrifice, and discipline that Chiang had repeatedly stressed in his speeches to the cadets and faculty at the Whampoa Academy. At the conclusion of the battle, Chiang Kai-shek gave the regiment a reward of 1,000 yuan on behalf of the Guomindang Central Committee and Soviet advisor Vasily Blyukher presented his sword to He Yingqin.[53] Five days after the battle, Chiang named He Yingqin overall combat commander of both training regiments.[54] March 13, the date of the battle at Mianhu, became a kind of anniversary for Chiang and He, which they often celebrated together with other veterans of the Whampoa force.[55] According to Li Zhonggong, who observed the relationship between the two men from 1926 to 1931, the victory at Mianhu brought He and Chiang as close together as Bao Shuya and Guan Zhong, famous statesmen and friends of the Warring States era (403–221 BC) who shared a strong professional and personal bond.[56]

## The Second Eastern Expedition: the Yang–Liu revolt and the battle at Huizhou

The success of the First Eastern Expedition gave the GMD military forces confidence and experience, but it did not remove all threats to the

[53] Xiong Zongren, *He Yingqin: xuanwozhong de lishi*, I, 165; John Erickson, *The Soviet High Command: A Military and Political History 1918–1941*, 3rd edn. (New York: Frank Cass, 2001), 230.
[54] *HYQJJ*, I, 77; Chen and Zhang, *Jiang Jieshi he huangpu xi*, 64.
[55] Li Qizhong, "Mianhu zhanyi zhong yilin banzhua" [Details of the Battle at Mianhu], *Wenshi ziliao xuanji*, 77 (n.d.), 118. Every ten years on the anniversary of the battle at Mianhu, He and Chiang made speeches or published writings on the importance of the victory there. See Chen Yuquan, "He Yingqin yu huangpu junxiao" [He Yingqin and the Whampoa Military Academy], Part II, *Huangpu*, 1 (2011), 21.
[56] Li Zhonggong, "Wosuo zhidao de He Yingqin," 207. Li uses the following phrase to describe Chiang's feelings for He Yingqin: "My parents gave life to me, but only Bao Shu [He Yingqin] really knows me" (*shengwozhe fumu, zhiwozhe baoshu*). Li Yuan cites a slightly different version: "My parents gave life to me, but only Jing Zhi [He Yingqin] really knows me": Li Yuan, *Jiang Jieshi he He Yingqin*, 43.

revolutionary government. With Chen Jiongming temporarily in retreat from eastern Guangdong, new challenges emerged both from within the ranks of the revolutionary government itself and from a return of Chen Jiongming's forces, which precipitated a Second Eastern Expedition in the fall of 1925. Shortly after the conclusion of the First Eastern Expedition, the GMD reorganized its military forces to create the Party Army (*dangjun*) with two brigades. Chiang Kai-shek remained in overall command, but he appointed He Yingqin as commander of the first brigade.[57] Shortly thereafter, the force faced another significant challenge with the revolt of two of its most powerful regional commanders. Sun Yat-sen had welcomed alliances with regional commanders in order to strengthen his military position, but remained painfully aware of the risks. The First Eastern Expedition sent the most reliable military forces, the two Whampoa training regiments, into eastern Guangdong to deal with Chen Jiongming's forces, which left Guangzhou in the hands of Yang Ximin, commander of a force of Yunnan troops, and Liu Zhenhuan, commander of Guangxi troops. They had arrived in Guangdong in 1924 to join Sun Yat-sen's revolutionary movement, and together they formed the largest block of troops in Sun's military alliance. Drawn to Guangdong primarily for its wealth, they proved more interested in tapping the resources of the province than in pursuing the stated goals of Sun's organization. They remained appropriately respectful of Sun, but typically responded to orders only when these were accompanied by material incentives. When Sun Yat-sen traveled north in late 1924 and then died in early 1925, Yang and Liu began to openly explore alternative alliances with other regional figures such as Chen Jiongming, Tang Jiyao, and Duan Qirui. During the First Eastern Expedition, Yang had not followed through on his assignment to lead his troops to the east against Chen Jiongming and had instead remained in Guangzhou.[58]

When senior members of the GMD leadership met with Yang and Liu to discuss integrating their troops into the Party Army, Yang and Liu had already decided to break with the revolutionary government.[59] This once again placed the revolutionary base in jeopardy and called for immediate military action to secure control of Guangzhou. The Party Army and other loyal forces quickly withdrew from the areas that they had just occupied in eastern Guangdong in order to recover the capital. As a result, Chen Jiongming's forces returned to take control of eastern

[57] *HYQJJ*, I, 77.
[58] Sutton, *Provincial Militarism*, 276–84; and Li Qizhong, "Tongyi guangdong geming genjudi de zhanzheng" [The War to Unify the Guangdong Revolutionary Base], *Wenshi ziliao xuanji*, 2 (n.d.), 32.
[59] Li Qizhong, "Tongyi guangdong geming genjudi de zhanzheng," 34.

Guangdong, taking back the territory they had lost in the First Eastern Expedition.

Yang and Liu commanded a combined force of 20,000 to 30,000 soldiers, but the quality of these Yunnan and Guangxi troops varied.[60] Anticipating the attack, they prepared defensive positions in the mountains to the northeast of Guangzhou in the high ground around Baiyunshan, Longyantong, and Shougouling. A GMD force of approximately 30,000 soldiers approached Guangzhou from three directions in early June, with He Yingqin leading the first brigade of the Party Army along the Guangzhou–Jiulong railroad from the east and allied units from Guangdong and Hunan from the north and south. At the same time, the GMD organized a strike among railroad workers that cut off the rebels' access to Guizhou and Yunnan. Poor coordination between Yang and Liu resulted in a weak defense and their rapid collapse in the face of this well-organized assault. On June 11, He Yingqin ordered some of his force to attack at Longyantong, but the main force concentrated on Shougouling where they inflicted heavy losses on the Yang–Liu force. Many Yunnan and Guangxi soldiers surrendered or shed their uniforms to blend in with the local population, and the fighting ended by June 12. Yang and Liu fled to the British concession at Shamian.[61]

The quick suppression of the Yang–Liu revolt produced several results. First, it secured control of the GMD base in Guangzhou and increased the government's income, as Yang and Liu had been siphoning off significant tax revenues. Second, it confirmed the general strategy of the First Eastern Expedition, to seek a decisive battle with an assault on a fixed position. A history of military campaigns between 1924 and 1950 compiled under the auspices of the War History Bureau of the Ministry of National Defense described the battle and offered a critique, comparing the aggressive strategy of the Party Army favorably to the passive, defensive approach of the Yunnan and Guangxi forces.[62] As had been the case at Danshui and Mianhu, GMD military authorities believed that seeking "a quick battle for a decisive victory" (suzhan, sujue) had carried the day. Third, it validated Sun's strategy of forming alliances with regional commanders in order to build the revolutionary movement. Despite the risks of allying with forces of dubious loyalty to the GMD, the military force built around the Whampoa Academy had the ability to

[60] Xiong Zongren, *He Yingqin: xuanwozhong de lishi*, I, 172; Cherepanov, *As Military Advisor*, 139; and Sutton, *Provincial Militarism*, 285.
[61] *HYQJJ*, I, 78–79; Wilbur and How, *Missionaries of Revolution*, 153: Li Qigong, "Tongyi guangdong geming genjudi de zhanzheng," 35.
[62] Lt. Col. William Whitson, Patrick Yang, and Paul Lai, eds., *Military Campaigns in China: 1924–1950* (Taipei: Office of the Military Historian, 1966), "2. Canton Battle."

deal with those who broke ranks with the government. Moreover, while
Yang and Liu had revolted, Zhu Peide from Guangdong and Tan Yankai
from Hunan had remained steadfast, and others such as Li Jishen from
Guangxi soon joined the GMD alliance.[63] In his study of provincial militarism in Yunnan and southern China, Donald Sutton noted this as an
important transition marking the end of the truly independent militarist
or warlord and the beginning of a new phase of "residual warlordism."
The GMD military now began to operate under a modified system that
combined central and regional forces under a national military organization, which gave rise to the problem of regional "cliques" that resisted
Chiang's authority.[64] While it bolstered the forces' numbers, this "residual warlordism" posed a substantial challenge to the Nationalist military
over the next three decades. Victory in the First Eastern Expedition and
the rapid suppression of the Yang–Liu revolt demonstrated the risks of
this system, but also showed that the Whampoa force could adequately
deal with such problems.

In the midst of the suppression of the Yang–Liu revolt, events in Shanghai gave rise to a series of anti-imperialist demonstrations that would lead
to a bloody clash in Guangzhou. The CCP had been active among workers in Shanghai and other cities, organizing labor unions and strikes, one
of which took place at a Japanese textile factory where a guard fired on
some Chinese who had broken into the factory and destroyed machinery.
This tragedy triggered a round of larger demonstrations against foreign
imperialism in Shanghai, featuring large numbers of students, workers,
and supporters from other walks of life. The students in particular swelled
the ranks of the protestors and added to their sense of indignation. On
May 30, 1925, a British police inspector feared that the angry mob might
overwhelm his station and seize the weapons inside, so he ordered his
officers to fire on the crowd, killing four Chinese and wounding many
others. This May Thirtieth Incident spurred a surge of nationalistic
protest across the country.[65]

In Guangzhou, where the British and French concessions at Shamian
lay just across a narrow strip of water, students and labor organizers
held meetings and demonstrations in support of those who had died
in Shanghai. On June 23, He Yingqin led a group of 700 soldiers and
Whampoa cadets, joining a much larger crowd of students, workers,
shopkeepers, and others in an emotional protest march. They met in the
morning and began the march at about 2 p.m., intending to pass through
an area known as Shaji, which would take them past the West Bridge

[63] *HYQJJ*, I, 85.     [64] Sutton, *Provincial Militarism*, 288.
[65] Wilbur, *The Nationalist Revolution in China*, 21–23.

leading across the water to Shamian. Singing revolutionary songs and waving banners with patriotic slogans, those at the head of the group suddenly stopped as they heard noises that sounded like gunfire, which came from defensive positions the British and French had built on the other side of the water. Rifle and machine-gun fire continued for several minutes as the marchers broke in a panic and scrambled to escape or find cover. He Yingqin ordered his men not to return fire as they took up position behind the massive columns of an arcade on the far side of the street. When the firing stopped, more than sixty bodies lay in the street, including twenty-three soldiers and cadets, with countless more wounded.[66]

Three days later, He Yingqin gave a report to the committee investigating this "Shaji Massacre," detailing his eyewitness account. The British and French claimed that the demonstrators had fired first, but He Yingqin disputed this claim in his report. First, he pointed out that the demonstrators had made no preparations for an attack and even the soldiers and cadets had carried few firearms. British and French forces, by contrast, had prepared defensive fortifications and had substantial weaponry on hand. Second, the organization of the marchers suggested a standard demonstration rather than an attack, with students in the front ranks, shopkeepers and merchants following, and finally soldiers and cadets in the rear. If the Chinese had intended to start a fight or fire on the British and French, why would they put the soldiers at the rear of the formation? Moreover, a number of women and children had accompanied the marchers, which would have been unthinkable if they had anticipated a violent clash. Finally, He Yingqin asserted that had they intended to attack the foreigners at Shamian they certainly would have put forth a better effort than this. After all, he told the committee, the Party Army had successfully assaulted and captured well-defended cities such as Danshui. If they really wanted to overrun the British and French defenses at Shamian, it would have been a relatively easy task.[67] He Yingqin's anti-imperialist credentials had now been forged in blood, and he remained an outspoken critic of foreign imperialism in China for the rest of his life.

While the Shaji Massacre of June had a profound impact on He Yingqin and would sharpen his desire to solve the problem of foreign imperialism in China, he soon had more immediate concerns and responsibilities to deal with. In a move designed to impose greater central control and

---

[66] *HYQJJ*, I, 81–82.

[67] *HYQJJ*, I, 83. See also "The Report of the Commission for the Investigation of the Shakee Massacre, June 23 1925," in *US Military Intelligence Reports: China, 1911–1941* (Frederick, MD: University Publications of America, 1982), Reel XII, 0372.

standardization over the military, the revolutionary government created a Military Affairs Commission (*junshi weiyuanhui* or MAC) on which He Yingqin served as one of eight members. This body reorganized the GMD military forces under the title National Revolutionary Army. The two training regiments with reinforcements from a new group of academy graduates became the First Corps (*jun*) of the NRA under the command of Chiang Kai-shek with He Yingqin commanding its first division. Hunan forces under Tan Yankai, Yunnan forces under Zhu Peide, Guangdong forces under Li Jishen, and Fujian forces under Li Fulin became the Second, Third, Fourth, and Fifth Corps respectively.[68] This basic organization, featuring a core of professionally trained and well-equipped central troops with several larger regional forces all under the banner of a single national military force, would characterize the Nationalist military for decades to come. Under the overall command of Xu Chongzhi, the corps commanders of the newly organized NRA and their Soviet advisors now agreed that Chen Jiongming still posed the most serious threat and therefore planned a Second Eastern Expedition to reestablish control over eastern Guangdong and protect the base at Guangzhou.

Xu Chongzhi's position as commander of the NRA did not last long, and Chiang Kai-shek forced him into exile in August 1925 after linking Xu to the assassination of Liao Zhongkai. As minister of finance, Liao Zhongkai imposed policies designed to centralize revenue collection under Sun's government and prevent individual armies from collecting taxes directly. This aroused the anger of those who stood to lose out on Guangdong's lucrative tax revenues and resulted in the August 20 murder of Liao. He Yingqin took charge of security in Guangzhou in the wake of Liao's assassination, posting guards at various points in the city and enforcing a curfew.[69] Subsequent investigations linked the murderers to men who had close ties to Hu Hanmin and Xu Chongzhi. Further suspicion that Xu had been in touch with Guangdong warlord Chen Jiongming led Chiang Kai-shek and Wang Jingwei to expel Xu from Guangdong and to send Hu Hanmin to Moscow as a GMD representative.[70] This elevated Chiang to the highest echelon of party leadership, and he

---

[68] *HYQJJ*, I, 80; Qin Xiaoyi, ed., *Zongtong Jianggong dashi changbian chugao* [Preliminary Draft of President Chiang's Chronological Biography], 13 vols. (Taipei: Caituan faren zhongzheng wenjiao jijinhui, 1978), vol. I, 101. It is common to translate the Chinese term *jun* as "army," but "corps" is more accurate as each of these units operated with two to five divisions.

[69] *HYQJJ*, I, 84.

[70] Zhang Xianwen, ed., *Zhonghua minguo shigang* [An Outline History of the Republic of China] (Henan: Henan renmin chubanshe, 1985), 242–45; van de Ven, *War and Nationalism*, 89–90; Taylor, *Generalissimo*, 51–52.

took over as commander in chief of GMD military forces, a position he would occupy for most of the next several decades. In order to trap Chen's forces in southeastern Guangdong and to prevent them from withdrawing into Fujian or Jiangxi, Chiang planned to occupy a line of towns moving northeast through Huizhou, Wuhua, Xingning, and Meixian, all of which Chen's troops controlled.[71] If the NRA could capture these towns, it would be a relatively simple matter of mopping up the remnants of Chen's forces, which would put the GMD in control of most of the province and deter others from attacking.

Leaving one division of the First Corps in Guangzhou to protect the city, approximately 21,000 NRA troops moved east in three separate columns advancing toward Mei, Lu, and Feng counties, which Chen Jiongming once again controlled. He Yingqin's first column drew the assignment of capturing Huizhou, the initial objective of the campaign and a major stronghold that had a reputation as an "impregnable" city that no attacking army had conquered since the Tang dynasty. Lin Hu held the city with approximately 3,000 of Chen Jiongming's troops. As a result of its location, with the East River snaking around the west, south, and east of the city and mountains to the north, it posed a serious challenge for attacking armies. Huizhou featured surrounding walls 8 to 10 meters high, with numerous stone parapets from which the 3,000 defenders could fire down on attackers. Two divisions of the NRA's First Corps led the assault on Huizhou, with the support of regional forces from Hunan and Guangdong.[72]

After surveying the city's defenses from nearby hills, Chiang and his advisors placed mountain and field guns on three sides and divided the attacking force into three columns. Employing strategy and tactics similar to those used at Danshui, they identified a strip of land near the north gate as the best point of attack and organized a vanguard of 650 soldiers divided into 5 units to lead the ground assault while others provided cover fire or stood in reserve. A second attack force would concentrate on the south gate and Huicheng city to the southwest of Huizhou. He Yingqin chose the 650 men for the vanguard unit, and Chiang authorized cash rewards for those soldiers who succeeded in getting over the city walls. Prior to the attack, He Yingqin moved around to various locations outside the city to observe the battlefield from different angles and perspectives. He then ordered his men to practice techniques for scaling walls. At 9:30 a.m. on October 13, the first column forces opened an artillery barrage that lasted for several hours, concentrating fire on the southwest

[71] Cherepanov, *As Military Advisor*, 162.
[72] *HYQJJ*, I, 86–87; Wilbur and How, *Missionaries of Revolution*, 173.

corner of the city. At 2:00 p.m., under cover of machine-gun fire, the first vanguard unit attempted to scale the city walls near the southwest gate, using bamboo ladders as they had at Danshui.[73] The defenders had a clear field of fire and inflicted heavy casualties on the vanguard. In addition to rifle and machine-gun fire, soldiers atop the walls hurled stones and logs and poured burning liquid down at the attackers. The NRA forces withdrew at dusk, but sent another vanguard unit to assault the north gate under cover of darkness at 4:00 a.m. on October 14. Lin Hu's troops soaked cotton in oil and ignited it before dropping it down at the base of the wall, where it not only burned attacking soldiers but also engulfed the grass below in a "sea of flames."[74]

The tide of the battle turned on the afternoon of October 14 when the NRA directed an assault on the west gate of the city, which placed the glare of the sun directly in the eyes of the defenders. With the attention of the defending troops drawn to the west gate and with continued artillery support and cover fire from machine guns, He Yingqin personally led another attack on the north gate. After observing the battle from nearby high ground, he ordered all available soldiers to join the attack and concentrated his artillery to direct fire on the north gate. The attackers suffered heavy casualties, but at approximately 3:30 p.m. the first few soldiers managed to get over the wall and into the city. Defenders at the north gate fell back, which allowed the NRA to open the gates and ultimately capture Huizhou. Continuing the campaign to the east, the NRA captured other cities, including Shantou and Chao'an in early November, which brought the Second Eastern Expedition to a close.

Like the two earlier battles at Danshui and Mianhu, the victory at Huizhou demonstrated He Yingqin's capabilities as a combat commander, as well as validating the general strategy and tactics of the NRA. Many members of this young force took great pride in the capture of Huizhou in that, as one veteran of the battle put it, the city that none had conquered in 1,000 years fell to the NRA in 40 hours.[75] The War History Bureau of the Ministry of National Defense also offered a critique of the battle at

---

[73] *HYQJJ*, I, 88.

[74] Li Yuan, *Jiang Jieshi he He Yingqin*, 48; and Xiong Zongren, *He Yingqin: xuanwozhong de lishi*, I, 178–79. It is difficult to assess the number of casualties the NRA suffered at Huizhou, but in his memoir of the Eastern Expeditions Li Qizhong describes heavy casualties resulting from the aggressive ground assault, with corpses piling up "like mountains." See Li Qizhong, "Tongyi guangdong geming genjudi de zhanzheng," 37–38. Cherepanov offers no numbers, but describes the combat as "fierce": Cherepanov, *As Military Advisor*, 166.

[75] *HYQJJ*, I, 90.

Huizhou, describing it as evidence of "the spirit of revolution that could overcome everything."[76]

In the wake of the battle at Huizhou, NRA forces drove Chen Jiongming into exile in Hong Kong and secured control of Guangdong. The NRA expanded again in late 1925 to include a Sixth Corps and additional independent divisions now totaling approximately 58,000 men under arms, a far larger, better-armed, and more experienced force than the "cadet" army with which the GMD had begun the campaigns of 1925.[77] On December 10, with a further reorganization of the NRA, Chiang Kai-shek promoted He Yingqin to commander of the First Corps. He Yingqin remained in control of eastern Guangdong and took on the additional role of commandant of the Chaozhou branch of the Whampoa Military Academy, where he continued his work training new officers for the developing and expanding NRA.[78]

Beyond securing the base area in Guangdong, without which the GMD revolutionary movement would have been marginalized or even destroyed, the two Eastern Expeditions also dramatically changed the fortunes of the GMD. In the early months of 1925, the GMD found itself in a precarious position: Sun Yat-sen ailing and on his death bed, hostile regional military forces on all sides, a shortage of resources including weapons, and a novice military force with cadet officers. At the end of the year, the situation had changed considerably, with secure control over most of Guangdong, new access to revenue through taxation, thousands of weapons captured from enemy forces, and most importantly a substantially larger and battle-tested army. The Eastern Expeditions also had important consequences for He Yingqin, who played a significant role in these critical early days of the revolutionary movement and demonstrated his value to Chiang Kai-shek.

The victory in the First Eastern Expedition in the spring of 1925 marked the start of He Yingqin's rapid rise through the ranks of the NRA. Over the course of 1925, he commanded a regiment, brigade, division, and then the First Corps, emerging as one of the most important figures in the military, second only to Chiang himself. He's developing relationship with Chiang at Whampoa made a crucial difference that allowed him to rise as rapidly as he did through the ranks of the Chinese military. Both men had been cadets in Japan, although Chiang Kai-shek never completed his studies there, and they shared a common appreciation for the values of hard work, discipline, self-sacrifice,

[76] See Whitson, Yang, and Lai, eds., *Military Campaigns in China: 1924–1950*, "3. The Second Eastern Campaign."
[77] Wilbur and How, *Missionaries of Revolution*, 181.    [78] *HYQJJ*, I, 91.

aggressive spirit, and moral character. He Yingqin arrived at Whampoa with significant experience and skill in administrative affairs as a result of his time as commandant of the Guizhou Military Academy, but his performance as the commander of the First Training Regiment in the Eastern Expeditions confirmed Chiang's view of him as a capable officer and laid a solid foundation for future cooperation. Neither dynamic nor charismatic, He Yingqin fit the role of high-ranking subordinate or "right-hand man" to someone like Wang Wenhua or Chiang Kai-shek. Chiang sought out subordinates who shared his personal values, on whose loyalty he could depend, and who could carry out his orders successfully. Both men got what they wanted from this relationship. This combination of common education and training, shared personal values, and most importantly success in combat paved the way for He Yingqin's future career in the Nationalist military.

# 3 The Eastern Route Army in the Northern Expedition

On October 10, 1926, NRA forces engaged in the Northern Expedition seized control of Wuchang, one of three cities that make up the important Yangzi River city of Wuhan. The fact that this victory came on the anniversary of the 1911 Wuchang revolt, which sparked the chain of events that led to the end of the Qing dynasty, seemed a good omen for the revolutionaries. The occupation of Wuchang marked an important step in the military campaign, which would lead to the capture of Shanghai and Nanjing, a violent break with the CCP, and the establishment of the new government under Chiang Kai-shek and the GMD. On the same day that Wuchang fell, He Yingqin led his troops to a victory at a town called Yongding in Fujian. This lesser-known battle, approximately 500 miles to the southeast, proved equal in importance to the overall success of the Northern Expedition as the capture of Wuchang.

Historians have long regarded the Northern Expedition as an important moment in the Nationalist revolution and have chronicled it in a number of works.[1] Most have devoted their attention to the combat in Hunan, Hubei, and Jiangsu because it involved major cities, because NRA commander Chiang Kai-shek followed this route, and because it precipitated a split in the GMD with competing factions in Wuhan and Nanchang. Few who write about the Northern Expedition pay attention to the combat on the eastern front, from the Guangdong–Fujian border north through Zhejiang and Jiangsu. He Yingqin commanded forces on this front and his victories made a significant contribution to the overall military victory of the NRA in the Northern Expedition. In the course of the campaign, He Yingqin won important military battles and ensured the loyalty and support of the First Corps, without which Chiang would not have maintained his position as commander in chief of the NRA and the Northern Expedition. Building on his success in the Eastern

---

[1] On the Northern Expedition, see Donald Jordan, *The Northern Expedition: China's National Revolution of 1926–1928* (Honolulu: University of Hawaii Press, 1976), Wilbur, *The Nationalist Revolution in China*, and van de Ven, *War and Nationalism*.

Expeditions of the year before, victories on the eastern front again demonstrated his value to Chiang Kai-shek and added to his reputation as a combat commander. His work during the Northern Expedition propelled He Yingqin further up the ranks of the NRA and cemented his position as Chiang Kai-shek's right-hand man. It also contributed to the split between rival forces within the united front.

## The Guangdong–Fujian border

With the consolidation of the revolutionary base due to the successes of the Eastern Expeditions of 1925, the next phase of the revolution involved a military campaign to unify the country through the Northern Expedition. The initial plan called for a rapid advance north through Hunan into Hubei to capture the strategic tri-city area of Wuhan on the Yangzi River. From there, NRA forces would ally with Feng Yuxiang's National Pacification Army (*anguojun*) and together defeat Zhang Zuolin's Fengtian forces and capture Beijing. The NRA faced the combined forces of five major warlords, Wu Peifu, Sun Chuanfang, Zhang Zongchang, Zhang Zuolin, and Yan Xishan, an aggregate force that outnumbered the NRA by perhaps as much as ten to one. Chiang Kai-shek and the NRA corps commanders understood that success depended upon engaging these opponents individually, preventing them from combining forces, which would leave the NRA with little chance for victory. With this in mind, the NRA adopted the popular slogan "Overthrow Wu Peifu, compromise with Sun Chuanfang, forget about Zhang Zuolin."[2] Fortunately for the NRA, the various warlords did not typically support each other and their individual forces did not always fight with great discipline or conviction. Still, the threat of attack by more than one major warlord at a time remained a serious concern as the expedition began in the summer of 1926.

The Northern Expedition began in July with an initial thrust north to engage troops under the control of the "Scholar Warlord," Wu Peifu, who controlled Hunan and Hubei. Chiang took Li Zongren's Seventh Corps and Tang Shengzhi's Eighth Corps, both of which had joined the NRA that year, with him as he pushed into Hunan and Hubei. This presented Chiang with a problem, as the NRA advance rendered the revolutionary base in Guangdong vulnerable to attack from Sun Chuanfang, the governor of the "Five United Provinces" of Fujian, Jiangxi, Zhejiang, Jiangsu, and Anhui. In order to defend Guangzhou and avoid a two-front war, Chiang assigned He Yingqin to take up a position on

---

[2] *HYQJJ*, I, 97; He Yingqin, "Dongzheng beifa dao tongyi," 84.

the Guangdong–Fujian border. Realizing the importance of both fronts, Chiang divided his most reliable force, the First Corps with its numerous Whampoa Academy graduates, taking the first and second divisions with him into Hunan and leaving the third and fourteenth divisions under the command of He Yingqin in the east.

Chiang had multiple reasons for arranging his forces in this manner. First, it placed the two newest NRA corps under Tang and Li on the front lines during the early fighting in Hunan and Hubei, in order to test their reliability. It also preserved half of Chiang's valuable First Corps – namely the two divisions with He Yingqin and the twentieth division under Qian Dajun, which remained in Guangzhou – should things go badly for the NRA in Hunan. Moreover, it made sense to keep He Yingqin and some of the Whampoa forces in eastern Guangdong as they had experience operating there, having done so successfully the year before. Chiang needed a capable commander on the Guangdong–Fujian border, and he now relied on He Yingqin to take up the most important assignments. If He Yingqin's forces failed to defend the border, it would mean the loss of the revolutionary government's financial and political base, the likely defeat of the Northern Expedition, and the possible end of the NRA. At the time, the eastern front held tremendous significance, and the overall success of the Northern Expedition depended as much on the course of events in eastern Guangdong as in Hunan, Hubei, and Jiangxi.[3]

Chiang Kai-shek planned to eventually send He Yingqin's force up through Fujian into Zhejiang, but in the meantime Chiang gave He clear orders to avoid any action that might provoke Sun to attack and to wait until the situation in Hubei and Jiangxi clarified.[4] Chiang Kai-shek had made overtures to Sun Chuanfang and some of his subordinate commanders to gauge their interest in joining the NRA, but Sun preferred to position himself as the "neutral" defender of the people of his territory, declaring, "If no one attacks me, I will not attack them."[5] Despite Sun's benign assertions, He Yingqin set up defensive positions in eastern Guangdong stretching from Meixian across Chaozhou down to Shantou. The First Corps's third division garrisoned Meixian while the fourteenth division occupied Chaozhou. He placed a regiment at Huangfeng, established gun emplacements along the Mei and Han Rivers near the Fujian border, and even mined the rivers at strategic points.[6]

[3] Chen Sanpeng, "Beifa shiqi de min'ao bianzhanshi yu He Yingqin" [He Yingqin and the Fighting on the Fujian-Guangdong Border During the Northern Expedition], *Hanshan shifan xueyuan xuebao*, 1 (March 1995), 36–37.
[4] *HYQJJ*, I, 100.
[5] Liu Zhi, *Wode huiyi* [My Memoirs] (Taipei: Wenhai chubanshe, 1982), 37.
[6] Chen Sanpeng, "Beifa shiqi de min'ao bianzhanshi yu He Yingqin," 37.

Just a short distance across the border stood approximately 9,000 soldiers, all under the command of Zhou Yinren, Sun Chuanfang's commander in Fujian. Beyond these troops near the border, Zhou had a total of 22,000 troops at his disposal, which might launch an attack into Guangdong at any time.[7] Despite the disadvantage in numbers, He Yingqin benefited from some important defections. In late August, he had been in contact with Li Fengxiang, commander of Zhou Yinren's third division, along with two of Li's brigade commanders, Du Qiyun and Cao Wanshun. All three expressed an interest in joining the NRA, provided He Yingqin with intelligence about the deployment of Zhou's force, and revealed his plan for attack on Guangdong. Du and Cao accepted offers to join the NRA as division commanders and prepared to defect at the appropriate time, but Li Fengxiang made no commitment, preferring to wait and see how things developed.[8]

While NRA forces in Hubei laid siege to the walled city of Wuchang throughout September, He Yingqin waited for an attack on eastern Guangdong or for further orders from Chiang Kai-shek. In the meantime, he continued training cadets at the Chaozhou branch of the Whampoa Military Academy. Observing the situation in neighboring Hubei with increasing concern, Sun Chuanfang sent some of his forces from Jiangxi to the western border with Hubei in order to support Wu Peifu. This opened up the battle for Jiangxi, which centered on the city of Nanchang. NRA forces crossed into Jiangxi, spreading the battlefront across two provinces. With intense fighting at Wuchang and Nanchang, the success of the Northern Expedition hung in the balance.

Now that Sun Chuanfang's forces had engaged the NRA in Jiangxi, he ordered Zhou Yinren to proceed with an attack on Guangdong. Zhou had prepared a plan for a three-pronged thrust across the border with the main force moving through the border towns Yongding and Songkou and with the ultimate goal of capturing Shantou and Huizhou in eastern Guangdong. Well informed about Zhou's intentions as a result of

---

[7] Xiong Zongren, *He Yingqin: xuanwozhong de lishi*, I, 199; He Yingqin shangjiang jiuwu shouyan congshu bianji weiyuanhui, *Donglujun beifa zuozhan jishi* [Combat Record of the Eastern Route Army in the Northern Expedition] (hereafter *DLJBF*) (Taipei: Liming wenhua shiye youxian gongsi, 1984), 13–14. This sources indicates that Zhou Yinren had a five-to-one advantage in manpower, but this probably represents all forces available to Zhou in Fujian province. His advantage in actual forces on the border for an attack into Guangdong would likely have been closer to three to one. Other scholars argue that Zhou Yinren attacked Guangdong with approximately 30,000 soldiers; see Chen Sanpeng, "Beifa shiqi de min'ao bianzhanshi yu He Yingqin," 37; Yang Chenguang, "Beifa donglujun changjiang yinan zuozhan de zhanlue zhidao" [The Strategic Leadership of the Eastern Route Army South of the Yangzi River During the Northern Expedition], *Zhonghua junshi xuehui huikan*, 12 (September 2007), 90.

[8] *HYQJJ*, I, 101–02.

contacts with Cao Wanshun and Du Qiyun, He Yingqin and his Soviet advisor, Alexander Cherepanov, discussed how to defend against this attack. Outnumbered and outgunned, they knew they could not hold a broad defensive line across eastern Guangdong, so they agreed that they would have the advantage only if they switched from defense to offense and launched a surprise attack on Zhou's force at a time and place of their own choosing. Unfortunately, such a move meant crossing the border to attack in Fujian, which Chiang Kai-shek refused to allow. Even after learning of Zhou Yinren's plans to attack eastern Guangdong, Chiang rejected He Yingqin's request to launch a preemptive strike and repeated his order to avoid any offensive action that might have an adverse effect on the fighting in Jiangxi. Chiang directed He to maintain a defensive position on the border and to await further instructions as the situation changed.[9]

Convinced that the best chance for a successful defense against the attack lay in offensive operations across the Fujian border, He Yingqin pressed Chiang to change his orders. On September 18, he sent Chiang a lengthy telegram explaining why the situation called for offensive action, pointing out that the First Corps could take advantage of some key weaknesses of Zhou Yinren's force that would both ensure victory and in no way jeopardize the NRA position in Jiangxi. First, He Yingqin argued that his intelligence indicated that the people of the border area as a whole, and the numerous local militias in particular, did not support Zhou Yinren and would welcome an opportunity to turn on him. He Yingqin predicted that these groups, having suffered considerable expropriations at the hands of Zhou and Sun Chuanfang, would jump at the chance to support the NRA against Zhou's force. Second, he argued that Zhou's force faced a number of problems including poor logistics, supply, and a lack of unity and spirit. Most of Zhou's soldiers, He Yingqin claimed, came from the north and were not accustomed to the climate, food, and conditions in the south. If faced with a strong attack, he predicted, they would collapse quickly. Finally, he reminded Chiang that he had already been in contact with two of Zhou's brigade commanders, Du Qiyun and Cao Wanshun, who would switch sides, bringing their entire units to the NRA as soon as the fighting began.[10] Chiang accepted He Yingqin's argument and authorized the attack on Zhou Yinren in Fujian.

Chiang perhaps saw the logic of He Yingqin's plan and believed the attack would succeed, but he had other reasons to approve it. In addition to providing the details of Zhou Yinren's plan of attack, Du Qiyun and Cao Wanshun had also reported that Zhou had sent representatives to

[9] *DLJBF*, 15.    [10] *HYQJJ*, I, 104–05; *DLJBF*, 15–16.

Hong Kong to contact Chen Jiongming and propose a joint operation against the NRA. Having withdrawn from eastern Guangdong only a year before, Chen welcomed Zhou's overtures and arranged to send ammunition, medicines, and other supplies to Zhou's forces, which threatened to disrupt the First Corps's rear areas.[11] Chiang concluded that the situation indeed called for an aggressive action on the Guangdong–Fujian border, but he also understood that it came with substantial risk, as the battlefronts in Hubei and Jiangxi remained fluid. The continuing siege against Wu Peifu's forces at Wuchang and seesaw battles at Nanchang against Sun Chuanfang meant that the NRA had already engaged two major warlords at once with the outcome still undetermined. Should He Yingqin fail against Zhou Yinren's force, Sun Chuanfang would then attack Guangzhou, and the Northern Expedition would likely end in defeat.

Beyond the threat to the larger campaign, the fighting on the Guangdong–Fujian border also represented significant personal risk to Chiang Kai-shek. The First Corps stood out as one of the best units of the NRA and the only corps completely loyal to Chiang Kai-shek. As such, it served as a personal power base against other NRA commanders who led their own regional military forces. Chiang had split his First Corps at the start of the Northern Expedition, taking Wang Boling with him into Hubei and Jiangxi to command the first and second divisions, but found that Wang performed poorly in the attacks on Wuchang and Nanchang. At the very time that He Yingqin sent his message to Chiang explaining why he should attack into Fujian, Wang Boling led his divisions into Nanchang, temporarily taking the city, but he did not sufficiently secure it, repeating the mistake he had made at Danshui. Sun Chuanfang's nearby forces launched a counterattack for which Wang had not prepared and which drove NRA forces out of the city. Wang himself disappeared in action and did not reappear until March 1927, when Chiang relieved him of command.[12] In authorizing the two divisions of the First Corps under He Yingqin's command to attack Zhou Yinren in Fujian, Chiang Kai-shek risked what remained of his most important power base.[13]

### The battles at Yongding and Songkou

With Chiang's approval for the operation on the border, He Yingqin and his staff quickly devised a plan. Cao Wanshun and Du Qiyun had provided details on Zhou's plan, which divided his force into three columns

---

[11] *DLJBF*, 16.    [12] Tsung-jen Li, *Memoirs*, 190–91; *HYQJJ*, I, 113.
[13] Xiong Zongren, *He Yingqin: xuanwozhong de lishi*, I, 204.

advancing separately toward the border in the west through Shanghang, in the center through Yongding and Songkou, and in the east through Pinghe and Raoping. Armed with this information, He Yingqin planned a surprise, preemptive attack on Zhou's center column as it crossed the border on its way into Guangdong, targeting the town of Yongding. Once this center column, Zhou Yinren's main force, crossed into Guangdong, He Yingqin planned to strike its rear at Yongding, on the Fujian side of the border, then quickly turn south to crush its advance force at Songkou, back in Guangdong. This offered the NRA units the advantage of choosing the time and place of the battle against the larger enemy force and engaging the enemy before they even came close to the NRA garrisons at Chaozhou, Meixian, or Shantou. Zhou's decision to disperse his forces across the border offered He Yingqin the opportunity to concentrate his own smaller forces for a decisive attack on Zhou's main force and devastate his army.[14]

With only two undersized divisions and one regiment to defend eastern Guangdong, He Yingqin had to utilize every available soldier for the planned attack on Zhou's advancing force. Directing the operation from Shantou, he divided his two divisions into three columns, moving through Dapu, Raoping, and Pinghe to attack Yongding from the east. He also dispatched a smaller force of the ninth regiment to take up position outside Songkou, on the Guangdong side of the border. Leaving a small number of troops and units of cadets in training to defend Chaozhou, Meixian, and Shantou, He Yingqin left for the front.[15] By late September, he had his forces in place and ready to attack. He Yingqin contacted Cao Wanshun and Du Qiyun, asking them to meet with him at Sanheba in order to confirm their roles in the attack, but Cao and Du knew that Zhou suspected them of communicating with the NRA, so they sent representatives instead to give He Yingqin up-to-date information on the enemy force and its progress.[16]

As Zhou Yinren's troops moved south toward the border, He Yingqin sent a telegram to Chiang on October 3 asking for final permission to launch the attack. While Chiang Kai-shek had agreed to the attack in principle, he now hesitated and ordered He Yingqin to sit tight and avoid contact that might alter the situation and influence the fighting in Jiangxi. Zhou Yinren had already begun his move toward Guangdong and on October 6 took up residence in Yongding, a hilly border town on the Fujian side, with approximately 5,000 troops of his main column. A smaller advance force continued on to Songkou, about 60 kilometers

---

[14] Chen Sanpeng, "Beifa shiqi de min'ao bianzhanshi yu He Yingqin," 22–23.
[15] *DLJBF*, 17.    [16] *DLJBF*, 22–23.

to the south across the border in Guangdong. Concentrating the third and fourteenth divisions for an attack on Yongding, He Yingqin also ordered his forces near Songkou to be prepared to attack if Zhou Yinren's troops there attempted to go back across the border to return to Yongding.[17]

On October 8, He Yingqin again requested permission from Chiang to attack, spelling out the details of his plan for a decisive strike against Zhou's main force at Yongding and a second attack on the advance force at Songkou. Still focused on the continuing fighting at Wuchang and Nanchang, Chiang did not reply. Unable to wait any longer, He Yingqin went ahead with the attack on October 9, ordering the third and fourteenth divisions to attack Yongding from the southeast. The attack began as the fourteenth division made contact with enemy troops at Fengshi, just south of Yongding. After several hours of combat, Zhou Yinren's forces withdrew behind Yongding's walls. NRA forces surrounded Yongding, cutting off communications and preventing reinforcement, then began the assault on the town walls on October 10. Using the methods that had brought success at Danshui and Huizhou, He Yingqin concentrated his artillery on specific points of the walls in preparation for a ground assault. The assault on the southwest gate of the city wall eventually succeeded and, late in the afternoon of October 10, Zhou Yinren's forces surrendered. The NRA captured thousands of prisoners, but Zhou Yinren and several of his subordinates managed to slip out of the city in the confusion and escape. On the same day, the fifteenth anniversary of the 1911 revolt, NRA forces in Hubei successfully captured and held Wuchang, ending a month-long siege.[18]

Immediately following the victory at Yongding, He Yingqin turned his forces south to cross back into Guangdong for an attack on Songkou before Zhou Yinren could reassemble his forces and counterattack. The NRA ninth regiment held the southern bank of the Mei River, blocking the route into Guangdong toward Chaozhou and Meixian. He Yingqin divided his force into three columns, under Tan Shuqing, Feng Yipei, and Chen Yi, all rapidly converging on Songkou from the right, left, and center, respectively. The ninth regiment then crossed to the north bank of the Mei River to join that attack, moving quickly despite the difficult terrain and surprising the commander of Zhou's advance force, Liu Jun, on October 12. Rather than retreat and attempt to regroup with other units of Zhou Yinren's force, Liu Jun decided to dig in and defend

[17] *HYQJJ*, I, 109–10; *DLJBF*, 24–25; Wu Shufeng, ed., *Chen Cheng xiansheng huiyilu: beifa pingluan* [The Memoirs of Mr. Chen Cheng: The Northern Expedition] (Taipei xian xindian shi: Guoshiguan, 2005), 52.
[18] *HYQJJ*, I, 113–14.

his position. Meanwhile He's left and right columns advanced from the north, flanking Liu's positions. At dawn the next day, these two columns mounted a coordinated attack on Songkou, and by evening NRA forces had taken control of the town. Leaving a force to hold Songkou and guard against counterattack, He Yingqin sent other forces to pursue the fleeing enemy troops. The combined victories at Yongding and Songkou yielded approximately 4,000 prisoners, an equivalent number of rifles, and 10 artillery pieces. These gains came at a significant cost, as He's First Corps suffered nearly 1,000 casualties in the process.[19]

The destruction of Zhou Yinren's main force spelled the end of his time as the dominant force in southern Fujian. His eastern column met a similar fate, as NRA regiments moved against it around Pinghe and Raoping, killing several hundred soldiers and forcing the survivors to straggle back north to Zhangzhou. In the west, Li Fengxiang had long considered defecting to the NRA as had two of his brigade commanders, the aforementioned Du Qiyun and Cao Wanshun. When the fighting broke out at Yongding and Songkou, Li's force switched sides and attacked Zhou Yinren's other subordinate, Sun Yunfeng. As He Yingqin had predicted, many of the independent military forces on the border now saw fit to declare their support for the NRA, placing southern Fujian firmly in the hands of the revolutionaries.[20]

The victories on the Guangdong–Fujian border had important implications for the success of the Northern Expedition and the careers of He Yingqin and Chiang Kai-shek. While the fighting in Hubei and Jiangxi has overshadowed the victories of He and the First Corps at Yongding and Songkou, the latter played a critical role in the larger military campaign. The capture of Wuchang and Nanchang, both of which featured intense combat and seesaw battles that lasted for several weeks, represented important victories for the NRA, but as Hans van de Ven has pointed out, they came close to failure.[21] Had Zhou Yinren succeeded on the eastern front, it would likely have meant the destruction of the bulk of the NRA's First Corps, the exposure of the revolutionary base in Guangzhou to attack, and the loss of resource-rich eastern Guangdong, all of which would have had disastrous consequences for the NRA. Moreover, the victories at Yongding and Songkou took place as the fighting at Wuchang concluded, but the battle for Nanchang continued. News of defeat on the eastern front would have dealt a serious blow to the morale of the NRA troops in Jiangxi, allowed Sun Chuanfang

---

[19] *HYQJJ*, I, 116.
[20] Chen Sanpeng, "Beifa shiqi de min'ao bianzhanshi yu He Yingqin," 39.
[21] Van de ven, *War and Nationalism*, 107.

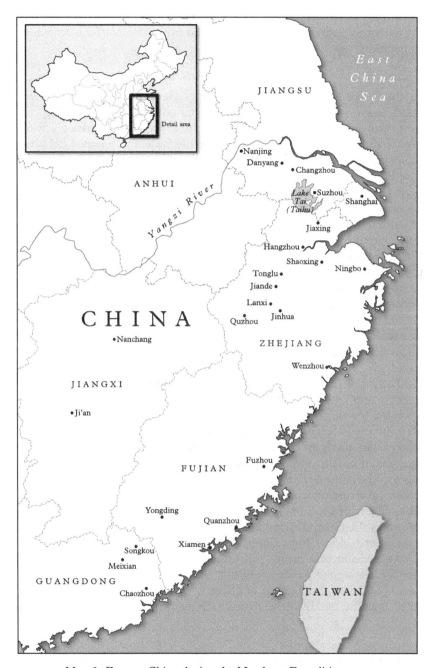

Map 3: Eastern China during the Northern Expedition

to commit additional forces to the fighting there, and possibly tipped the balance against the NRA and resulted in the defeat of the Northern Expedition.

The fighting on the eastern front again demonstrated He Yingqin's capabilities as a combat commander. With his own force stretched in a defensive line across eastern Guangdong, He Yingqin faced imminent attack from a much larger enemy. Making good use of the intelligence from Cao and Du, He developed an appropriate plan taking advantage of Zhou Yinren's decision to divide his force into separate columns separated by hundreds of kilometers. By concentrating its forces for a coordinated attack on the center column at Yongding and Songkou, the First Corps demonstrated the same tactics that had brought success in previous campaigns in eastern Guangdong. Commander of the NRA Seventh Corps Li Zongren later claimed that the fighting on the eastern front played little role in the Northern Expedition and described Zhou Yinren's troops as "so poor that they could not really fight."[22] In fact, the combat on the Guangdong–Fujian border featured tens of thousands of troops, resulted in thousands of casualties, and required quick and decisive action on the part of the First Corps. As Chen Chenguang has noted, the combat at Yongding and Songkou did not match the size and scale of the battles in Hunan, Hubei, and Jiangxi, but He Yingqin's forces defeated a much larger enemy force and won an important strategic victory.[23]

The success of the First Corps under He Yingqin had important consequences for Chiang Kai-shek, whose position as NRA commander rested upon the foundation of the Whampoa Military Academy and its graduates who made up the First Corps. In 1926, the NRA's initial eight corps stood as an amalgam of regional forces featuring significant differences in terms of quality, numbers, and dedication to the cause. Some of the other corps commanders, Li Zongren and Tang Shengzhi in particular, would subsequently challenge Chiang's position as overall commander. The officers of the First Corps, the foundation of what would later be known as the Central Army, served not only as Chiang's power base *vis à vis* other regional commanders but also as a vehicle for implementing Chiang's vision of a strong and united Chinese state. Michael Richard Gibson has argued persuasively that this force, under the overall command of Chiang and a group of fifteen or so key officers of the "Nanjing elite," spearheaded the drive to unify China by force of arms and to build

[22] Tsung-jen Li, *Memoirs*, 199.
[23] Yang Chenguang, "Beifa donglujun changjiang yinan zuozhan de zhanlue zhidao," 103–04.

the republic.[24] This group of military officers, of which He Yingqin was the most prominent, worked with Chiang to achieve their revolutionary goals and formed the driving force behind the Nationalist Revolution of the 1920s and 1930s. The success of the First Corps on the eastern front preserved Chiang's power base and launched him on the path to becoming paramount leader during the Nationalist period. Given the mediocre performance of the first and second divisions of the First Corps in Hubei and Jiangxi, He's strong showing on the Guangdong–Fujian border took on even greater importance in solidifying Chiang's position as commander in chief.

Finally, He Yingqin's performance on the eastern front further strengthened his developing relationship with Chiang Kai-shek. Like others, Chiang valued regional connections and school ties in his professional relationships, but he did not necessarily place them before competence. It is true that He Yingqin shared a similar set of values with Chiang; they had the common experience of study in Japan; and they had worked together closely at the Whampoa Military Academy. Yet this does not explain why He Yingqin rose rapidly alongside Chiang over the course of the 1920s and remained with him throughout the Nationalist period. In the early years of working with Chiang, He Yingqin demonstrated a professionalism and reliability that made him a valuable subordinate. Again, the contrast with another officer in the First Corps is striking. Wang Boling, commander of the two First Corps units that fought in Hubei, also had a long personal and professional relationship with Chiang, studied in Japan, served on the faculty at the Whampoa Military Academy, and participated in the Eastern and Northern Expeditions. Wang, however, performed poorly in Hubei and actually went missing in action during the early fighting at Wuchang. Despite their friendship and personal connection, Chiang Kai-shek did not hesitate to remove Wang Boling from his command, demote him to instructional positions at the Central Military Academy, and restrict him to minor positions thereafter.[25] He Yingqin's performance in the military campaigns of 1925–26, during which he twice defended the revolutionary government's base in Guangdong against numerically superior opponents, demonstrated his ability and solidified his relationship with Chiang as a leading member of the "Nanjing elite."

---

[24] Michael Richard Gibson, "Chiang Kai-shek's Central Army, 1924–1938" (Ph.D. dissertation, George Washington University, Washington, DC), 4–9.

[25] Gu Yiping, "Wang Boling qiren qishi" [Wang Boling: The Man and His Work], *Renwu chunqiu*, 3, 1 (2003), 12–14.

## The Fujian and Zhejiang campaigns

Following the victories on the Guangdong–Fujian border, Chiang Kai-shek committed to a plan to occupy the southeast and to consolidate NRA control south of the Yangzi River. This meant a rapid move through Fujian into Zhejiang and Jiangsu to occupy major urban areas around Hangzhou, Shanghai, and Nanjing. Accordingly, on October 16 Chiang appointed He Yingqin commander of the Eastern Route Army (*donglujun* or ERA) and directed him to lead his force through Fujian and into Zhejiang. The Eastern Route Army consisted of the original two divisions of the First Corps, the third and fourteenth; the Seventeenth Corps under the command of Cao Wanshun; a newly organized force under Tan Shuqing; and one division from the Fourteenth Corps.[26] This increased the size of He's command, but it included large numbers of Fujian troops who had defected to the NRA, which posed complications for He as the force moved north toward Zhejiang.

Following his defeat in Fujian and Jiangxi, Sun Chuanfang withdrew to Nanjing and pulled his forces back into Zhejiang. Zhou Yinren took up a position in Yong'an, Fujian, but after the defeats at the border he lacked sufficient manpower and resources to mount an effective defense or lead a counterattack. A few units delayed their withdrawal and engaged the ERA in skirmishes on the Fujian side of the border, but quickly fell back on Zhangzhou and Quanzhou. A few thousand of Zhou Yinren's troops remained there under the command of Zhang Yi, hoping to block the ERA advance. Shortly thereafter, on October 18, Sun Chuanfang sent a telegram to Zhang Yi authorizing his retreat to Zhejiang should Zhang conclude that his force could not hold the line in Fujian. Zhang promptly moved his troops north, yielding Fujian to the ERA.[27]

As He Yingqin realized that enemy forces had pulled back and had little interest in defending Fujian, he directed his forces to move steadily north up the coast. In early November, they advanced as far as Quanzhou, and in early December the ERA marched into Fuzhou with little resistance. Sun Chuanfang's forces posed no obstacle to the ERA's advance into Fujian, but the need to deal with surrendering or defecting units complicated the mission and forced He Yingqin to delay his advance. The ERA had to reorganize and incorporate as many as 10,000 new soldiers, some from the ranks of Zhou Yinren's forces and others from local militia or border defense forces. In some cases entire units and their officers switched sides. At various points in the campaign, former Sun Chuanfang subordinates such as Li Shengchun, Chen Yi, Zhou Fengqi,

---

[26] *HYQJJ*, I, 117; *DLJBF*, 34.    [27] *DLJBF*, 35.

and Fujian naval commander Lin Zhiyuan joined the ranks of the NRA, bringing their units with them. The defectors and new additions formed a large part of the ERA, which forced He Yingqin to proceed north toward Zhejiang with great care and at a measured pace, spending much of December reorganizing his force and consolidating his control over Fujian. His initial orders had been to defend the Guangdong–Fujian border and there had been no detailed plan for a rapid advance into Fujian and Zhejiang. The caution he exercised proved appropriate as some of the newly reorganized units showed a tendency to resist NRA authority. He Yingqin would later relieve Li Shengchun of his command and disarm his troops because of his unwillingness to follow orders.[28] As a result, He Yingqin's advance through Fujian took longer than Chiang Kai-shek had expected.

Chiang Kai-shek, in contrast, urged speed and on December 20 sent a telegram to He Yingqin with orders to move through Fujian and into Zhejiang as soon as possible. To support He Yingqin's ERA, Chiang appointed Bai Chongxi as Eastern Route Army advance commander (*donglujun qiandi zongzhihui*) with command over the first and second divisions of the First Corps along with two additional divisions, and ordered Bai to lead this force from Jiangxi east into Fujian.[29] From there Bai's force would meet up with He's ERA units and converge on Hangzhou in preparation for the attack on Shanghai and Nanjing.[30] On January 6, following a meeting of military officials in Nanchang, Chiang reorganized the rest of the NRA into the Western Route Army and the Center Army, the latter further divided into the right- and left-bank (of the Yangzi River) columns.[31]

As the ERA forces moved farther north into Zhejiang, they met heavy resistance from several regiments of Sun Chuanfang's forces in the area around Quzhou in central Zhejiang. Zhou Fengqi, a former Sun Chuanfang officer who had joined the NRA and now commanded the Twenty-Sixth Corps, reported that Sun had approximately eight regiments and twenty artillery pieces organized in a defensive line across Zhejiang from Wenzhou to Jinhua.[32] He Yingqin sent a telegram to Bai Chongxi, asking him to send support quickly from Jiangxi, as some advance units of the ERA had already made contact with enemy forces around Quzhou. Though some have implied that Bai's appointment

[28] *DLJBF*, 39–44.
[29] Guo Tingyi and Jia Tingshi, eds., *Bai Chongxi xiansheng fangwen jilu* [A Record of Interviews with Bai Chongxi], 2 vols. (Taipei: Zhongyang yanjiuyuan jindaishi yanjiusuo, 1984), vol. I, 47.
[30] Tsung-jen Li, *Memoirs*, 198; *HYQJJ*, I, 125.
[31] *HYQJJ*, I, 129–31; Tsung-jen Li, *Memoirs*, 198–99.     [32] *DLJBF*, 54, 59.

as advance commander amounted to a replacement of He Yingqin as commander of the ERA, he clearly fell under He's authority as overall commander.[33] According to Bai, Chiang specifically questioned him on this point, asking him whether he would accept a position subordinate to He, and Bai agreed without hesitation.[34] As it turned out, He and Bai operated independently and more or less as equals, at times holding different views of the appropriate tactical approach. While Bai Chongxi favored a rapid advance, He Yingqin believed that moving too quickly would stretch out NRA forces and leave them vulnerable to counterattack or would provoke Zhang Zongchang to send his Shandong Army forces to support Sun Chuanfang's troops around Shanghai and Nanjing.[35] His request for support from Bai Chongxi reflected his view that the two ERA units, his own Fujian force and Bai's units in Jiangxi, should advance with carefully coordinated movements to maximize their strength. He Yingqin fully embraced the "Whampoa spirit," which called for aggressive attacks when facing a larger and better-armed force, but he also believed in careful preparation and avoiding situations that rendered his force vulnerable to attack. He favored all-out frontal assaults when attacking a fixed defensive position, but the battlefields of Fujian and Zhejiang proved fluid, leading He Yingqin to advocate caution rather than a rash advance.

With regard to the Zhejiang campaign, He Yingqin envisioned two possible scenarios: either Sun Chuanfang would meet the advancing NRA with a large force for a decisive battle in central Zhejiang or he would take a defensive position around Hangzhou, Shanghai, and Nanjing. In the event of the former, He Yingqin advocated avoiding a major battle until multiple NRA forces, or at least the two parts of the ERA, could coordinate and support each other. Should Sun choose the latter course, He Yingqin believed that both ERA forces should advance together and converge on Hangzhou for a coordinated attack. In order to avoid any provocative action until they knew Sun's intentions, He Yingqin contacted General Cheng Qian, commander of the right-bank column of the Center Army, urging him not to enter the Anhui border region until Zhejiang had been cleared of enemy forces. He argued that to do otherwise might expand the battlefield before the NRA could make

---

[33] Donald Jordan wrote that Bai took command of all ERA forces: Jordan, *The Northern Expedition*, 103–04. Li Zongren also asserts that Bai Chongxi led all ERA troops: Tsung-jen Li, *Memoirs*, 203 (Li Zongren is the Pinyin transliteration, while Li Tsung-jen is the Wade–Giles transliteration). Edward Dreyer describes Bai as taking "overall command of the NRA campaign in Chekiang": Dreyer, *China at War*, 138. See also Wilbur, *The Nationalist Revolution in China*, 85.

[34] Guo Tingyi and Jia Tingshi, eds., *Bai Chongxi xiansheng*, 47–48.

[35] *DLJBF*, 52.

adequate plans and would have a negative impact on the situation in Zhejiang.[36]

Bai Chongxi quickly moved his forces toward Quzhou and began planning for offensive action against the enemy forces in the area. Intelligence indicated that Sun Chuanfang had 10,000-odd troops in the area around Quzhou waiting for supplies, and Bai Chongxi saw this as an opportunity to deal a decisive blow, which would clear the way for an attack on Hangzhou. He believed it essential to take control of western Zhejiang and feared that if he delayed he might lose this advantage and then find his force outnumbered and outgunned. He therefore concluded that his force should attack Jiande and Lanxi in order to clear out enemy forces from western Zhejiang. The news that enemy units in southern Anhui, which otherwise might have crossed the border and attacked Bai's units in western Zhejiang, had switched sides and joined the NRA made him even more determined to take the offensive.[37]

He Yingqin disagreed. The enemy forces in western Zhejiang outnumbered Bai's force, and He viewed an attack as an unwarranted risk, which might jeopardize their progress toward the more important cities of Hangzhou, Nanjing, and Shanghai. On January 22, as Bai prepared his forces to attack enemy positions around Quzhou, He Yingqin sent him a telegram pointing out that it would be better to wait until He himself arrived and then coordinate their forces prior to any attack.[38] Cherepanov had similar concerns and expressed them to Bai Chongxi's Soviet advisor, V. N. Panyukov, in the hope that Bai would slow his movement.[39] He Yingqin had no qualms about attacking forces of greater size, as he had done so on multiple occasions with success, but he also believed in applying maximum force whenever possible. Moreover, he still faced problems in Fujian that complicated his advance into Zhejiang. In late January 1927 there remained a significant number of new units that had switched allegiance to the NRA but had not yet been adequately reorganized into He's ERA. Concerned with possible disorder among his forces as he entered Zhejiang, He Yingqin ordered Cao Wanshun to notify all new units that now accepted the authority of the NRA to submit information on their numbers and armaments as soon as possible.[40] Still trying to establish firm control of Fujian and to put his own rapidly growing force in order, He Yingqin did not yet feel prepared for an aggressive operation in Zhejiang.

Despite He Yingqin's concerns, Bai Chongxi declined to wait and went ahead with the attack on January 29. Within a matter of days his troops

[36] *DLJBF*, 52.    [37] *DLJBF*, 61.    [38] *DLJBF*, 62–63.
[39] Wilbur and How, *Missionaries of Revolution*, 374, 387.    [40] *DLJBF*, 66.

crushed enemy units at Jiande and Lanxi, an operation that Donald Jordan described as a decisive blow from which Sun Chuanfang never recovered.[41] Even as news of Bai's victory reached He, still in Fujian but making his way north along the coast, he again urged Bai to exercise caution and wait for the Fujian force to arrive in Zhejiang. He pointed out that the flat terrain of the plains of central Zhejiang favored the enemy, which could apply its artillery more effectively and perhaps deal a damaging defeat to Bai's army. He also warned that, if Bai pushed too deeply into Zhejiang, the remaining enemy units might fall back from their current positions to Hangzhou, acquire support from Zhang Zongchang's Shandong troops, and force a prolonged siege of the city. The best course of action, He Yingqin argued, was for Bai to wait until He Yingqin arrived from Fujian in order to concentrate their full force against the enemy.[42]

Both men had valid points. Bai's victory at Jiande and Lanxi indeed secured his control of western Zhejiang and the approach to Hangzhou, perhaps causing He Yingqin some chagrin. Yet it also triggered a counterattack from Zhou Yinren's remaining forces in the area, as He Yingqin had predicted. As Bai's forces advanced north toward Hangzhou, three divisions of enemy troops attacked them at Tonglu. Outnumbered nearly three to one, Bai's forces fought an intense battle that lasted four days and nearly ended in defeat. Liu Zhi, commander of the first division of the First Corps, led a flanking maneuver that turned the tide of the battle and delivered an ERA victory.[43] This marked the end of serious fighting in Zhejiang, as the remainder of Sun Chuanfang's forces either fled or withdrew to the defensive line between Shanghai and Nanjing. Bai Chongxi then occupied Hangzhou with little resistance on February 18. He Yingqin joined him there three days later.[44]

Chiang Kai-shek gave the order for the capture of Shanghai and Nanjing in late February so planning for the Jiangsu campaign began as soon as He Yingqin arrived in Hangzhou. Panyukov suggested leaving a small force at Hangzhou while the ERA main force drove north toward Changzhou in order to cut the Nanjing–Shanghai railroad line. This would prevent Sun Chuanfang from getting any supplies or reinforcements before the attack on Shanghai. Bai Chongxi agreed in principle, but suggested that, while one group of ERA forces severed the rail line, another should advance directly on Shanghai. ERA advance units had already progressed as far as Jiaxing, some 60 miles from Shanghai. He Yingqin agreed with Bai and divided the ERA into six

[41]  Jordan, *The Northern Expedition*, 103–04.    [42]  *DLJBF*, 65.
[43]  Liu Zhi, *Wode huiyi*, 45–46; *DLJBF*, 66–67.    [44]  Tsung-jen Li, *Memoirs*, 203.

columns, three under Bai and three under himself. In mid March, Bai Chongxi led the first, second, and third columns toward Shanghai along the railway while He Yingqin moved the fourth, fifth, and sixth columns north toward Changzhou, Danyang, and the area west of Lake Tai.[45] Meanwhile, the right-bank column of the NRA Center Army, under Cheng Qian's command, advanced along the south bank of the Yangzi River from Anhui, executing a pincer movement targeting Nanjing. The left- or north-bank column would cut the Tianjin–Shanghai railroad.[46]

Remnants of Sun Chuanfang's army stood ready to defend Shanghai with support from Zhang Zongchang's Eighth Army from Shandong. Some intense fighting took place at Songjiang, the last defensive outpost before Shanghai, but enemy forces quickly withdrew in the face of Bai Chongxi's three columns, clearing the road to Shanghai. Zhang Zongchang moved his forces to the north bank of the Yangzi River, Sun Chuanfang's commander Bi Shucheng surrendered, and naval commander Yang Shuzhuang committed his fleet in support of the NRA. Setting out on March 13, the first anniversary of the important victory at Mianhu, He Yingqin's columns moved steadily north to occupy both Changzhou and Danyang, severing the rail link between Nanjing and Shanghai. This series of events effectively rendered Shanghai defenseless, allowing Bai Chongxi to march his force into the city on March 22. Chiang appointed Bai Shanghai garrison commander and ordered all other available units to concentrate on Nanjing.[47]

He Yingqin's fourth, fifth, and sixth columns approached Nanjing from the east, arriving at Zhenjiang, less than 50 miles downriver from Nanjing, on March 22. Always cautious and wary of counterattack, He Yingqin left his fifth and sixth columns at strategic points outside the city to await orders while he led the fourth column into Nanjing on March 25. Cheng Qian's right-bank column had arrived first, occupying Nanjing on March 24 as the last northern troops fled. On that day, violence broke out, and NRA soldiers looted consulates, injuring and killing several foreigners. In response to this Nanjing Incident, British and American naval vessels bombarded the city for hours, resulting in dozens of Chinese casualties. Li Zongren blamed communist elements of Cheng Qian's Sixth Corps for the violence, as did prominent Taiwan historian Guo Tingyi. Donald Jordan sees no conspiracy or prearranged

---

[45] Guo Tingyi and Jia Tingshi, eds., *Bai Chongxi xiansheng*, 51–52; Tsung-jen Li, *Memoirs*, 203–04; *DLJBF*, 77–78.
[46] *DLJBF*, 78; Wilbur and How, *Missionaries of Revolution*, 398.
[47] *DLJBF*, 80–82; Wilbur and How, *Missionaries of Revolution*, 398.

plot, but rather describes it as a rare breakdown of discipline in the NRA, which underscores its diverse nature and internal disunity.[48]

### He Yingqin and the April 1927 purge

With the capture of the Wuhan tri-city area in Hubei and Nanchang in Jiangxi, the Northern Expedition had created rival power centers within the GMD and NRA. Since the beginning of the CCP–GMD united front in 1924, the two parties had managed to concentrate on the common goal of overthrowing the regional warlords and uniting China through force of arms. The GMD itself had numerous factions and their differences began to reemerge as the campaign progressed, with a series of important issues dividing them. Leaving the original revolutionary base behind, GMD leaders moved north to establish new bases in November and December 1926. One group, the GMD "left" including Xu Qian, Sun Ke, Song Ziwen (T. V. Soong), Deng Yanda, and ultimately Wang Jingwei, arrived at Wuhan. They enjoyed the support of the CCP and chief Soviet advisor Mikhail Borodin and supported the CCP and Soviet view that working among labor unions to organize strikes and creating peasant associations to foment unrest in rural areas stood as important parts of the campaign to overthrow the warlords. Chiang Kai-shek, Jiang Jinjiang, Tan Yankai, and others who remained wary of the CCP and Soviet influence on the movement stayed at Nanchang. They worried that the labor movement and peasant organizations would interfere with military operations, alienate important sectors of Chinese society and the economy, and possibly invite foreign intervention.[49]

The military campaigns of the Northern Expedition had a significant impact on the dispute between Wuhan and Nanchang. In addition to holding differing views of labor and peasant unrest, Wuhan and Nanchang authorities disagreed on military strategy. Soviet advisors argued in favor of a strike north to link up with Feng Yuxiang, a progressive northern warlord who had accepted Soviet support, in order to launch a coordinated attack on Zhang Zuolin and drive toward Beijing. Chiang and his supporters at Nanchang favored a move to the east in order to capture Shanghai and Nanjing. This would provide the revolutionary

[48] Tsung-jen Li, *Memoirs*, 206; Guo Tingyi and Jia Tingshi, eds., *Bai Chongxi xiansheng*, 572–73; Jordan, *The Northern Expedition*, 116–17. Xiong Zongren, He Yingqin's biographer from the PRC, downplays the attacks on the consulates and foreign property. He suggests that the "incident" stemmed from the desire of the Americans and British to "speed up the GMD right wing's counterrevolution" and killed 2,000 Chinese citizens: Xiong Zongren, *He Yingqin: xuanwozhong de lishi*, I, 211.
[49] On the Wuhan–Nanchang rift, see van de Ven, *War and Nationalism*, 94–130; Wilbur, *The Nationalist Revolution in China*, 77–133.

government with new sources of revenue and allow the NRA to consolidate its control over China south of the Yangzi River before resuming the military campaign against the northern warlords. Chiang essentially forced the issue in December 1926, when he sent additional forces under Bai Chongxi to the east to support He Yingqin and the ERA on its march through Zhejiang toward Shanghai and Nanjing. In doing so, he dramatically altered the military situation and his relationship with the Wuhan authorities.[50]

With the leadership of the GMD split between the two cities, each group established a new political body claiming to represent the highest authority of the GMD. In Wuhan a "Provisional Joint Council" and in Nanchang a "Provisional Central Political Council" each laid claim to supreme party authority. A military conference in Nanchang in January 1928 approved Chiang's military plan to capture Shanghai and Nanjing, but when Chiang visited Wuhan days later for discussions the two sides grew even further apart. Chiang returned to Nanchang unsure of the proper course of action but convinced that Wuhan's leaders and the CCP were seeking to remove him as military commander. In the ensuing months, as Chiang's forces moved closer to Shanghai and Nanjing, Wuhan authorities took steps to reduce his political and military authority. Decrying Chiang's emerging "military dictatorship," Wuhan's leaders accused him of setting himself up as a new warlord. In response, Chiang and his supporters alleged CCP and Soviet attempts to take over the movement and establish control over the GMD. On April 1, the Provisional Joint Council in Wuhan relieved Chiang of his position as commander in chief of the NRA.[51]

In his research on the Nationalist revolution and Northern Expedition, Hans van de Ven makes important points about the split between the GMD factions and Chiang's purge of CCP members. First, they did not come as a result of a master plan devised at an earlier date, but rather came as the result of gradually developing anxieties and personal rivalries inherent in the revolutionary movement. Second, the brutal assaults on CCP members and their supporters took place in the context of ongoing violence in the cities of the lower Yangzi region. He describes frequent violent clashes between GMD forces and labor unions in areas such as Shanghai, Nanjing, Hangzhou, and Ningbo, and as far away as Sichuan and Fujian.[52] It is important to understand this in order to see that the events of April 1927 had as much to do with military affairs as they did with

---

[50] Van de Ven, *War and Nationalism*, 107.
[51] Taylor, *Generalissimo*, 63–64; Furuya, *Chiang Kai-shek*, 196–97; Qin Xiaoyi, *Zongtong Jianggong*, I, 145.
[52] Van de Ven, *War and Nationalism*, 118–19.

politics or ideology. The chaotic scenes in Shanghai, Nanjing, and other cities, combined with clear indications that Wuhan authorities sought Chiang's removal, amounted to a serious threat to the mission of military unification, which Chiang Kai-shek and He Yingqin took seriously.

The occupation of Shanghai and Nanjing in late March 1927, accomplished largely through the efforts of He Yingqin, Bai Chongxi, and the ERA, set the stage for the violent upheaval that followed in April. Within three weeks of his arrival at Shanghai, Chiang presided over a bloody purge designed to eliminate the CCP and Soviet advisors from the government and the NRA, to consolidate his hold on the lower Yangzi River region, and to force the Wuhan faction to seek reconciliation. In order to succeed, Chiang needed the support of that portion of the NRA that occupied Shanghai and Nanjing, namely those units of the ERA under the command of He and Bai.

From its earliest days, the NRA had never been a coherent military force, but rather a patchwork of regional military forces and commanders built around a core GMD force that originated at the Whampoa Military Academy. The original NRA of eight corps expanded dramatically during the first phase of the Northern Expedition to at least thirty-four corps over the course of several months, as the NRA moved through Hunan, Hubei, Jiangxi, Fujian, and Zhejiang, and into Jiangsu and Anhui.[53] Adding new brigades, regiments, divisions, and entire corps as local defense units and former warlord armies threw their lot in with the NRA strengthened the force in terms of manpower, but exacerbated the regional and personal divisions within the movement. In the context of the rapidly developing split between GMD leaders at Wuhan and those now in Shanghai and Nanjing, it remained unclear which NRA units would side with which faction.

At this critical moment, Chiang Kai-shek had to carefully evaluate the condition of the military forces under his command, meaning those occupying the lower Yangzi River region. Cheng Qian's Sixth Corps and Tan Yankai's Second Corps had been the first to occupy Nanjing, followed soon thereafter by part of He Yingqin's ERA. Tan openly sided with Wuhan while Cheng Qian had a reputation for being pro-communist and also maintained ties to the Wuhan faction. In Shanghai, Chiang relied on Guangxi leader Bai Chongxi, who commanded the first and second divisions of the First Corps and other units that had participated in the campaigns in Zhejiang and Jiangsu. These included newcomers to the ranks of the NRA such as the Twenty-Sixth Corps under the command of Zhou Fengqi, until recently part of Sun Chuanfang's force in Fujian.

---

[53]  Gibson, "Chiang Kai-shek's Central Army," 117.

Li Zongren's Seventh Corps approached from the west and took up supporting positions in and around Shanghai.

Chiang understood that he could not count on the loyalty of all of these commanders and knew that Wuhan leaders were actively seeking their support as well. For example, Wuhan authorities urged Cheng Qian to arrest Chiang Kai-shek in Nanjing, but Cheng ignored the order and perhaps even told Chiang about it. Li Zongren recalled that in late March 1927, while on a visit to Wuhan, Mikhail Borodin had attempted unsuccessfully to convince Li to replace Chiang as commander in chief of the NRA and that Chiang knew all about it. Li also claimed that Third Corps commander Zhu Peide strongly opposed Chiang and supported Wuhan in the conflict.[54] Following the purge, Zhu penned a ten-page letter to He Yingqin in which he complained bitterly about Chiang's "discrimination against his troops" and urged He to side with Wuhan. He Yingqin told Li Zongren that he had shown the letter to Chiang Kai-shek. On March 28, Xue Yue, commander of the second division of the First Corps, met with CCP leader Chen Duxiu in Shanghai and offered to arrest Chiang. Chen rejected the offer.[55]

While some NRA commanders either wavered or decided to cast their support behind the Wuhan leadership, Chiang believed he could be absolutely certain of the loyalty of the First Corps, under the command of He Yingqin. Most of the First Corps officers felt strong personal and professional ties to Chiang, informally referring to him as the "commandant" (xiaozhang) rather than "commander in chief" (zongsiling). The First Corps had served as the strongest and most reliable unit under Chiang's command dating back to its roots as the Whampoa training regiments and Party Army.

As commander of the ERA and First Corps, He Yingqin played an important role in the purge of CCP members at Nanjing. Within the GMD, he occupied a centrist position with regard to the Soviet Union and the CCP, similar to Chiang Kai-shek. His early anti-imperialist attitudes dated back to his days at the Guizhou Military Academy and his work with the YGA. At the Whampoa Military Academy, he had worked constructively and cooperatively with Soviet advisors and CCP members, including Zhou Enlai, who served as the chief political officer for the NRA First Corps. He Yingqin found a good deal of common ground between the GMD and the CCP, as he strongly opposed foreign imperialism in China, believed that China must be unified under a central government

---

[54] Taylor, *Generalissimo*, 65. Taylor does not make the source of this information clear. See also Tsung-jen Li, *Memoirs*, 201–02, 206.
[55] Tsung-jen Li, *Memoirs*, 214.

to free it from the grip of regional militarists, and looked forward to building a new society and government. Yet by the time of the Northern Expedition He Yingqin had begun to change his views of the CCP and the Soviet influence in China. During the Zhongshan Boat Incident of March 1926, when Chiang suspected a plot to kidnap him and considered resigning his positions, he had consulted with He Yingqin, then a division commander stationed at Shantou, via telegram. He Yingqin responded immediately with a pledge of full support for Chiang and suggested that he come to eastern Guangdong to take command of He's troops and meet the threat with force. Some have argued that this strong show of support not only encouraged Chiang to take aggressive action against his alleged kidnappers, but also led Chiang to name He Yingqin commander of the Eastern Route Army in the upcoming Northern Expedition.[56] In early 1927, amid the growing rift between GMD authorities at Wuhan and Nanchang, He Yingqin again made clear his support for Chiang against both Wuhan and the CCP. In February 1927, Chiang ordered Li Zhonggong, a secretary in Chiang's military headquarters at Nanchang, to send a telegram to He in Hangzhou asking him his views on Wuhan's recent actions. Again, He Yingqin responded with full support and urged Chiang to break relations with Wuhan and "purge the party" (qingdang).[57]

Owen Lattimore, a longtime China scholar and American advisor to Chiang Kai-shek during the Pacific War, described He Yingqin as one of the most "reactionary generals" in the Chinese military, citing his status as a large landowner and a Roman Catholic to suggest that he opposed more progressive forces in China and stood rigidly opposed to reform.[58] American diplomats in the 1940s believed that He Yingqin's anti-communism amounted to "an obsession" and suspected that he had greater interest in liquidating the communists than in defeating the Japanese.[59] While there is no doubt about He's record of opposition to the CCP, it is important to understand that his views stemmed directly from his belief that the actions of the Wuhan authorities and the CCP endangered the military campaign against the warlords that had to pre-cede any substantial reform. He had previously worked constructively with CCP members and Soviet advisors but, as he came to believe they

---

[56] Li Zhonggong, "Wosuo zhidao de He Yingqin," 208–09. Li claims that this information came to him through He Yingqin's brother, He Jiwu, who learned of it from He Yingqin.

[57] Li Zhonggong, "Wosuo zhidao de He Yingqin," 209.

[58] Lattimore, China Memoirs, 154.

[59] United States Department of State, Papers Relating to the Foreign Relations of the United States, 1944, vol. VI, Far East: China (hereafter FRUS with year and volume number) (Washington, DC: Government Printing Office, 1967), 786.

posed a threat to the central mission of unification of the country, he stood ready to support Chiang Kai-shek in his decision to break with Wuhan and expel the CCP and Soviet advisors from China. On April 2, He Yingqin attended a critical meeting in the Longhua neighborhood of Shanghai at which Chiang, Bai Chongxi, Li Zongren, Cai Yuanpei, Wu Zhihui, and others discussed the purge. He Yingqin supported a break with the CCP, pointing to the Nanjing Incident of March 24 and blaming communist elements for inciting local thugs to attack Westerners. He Yingqin's concerns appear more practical than ideological and revolved around preserving order and avoiding foreign intervention.[60]

While He Yingqin supported Chiang in this developing conflict, some middle- and lower-level officers in the first and second divisions of the First Corps had pro-communist or pro-Wuhan sympathies, which led Chiang and He to question their loyalty. Li Zongren made numerous references to this issue, later claiming that both the First Corps and the Sixth Corps (under Cheng Qian) which garrisoned Nanjing in late March 1927 were "unreliable" due to communist infiltration of the officer corps. He identified division commanders Xue Yue (first division) and Yan Zhong (twenty-first division) in particular. He described second division commander Liu Zhi as loyal, but stated that Liu could not control his subordinate officers, who tended to support Wuhan. According to Li, things had gotten so out of hand that, when he met Chiang Kai-shek in Shanghai on March 28, he found the commander in chief despondent over the condition of the First Corps and contemplating resigning his position. Li claimed that Chiang showed him a letter from He Yingqin who had himself asked to resign due to his inability to control the First Corps, which guarded the Nanjing–Shanghai railroad and were now allegedly "completely out of control."[61]

While it is likely that some First Corps officers had sympathies for their colleagues in Wuhan or in the CCP, Li exaggerated the state of the First Corps. In his analysis of the communist movement in Shanghai, Steve A. Smith finds little evidence to suggest that the First Corps officers might reject the authority of their commanders or that Communist Party members in the NRA could convince them to break with Chiang Kai-shek and He Yingqin. Likewise, C. Martin Wilbur and Julie Lien-ying How estimate that the entire NRA included a mere 1,000 CCP members, so there is no reason to believe the First Corps, or any other unit of the NRA, might fall under the control of the CCP or its supporters. Indeed,

[60] Guo Tingyi and Jia Tingshi, eds., *Bai Chongxi xiansheng*, 73; Li Yuan, *Jiang Jieshi he He Yingqin*, 73; Qin Xiaoyi, *Zongtong Jianggong*, I, 145.
[61] Tsung-jen Li, *Memoirs*, 207.

First Corps units continued to obey orders, and the balance of military forces in Shanghai heavily favored Chiang and his supporters. Aside from Li Zongren's memoir, there are no other references to He Yingqin's letter of resignation or Liu Zhi's inability to control the officers in his division. Li Zongren himself later concluded that the degree of CCP infiltration had been exaggerated.[62]

At the same time, it seems clear that Chiang perceived evidence of dissension within the ranks of the First Corps. Some officers perhaps favored reconciliation and expressed this view openly, leading Chiang to question their loyalty in this time of crisis. Bai Chongxi recalled that, sometime around early April, Chiang Kai-shek assembled the officers of the first and second divisions of the First Corps and "admonished them" (*xunhua*). Since many of lower-ranking officers had been members of the Young Soldiers Alliance, a CCP-affiliated organization active at the Whampoa Academy, they questioned Chiang or "called him to account" (*zewen*) for his anti-CCP and anti-Wuhan comments. According to Bai, this led Chiang to doubt their loyalty.[63] Chiang noted in his diary that on April 10 he had addressed a group of cadets from the Wuhan branch of the Central Military Academy and came away from the meeting feeling that CCP members had persecuted or pressured many of the cadets.[64] While the degree of the threat is not clear, there is no doubt that Chiang worried about communist influence and support for Wuhan among the First Corps officers and enlisted men. This had as much to do with Chiang's rivalry with the Wuhan government as with his concerns about the CCP. Michael Richard Gibson's study of Chiang's Central Army describes the split between Wuhan and Nanjing as a "mutiny within the armed forces," and it seems likely that Chiang and He Yingqin saw it in a similar light.[65]

In order to deal with this potential problem, Chiang and He conducted a small-scale purge of a handful of First Corps officers in early April. Chiang transferred two division commanders, Xue Yue and Yan Zhong, to Guangdong, dismissed a handful of lower-ranking officers, and disbanded the political departments of the first and second divisions.[66] Xue Yue had close ties to the officers of the Fourth Corps, which supported Wuhan, but some have suggested that his transfer stemmed not

---

[62] Wilbur and How, *Missionaries of Revolution*, 379; Steve A. Smith, *A Road Is Made: Communism in Shanghai 1920–1927* (Honolulu: University of Hawaii Press, 2000), 196–97; Tsung-jen Li, *Memoirs*, 208.

[63] Guo Tingyi and Jia Tingshi, eds., *Bai Chongxi xiansheng*, 74.

[64] Qin Xiaoyi, *Zongtong Jianggong*, I, 153.

[65] Gibson, "Chiang Kai-shek's Central Army," 121.

[66] Furuya, *Chiang Kai-shek*, 206, Gibson, "Chiang Kai-shek's Central Army," 122.

from a pro-CCP or pro-Wuhan stance but rather from a "difference of opinion" with Bai Chongxi. The fact that Xue Yue helped suppress the CCP uprising at Guangzhou reinforces the view that he lost his position for other reasons.[67] Yan Zhong had worked closely with Deng Yanda, a member of the Wuhan faction's Provisional Joint Council and one of the most vocal critics of Chiang's "military dictatorship."[68] Zeng Kuoqing, secretary of the political department of the Whampoa Military Academy, served Chiang as a conduit through which to contact Whampoa Academy graduates who leaned toward the CCP or the Wuhan government. In late March, Chiang gave Zeng a handwritten letter to deliver to Yan Zhong, instructing him to bring all CCP members or sympathizers in his division to Shanghai under armed escort. Before Zeng had time to reach Yan Zhong and deliver the letter, Chiang sent an officer to catch up to Zeng and rescind the order. Though he received no explanation, Zeng surmised that Chiang had changed his mind out of fear that the order would warn CCP members of the upcoming purge. Perhaps Chiang had also changed his mind about Yan Zhong and decided to include him in the purge of the First Corps.[69] Interestingly, the purge involved only the two First Corps divisions in Shanghai, which had fought under Chiang's command in Jiangxi and then under Bai Chongxi in Zhejiang and Jiangsu. It did not involve the third or fourteenth divisions under He Yingqin's command in and around Nanjing, which had been on their own since the start of the Northern Expedition and isolated to a certain extent from the developing split.

With the preliminary purge of the First Corps complete, Chiang Kaishek found himself in a stronger position to conduct the larger purge of CCP and pro-Wuhan elements in Nanjing and Shanghai. In Nanjing, He Yingqin's two divisions occupied the city along with Cheng Qian's Sixth Corps and Tan Yankai's Second Corps. Since Cheng and Tan both leaned toward Wuhan in the dispute, Chiang feared that he did not have sufficient strength to deal with these two corps should they come out in open support for Wuhan once the purge began. This required a redeployment of troops in and around Nanjing and Shanghai, designed to move less trustworthy units out and replace them with the most reliable forces in preparation for the larger purge of the CCP and complete break with Wuhan. Chiang sent Cheng's Sixth and Tan's Second Corps out of Nanjing to take up positions to the north along the Yangzi River in order

---

[67]  Boorman, *Biographical Dictionary of Republican China*, II, 153–54.
[68]  Xiong Zongren, *He Yingqin: xuanwozhong de lishi*, I, 216; Gibson, "Chiang Kai-shek's Central Army," 122.
[69]  Zeng Kuoqing, "Huangpu tongxuehui shimo" [The Whole Story of the Whampoa Military Academy Alumni Association], *Wenshi ziliao xuanji*, 19 (n.d.), 176–77.

to guard against attack from Sun Chuanfang or Zhang Zongchang. Only three regiments of the Sixth Corps temporarily remained in the city to maintain order. The newly purged first and second divisions of the First Corps then moved from Shanghai to Nanjing on April 8, returning to He Yingqin's command and rejoining the third and fourteenth divisions, which occupied Nanjing and strategic points on the Nanjing–Shanghai railroad. In Shanghai, Zhou Fengqi's Twenty-Sixth Corps arrived to take control of the city under Bai Chongxi's direction as Shanghai garrison commander. He Yingqin's First Corps and the Twenty-Sixth Corps, which he had reorganized and integrated into the NRA, took up the most important duties in Shanghai and Nanjing as the date of the purge approached.[70] He Yingqin now had four divisions of First Corps troops under his command for the first time since the Northern Expedition began.

He Yingqin and Chiang Kai-shek arrived in Nanjing together on April 9 and promptly set matters in motion. Chiang sent telegrams to several prominent NRA and GMD officials including Wang Jingwei, Tan Yankai, Cheng Qian, Hu Hanmin, Zhu Peide, and others, inviting them to Nanjing to discuss party unity and plan for continuing the Northern Expedition. Meanwhile, He Yingqin ordered his troops to sever the Nanjing–Shanghai railroad in order to prevent other units, Cheng Qian's Sixth Corps in particular, from returning to Nanjing. He then had his First Corps disarm the three regiments of the Sixth Corps that had remained in the city.[71] Violence broke out on April 9 as members of the Sun Yat-sen Study Society, a right-wing student organization, armed themselves with sticks and small arms to break up a public event organized to celebrate the return of Wang Jingwei, a longtime leading figure in the GMD who had been in Europe since 1926. When Wang arrived in Shanghai on April 1, Chiang welcomed him and sought to persuade him to go to Nanjing and join in the struggle against the Wuhan faction. Wang secretly left Shanghai that evening, sailing upriver to take over political authority at Wuhan. When protesters appeared on April 10 to demand punishment for those who had attacked the welcome event, He Yingqin posted his troops around the Jiangsu Provincial GMD Party Office and ordered others to close down the Nanjing branch office of the CCP. This resulted in more violent clashes and arrests of CCP supporters and labor

[70] Wilbur and How, *Missionaries of Revolution*, 405; Chen and Zhang, *Jiang Jieshi he huangpu xi*, 84–85.
[71] Qin Xiaoyi, *Zongtong Jianggong*, I, 146; Xiong Zongren, *He Yingqin: xuanwozhong de lishi*, I, 218–19.

organizers, leading some to describe April 10–11 in Nanjing as "days of terror."[72] The purge had begun in earnest.

As dawn broke in Shanghai on the morning of April 12, Bai Chongxi executed a prearranged plan in coordination with the Green Gang, a Shanghai-based criminal organization, to attack CCP members and their supporters and to crush the labor movement. The violence and bloodshed spread to multiple cities and reverberated across China for the next several months.

The capture of Shanghai and Nanjing brought to a close the first phase of the Northern Expedition and set the stage for the dramatic break between the GMD and the CCP. Perhaps because of the tumultuous events that followed in the spring and summer of 1927, observers have tended to emphasize the political aspects of the Northern Expedition. A number of scholars, such as Donald Jordan, Michael Richard Gibson, and Hsi-sheng Ch'i, have argued persuasively that the military played a dominant role in this phase of the Chinese revolution, but the political and ideological struggles of the main parties have garnered the majority of scholarly interest.[73] Even among those who pay attention to the military aspects of the Northern Expedition, there is a tendency to overlook the eastern front.

A closer look indicates that the eastern front of the Northern Expedition played a vital role in the overall success of the campaign and in He Yingqin's rise to national prominence in the NRA and the emerging Nationalist regime. Over the course of several months between the summer of 1926 and the spring of 1927, the revolutionary government broke out of its base area in Guangdong, defeated numerically superior warlord forces in several southern provinces, and took control of the lower Yangzi River basin. He Yingqin's ERA, the smallest of the NRA main force units, drew the assignment of defending the Guangdong base, but later launched offensive operations in Fujian, Zhejiang, and Jiangsu that led to the capture of Shanghai and Nanjing. Chiang Kai-shek and the leaders of the NRA found themselves in a tense situation in the spring of 1927 as internal divisions split an already fragmented force, but the movement undoubtedly stood in a better position than it had six months earlier. The military victories in Hubei and Jiangxi contributed to this development, but no more than the military success of He Yingqin and the ERA in

[72] Xiong Zongren, *He Yingqin: xuanwozhong de lishi*, I, 219; Jordan, *The Northern Expedition*, 122–23; Wilbur and How, *Missionaries of Revolution*, 405.

[73] Jordan, *The Northern Expedition*, xi; Gibson, "Chiang Kai-shek's Central Army," 4–8; Hsi-sheng Ch'i, *Nationalist China at War: Military Defeats and Political Collapse, 1937–1945* (Ann Arbor: University of Michigan Press, 1982), ch. 1.

the battles on the Guangdong–Fujian border. Without these victories, the history of the Northern Expedition and the Nationalist period would be quite different. Moreover, during the break with GMD officials in Wuhan and the April 1927 purge of CCP members, He Yingqin and Bai Chongxi played key roles in coordinating and executing the plan in Nanjing and Shanghai, respectively. Their support proved indispensable to Chiang.

The success on the eastern front of the Northern Expedition also served as an important factor in He Yingqin's relationship with Chiang Kai-shek. He's success on the eastern front reinforced Chiang's confidence in his abilities as field commander, as he now led larger forces with great success. All the more important as deep fissures emerged in the NRA camp, Chiang put He Yingqin in command of what he originally believed to be the most reliable forces in the NRA, the First Corps. Little did Chiang know that in the months that followed his relationship with He Yingqin was about to face an important turning point that would lead it into a complicated new phase.

# 4 "Without Chiang Kai-shek, there is no He Yingqin!"

Four months after the violent split between the GMD and the CCP, Chiang Kai-shek stepped down as commander in chief of the NRA. His subordinate officers, including He Yingqin, faced the task of bringing together the factions of the GMD and completing the Northern Expedition. At this critical moment, Sun Chuanfang launched a massive assault across the Yangzi River aimed at destroying the NRA and capturing Nanjing. Under the joint command of He Yingqin, Li Zongren, and Bai Chongxi, the NRA fought a fierce three-day battle around the town of Longtan, the outcome of which would determine whether the revolution would continue or end on the muddy banks of the Yangzi. He Yingqin's participation in the victory at Longtan, and the preservation of the NRA and its mission, should have been one of the most celebrated events of his career. Instead, it caused a serious rupture in his relationship with Chiang Kai-shek and nearly cost him that career.

## Resuming the Northern Expedition

As the dust settled in Nanjing and Shanghai in the wake of the violent purge of the communists in April 1927, He Yingqin prepared to resume the Northern Expedition. Within the NRA, he occupied a stronger position than ever as his work on the eastern front and his support for Chiang in the purge again demonstrated his value to the commander in chief. He Yingqin commanded the First Corps in control of Nanjing, which Chiang proclaimed the capital of the Republic of China on April 18. The First Corps also controlled the Nanjing–Shanghai railroad, securing the NRA's base in the lower Yangzi River area. Along with Bai Chongxi and Li Zongren, who had also supported Chiang during the purge, He Yingqin stood out as one of Chiang's most important subordinate officers.

While He Yingqin's personal and professional position continued to improve, the movement as a whole faced a difficult situation. The purge had placed the Nanjing and Wuhan factions of the GMD at even greater odds and, while there had thus far been no cases of NRA forces shooting at each other, the possibility now loomed large. At Wuhan, Tang Shengzhi's Eighth Corps, Tan Yankai's Second Corps, and Li Jishen's Fourth Corps all supported Wang Jingwei and the Wuhan regime, which might begin an "eastern expedition" against Nanjing at any time. To the north, warlords Sun Chuanfang and Zhang Zongchang still posed a threat, making a resumption of the Northern Expedition a priority for the Nanjing leadership. Finally, though driven underground, the CCP survived and would launch a series of armed uprisings in southern China over the course of 1927. Against these considerable forces, Chiang enjoyed the support of He Yingqin's First Corps, Li Zongren's Seventh Corps, and a few other corps and independent divisions and regiments.

The formal split with the CCP and Wuhan necessitated changes to the NRA, essentially a reorganization of those units that remained firmly on the side of the Nanjing authorities. In late April, He Yingqin met with Chiang to discuss the reorganization, without including Li or Bai. Chiang remained wary of them even though they had both sided with him in the dispute with the CCP and Wuhan, and Bai in particular had presided over the purge in Shanghai. They commanded the Seventh Corps from Guangxi, a strong regional force within the NRA commonly known as the "Guangxi Clique." Even after the purge, the NRA remained a fragmented force, rife with rivalries and personal jealousies among commanders. Li Zongren made no secret of his resentment of what he regarded as favorable treatment of the First Corps at the expense of his Seventh Corps, which fueled Chiang's suspicions about the independent nature of the Guangxi Clique.[1] He Yingqin and Chiang discussed using the reorganization of the force as a way to weaken Li's position and to bring the Seventh Corps more firmly under Chiang's control, perhaps staffing it with officers from the Whampoa Academy who had strong allegiance to Chiang. Rumors of such changes circulated within the NRA, arousing suspicions within the Guangxi Clique that Chiang intended eventually to take control of the Seventh Corps.[2] These tensions within the remaining units of the NRA meant that, as the campaign continued, Chiang could be sure of the loyalty only of the First Corps under He Yingqin's command. The reorganization of the NRA began on May 1, 1927, when Chiang created three route armies (*lujun*) in preparation for crossing the Yangzi River and resuming the Northern Expedition. He Yingqin commanded the First Route Army, which included the

[1] Tsung-jen Li, *Memoirs*, 171, 193. In his memoirs Li is consistently critical of the First Corps and He Yingqin.
[2] Xiong Zongren, *He Yingqin: xuanwozhong de lishi*, I, 220.

First, Fourteenth, Seventeenth, and Twenty-Sixth Corps. Bai Chongxi commanded the Second Route Army with two corps and Li Zongren the Third Route Army with another four corps. Chiang Kai-shek remained commander in chief.[3]

Chiang Kai-shek and He Yingqin saw Sun Chuanfang and Zhang Zongchang as the greatest threats to Nanjing and therefore began making plans to attack them and resume the Northern Expedition. Chiang had information indicating that Tang Shengzhi, commander of the strongest force aligned with Wuhan, had been in contact with Sun Chuanfang and Zhang Zongchang to organize a coordinated attack on Nanjing.[4] Indeed, Sun Chuanfang began shelling NRA positions on the southern bank of the Yangzi River and giving every indication that he intended to attack. On the north bank of the river, approximately 50,000 of Sun's soldiers controlled the area roughly from the city of Yangzhou in western Jiangsu to the coast. Zhang Zongchang's much larger force of 150,000 controlled the area west of Yangzhou, primarily in Anhui province. Taking advantage of the disorder within the NRA following the chaotic events of April, Sun and Zhang prepared to cross the river, hoping to crush NRA forces in Jiangsu, end the threat to Zhang's base in Shandong, and restore Sun's control over his "Five United Provinces."[5]

Chiang's general plan called for each of the three route armies to cross the river independently, to coordinate with each other as needed to sweep enemy forces out of Jiangsu and Anhui, and to secure control of the southern section of the Tianjin–Shanghai railroad and the eastern section of the Long–Hai railroad, the main north–south and east–west transportation arteries. The Third Route Army would advance on the western front into Anhui, and the Second Route Army into central and eastern Jiangsu, while He Yingqin's First Route Army would form the eastern or right wing of the campaign and advance up the eastern side of Jiangsu, capturing important cities and towns along the way and driving enemy forces north.[6] As he considered the situation, He Yingqin concluded that all plans must make the security of the base area around Nanjing and Shanghai a top priority. Specifically, he wanted to ensure that the NRA did not fall victim to a flanking maneuver or face an attack from Tang Shengzhi's Eighth Corps from the west, as the route armies pushed north. In order to defend the base area, he favored an aggressive assault across the river, employing a strategy of "active defense," taking the fight to the enemy for a quick and decisive battle. He left the Twenty-Sixth Corps to the south of the river under the command of Zhou Fengqi

---

[3]  Guo Tingyi and Jia Tingshi, eds., *Bai Chongxi xiansheng*, 60–61.
[4]  *HYQJJ*, I, 146.     [5]  *DLJBF*, 88.     [6]  *DLJBF*, 93; *HYQJJ*, I, 155.

and divided the rest of the First Route Army into four columns for the move across the river.[7]

The operation began smoothly with the four columns of the First Route Army crossing the Yangzi at Zhenjiang on May 20 and advancing north and east through Jiangsu. As he had done when moving through Fujian, He Yingqin proceeded as quickly as he could, but remained careful to protect his lines of supply and to guard against ambush or counterattack. Some serious fighting took place as the enemy destroyed bridges and staged a defense at Shaobo near Lake Gaoyou, but for the most part Sun's forces withdrew in the face of the NRA advance and pulled back into Shandong either on foot or by boat. Eventually the First Route Army captured Haizhou, on the Jiangsu–Shandong border, while the Second and Third Route Armies pushed north and east through Anhui and Jiangsu, capturing Xuzhou on June 2, where the major rail lines intersected.[8]

While the three route armies pushed north through Anhui and Jiangsu, both Wuhan and Nanjing sought to win the support of the major regional military leaders in north China, especially Feng Yuxiang, commander of the National People's Army (*guominjun*), who controlled Shaanxi and Gansu. Feng had previously shown a willingness to cooperate with the GMD and had accepted military aid from the Soviet Union. As NRA forces captured Xuzhou in early June 1927, Feng's forces occupied Zhengzhou in northern Henan, an important city on the Long–Hai railroad, and both GMD camps hoped to secure his support as his military force would swing significant advantage to whichever group he chose. From the start of the Northern Expedition, the GMD plan had been to have the NRA fight its way north to link up with Feng's forces in preparation for a campaign against Zhang Zuolin, who controlled Manchuria and parts of north China. Feng had largely stayed out of the dispute, but opened discussions with both camps in June. Wuhan officials including Wang Jingwei, Tang Shengzhi, and Tan Yankai met with Feng in Zhengzhou on June 10–12, hoping that Feng's previous relationship with the Soviet Union might lead him to support their view of continuing the united front with the CCP and Soviet advisors.[9]

Wuhan's leaders conceded to Feng's demands for military and political authority in Henan, Shaanxi, and Gansu, but he made no commitment to support Wuhan against the Nanjing faction. A week later he boarded a train and met with Chiang Kai-shek at Xuzhou. Chiang offered Feng a similar package of political and military authority, including positions

---

[7] *DLJBF*, 91.    [8] *DLJBF*, 92–95.

[9] James Sheridan, *Chinese Warlord: The Career of Feng Yü-Hsiang* (Stanford: Stanford University Press, 1966), 220–25.

on the Military Affairs Commission and as governor of Henan province. More importantly, with the new revenue base in the lower Yangzi River, Chiang could promise greater financial support in the form of a monthly subsidy. Feng returned to Zhengzhou and announced his support for Chiang and Nanjing, expelled the communists from his force, and urged the Wuhan authorities to join with the Nanjing leaders. As Edward Dreyer put it, Feng's declaration "kicked the military props from under the Wuhan government," leaving its leaders little choice but to seek reconciliation with Chiang.[10] Shortly after Feng's announcement, the longtime militarist from Shanxi province Yan Xishan followed suit and accepted a similar deal with Chiang Kai-shek.[11]

Adding the combined forces of Feng Yuxiang's National People's Army and Yan Xishan's Northwest Army tipped the balance of power decisively in Nanjing's favor and improved the NRA's chances of a successful campaign to crush Sun Chuanfang, Zhang Zongchang, and Zhang Zuolin. It also prompted Wuhan military leaders Tang Shengzhi and Zhang Fakui to organize their forces for an "eastern expedition," attacking downriver in a last-ditch effort to destroy the Nanjing government and settle the dispute on Wuhan's terms. In order to meet this threat, Chiang Kai-shek ordered He Yingqin to shift some First Route Army units back to the lower Yangzi to defend the base. He Yingqin personally led three divisions back to Yangzhou, Zhenjiang, and Nanjing, leaving the remainder of the First Route Army under the command of Cao Wanshun in northeastern Jiangsu to continue the advance into Shandong. Li Zongren detached his Seventh Corps from the Second Route Army and sent it west of Nanjing to take up positions at Anqing and Wuhu, forming a first line of defense against an attack downriver from Wuhan.[12] He Yingqin returned to Nanjing in time to be named one of seven members of the new Military Affairs Commission on July 4.[13]

The attack never materialized since the Wuhan authorities decided instead to conduct their own purge of communists and seek reconciliation with Nanjing. Continuing disagreements over the role of social revolution in the movement, and Comintern agent M. N. Roy's decision to reveal to Wang Jingwei that Stalin had ordered CCP members to replace the current Wuhan leadership and to create their own independent military corps, doomed the fragile relationship, which had survived the violence of April. In mid July the Wuhan government expelled communists from

[10] Dreyer, *China at War*, 146.
[11] Sheridan, *Chinese Warlord*, 226–28; Taylor, *Generalissimo*, 70–71.
[12] *HYQJJ*, I, 161–62; Tsung-jen Li, *Memoirs*, 218; Gibson, "Chiang Kai-shek's Central Army," 132.
[13] *HYQJJ*, I, 163.

its ranks and sent Soviet advisors home. Wang Jingwei initiated new contacts with Nanjing with an eye toward reuniting the feuding factions of the GMD.[14]

Sun Chuanfang, who had seen the NRA drive his forces from the Guangdong–Fujian border all the way north into Shandong, now saw an opportunity to counterattack, turn the tide of battle, and perhaps regain some or all of his "Five United Provinces." As He Yingqin and Li Zongren shifted their forces to the west in anticipation of an attack from Wuhan, they weakened the NRA position in Jiangsu north of the Yangzi River. With the NRA now forced to spread its forces across two fronts, Sun Chuanfang attacked Xuzhou on July 24. The Tenth Corps of Li Zongren's Third Route Army, under the command of Wang Tianpei, found itself outnumbered, outgunned, and unable to repel the attack. With his most reliable First Corps now defending the base area south of the Yangzi, on July 29 Chiang attempted a counterattack on Xuzhou with units of the Second and Third Route Armies, but failed to retake the city. Still concerned about a possible attack from Wuhan, Chiang ordered all NRA forces to pull back south of the Yangzi. Furious with this setback, on August 10 he ordered Wang Tianpei's arrest.[15]

## Chiang steps down

Returning to Nanjing after the failed attempt to recapture Xuzhou, Chiang Kai-shek faced threats from all sides. To the north, the forces of Sun Chuanfang and Zhang Zongchang stood just across the river, poised for an attack on the new capital. To the west, Tang Shengzhi, Zhang Fakui, and other supporters of the Wuhan faction still threatened to launch an "eastern expedition" against Nanjing, keeping alive the danger of a two-front war. Wang Jingwei and the Wuhan authorities had already broken off relations with the Soviets, purged CCP members from their ranks, and accepted Nanjing's offer of negotiations, but Wang demanded that Chiang Kai-shek step down as commander in chief of the NRA and relinquish his political positions as a precursor to any concrete co-operation between Wuhan and Nanjing. To the south, the CCP began a series of armed attacks, including the Nanchang and the Autumn Harvest Uprisings, designed to seize control of urban areas. Moreover, within the NRA units that remained loyal to Chiang, regional and factional divisions threatened the vitality of the force. Under these circumstances, Chiang

[14] Wilbur and How, *Missionaries of Revolution*, 418; Taylor, *Generalissimo*, 70; F. F. Liu, *Military History of Modern China*, 46.
[15] *HYQJJ*, I, 163–64; Li Zhongming, *He Yingqin dazhuan* [Biography of He Yingqin] (Beijing: Tuanjie chubanshe, 2008), 43–44.

Kai-shek announced his decision to "step down" (*xiaye*) from his position as commander of the National Revolutionary Army on August 13, 1927.

Chiang claimed that he did so in order to preserve party unity and heal the rift between factions of the movement, but additional factors undoubtedly played a role.[16] Though both would deny it in later years, many believe that Bai Chongxi and Li Zongren forced Chiang to step down.[17] In particular, they resented Chiang's practice of reserving the best recruits and supplies for his First Corps and those units under the command of Whampoa Academy graduates. For example, the units serving under Zhou Fengqi and Cao Wanshun, which had switched allegiance from Zhou Yinren to the NRA in late 1926, both found their way under the command of He Yingqin and the ERA, as did the bulk of captured weapons and ammunition. Bai and Li correctly interpreted this as Chiang's attempt to maintain a preponderance of military strength within the NRA, thereby keeping the Guangxi forces in an inferior position.[18] Others have downplayed external pressure or coercion as a factor in Chiang's decision, seeing it instead as a strategic and temporary move. Jay Taylor argues that Chiang saw this as "a good time" to resign because he would gain the moral high ground in presenting himself as a selfless servant of the revolution. Confident that the other commanders would soon find they could not complete the task without him, Chiang felt sure that they would eventually ask him to resume command.[19] These two views are not mutually exclusive, and Zhao Suisheng has argued that both played a role in Chiang's decision.[20]

Li Zhonggong, a secretary of the GMD Central Executive Committee, provides an insider's account of Chiang's resignation that gives He Yingqin a pivotal role.[21] According to Li, Chiang did not want to step down and took this dramatic step only when confronted with He's refusal to support him against Li Zongren and Bai Chongxi. When Chiang

[16] The text of Chiang's resignation declaration appears in Qin Xiaoyi, *Zongtong Jianggong*, I, 177–81.
[17] Tsung-jen Li, *Memoirs*, 221–22; Guo Tingyi and Jia Tingshi, eds., *Bai Chongxi xiansheng*, 63–64; Guo Tingyi, *Jindai zhongguo shigang* [An Outline of Modern Chinese History], 2 vols. (Xianggang: Zhongwen daxue chubanshe, 1980), vol. II, 481; Guo Xuyin, ed., *Guomindang paixi douzhengshi* [A History of the Struggle Between Guomindang Factions] (Shanghai: Shanghai renmin chubanshe, 1992), 325.
[18] Zeng Kuoqing, "Jiang Jieshi diyici xiaye yu fuzhi de jingguo" [The First Time Chiang Kai-shek Stepped Down and Then Returned to His Position], *Wenshi ziliao xuanji*, 38 (n.d.), 46.
[19] Taylor, *Generalissimo*, 72–73.
[20] Suisheng Zhao, *Power by Design: Constitution-Making in Nationalist China* (Honolulu: University of Hawaii Press, 1996), 99–100.
[21] Li Zhonggong, "Wosuo zhidao de He Yingqin," 210.

returned to Nanjing after the defeat at Xuzhou, he had already decided to send troops to Jiujiang, just downriver from Wuhan, in preparation for an attack on Tang Shengzhi and other forces supporting the Wuhan faction. On August 12, Chiang met with Bai Chongxi and He Yingqin to explain his view that the first step in resuming the Northern Expedition must be to crush Wuhan's forces in order to unite the NRA before turning to deal with Sun Chuanfang and Zhang Zongchang. Bai Chongxi agreed on the need to repair the Wuhan–Nanjing split, but disagreed with Chiang's plan to attack Wuhan. Chiang angrily retorted that, if they did not agree with his plan, he might resign and leave Bai and the other commanders to deal with the situation. Chiang had predicted that a threat to step down would bring the others around to his view, so his personal secretary Chen Bulei had reportedly drafted a letter of resignation for Chiang on the train journey back to Nanjing. Chiang viewed his own position as central to the success of the movement and no doubt expected Bai to accept his plan for a "western expedition" against Wuhan. Instead, Bai took advantage of Chiang's threat and suggested that party unity should be the top priority and Chiang's departure might indeed be the best solution to the problem.[22]

That Li Zongren or Bai Chongxi, leaders of the Guangxi Clique with its base in the Seventh Corps, pressed Chiang to step down is not surprising. This had long been a cause of concern for Chiang, who believed that Wang Jingwei had been in contact with Li Zongren with a plan to take command of the NRA.[23] In fact, shortly after the purge of April 1927, in which Bai and the Seventh Corps had played a central role in Shanghai, Chiang confidentially suggested to He Yingqin that they look for opportunities to reorganize the NRA in ways that would weaken the Seventh Corps and undermine the Guangxi Clique's military base. He Yingqin thought about it carefully, but ultimately expressed his reservations to Chiang, pointing out the substantial risks. He did not believe that their own First Corps gave them sufficient military force to deal with the Seventh Corps if the "reorganization" brought a strong reaction from Bai and Li. Moreover, He Yingqin did not want to risk further fragmenting an already tenuous alliance of different forces within the NRA at a time when they seemed poised for a successful completion of the Northern Expedition. Chiang did not force the issue, but remained wary of Bai and Li.[24]

At the August 12 meeting, when Chiang realized that Bai intended to accept his threat to step down, he turned and looked at He Yingqin,

[22] Li Zhonggong, "Wosuo zhidao de He Yingqin," 210; Tsung-jen Li, *Memoirs*, 222.
[23] Qin Xiaoyi, *Zongtong Jianggong*, I, 176.    [24] Li Yuan, *Jiang Jieshi he He Yingqin*, 80.

expecting him to reject this proposal and insist that Chiang remain in command. Who among the NRA commanders, if not He Yingqin, could Chiang truly rely on? Having worked closely with Chiang since their days at Whampoa, led elements of the First Corps in the Eastern and Northern Expeditions, and supported Chiang during the purge of the army and party, He Yingqin now stood silent. He did not voice agreement with Bai's view that Chiang's absence would mend the rift in the party and army nor did he lend support for Chiang to maintain his position and lead the campaign against Wuhan. He simply remained silent and did not meet Chiang's eyes.[25] Shocked at He Yingqin's silence, which gave tacit support to Bai's suggestion, Chiang felt he had no choice but to follow through on his threat and resign. He did so the next day, withdrawing to his ancestral home at Xikou in Fenghua county, Zhejiang, before eventually heading to Japan for an extended stay. Before leaving Nanjing, he met with He Yingqin, Bai Chongxi, and Li Zongren, explaining that they would act as a triumvirate to jointly chair the MAC and command the NRA. He instructed them to regroup their forces and resume the Northern Expedition with an attack north across the Yangzi River.[26]

He Yingqin left little indication as to why he acted as he did in August 1927. It is possible to see He Yingqin's failure to support Chiang as an attempt to step out from behind Chiang and stand on his own as commander of the NRA. Yet such a bold move would mark a dramatic departure from his earlier experience and character. Reserved and introverted, He Yingqin had long been accustomed to the role of "right-hand man" or top subordinate to another prominent officer. He had played this role in his early years in the Guizhou Army where he served as Wang Wenhua's trusted right-hand man in the struggle against Liu Xianshi. He Yingqin excelled in this capacity, commanding the Guizhou Military Academy, organizing cadets in opposition to Liu Xianshi, and even plotting and participating in the Minjiu Incident of 1920. While this experience ended with his near-fatal wounding and expulsion from his native province, He Yingqin had quickly recovered and found a similar position at the Whampoa Academy under Chiang Kai-shek. By the summer of 1927, He Yingqin had clearly settled in as Chiang's right-hand man, commanding his best and most loyal troops, the First Corps.

There is little evidence to suggest that He Yingqin sought to usurp Chiang's position. In Chiang's absence, He Yingqin did nothing to try to

---

[25]  Li Zhonggong, "Wosuo zhidao de He Yingqin," 210; Li Zhongming, *He Yingqin dazhuan*, 226.

[26]  Guo Tingyi and Jia Tingshi, eds., *Bai Chongxi xiansheng*, 64.

assert himself above his co-commanders, Bai Chongxi and Li Zongren, and in fact worked with them cooperatively and successfully. It is more likely that He Yingqin saw this as a temporary expedient, designed to restore unity to the NRA, to avoid a potentially disastrous two-front war, and to return to the most important task of unifying the country through force of arms. He Yingqin had fully absorbed the "Whampoa spirit" of self-sacrifice and dedication to duty and saw this as the moment when Chiang Kai-shek had to do what was best for the party, the army, and the nation. Most of Chiang's supporters viewed his absence as temporary and envisioned his return after an appropriate period of healing within the party and army. In fact, on August 16, just days after Chiang's resignation, He Yingqin sent a telegram to Chiang, requesting him to return to resume his position as commander in chief.[27] There is no doubt, however, that Chiang believed that He Yingqin had betrayed him in siding with the Guangxi Clique at this critical moment.[28]

He Yingqin retained command of the First Corps after Chiang's departure, but he quickly discovered that this meant little if he could not count on the loyalty of the Whampoa Military Academy graduates who served as officers at all levels of the First Corps and other units. Many of these graduates belonged to the Whampoa Military Academy Alumni Association or WMAAA (*huangpu tongxuehui*), a powerful organization within the NRA that remained fiercely loyal to the "commandant," Chiang Kai-shek. As he departed from Nanjing, Chiang appointed Zhu Shaoliang as head of the WMAAA and ordered him to move its headquarters to Hangzhou, away from He, Bai, and Li, who remained in the capital. Chiang charged Zhu with the mission of organizing the alumni, especially those in the First Corps, in order to preserve and develop its strength in preparation for Chiang's return. In essence, this meant avoiding any action or directive from He Yingqin that might weaken or deplete the First Corps. Chiang had no doubts that Bai and Li would take advantage of his absence and try to manipulate He Yingqin in order to strengthen their own position in the NRA vis à vis the First Corps. As a part of this plan, Zhu Shaoliang organized approximately 1,000 Whampoa graduates who had not yet been assigned work and formed a new unit to operate independently under Chiang's command.[29]

---

[27] *HYQJJ*, I, 171.

[28] In the aftermath of this incident, Chiang used the word "traitor" (*hanjian*) to describe He Yingqin. See Wang Zhenhua, ed., *Jiang zhongzheng zongtong dang'an: shilüe gaoben* [The Chiang Kai-shek Collections: The Chronological Events] (hereafter *SLGB*), 81 vols. (Taipei: Guoshiguan, 2003), vol. II, September 6, 1927, 15.

[29] Zeng Kuoqing, "Huangpu tongxuehui shimo," 178; Zeng Kuoqing, "Jiang Jieshi diyici xiaye," 47.

Almost immediately upon taking up his position as one of the three chairs of the MAC, He Yingqin had to confront attempts on the part of Bai and Li to address the issue of resource allocation, which had long been a source of resentment. Over the course of the Northern Expedition, Chiang had organized emerging classes of Whampoa graduates to create several "supplemental regiments" (*buchongtuan*) under his own command. Bai and Li naturally saw this as a prime example of Chiang behaving selfishly to bolster his own military position rather than acting as commander in chief with the welfare of the entire NRA in mind. They pressed He Yingqin to break up these regiments and distribute them to other corps. He Yingqin saw the logic of this proposal and agreed. When Chiang learned of this order he moved quickly to block it, sending Whampoa officers from these supplemental regiments to He Yingqin to inform him that they would resign rather than accept reassignment. When some of the these officers expressed reluctance to disobey orders from He Yingqin, Chiang told them that the supplemental regiments must be preserved and that desperate times called for desperate measures.[30] This amounted to He Yingqin's first indication that life without Chiang Kai-shek would prove difficult.

A second lesson came shortly thereafter when He Yingqin discovered that the regular units of the First Corps might not follow his orders. Chiang's departure smoothed over the differences between Nanjing and Wuhan and allowed the new leadership under Bai, Li, and He to turn to planning for the resumption of the Northern Expedition against Sun Chuanfang and Zhang Zongchang. Yet, when He Yingqin gave orders for units of the First Corps to prepare to cross the Yangzi River to attack Sun Chuanfang, Zhu Shaoliang organized a meeting of First Corps officers at the regimental level and above, all Whampoa graduates. To keep the meeting secret, rather than send telegrams to summon the officers, Zhu Shaoliang rode the train from Nanjing to Shanghai, getting off at stations near First Corps units in order to speak personally with the officers. Though Zhu chaired the meeting, deputy commander of the first division Hu Zongnan did most of the talking, voicing the sentiments of most in attendance. Hu interpreted the order as an attempt on the part of Bai Chongxi and Li Zongren to weaken Chiang's power base by sending the First Corps to bear the brunt of the fighting against Sun Chuanfang. Committing the First Corps to battle on the north bank of the Yangzi River at this time, he argued, would place the Nanjing–Shanghai base area in jeopardy and perhaps endanger the Northern Expedition. He expected that Chiang would be back to duty soon and advocated that the

---

[30] Zeng Kuoqing, "Jiang Jieshi diyici xiaye," 47.

First Corps officers delay until Chiang's return. The group agreed and resolved to refuse to obey the order.[31]

Zhu Shaoliang then met with He Yingqin to inform him of the situation. Zhu had known He for many years and the two had a common history. They had both attended the Shikan Gakko in Japan and had served together in Guizhou under Wang Wenhua. Zhu explained the views of the First Corps officers and told He Yingqin that when Chiang Kai-shek had departed from Nanjing he had ordered Zhu to use the WMAAA to preserve the First Corps. He warned He Yingqin to be careful in his dealings with Bai Chongxi and Li Zongren, who would try to manipulate him to their own advantage.[32] Confronted with this stark demonstration of resistance from his own officers, He Yingqin found himself in a dangerous situation. He did not realize the depth of Chiang Kai-shek's anger and disappointment at his failure to support him, and he now found himself caught between Bai and Li on one hand and the Whampoa officers of the First Corps on the other.

### The battle at Longtan

While He Yingqin grappled with the complicated politics of commanding the NRA, in mid August signs indicated that Sun Chuanfang and Zhang Zongchang planned to take advantage of the disorder within the revolutionary forces and attack the southern bank of the Yangzi River. Sun's troops began shelling at different points along the river, hoping to confuse the NRA as to the exact location at which his troops would cross the Yangzi.[33] In response, the NRA's three route armies took a defensive position along the southern bank, utilizing the water as a barrier against attack from the north. Bai Chongxi's Second Route Army took responsibility for Anhui and the western front, deploying troops from Hefei and west upriver. Li Zongren stationed his Third Route Army in the middle Yangzi, between Hefei and Nanjing. This left He Yingqin and the First Route Army with greatest responsibility for defending the base area of the lower Yangzi, essentially Nanjing, Zhenjiang, Shanghai, and the Nanjing–Shanghai railroad that connected them.[34] With such a vast area to cover, nearly 200 miles, and with limited troop strength at his

---

[31] Li Yuan, *Jiang Jieshi he He Yingqin*, 82–83; Zeng Kuoqing, "Jiang Jieshi diyici xiaye," 47–48.

[32] Li Zhongming, *He Yingqin dazhuan*, 46–47; Zeng Kuoqing, "Jiang Jieshi diyici xiaye," 47.

[33] Guofangbu shizhengju, *Beifa zhanshi* [A History of the Northern Expedition] (hereafter *BFZS*), 5 vols. (Taipei: Guofangbu shizhengju, 1967), vol. III, 865–66.

[34] Guo Tingyi and Jia Tingshi, eds., *Bai Chongxi xiansheng*, 64–65.

disposal, He Yingqin decided to post small units at various points along the river to keep watch for an attacking force, while stationing his main forces at points along the Nanjing–Shanghai railroad. These main forces could then move east or west along the railroad as needed in the event of an attack.[35]

Meanwhile, Sun Chuanfang targeted the area between Nanjing and Zhenjiang. The actual attack came on the night of August 25–26, when Sun took advantage of darkness and heavy fog to ferry a large force across the river, landing near Longtan, a town on the Nanjing–Shanghai railroad line. Once in control of Longtan, Sun's troops could move either west against Nanjing or east against Shanghai. The attacking force landed on the south bank of the river in territory under the control of He Yingqin's First Route Army. Troops stationed on the riverbank saw the boats as they approached the shore, raised the alarm, and opened fire on the enemy. By the afternoon of August 26, Sun's troops had overwhelmed the thinly stretched NRA units and taken control of Longtan and Qixia to the west, driving NRA forces back toward Nanjing and cutting transportation and communication lines.[36]

When news of the attack arrived in Nanjing, He Yingqin and Li Zongren immediately rushed reinforcements from the First and Seventh Corps to Wulongshan and Qixia, the area between Nanjing and Longtan.[37] The first division had held its ground at Wulongshan and together with these reinforcements organized a counterattack on Qixia. Over the course of August 27, the NRA pushed east along the river and regained control of Qixia and the Longtan train station.[38] Yet with no way to stop Sun from bringing more troops across the river, the NRA eventually faced an overwhelming force of 60,000 to 70,000 troops on the southern bank, which again drove the NRA from the area around Longtan and Qixia. On August 28, Sun's troops secured control of the Longtan train station, again cutting the railway between Nanjing and Shanghai, and began pushing east along the river toward Nanjing. Sun Chuanfang established his operational headquarters in a Longtan cement factory.[39]

The battle at Longtan developed on two fronts, with He Yingqin and Li Zongren directing operations in the west from Nanjing and Bai Chongxi

[35] *DLJBF*, 105.
[36] Guo Tingyi and Jia Tingshi, eds., *Bai Chongxi xiansheng*, 69; *DLJBF*, 106–07; *HYQJJ*, I, 173; Wu Shufeng, ed., *Chen Cheng: beifa pingluan*, 66; Li Zhongming, *He Yingqin dazhuan*, 49.
[37] *BFZS*, III, 868–69.    [38] *BFZS*, III, 877.
[39] *DLJBF*, 107–10; *HYQJJ*, I, 174–76; Wu Shufeng, ed., *Chen Cheng: beifa pingluan*, 67–68.

commanding First Corps forces to the east. Though he had been away from Nanjing when the attack began, Bai ended up playing a central role in organizing its defense. Chiang Kai-shek had forged relationships with prominent members of the Shanghai business community, as well as underworld organizations such as the Green Gang, and had developed methods for acquiring revenue.[40] Following his resignation, the NRA leadership found it difficult to procure sufficient funds to pay and provide for its troops. Just prior to the attack, Bai had been in Shanghai to negotiate further loans from some of the city's biggest banks. On his return trip to Nanjing, his train stopped at Wuxi station where he learned of Sun's attack. Unable to continue west because Sun's forces had severed the rail line and with no way to contact Li Zongren or He Yingqin as phone lines to Nanjing had also been cut, NRA units could not coordinate a defense. Bai eventually managed to make phone contact with NRA units in Shanghai, which established wireless radio contact with Nanjing. He learned that the MAC had directed him to take command of all NRA forces east of Zhenjiang, but for most of the battle the commanders had difficulty communicating with each other and essentially fought independently.[41]

Eventually, Bai managed to contact two First Corps division commanders, Wei Lihuang of the fourteenth division, nearly 60 miles away at Zhenjiang, and Liu Zhi of the second division at Changzhou, 25 miles away. He ordered both commanders to organize their units for a counterattack on Longtan right away.[42] A group of First Corps officers again met to discuss whether or not to obey Bai Chongxi's orders. Although wary of submitting to Bai's authority, because the attack threatened the very existence of the government and army they agreed that this situation overrode Chiang's direction that they preserve First Corps troop strength, and they committed their troops to the battle.[43] Bai also contacted Yang Shuzhuang, commander of NRA naval forces, urging him to block Sun's troops from continuing to cross the river. Yang explained that he did not have enough vessels to do so, but eventually arranged his forces to fire both on troops crossing the river and on Sun's positions on the south bank of the river.[44]

---

[40]  See Parks Coble, *The Shanghai Capitalists and the National Government, 1927–1937* (Cambridge, MA: Council on East Asian Studies, Harvard University Press, 1980).

[41]  Guo Tingyi and Jia Tingshi, eds., *Bai Chongxi xiansheng*, 67–68; *BFZS*, III, 869.

[42]  Guo Tingyi and Jia Tingshi, eds., *Bai Chongxi xiansheng*, 67–68; Liu Zhi, *Wode huiyi*, 58; Xiong Zongren, *He Yingqin: xuanwozhong de lishi*, I, 232.

[43]  Tsung-jen Li, *Memoirs*, 230; Li Zhongming, *He Yingqin dazhuan*, 50; Li Yuan, *Jiang Jieshi he He Yingqin*, 85.

[44]  Guo Tingyi and Jia Tingshi, eds., *Bai Chongxi xiansheng*, 68–69.

Early in the morning of August 29, He Yingqin learned through scattered reports filtering into Nanjing that Sun's forces had recaptured the Longtan train station. Moreover, units of the First and Seventh Corps had been driven back and began to appear on the eastern edge of Nanjing.[45] Still unable to communicate directly with Bai Chongxi and NRA units to the east of Longtan, He Yingqin and Li Zongren managed to establish indirect contact with Bai, passing messages through various units via telephone and wireless radio. Together they drew up a general plan for an all-out counterattack to begin at dawn on August 30, sending all available NRA forces toward Longtan in three separate columns. He Yingqin led the first division of the First Corps from the eastern suburbs of Nanjing in an attack on Longtan from the southwest. Xia Wei led Li Zongren's Seventh Corps and the Seventeenth Corps east along the river bank and the railroad tracks, attacking Longtan from the west. On the other side of Longtan, Bai Chongxi led the second and fourteenth divisions of the First Corps attacking west from Zhenjiang, catching Sun's force in the middle of this three-pronged attack.[46]

Li Zongren's memoir includes a passage in which he describes a visit to He Yingqin's headquarters in Nanjing in the early morning of August 29. Hoping to discuss the situation and develop a plan for a counterattack, Li claims that he found He Yingqin and his staff packing to withdraw from Nanjing. When Li asked He Yingqin why he felt he needed to retreat, He told him that "ever since the resignation of the commander in chief, my army [the First Corps] has lost its will to fight; what else can I do?" Only after Li had chastised him and demonstrated his own "firm manner" did He Yingqin agree to stay and participate in the counterattack. Li also complains that He Yingqin refused to give Li's forces adequate ammunition for the counterattack and suggests that He's timid nature led his troops to refer to him as "Grandma."[47] Criticism of the First Corps and He Yingqin are common in Li's account of the Northern Expedition, which tends to emphasize the contributions of his own Seventh Corps. Indeed, Li's advice to He on August 29 included pulling out First Corps units from the battle and replacing them with units of the Seventh and Nineteenth Corps from Li's Third Route Army.[48] Li's account suggests that He Yingqin's inclination to leave Nanjing reflects his weakness as a commander and a preference for avoiding combat. Given He Yingqin's record in previous battles at Danshui, Mianhu, Huizhou, Yongding, and Songkou, this seems unlikely. Finally, Li's claims that only after he insisted did He Yingqin agree to

[45]  *BFZS*, III, 883.      [46]  *DLJBF*, 111.
[47]  Tsung-jen Li, *Memoirs*, 231–32.      [48]  Tsung-jen Li, *Memoirs*, 231.

stay and defend the capital seem farfetched. It is unlikely that a few harsh words from Li Zongren would convince He Yingqin to change his plans. In concluding his remarks about the battle at Longtan, Li states that, had he not visited He on the morning of August 29, the entire First Corps would have withdrawn to Hangzhou and the capital would have been lost. This is likely an exaggeration that, as in other cases in his memoir, emphasizes his own role to the detriment of others.[49]

He Yingqin may or may not have learned of the meeting of First Corps officers to discuss whether to obey Bai Chongxi's orders when the attack began, but by August 29 when he met with Li Zongren there could be no doubt that the First Corps had demonstrated its willingness to fight. Indeed, in the early phase of the fighting He Yingqin had already successfully ordered additional First Corps units to support NRA forces at Wulongshan and Qixia, suggesting that the Whampoa Academy officers, whatever their views prior to Sun's attack, stood ready to accept orders and fight. Moreover, though the various NRA units had difficulty communicating, He Yingqin knew that Bai Chongxi had taken command of the second and fourteenth divisions to the east, which had begun to advance on Longtan. On the morning of August 29, following his meeting with Li Zongren and with the news that Sun Chuanfang's forces had once again captured Longtan station, He Yingqin went to the Qilin Gate on the eastern side of Nanjing to reorganize his troops in preparation for an all-out counterassault. He met with available division commanders to discuss a plan of attack and reorganized troops that had fallen back on Nanjing. He even identified wounded soldiers still able to fight and incorporated them into the force that now moved west toward Longtan. To prevent further loss of ground, he sent ahead orders to all First Route Army units prohibiting retreat and directed those falling back on the capital to remain in place and await orders.[50]

In the early hours before dawn on August 30, He Yingqin led his troops from the east side of the capital, moving northeast toward Longtan. According the plan, Xia Wei and Bai Chongxi did likewise, converging on the enemy force from three sides, occupying the high ground surrounding Longtan. Sun Chuanfang had committed the majority of his force to the attack, which left him with few reinforcements to support his position. Moreover, in order to motivate his men, he had ordered nearly all of the vessels that had transported his troops across the river to return to the

---

[49] Tsung-jen Li, *Memoirs*, 233. Gibson reached a similar conclusion about Li Zongren's tendency to exaggerate his own position in his memoirs. See Gibson, "Chiang Kai-shek's Central Army," 136 n. 25.

[50] *DLJBF*, 110–11; *HYQJJ*, I, 178; *BFZS*, III, 883; He Yingqin, "Dongzheng beifa dao tongyi," 85.

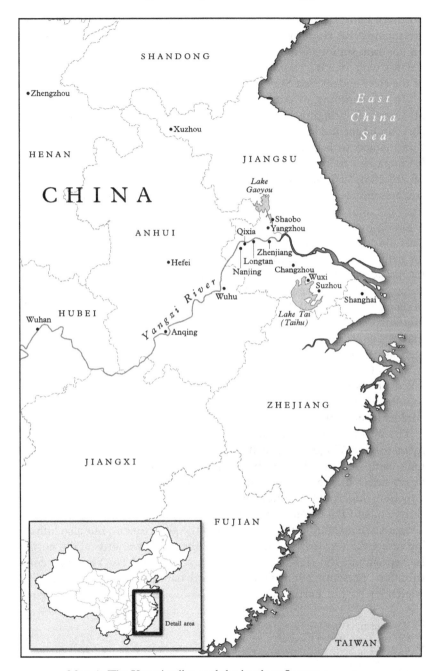

Map 4: The Yangzi valley and the battle at Longtan

northern bank. The fighting on August 30 raged around Longtan as the advancing NRA columns pressed in on Sun's force, gradually converging on the train station. With no retreat possible, Sun's men put up a strong defense with their backs at the river. NRA naval forces established control of the river and shelled Sun's forces, adding to the pressure.[51]

On the morning of August 31, He Yingqin and Bai Chongxi met at Longtan, bringing their combined forces to bear on the town, surrounding it and leaving no avenue for retreat. Like a cornered animal, Sun reacted with a fierce counterattack on the Longtan train station, leading to several hours of intense combat. In an uncharacteristic display of emotion that perhaps demonstrates the sense of emergency that surrounded the entire battle, He Yingqin moved up and down the front lines haranguing his troops to maintain their positions, allegedly even wielding his sidearm and threatening to shoot himself if they failed.[52] Surrounded and with only a small number of boats on hand to ferry his men across the river, Sun Chuanfang escaped with several thousand troops, leaving the bulk of his defeated force on the south bank of the Yangzi River. Over the course of the six-day battle, NRA forces inflicted perhaps as many as 10,000 casualties on Sun's army and in the end took 30,000 prisoners and captured large quantities of rifles, ammunition, machine guns, and artillery pieces. Estimates of NRA casualties ran as high as 10,000.[53] Liu Zhi, commander of the second division fighting with Bai Chongxi to the east of Longtan, reported one-third of his force killed or wounded over the course of the battle.[54] Some said that six months after the battle passengers on trains passing through Longtan could still smell the rotting corpses of soldiers from both sides.[55]

The victory at Longtan might have seemed like a crowning achievement for He Yingqin. Once the exhaustion and tension of the week-long campaign faded away, he could look back on this battle as one of his finest moments as a combat commander. Despite commanding a faction-ridden force without its commander in chief, He Yingqin, Li Zongren, and Bai Chongxi had pulled together and successfully defeated a large-scale assault, not only protecting the government, but also inflicting severe damage on the army of one of the major warlords of the north. In September, the Nanjing government recognized He Yingqin's contribution, presenting him with an award banner that proclaimed him "defender of the party and nation" (hanwei dangguo).[56] He Yingqin

---

[51] Wu Shufeng, ed., Chen Cheng: beifa pingluan, 68.
[52] Jordan, The Northern Expedition, 140.
[53] Jordan, The Northern Expedition, 141.     [54] Liu Zhi, Wode huiyi, 59.
[55] Guo Tingyi and Jia Tingshi, eds., Bai Chongxi xiansheng, 71.
[56] HYQJJ, I, 185.

sent a telegram to Chiang Kai-shek in Japan reporting the news of the victory at Longtan. Chiang sent his own telegram of congratulations in which he praised the work of the First and Seventh Corps and compared the victory at Longtan to other milestone victories, including the battles at Mianhu and Songkou, which He Yingqin had delivered for the NRA. Of the three route army commanders, Chiang mentioned only He Yingqin.[57] The First Corps, of which He Yingqin remained in command, incorporated a number of units captured at Longtan and increased its manpower by 50 percent, which He Yingqin no doubt believed would please Chiang Kai-shek.[58]

The prospects of the Nanjing government and the NRA as a whole seemed to revive with the victory at Longtan. This, combined with Chiang's temporary absence from the scene, now seemed to clear the path for unification of the leadership as most of those who supported the Wuhan faction now made their way to Nanjing to create a new government in September. Tang Shengzhi refused reconciliation, but when he found himself surrounded by hostile forces he formally "retired" and left for Japan.[59] With the western front secure, NRA forces crossed the Yangzi River to resume the Northern Expedition against the remnants of Sun's battered force and Zhang Zongchang's Shandong Army. He Yingqin's First Route Army and Li Zongren's Third Route Army moved north, clearing Jiangsu of enemy troops and recapturing Xuzhou on December 16. Meanwhile, the major commanders began negotiations with Chiang Kai-shek, which produced an agreement for his return as commander in chief. Based on the slogan "divided and cooperative rule" (fenzhi hezuo), the deal called for the commanders to accept Chiang's return to his post as commander in chief of the NRA and acknowledge the legitimacy of the government in Nanjing. In return, Chiang agreed to recognize the regional power bases of each of the major commanders through the creation of four branch political councils under Li Jishen, Li Zongren, Feng Yuxiang, and Yan Xishan.[60] On December 20, He Yingqin sent another telegram to Chiang, asking him to return to duty, one of many such telegrams that preceded Chiang's return.[61] Having returned from Japan and announced his plans to marry Song Meiling, Chiang Kai-shek agreed to resume command in January 1928.

[57] *HYQJJ*, I, 184.

[58] Gibson, "Chiang Kai-shek's Central Army," 138.      [59] Dreyer, *China at War*, 148.

[60] Tsung-jen Li, *Memoirs*, 243–44; Zeng Kuoqing, "Jiang Jieshi diyici," 49–50.

[61] He Yingqin, "Qing Jiang zongsiling fuzhi wancheng beifa shang zhongyang dian" [Telegram Inviting Commander Jiang to Return and Complete the Northern Expedition], in He Yingqin, ed., *Weibang bainian ji* [A Century of Service to the State] (Taipei: Liming wenhua shiye gufen youxian gongsi, 1987), 709–10.

## The rift

As Nanjing prepared for Chiang's return to duty, He Yingqin must have understood that his decision to remain silent and acquiesce to Bai Chongxi's suggestion that Chiang step down as commander in chief had damaged his relationship with Chiang. In Chiang's absence, He Yingqin learned that he could not control the Whampoa Academy officers who commanded the First Corps and that he needed Chiang in order to maintain his own position as its commander. He did not, however, realize how deeply his silence at that meeting and his subsequent cooperation with Li Zongren and Bai Chongxi had hurt Chiang. What he viewed as a temporary sacrifice on Chiang's part for the good of the army, party, and nation, Chiang Kai-shek interpreted as a personal betrayal. In early September 1927, Chiang privately referred to He Yingqin as a "traitor" (*hanjian*).[62] As he awaited Chiang's return, He Yingqin no doubt hoped that his success in leading the First Corps during the battle of Long-tan had helped him win the trust of the First Corps officers and would go a long way toward restoring his relationship with Chiang. If this is indeed what he thought, a rude awakening accompanied Chiang's return in January 1928.

Returning first to Shanghai, Chiang remained cool toward He Yingqin, but prepared to resume their previous professional and personal relationship. In a letter to Li Zongren, Li Jishen, and other NRA commanders, Chiang hinted at both his sense of betrayal and his willingness to make amends, writing that "if He Yingqin will just obey me, then we will work together and never part ways."[63] Shortly after Chiang's return in early 1928, he summoned Li Zhonggong, now working under He Yingqin's brother-in-law Wang Boqun in the Ministry of Communications, to his temporary residence in the French Concession. Li had worked with both He Yingqin and Chiang Kai-shek, and served as an intermediary of sorts after Chiang's return. After discussing Li's position as a secretary to the GMD Central Executive Committee (CEC), Chiang asked if Li had seen He Yingqin. Li told him that He Yingqin was in Shanghai too, but that he had not seen him. Chiang became angry and complained that all the other commanders, presumably Li Zongren, Feng Yuxiang, and Yan Xishan, had sent telegrams to Chiang welcoming him back to duty and pledging their full loyalty and support. As he now prepared to return to Nan-jing, only He Yingqin, his longest-serving and most trusted subordinate, had failed to do so.[64] He Yingqin had twice sent telegrams requesting Chiang's return, in August and December 1927, but his failure to send

---

[62] *SLGB*, II, September 6, 1927, 15.     [63] Zeng Kuoqing, "Jiang Jieshi diyici," 50.
[64] Li Zhonggong, "Wosuo zhidao de He Yingqin," 210.

an additional message once Chiang returned rekindled the latter's ire. Li Zhonggong tried to smooth things over, explaining that He Yingqin did not understand the political issues within the NRA, and promised to go talk to He Yingqin.[65]

After his meeting with Chiang, Li Zhonggong visited He Yingqin, who had gone to Shanghai, and relayed to him the details of Chiang's anger. This news stunned He Yingqin, who explained that he had consulted with his subordinate officers Liu Zhi, Gu Zhutong, and others before sending a message to Chiang on their behalf. As he had not yet heard back from them, he had not sent a message of welcome to Chiang. Li explained that Chiang still bore a grudge about He Yingqin's cooperation with Li Zongren and Bai Chongxi and urged him to send a telegram pledging support and loyalty right away. He Yingqin agreed and asked Li to draft a copy and send it immediately.[66] The telegram did little to soothe Chiang's anger, which reached a climax a few days later. In early February, Chiang visited the headquarters of the First Route Army at Xuzhou, taking the staff by surprise. When Chiang asked for He Yingqin, they responded that he had gone hunting and had not yet returned. Infuriated, Chiang pounded the table and yelled that Xuzhou was still the front line of battle and the fact that He Yingqin had left his post amounted to grounds for dismissal. Chiang then announced that he intended to remove He Yingqin from his command over the First Route Army and make him chief of staff. Nominally, this amounted to a promotion, but in reality it deprived He of direct command over troops. All involved understood what this meant: it was no ordinary military transfer. Chiang then sent a telegram to Li Zhonggong and Wang Boqun summoning them to Xuzhou immediately to help him deal with this deeply personal and professional issue. He sent a second telegram to his headquarters in Nanjing, ordering the removal of guards from He Yingqin's residence.[67]

Back in Nanjing, Li Zhonggong prepared to travel to Xuzhou on a special train car as soon as he received Chiang's telegram. Li and Wang Boqun shared a residence, but Wang was suffering from an illness and could not travel. As he packed, Li received a telephone call from Wang Wenxiang, Wang Boqun's sister and He Yingqin's wife. She told Li that the guards stationed at their Nanjing residence had left their posts and wanted to know what had happened. Li asked about He Yingqin's where-abouts, but all Wang Wenxiang could tell him was that she had dispatched

---

[65] Li Zhonggong, "Wosuo zhidao de He Yingqin," 210.

[66] Li Zhonggong, "Wosuo zhidao de He Yingqin," 210–11.

[67] Fang Yonggang, "Jiang Jieshi diaojiao He Yingqin" [Chiang Kai-shek Disciplines He Yingqin], *Moulüe tiandi*, 6 (2008), 59.

men to find him.[68] He Yingqin, who had been in Nanjing when Chiang visited the First Corps headquarters, appeared at Wang and Li's residence in a state of great anxiety. He had learned of Chiang's decision to take away his command and demanded to know "what on earth is old Chiang doing!" He complained that he had now lost face and could not accept the chief of staff position. Li Zhonggong calmed him down and explained that Chiang was deeply upset at He Yingqin's actions, but that the two men had a long history of working together and would eventually work things out. Offering some broader insight into the issue, Li told He that the key issue stemmed from his decision to side with the Guangxi Clique against Chiang. This lay at the heart of Chiang's discontent, and He Yingqin had to handle it carefully in order to make amends. He Yingqin saw the logic of this view, agreed to accept the new assignment, and penned a letter to Chiang asking to be relieved of command of the First Corps.[69]

Word of He Yingqin's "promotion" had spread rapidly through the NRA. That evening as Li Zhonggong boarded the train for Xuzhou, he overheard other officers sniggering over He's "head-first fall." Upon arriving at Xuzhou, he immediately went to see Chiang at the Xuzhou Hotel where Chiang asked if Li had spoken to He Yingqin. Li explained that he had done so, and the latter now understood his mistake and would gladly accept his new post as Chiang's chief of staff. This mollified Chiang somewhat, but he stressed to Li that they must ensure that He Yingqin fully comprehended that this was not so much about He's failure to send a telegram as about his cooperation with Chiang's rivals. From Chiang's perspective, He Yingqin had abandoned him to side with Bai Chongxi and Li Zongren, who had then used He to weaken Chiang and the position of the First Corps in the NRA. How, Chiang wondered, could He Yingqin not see this? "You go tell Jingzhi [He Yingqin's courtesy name] to make no mistake," Chiang ranted at Li, "that when Li and Bai pressured me to step down, with just one phrase [of support] from him I would not have had to do it!" Several times in the course of his conversation with Li Zhonggong he emphatically declared that "without Chiang Kai-shek, there is no He Yingqin! He must know this!"[70]

---

[68]  Li Zhonggong, "Wosuo zhidao de He Yingqin," 211; Fang Yonggang, "Jiang Jieshi diaojiao He Yingqin," 59–60.

[69]  Li Zhonggong, "Wosuo zhidao de He Yingqin," 211. See reference to He Yingqin's letter of resignation in *SLGB*, II, February 11, 1928, 413–14.

[70]  Li Zhonggong, "Wosuo zhidao de He Yingqin," 212. Some have suggested that Chiang removed He Yingqin from his command as a warning to other commanders, in essence "killing a chicken to scare the monkeys." See Fang Yonggang, "Jiang Jieshi diaojiao He Yingqin," 60.

The more Chiang spoke, the more Li understood the great sense of disappointment and anger Chiang felt about He Yingqin's failure to support him against the Guangxi Clique. He stressed to Chiang that He Yingqin's actions did not represent disloyalty, but rather the simple fact that he did not understand the political issues of the NRA and failed to grasp the complicated relationships that constituted the larger picture of the revolution. "He Yingqin has served under you for a long time and you know that he is loyal to you like no other," Li explained to Chiang; "he is like your arms in that he will do whatever you ask."[71] At this explanation, Chiang relented and let go of some of his anger. Reviewing the close bond he felt with He Yingqin, Chiang felt the need to express his feelings to his comrade. Sitting down at his desk, Chiang penned a twelve-page letter to He Yingqin and gave it to Li Zhonggong to deliver personally. "He Yingqin does not understand politics," Chiang agreed with Li, "so you and Wang Boqun must help him with this."[72]

On the train back to Nanjing, Li read the letter carefully. It began with a review of their long working relationship, harking back to their battles at Danshui, Mianhu, and Huizhou. In a reference to He Yingqin's collaboration with Bai and Li, Chiang explained that the revolutionary environment remained fraught with complications and they must be careful at all times. The Guangxi Clique had been sowing dissension within the NRA, and Chiang needed time to deal with this problem. Once he resolved this issue, Chiang promised to call He back to command the Whampoa forces. Unexpectedly, at the third station out of Xuzhou, an army officer boarded the train with an order from Chiang Kai-shek to take back the letter from Li Zhonggong, without offering any explanation. Li turned the letter over to the man, but when he arrived in Nanjing he related most of its contents to He. A few weeks later Chiang formally appointed He Yingqin as chief of staff to the commander of the NRA, a position with no direct command over troops. Sick at heart over recent events, He Yingqin asked for two months' leave before taking up his new duties.[73]

For the second time in his career, He Yingqin had seemingly lost his position as favored subordinate to a military commander. Years earlier, after his near-fatal wounding in Kunming, He Yingqin had gone to Shanghai to recuperate, spending long hours contemplating his future. Having developed a close personal and professional relationship with Wang Wenhua, rising through the ranks of the Guizhou Army, and

[71] Li Zhonggong, "Wosuo zhidao de He Yingqin," 213.
[72] Li Zhonggong, "Wosuo zhidao de He Yingqin," 213.
[73] Li Zhonggong, "Wosuo zhidao de He Yingqin," 213–14.

engaging in the revolutionary movement in Guizhou, he had suddenly found himself without a position, patron, or prospects. Eventually, through family and professional connections, he had taken a position at the Whampoa Military Academy and begun a close association with a new patron and a new national revolutionary movement. After four years of hard work and success on the battlefield, that situation had now potentially come to an end. He had thrived in a position as the "right-hand man" to a top commanding officer, a position "under 1 and over 10,000" (*yiren zhixia, wanren zhishang*), as the Chinese saying goes, but, having lost Chiang's trust, his prospects with the NRA seemed dim.

During his leave of absence, He Yingqin occupied himself with his usual hobbies, such as going dancing with his wife, visiting friends and relatives, and hunting in the area around Shanghai. He did make one major change that would be an important part of his private life going forward. At Wang Wenxiang's urging, he began to attend Catholic services and eventually embraced his wife's faith. He had grown up in Guizhou where a number of prominent families, including his in-laws, had converted to Catholicism, but up to this point He Yingqin had shown little interest in Western religion. His spiritual views had remained rooted in Chinese tradition and his intellectual focus always on his professional career, but he now found comfort in his wife's religion. This conversion came perhaps as a result of his despondency over his break with Chiang Kai-shek and loss of his position as army commander, providing a source of comfort in a time of emotional difficulty.[74] Always a private man, He Yingqin left few clues as to his motives, and outwardly he remained the same stoic, disciplined, and reserved individual cut from traditional Confucian cloth. The leap to Catholicism might have been easy, given the church's emphasis on personal responsibility, self-discipline, and concern for society as a whole, which dovetailed nicely with his own martial values and revolutionary goals. Later in life he wore this faith more openly and played an active role in an international Christian movement, Frank Buchman's call for "Moral Re-armament."

While He Yingqin passed the time in Shanghai, wondering what lay ahead in his professional career, Chiang Kai-shek resumed command of the NRA only to face significant challenges. The Northern Expedition had whittled down the number of major and minor warlords who opposed the GMD's revolutionary movement, but had not provided genuine unity. Chiang's return to duty as commander in chief, and his main political rival Wang Jingwei's departure for Europe, marked his rise to

[74] Xiong Zongren, *He Yingqin: xuanwozhong de lishi*, I, 244; Li Zhongming, *He Yingqin dazhuan*, 57.

both political and military dominance within the GMD and set the stage for the final campaigns of the Northern Expedition. Chiang reorganized the NRA, abolishing the route armies in late February 1928 and creating four group armies (*jituanjun*). The former First Route Army became the First Group Army, which included the original Whampoa units of the old First Corps and many new units added from various regional forces which the NRA had defeated or coopted on its march to the north. Chiang divided the First Group Army into separate "columns" (*zong-dui*) under the command of Liu Zhi, Chen Diaoyuan, and He Huizu. Painfully aware that he still presided over a delicate balance of regional armies, Chiang recognized the existing regional divisions, renaming Feng Yuxiang's Northwest Army in Shaanxi and Henan as the Second Group Army, Yan Xishan's Shanxi force as the Third Group Army, and Li Zongren's forces in Guangxi, Hunan, and Hubei as the Fourth Group Army. Chiang occupied the chair of the GMD Central Political Council (CPC) but, again bowing to the realities of the situation, he distributed political power along regional lines by appointing other commanders as "branch chairs" of the CPC and granting them virtual autonomy. Feng Yuxiang chaired the CPC branch at Kaifeng, Yan Xishan the branch at Taiyuan, Li Zongren the branch at Wuhan, and Li Jishen the branch at Guangzhou.[75] As he reorganized the NRA, Chiang also reconsidered He Yingqin's role. Having let go of most of his anger, Chiang now wanted others to understand that He Yingqin again had his support. As He Yingqin took up his duties as chief of staff on March 7, Chiang gave orders that everyone should know that He was his "right-hand man" (*guxiong shouzu*) and that He would now take over all rear-area responsibilities.[76]

In early April, the First and Second Group Armies began the final phase of the Northern Expedition, pushing north and east, converging on Shandong where the remnants of Sun Chuanfang's force made a brief stand before withdrawing across the Yellow River. The Japanese government feared that the conflict posed a danger to Japanese citizens living and working in Shandong and dispatched 5,000 troops to Jinan to protect them. Minor clashes escalated into the infamous Jinan Incident which resulted in more than 4,000 Chinese casualties. Chiang understood the necessity of avoiding war with Japan and agreed to a settlement

---

[75] Lloyd Eastman, "Nationalist China During the Nanking Decade 1927–1937," in Fairbank and Feuerwerker, eds., *Republican China 1912–1949, Part 2*, 125; Gibson, "Chiang Kai-shek's Central Army," 170–71; *HYQJJ*, I, 199–201; Furuya, *Chiang Kai-shek*, 238; Dreyer, *China at War*, 148–49.

[76] *SLGB*, II, March 7, 1928, 485.

that included the withdrawal of Japanese forces from Shandong.[77] Two months later, the Japanese military again indicated its willingness to take provocative action in China with the assassination of Zhang Zuolin in the hope that it would foment chaos and serve as an excuse for the Japanese Guandong Army to seize control of Manchuria. The plan backfired when Zhang's son Zhang Xueliang, new "warlord" of Manchuria and commander of the National Pacification Army (*anguojun*), declared his loyalty to Chiang Kai-shek and the GMD.[78] Forces of the Third and Fourth Group Armies marched into Beijing, soon renamed Beiping, in early July to complete the nominal unification of China.

Few failed to recognize that China remained divided along regional lines and that the commanders of the four group armies did not necessarily accept Chiang's military and political authority. Chiang consented to this temporary division of military and political power for the time being, yet he wasted little time before planning action against the "new warlords" he believed now stood in the way of military unification and centralization, a prerequisite to nation-building. With this in mind, he again turned to his former "right-hand man," He Yingqin, whose support he could not easily do without.

Some have seen the rift between Chiang Kai-shek and He Yingqin as a turning point after which Chiang never fully trusted He again. However, the evidence indicates that the two men quickly returned to their previous close professional relationship, and He Yingqin continued his rise through the ranks of the NRA. More accurately, the events of the fall and winter of 1927–28 demonstrated to both He Yingqin and Chiang Kai-shek how much they needed each other. Without He's support, Chiang found himself at a disadvantage against his main rivals within the NRA. Without Chiang's support, He Yingqin found himself unable to command the First Corps or Whampoa units of the Central Army. Rather than a dispute that created lingering distrust, this produced a clear understanding on the part of both men that they depended on each other and that their fates had become intertwined. Within months of Chiang's return to duty in January 1928, the two men resumed working closely together and Chiang continued to call on He Yingqin to handle the most important issues of the day.

[77] Furuya, *Chiang Kai-shek*, 239–49; Taylor, *Generalissimo*, 78–82.
[78] Taylor, *Generalissimo*, 83.

# 5    Reorganization and its discontents

On February 3, 1929, a central radio broadcast carried He Yingqin's speech to the far corners of China. Addressing a national audience of soldiers and civilians alike, he posed a series of questions, asking: did they want to rescue the nation? Did they want to relieve the suffering of the people? Raise the status of soldiers? Realize genuine unity? End internal conflict and civil war? Engage in construction projects? Preserve order in Chinese society? Strengthen national defense? If they answered yes to any of these questions, then they must support the essential task of reorganizing and demobilizing large parts of China's armed forces. Otherwise, he concluded, the Nationalist revolution would fail.[1]

In the early years after the establishment of the new government in Nanjing, He Yingqin and Chiang Kai-shek had hoped to begin a period of nation-building, modernization, and national revitalization. As a first step in this process, they initiated a movement to reorganize China's armed forces in order to reduce the overall number of soldiers and bring them all under central control. Instead of moving toward their goals, they confronted a series of military challenges from a variety of internal opponents, which forced them to spend the years 1928–30 working to defend and extend Nanjing's authority over regional military commanders.

Following He Yingqin's "promotion" to Chiang's chief of staff, which deprived him of command over troops, his career within the NRA, or what most now called the "Nationalist army" (*guojun*), seemed unclear.[2] Chiang had bristled at He Yingqin's cooperation with the Guangxi Clique in late 1927, but he also understood that he needed He Yingqin in order to accomplish his goals of extending central authority over regional

---

[1] "Guojun bianqian shishi zhi yiyi" [The Significance of Reorganization and Demobilization of the National Army], in He Yingqin, *He zongzhang Yingqin yanlun xuanji* [Selected Speeches of General He Yingqin] (hereafter *HZZYQYLXJ*) (China: n.p., 1939), 1–6.
[2] The GMD military force retained the name "National Revolutionary Army" but most referred to it with the shorter name "National army." This study uses the term "Nationalist army," which follows the convention of Western writing on the topic and reflects the fact that it remained a military force of the Nationalist Party.

forces. He Yingqin quickly returned to his former role, supporting Chiang's attempts to defeat regional opponents, impose unity on the country, and build a new nation. First, he presided over the movement to reorganize and demobilize parts of the Nationalist army. Together, He Yingqin and Chiang Kai-shek pushed regional commanders to join them in dramatically reducing the size of their militaries and put them under central command in order to cut government expenses and achieve genuine unification. Second, when this effort triggered a series of revolts in Hunan, Hubei, and Guangxi, He Yingqin played a critical role in defeating regional commanders who resisted Chiang's central authority. He also played a decisive role in defeating a coalition of major warlords in the Central Plains War of 1930, suppressing the last military attempt to drive Chiang from power within the Nationalist camp and expanding his territorial base. In early 1930, Chiang named him minister of military administration (*junzhengbu buzhang*), a position he would hold for fourteen years. This clearly positioned He Yingqin as second only to Chiang in the Nationalist military hierarchy.

### Reorganization and demobilization of the Nationalist army

In early 1928, Chiang had nominally completed the Northern Expedition, unified the country, and established a new capital at Nanjing. In reality, he faced continued division within the ranks of his army as the regional commanders he had appointed to chair the branch political councils still loomed as potential threats to central authority. Genuine unification remained elusive and Nanjing continued to pursue the goal of extending central political and military control. With this in mind, Chiang Kai-shek and He Yingqin began discussing the need to reduce the size of China's military with a series of attempts to "reorganize and demobilize" (*bianqian*) the four group armies. Chiang's critics tend to see this as an attempt to weaken his internal rivals, namely the four group army commanders, in order to consolidate his own power under a military dictatorship.[3] Chiang and his supporters argued that building a modern, unified state required a disciplined and truly national military force, looking to the examples of Germany and Japan, where strong, centralized militaries formed the basis of the creation of

---

[3] Lloyd Eastman describes contemporary views of Chiang's attempts at reorganization and demobilization in "Nationalist China During the Nanking Decade," 125–26. Captain Parker Tenney, assistant military attaché in China, described the effort as a "failure" due in part to its "wide scope" and lack of "machinery for its execution." See *US Military Intelligence Reports, China, 1911–1941*, Reel VI, 0058.

modern governments, as models for China.[4] Indeed, when speaking on the topic, Chiang specifically praised Japanese regional "militarists" who had overthrown the shogun in the 1868 Meiji Restoration and turned over complete military authority to the central government.[5] Chiang and He Yingqin consistently stressed the need to reorganize and demobilize the Nationalist army not as a way to weaken their rivals, but as a part of their revolutionary vision for building a modern state and society.

Chiang began with attempts to transform his own First Group Army. Over the course of the Eastern and Northern Expeditions, Chiang Kai-shek had expanded his military base, building around the Whampoa troops, which had served as his most loyal forces. These troops remained the core of his First Group Army, which he reorganized into four divisions, but he also incorporated numerous provincial forces that had joined the NRA in the course of the fighting since 1925. In order to ensure their loyalty and effectiveness, Chiang instituted what Michael Richard Gibson calls the "command switch," which involved rotating officers across different units. In 1928, the Whampoa Academy moved to Nanjing and took the new name Central Military Academy (CMA), but its graduates continued to serve in these new provincial units, rotating the existing officers to other units. Believing that a modern army should have officers with standardized training who could serve effectively in any unit, Chiang switched officers as often as possible. In addition to placing his trained and trusted officers in these former provincial units, he also ensured with this practice that no officers would rise up through the ranks in a single unit and establish a separate power base. This expanded Chiang's military base, strengthening what many call Nanjing's "central army."[6]

Reorganization and transferring officers played an important role in Chiang's plans for the Nationalist army in 1928–29, but most of the discussion at the time revolved around the issue of demobilization or force reduction. Chiang and He Yingqin consistently emphasized demobilization as a part of state-building, arguing that if China were to have any hope of building a stable government that would respond to the needs of the people, it needed to dramatically reduce the size and cost of the military. In this light, reorganization and demobilization had as much to do with financial retrenchment as with center–region relations.

To address the challenge of demobilization and asserting central authority over regional forces, in June 1928 Chiang Kai-shek turned to He Yingqin, appointing him to chair preparatory meetings on the issue.

[4]  Taylor, *Generalissimo*, 85.
[5]  "Speech of Chiang Kai-shek at the Opening of the Disbandment Conference," in *US Military Intelligence Reports: China, 1911–1941*, Reel VI, 0034.
[6]  Gibson, "Chiang Kai-shek's Central Army," 154–55.

Several factors led Chiang to put aside his anger about He's failure to support him in late 1927 and to rely heavily on him once again. Certainly, Chiang knew He as a capable and reliable officer who had served under his command since the early days at the Whampoa Military Academy and had proven himself as a combat commander in the Eastern and Northern Expeditions, delivering critical victories with the fate of the revolution on the line. He Yingqin also shared the belief that China must be unified by force of arms and that a modern, centralized, and disciplined force must serve as the cornerstone of a new China. Ironically, the very issues that caused the rift in their relationship also helped draw the two men back together. He Yingqin came from southwest China and had ties to other regional leaders in Guizhou, Yunnan, and Sichuan. He had also worked effectively with both Li Zongren and Bai Chongxi, leaders of the Guangxi Clique, on the eastern front of the Northern Expedition and the critical battle at Longtan. Despite his anger over He's cooperation with Li and Bai back in 1927–28, Chiang knew these connections might prove helpful in his attempts to bring the various regional commanders under central authority.[7] For his part, He Yingqin had few options other than to accept his new assignment as chief of staff and to look for an opportunity to repair their relationship. When Chiang tapped him to work on the issue of demobilization, He Yingqin set to the task. Work on the demobilization issue served as the vehicle for He Yingqin's return to Chiang's good graces, and for the next several years He Yingqin concentrated on executing Chiang's policies vis à vis regional military commanders, the CCP, and the Japanese.

The first discussions of demobilization took place in late June, when He Yingqin attended a meeting of the Military Affairs Commission on the topic of military reductions. He delivered a report on the state of the Nationalist army, parts of which he would repeat again and again at different times and in different venues over the next year. According to his statistics, the total number of men under arms in the four group armies and known regional forces had exceeded 2 million, with annual military expenditures exceeding 800 million yuan. He estimated annual government revenues at 500 million yuan, creating an untenable financial situation. In order to rectify this situation, He Yingqin proposed a preliminary plan for demobilization and reorganization that included making the division, rather than the corps, the basic unit of the Nationalist army and compensating demobilized soldiers with 20 *mou* of land to farm. He followed up in early July with a formal meeting of officers from the First Group Army to discuss demobilization. He informed them that

---

[7]  Li Zhongming, *He Yingqin dazhuan*, 58.

they, the core of the central army, would serve as role models for reorganization and went over procedures for demobilizing officers and enlisted men.[8]

Throughout 1928 He Yingqin promoted demobilization, addressing senior officials and military commanders and emphasizing the need to reduce current military expenditure, which endangered the ability of the new government to operate. At a meeting honoring Sun Yat-sen on July 2, He Yingqin invoked Sun's dream of a united, modern republic to call on the military commanders to reduce the number of troops by at least half and strictly limit expenditure.[9] He followed up with a telegram to the four group army commanders, stressing the need to demobilize large numbers of soldiers and officers in order to ease the government's financial burden.[10] Chiang proposed a formal conference to discuss reorganization and demobilization and offered to begin the process with his own First Army Group.[11] Several days later Chiang convened a formal meeting at Tangshan, east of Beiping, to discuss the initial plans for demobilization. Feng Yuxiang, Yan Xishan, and Li Zongren all attended and agreed in principle with the need to reduce the size of the overall force and to reorganize their armies to make the division the basic organizational unit.[12] He Yingqin presented the assembled officers with a "Plan for Military Reorganization" (junshi zhengli'an), which outlined the broad objectives of reorganizing the four group armies into a single Nationalist army of sixty divisions, all under a centralized system of organization, training, and discipline. To improve this reduced force, officers and enlisted men who remained would receive additional training at one of several military academies in China or abroad. Those present accepted this plan and created a committee, which included Feng, Yan, and Li, to oversee its implementation. At the end of the meeting on July 13, Chiang drafted a circular letter in which he reiterated the financial rationale for demobilization, reemphasized the need for central command over the national military, and announced plans to convene a formal Reorganization and Demobilization Conference (bianqian huiyi). He sent the letter to all senior military officials.[13]

[8] *HYQJJ*, I, 202–03.    [9] *HYQJJ*, I, 203–04.
[10] Van de Ven, *War and Nationalism*, 134; Li Yuan, *Jiang Jieshi he He Yingqin*, 96.
[11] "Disbandment of Troops in the Chinese Armies," in *US Military Intelligence Reports: China, 1911–1941*, Reel VIII, 0330.
[12] *HYQJJ*, I, 209; Tsung-jen Li, *Memoirs*, 257.
[13] Li Baoming, *"Guojiahua" mingyixia de "sishuhua": Jiang Jieshi dui guomin gemingjun de kongzhi yanjiu* ["Privatization" in the Name of "Nationalization": A Study of Chiang Kai-shek's Control of the National Revolutionary Army] (Beijing: Shehui kexue wenxian chubanshe, 2010), 53; van de Ven, *War and Nationalism*, 134–35; Li Yuan, *Jiang Jieshi he He Yingqin*, 96.

With the tacit acceptance of the commanders of the four group armies, Chiang and He Yingqin presented the plan to the GMD Central Executive Committee in mid August 1928. A week before the full session, He Yingqin reported on the details of the Plan for Military Reorganization to the CEC standing committee and an additional audience of party members, military officials, and other experts. This report included the same main points discussed and agreed upon at the Tangshan meeting, emphasizing the need for financial retrenchment and central command and training, but it went into details on procedures for dealing with military education, wounded soldiers, arms and ammunition factories, supply, sanitation, and horses. The CEC standing committee accepted the plan and put it on the agenda for the upcoming plenary session. At that session, the CEC approved the plan as a set of guiding principles for the reorganization of the army, stipulating that the central government must have complete political and military authority and must eliminate all vestiges of old regional or individual systems and practices. It called for the rapid organization of a new, but smaller Nationalist army with a limit on expenditure, not to exceed 50 percent of the annual budget. All military training for this force would be centrally controlled, and the development of an air force and navy would follow.[14]

Once the plan for reorganization and demobilization passed through the CEC, He Yingqin wasted no time pushing for immediate implementation. In order encourage popular support, He Yingqin spoke frequently about the need for demobilization and reported on its progress. In late August he traveled to Shanghai to address a group of officers from the former Fourteenth Corps, a provincial unit now under central control, newly reorganized as the fifth division of the Nationalist army.[15] He praised them for their dedicated efforts since joining the revolution and announced that one of the division's brigades would soon deploy to Jiangxi to engage in "bandit suppression" against the CCP rural base. After expressing his belief in the need to work toward unification of the nation and centralization of political and military authority, He Yingqin closed his remarks to the officers with a version of a phrase Mao Zedong would make famous, "Serve the people!" (*weimin fuwu*).[16]

Chiang Kai-shek and He Yingqin succeeded in pushing the plan for military reorganization through the GMD, but the real question remained: would the regional commanders follow through on implementation, submit to Nanjing's central authority, and truly pare down

---

[14] *HYQJJ*, I, 204–05.
[15] See chart in Gibson, "Chiang Kai-shek's Central Army," 161.
[16] *HYQJJ*, I, 205–06.

their forces to the required levels? None had argued against it in principle, but it remained unclear if they would act on it. In early September, He Yingqin held a press conference and informed reporters that demobilization had made significant strides. According to He's remarks, the First Army Group under Chiang's command had already cut 100,000 soldiers and the four group armies had shed approximately 340,000 soldiers from their collective ranks. This may be an exaggeration or it might simply reflect cuts to provincial forces deemed unreliable. Still, Chiang Kai-shek approved of He Yingqin's efforts and in mid October the CEC standing committee appointed him supervisor of training for the new Nationalist army (*xunlian zonglan*).[17]

In anticipation of the start of the formal Reorganization and Demobilization Conference set to convene on New Year's Day 1929, He Yingqin chaired meetings of a preparatory committee, which again included the group army commanders Feng Yuxiang, Yan Xishan, and Li Zongren. The committee opened with preliminary discussion of the specifics of the reorganization and encouraged each committee member to offer a plan for reducing the size of his own forces.[18] In separate conversations with both Feng and Yan, He Yingqin conveyed that Chiang Kai-shek hoped that each of them would offer a concrete plan for reducing the group armies and for identifying which soldiers and officers they should demobilize. Feng Yuxiang favored reorganizing troops with the best training, discipline, and arms while demobilizing those with inadequate training and poor discipline and lacking weapons. Specifically, he recommended reorganizing the First (Chiang's) and Second (Feng's) Group Armies into twelve divisions each and the Third (Yan's) and Fourth (Li's) into eight divisions each, with an additional eight divisions composed of other assorted regional forces. Yan Xishan remained quiet during many of the nine meetings of the preparatory committee, but at He Yingqin's urging eventually proposed an alternative to Feng's plan in which the First and Second Group Armies would have ten divisions each while the Third and Fourth Group Armies again would have eight divisions each. This plan, not surprisingly, reduced the numerical advantage of Chiang's and Feng's forces vis à vis those under Yan's command.[19]

On January 1, 1929, the day the Reorganization and Demobilization Conference formally opened, He Yingqin authored a lengthy editorial

[17] *HYQJJ*, I, 206–08; Xiong Zongren, *He Yingqin: xuanwozhong de lishi*, I, 248; Diana Lary, *Region and Nation: The Kwangsi Clique in Chinese Politics, 1925–1937* (London: Cambridge University Press, 1974), 133.

[18] *HYQJJ*, I, 208–09.

[19] Li Baoming, *"Guojiahua" mingyixia de "sishuhua,"* 58; Li Zhongming, *He Yingqin dazhuan*, 61–62; Li Yuan, *Jiang Jieshi he He Yingqin*, 96–97.

in a special edition of the *Shanghai Republican Daily* in which he placed the issue within the larger context of nation-building. Under the title "Several Critical Problems in Constructing the New China," the piece touched on a variety of issues but focused on the critical themes of financial retrenchment and centralization. He Yingqin argued that, in order to meet the needs of its people, the country required unity above all else and that regional civil officials and military officers must respect the authority of the central government. Central authorities must have the power to appoint and dismiss officers, to move military units across China, to allocate supplies and resources, and to oversee training and discipline. Speaking specifically to the issues before the Reorganization and Demobilization Conference, He Yingqin stated that despite recent progress the current total troop level of 1.6 million men (down from 2.2 million several months earlier) remained an impossible burden and consumed more than 70 percent of the annual budget. In order to "save the nation and the revolution," ideally the government had to limit the military budget to 33 percent, or at the absolute highest 50 percent, of the annual budget. This task required finding alternative work for demobilized soldiers who would otherwise simply turn to banditry. There remained much to do, He Yingqin admitted, but no task loomed as large as dealing with the problem of the bloated armed forces.[20]

The formal meeting of the Reorganization and Demobilization Conference in Nanjing brought together members of the CEC, commanders of the four group armies, and their field commanders, along with an assortment of other military officers and political officials. The conference convened with the expressed intention of reducing the size of the military, reorganizing it into a strong force for national defense, establishing central control, and creating plans for dealing with demobilized officers and enlisted men. Over the course of several sessions Chiang Kai-shek, He Yingqin, and others made formal remarks on the state of the military and stressed the need for demobilization. The most dramatic remarks came from Minister of Finance Song Ziwen, who predicted financial disaster if the government failed to rein in military spending.[21]

When the conference concluded on January 25, delegates had arrived at a number of resolutions. First, they agreed to eliminate the current position of group army commander, to place all military forces under central authority, and to create six "demobilization zones" and regional branches of the demobilization committee to carry out force reductions.

[20] He Yingqin, "Jianshe xinzhongguo de jige qieyao wenti" [Several Critical Problems in Constructing the New China], in *HZZYQYLXJ*, 1–15.
[21] "National Military Reorganization and Disbandment Conference," in *US Military Intelligence Reports: China, 1911–1941*, Reel VI, 0034.

The results would create an army of at most 65 divisions of 11,000 soldiers each and ensure that the military budget could not exceed 40 percent of the government's annual budget.[22] In a widely circulated open telegram at the end of the conference, Feng, Yan, and Li pledged their sincerity in pursuing demobilization and the cause of building a truly national army.[23] Despite their acceptance of the conference's conclusions, both Feng Yuxiang and Yan Xishan had reservations and balked at the plan. According to Li Zongren, they believed that Chiang intended to avoid reducing his own First Group Army while targeting their Second and Third Group Armies for large-scale reductions. Before the conference completed its sessions, Yan left Nanjing to return to his base in Shanxi, claiming urgent business, and Feng feigned illness and departed as well.[24]

After the conference, He Yingqin continued to build momentum for the movement through public speeches stressing the importance and urgency of demobilization. On February 3 the Central Radio Broadcast Station in Guangzhou carried his speech entitled "The Significance of Reorganization and Demobilization," in which he again described the financial burdens of maintaining a large military force during peacetime that drained resources from much-needed construction of public works and increased the burden on the common people. He repeated his view of demobilization as essential to the preservation of the revolution and the salvation of the nation. In concluding, he revealed his doubts that Feng, Yan, and Li would comply, warning that a "small group of ambitious people who sought only personal gain" hoped to derail the work of the Reorganization and Demobilization Conference. All true military men, he stressed, had a heavy responsibility to carry out the task of demobilization and make the army a truly national force.[25]

Most describe the conference as a failure as it did not lead to large-scale demobilization or dramatically improve central authority.[26] It did,

[22] "National Military Reorganization and Disbandment Conference," in *US Military Intelligence Reports: China, 1911–1941*, Reel VI, 0034.
[23] "Circular Telegram Issued at the Conclusion of the Conference Pledging Faithful Carrying Out of the Resolutions Adopted," in *US Military Intelligence Reports: China, 1911–1941*, Reel VI, 0057.
[24] Tsung-jen Li, *Memoirs*, 261; Li Baoming, *"Guojiahua" mingyixia de "sishuhua,"* 59 n. 2. Li Baoming claims that both men left Nanjing on January 29, after the final sessions of the conference.
[25] He Yingqin, "Bianqian shishi zhi yiyi" [The Significance of Reorganization and Demobilization], in *HZZYQYLXJ*, 16–23.
[26] F. F. Liu, *Military History of Modern China*, 73–74; Sheridan, *Chinese Warlord*, 243. See remarks by Captain Parker G. Tenney, Assistant Military Attaché, in "National Military Reorganization and Disbandment Conference," in *US Military Intelligence Reports: China, 1911–1941*, Reel VI, 0058.

however, position Chiang Kai-shek and He Yingqin as pursuing policies in the nation's best interests and established Feng, Yan, and Li as "new warlords" who clung to their private armies and opposed national unity. It also set the stage for what might be called the final part of the Northern Expedition, in which Chiang and his central army vastly expanded Nanjing's territorial base.

## The Hunan Incident and the 1929 revolts

It is possible that Chiang Kai-shek never expected the Reorganization and Demobilization Conference to achieve its stated goals, but rather intended it to bring about a final clash of center against region. If so, he succeeded, as the conference increased suspicions that Chiang intended to chip away at the strength of the other group armies and triggered a series of challenges to Nanjing's authority on the part of regional commanders over the next two years. The revolts began with the Hunan Incident of February 1929, a dispute over control of that province. In the spring of 1928, Chiang Kai-shek appointed Lu Diping governor of Hunan, who dutifully passed on tax revenue collected in Hunan to the central government in Nanjing. Some generals in Li Zongren's Fourth Group Army, including Xia Wei, Hu Zongduo, and Tao Jun, sought to ensure their autonomy from Chiang by leading their forces into Changsha to take control of Hunan. Lu Diping fled in the face of their advance, so the Guangxi commanders appointed He Jian as the new governor in defiance of Nanjing's authority.[27] Some have seen Li Zongren, chair of the Wuhan Branch of the Political Council, as the architect of the Hunan Incident, aiming to take control of Hunan's resources and preserve his autonomy.[28] Li later claimed that the generals had acted without his knowledge or permission, but that they did so only as a preemptive measure in anticipation of an attack from Chiang Kai-shek's forces. They claimed that Chiang had sent a secret shipment of arms and ammunition to Lu Diping at Changsha as a part of the preparation for the attack on Wuhan intended to destroy Li's force and take control of Hunan and Hubei.[29]

---

[27] Tsung-jen Li, *Memoirs*, 266–67.

[28] Dreyer, *China at War*, 152; Sheridan, *Chinese Warlord*, 253; van de Ven, *War and Nationalism*, 137.

[29] Tsung-jen Li, *Memoirs*, 266–67. Factional alliances and personal relationships might also have played a role in the Hunan Incident. Lu Diping had ties to Tan Yankai, who had supported the Wuhan faction of the GMD. This put him at odds with the generals of the Fourth Group Army's Guangxi Clique, which had sided with Nanjing. He Jian might also have had an axe to grind against Lu, since He Jian's benefactor Tang Shengzhi, had earlier clashed with Lu's benefactor, Tan Yankai.

Regardless of their motives, this action on the part of Li Zongren and the Wuhan Branch of the Political Council presented Chiang with a direct challenge that he felt he could not ignore. Michael Richard Gibson has argued that Chiang welcomed the opportunity to use military force against Li Zongren and the Guangxi Clique in order to expand his base of operations and resources. Located upriver from Nanjing and Shanghai, Wuhan had important strategic value to Chiang, giving him greater security and stronger control over a larger financial base in the lower and middle Yangzi River region. This included the Hanyang arsenal at Hankou, China's premier producer of arms and ammunition.[30] In late February, He Yingqin traveled to Hunan on behalf of Chiang Kai-shek for talks with Xia Wei and Hu Zongduo. There is no record of their conversation, but afterwards He Yingqin told reporters that the central government had no intention of using military force to resolve the issue.[31] In fact, his meetings with the Guangxi Clique generals served only to buy Nanjing authorities a little time to prepare a military campaign against Li and Wuhan. On March 14, the Nanjing government signaled its readiness for such a campaign when it abruptly abolished all branch political councils and ordered Guangxi forces to withdraw from Changsha.[32]

In order to maximize Nanjing's chances for success, He Yingqin first sought to win the support of other regional military commanders, thereby isolating the Guangxi forces and preventing a two-front conflict. He visited Feng Yuxiang and helped convince him to send six divisions of his Second Army Group to support Nanjing's attack on Wuhan. James Sheridan and Li Zongren both note that another Nationalist official, Li Shaozi, visited Feng on Nanjing's behalf, but more recent accounts suggest that He Yingqin traveled to Shaanxi to talk with Feng in person, which is much more in keeping with He's activities of the time.[33] He Yingqin also met with leaders from Yunnan, Guizhou, and Sichuan to get their nominal support for the Nanjing government, or at the very least a promise to maintain neutrality.[34] Based on rumors that circulated at the time, some suggest that Chiang Kai-shek paid Feng a 2-million-yuan bribe and promised him control over parts of Shandong that the Japanese had occupied in 1928 in order to persuade Feng to support

[30] Gibson, "Chiang Kai-shek's Central Army," 173–74.
[31] *HYQJJ*, I, 213.     [32] Furuya, *Chiang Kai-shek*, 274.
[33] Sheridan, *Chinese Warlord*, 254; Tsung-jen Li, *Memoirs*, 268; Xiong Zongren, *He Yingqin: xuanwozhong de lishi*, I, 250; Li Yuan, *Jiang Jieshi he He Yingqin*, 98.
[34] Xiong Zongren, *He Yingqin: xuanwozhong de lishi*, I, 250; Li Yuan, *Jiang Jieshi he He Yingqin*, 98.

Nanjing against Li Zongren.[35] Others argue that these claims are exaggerated, and Li Zongren himself suggested that Feng required little convincing and willingly committed six divisions of his force to the task of weakening a regional rival.[36]

Having isolating the Guangxi forces, on March 2 Chiang ordered the First Group Army to take up positions for an attack on Wuhan and appointed He Yingqin to supervise the preparations. Continuing his public statements in favor of central authority, He Yingqin addressed the Third GMD Congress two weeks later, arguing that beyond defeating the warlords, old or new, the Nationalist army must eliminate the environment in which warlordism existed. All military forces in China, he emphasized, must be responsible to the party and the people.[37] Meanwhile, preparations for the attack progressed rapidly, with three columns of Chiang's central army under Zhu Peide and Liu Zhi and six divisions of Feng's Second Group Army under Han Fuju set to advance on Wuhan from three directions.[38] Chiang Kai-shek gave the order to begin the attack in late March and the battle proved a short affair. He Jian announced his support for the Nanjing government and, rather than fight, Li Zongren's Guangxi forces withdrew, allowing Nanjing to capture Changsha and march into Wuhan on April 5.[39] Generals Hu Zongduo, Xia Wei, and Tao Jun announced their retirements, and Li Zongren went into temporary exile in Hong Kong.

The successful resolution of the Hunan Incident opened the door for Chiang to extend his control over Hunan and Hubei. Shortly after the defeat of Li's forces, he sent He Yingqin to Wuhan in early May as chair of the demobilization committee and newly appointed supervisor of military training and education, with orders to restructure the political and military forces in these two provinces. Reorganizing surrendered units of Li's Fourth Army Group, He Yingqin created six new divisions to serve in Chiang's central army.[40] The campaign against Li and the rapid reorganization of the Hunan and Hubei forces served notice to other regional military commanders that Chiang would now take direct action against any forces that resisted central authority. Feng Yuxiang had supported Chiang against Li Zongren in part because he anticipated acquiring control of Shandong, which would give him access to rail lines and seaports that would ease the isolation of his base in Shaanxi and open up new

---

[35] Van de Ven, *War and Nationalism*, 137; Dreyer, *China at War*, 152; Eastman, "Nationalist China During the Nanking Decade," 126.

[36] Sheridan, *Chinese Warlord*, 254; Tsung-jen Li, *Memoirs*, 267.

[37] *HYQJJ*, I, 214–15.

[38] Li Zhongming, *He Yingqin dazhuan*, 64.    [39] Liu Zhi, *Wode huiyi*, 69.

[40] *HYQJJ*, I, 217–18; Li Zhongming, *He Yingqin dazhuan*, 64.

sources of revenue. When Chiang first asked the Japanese to delay their withdrawal from Shandong and then ordered Chen Diaoyuan's forces to seize the rail line between Jinan and Qingdao in April, Feng quickly understood that Chiang had no intention of allowing him to take control of Shandong. Feng called a meeting of his senior officers at Kaifeng and concluded that he could not contest the issue, as Chiang's forces outnumbered his own in Shandong. Instead, he pulled his forces back toward Henan and Shaanxi, destroying rail lines in the process to obstruct any advance by central army forces.[41] This act alone represented a clear break in relations between Feng and Chiang, but in late May a group of Feng's subordinates made it official with a circular telegram that criticized Chiang Kai-shek for his dictatorial rule. The officers demanded that Chiang resign and asked Feng Yuxiang to lead a revolt against Nanjing. Feng accepted the invitation and announced his command of a new force called the Northwest Army for the Protection of the Party and National Salvation.[42]

With trouble brewing to the northwest, Chiang Kai-shek called He Yingqin back to Nanjing to report on the reorganization of forces in Hubei and to discuss the situation. They decided on a military campaign against Feng, and on May 22 He Yingqin addressed reporters at a news conference to report details on the extensive damage Feng's troops had done to the Ping–Han (Beiping–Hankou) and Long–Hai (Lanzhou–Lianyungang) railroads. This had caused tremendous damage that would take a long time to repair, He Yingqin reported, and clearly indicated Feng's intention to resist national unification. He also linked Feng to the Soviet Union and the forces of foreign imperialism, claiming that Feng was only waiting for an expected shipment of money and weapons from the Soviets before linking up with Li Zongren to launch another revolt against the central government. Two days later, the GMD expelled Feng Yuxiang from the party and all positions of authority. He Yingqin then returned to Wuhan as commander of the Wuhan field headquarters with an additional 60,000 troops to secure Hubei against an attack from Shaanxi.[43]

As had been the case in preparing to deal with Li Zongren's revolt just months earlier, Nanjing took a two-pronged approach to dealing with the potential threat. On the one hand, He Yingqin prepared a plan for military action involving a multicolumn push into Shaanxi to attack Xi'an from the east. On the other hand, he made overtures to some

[41] Gibson, "Chiang Kai-shek's Central Army," 180; *HYQJJ*, I, 218; Sheridan, *Chinese Warlord*, 255–59; Furuya, *Chiang Kai-shek*, 275.
[42] Sheridan, *Chinese Warlord*, 260.    [43] *HYQJJ*, I, 219–20.

Map 5: Central China during the Central Plains War

of Feng's top generals, including Shi Yousan and Han Fuju. The latter effort brought results when in late May Shi Yousan's secretary Liu Yidan arrived in Wuhan with a letter indicating that Shi and Han had broken with Feng and would support the central government, bringing nearly 100,000 of Feng's best troops with them. Facing the crippling loss of nearly one-third of his army, Feng promptly announced his "retirement" and took refuge with Yan Xishan, who gave him sanctuary in Taiyuan.[44] Remaining neutral in these conflicts, Yan shielded Feng perhaps knowing that Feng would be among Chiang's next targets and hoping that the threat of a Yan–Feng alliance would deter an attack from Nanjing.[45]

With Li Zongren and Feng Yuxiang in seclusion at least temporarily, Chiang and He Yingqin returned to the task of promoting demobilization and centralization. In early July, He Yingqin gave a press conference at the Wuhan field headquarters in which he attempted to enlist the support of the media with a speech on "The Responsibility of News Reporters." Telling them that they played a major role in moving the nation forward, He Yingqin explained that foreign imperialists posed the greatest threat to China because they supported regional warlords, local tyrants, and other feudal forces. Through their writing, he argued, journalists could guide the people to support central authority and oppose foreign imperialism, thereby contributing to building a peaceful and unified China.[46] Chiang Kai-shek and He Yingqin then organized a second Reorganization and Demobilization Conference in August, at which the chairs of the various demobilization zones met to discuss further details and to report on progress thus far. He Yingqin, chair of both the central and first demobilization zones, the latter chair taken from Li Zongren after the Hunan Incident, reported that the nine corps of the old First Group Army had been reorganized into thirteen divisions with additional smaller specialty units attached. In the process, more than 12,000 officers and enlisted men had returned to civilian life. Similarly, he reported the reorganization of Hubei forces, under his command following his defeat of the Guangxi Clique, into 12 divisions and the demobilization of 19,000 men. That meant a total of 31,000 troops removed from the military payroll.[47] Although touting force reduction, this report implicitly indicated an expansion of Chiang's territorial base to include Hunan, Hubei,

[44] *HYQJJ*, I, 220–21; Sheridan, *Chinese Warlord*, 261–62.
[45] Donald G. Gillin, *Warlord: Yen His-shan in Shansi Province, 1911–1949* (Princeton: Princeton University Press, 1967), 111–12; van de Ven, *War and Nationalism*, 138.
[46] He Yingqin, "Xinwen jizhe de zeren" [The Responsibility of News Reporters], July 5, 1929, in *HZZYQYLXJ*, 78–84.
[47] *HYQJJ*, I, 221; "The Second Reorganization and Disbandment Conference," in *US Military Intelligence Reports: China, 1911–1941*, Reel VI, 0058.

Jiangxi, and Henan, along with a significant growth in the ranks of his central army.[48] The delegates adopted a strict separation of political and military authority, stipulating that no governor could hold a military position in the same province and barring division commanders from holding political office.[49] Chiang Kai-shek closed the conference with exhortations for all to adhere to these stipulations, using the terms "revolutionary" and "counterrevolutionary" to distinguish those who supported it from those who opposed it.[50]

Over the course of 1928–29, He Yingqin again demonstrated his value to Chiang, this time as a vocal proponent of Chiang's position on demobilization and centralization and as a field commander in the campaigns against Li and Feng. Despite their success over these two years, the threat of further revolt hung in the air in the summer and fall of 1929. Chiang and He had every reason to believe that Feng and Yan would eventually launch a joint military action against Nanjing, and the Guangxi commanders Li Zongren and Bai Chongxi, though in temporary exile in Hong Kong, harbored strong animosities toward Chiang and would undoubtedly seek an opportunity to strike back. In mid September, at this time of tension and anxiety as they waited for the next revolt, news arrived from Guizhou that He Yingqin's father, He Qimin, had passed away. He Yingqin felt a strong obligation to return to his ancestral home and participate in the funeral ceremonies, so he immediately requested a leave of absence. Anticipating that another major conflict would start any day, Chiang did not want to lose his most reliable subordinate for an extended period and asked He Yingqin to drop his request in order to put his duty to his country and to his commander first. Specifically, Chiang appealed to He Yingqin's sense of duty and asked him to "substitute loyalty for filial piety" (*yixiao zuozhong*). He Yingqin could not refuse his commander's request, and so he put aside his personal desire to return home to honor his father and remained in Nanjing.[51]

Chiang's reluctance to allow He Yingqin to go to Guizhou after his father's death proved prescient when just days later Zhang Fakui, commander of multiple Nationalist divisions in Guangdong, denounced Chiang and revolted against Nanjing. Zhang, who had supported the suppression of Li's Guangxi Army in Hubei just months earlier, now moved his forces from Hubei across Hunan into Guangxi to ally with elements of the Guangxi Clique to attack central army units in

[48] Gibson, "Chiang Kai-shek's Central Army," 186–87.
[49] Li Baoming, *"Guojiahua" mingyixia de "sishuhua,"* 68.
[50] Li Zhongming, *He Yingqin dazhuan*, 66.
[51] Li Zhongming, *He Yingqin dazhuan*, 66: Xiong Zongren, *He Yingqin: xuanwozhong de lishi*, I, 251; Li Yuan, *Jiang Jieshi he He Yingqin*, 99.

Guangdong.[52] Less than one month later, another revolt in the north appeared imminent when a group of twenty-seven officers of Feng Yuxiang's Northwest Army issued a circular telegram announcing a new force in opposition to Nanjing, with Yan Xishan as commander and Feng as deputy commander. This force moved east along the Long–Hai railroad and other routes, preparing to engage Chiang's central army forces on several fronts in Shaanxi and western Henan. Chiang directed units from Xuchang, establishing a defensive line across northwestern Henan, while He Yingqin assumed command of the Kaifeng field headquarters.[53] In the middle of the fighting on October 26–27, He and Chiang returned to Nanjing for a specially arranged ceremony for He Qimin, which a number of prominent GMD and Nationalist army officials attended.[54]

The twenty-seven officers named Yan Xishan as commander of this anti-Chiang force, but he remained careful to avoid open commitment to either side in this conflict, preferring to wait to see how things developed. As the fighting against Feng Yuxiang continued in Henan, He Yingqin made two trips to Taiyuan to speak with Yan Xishan to try to win his support. In late October, he delivered the news that Chiang had appointed Yan commander of all land, air, and naval forces.[55] He Yingqin followed up with a second visit in November, urging adherence to Nanjing's authority and returning to the issue of demobilization. On November 12, He Yingqin delivered a speech commemorating the anniversary of Sun Yat-sen's birthday, in which he listed the most critical problems China faced. First, the existence of too many soldiers placed an impossible burden on the backs of the common people. Second, China had too many private military forces that were acting on behalf of individuals and not the nation. All private armies must become national armies, he argued, a process that must begin with a thorough implementation of the demobilization plan adopted at the January 1929 Reorganization and Demobilization Conference.[56] There is no record of Yan Xishan's reaction to these remarks, but he remained reluctant to commit to either side and continued to straddle the fence between Feng Yuxiang and Chiang Kai-shek.

[52] *HYQJJ*, I, 223; Sheridan, *Chinese Warlord*, 263–64; Furuya, *Chiang Kai-shek*, 280.
[53] *HYQJJ*, I, 222.
[54] Xiong Zongren, *He Yingqin: xuanwozhong de lishi*, I, 251–52; Li Yuan, *Jiang Jieshi he He Yingqin*, 99–100.
[55] Li Baoming, *"Guojiahua" mingyixia de "sishuhua,"* 70; Li Yuan, *Jiang Jieshi he He Yingqin*, 100.
[56] He Yingqin, "Zai shanxisheng dangbu zongli danchen jinianhui yanci" [Speech at the Shanxi Provincial Party Office Commemorating the Anniversary of Sun Yat-sen's Birthday], November 12, 1929, in *HZZYQYLXJ*, 90–93.

In late November Chiang sent He Yingqin south to establish and command the Guangzhou field headquarters from which he could direct combat operations against Zhang Fakui, taking along several additional divisions of central army troops. He arrived on December 2 and met with unit commanders to plan the campaign along the Bei River, north of Guangzhou. In a swift and well-planned campaign, He's divisions defeated Zhang's forces and pushed west to capture Wuzhou in Guangxi. From there, He Yingqin's units separated and threatened to march south toward Nanning and north toward Guilin, essentially ending the danger to Guangzhou. With the successful suppression of Zhang's revolt, He Yingqin boarded a ship for Shanghai en route back to Nanjing.[57]

After returning to the capital He Yingqin had little time to rest or savor his recent accomplishments, as yet another regional militarist revolted against Nanjing's authority. From his position at Zhengzhou, Tang Shengzhi denounced Chiang Kai-shek and took control of the southern portion of the Ping–Han railroad and threatened to attack Wuhan. Chiang immediately dispatched He Yingqin back to Wuhan to again take over command of the Wuhan field headquarters and direct central army units in southern Henan against Tang.[58] Reaching Wuhan just as a snowstorm engulfed the area, He Yingqin once again publicly stressed the importance of eliminating regional factions and individual cliques in order to forge a truly national military force. In a speech on January 1, 1930, he echoed Chiang's remarks at the conclusion of the second Reorganization and Demobilization Conference, identifying two groups in China: one that accepted the plan for reorganization and demobilization of China's military forces (revolutionary) and one that feared it and sought to destroy the unity of the party and the nation (counterrevolutionary).[59] He then set to the business at hand, planning a military campaign from Wuhan into southern Henan designed to surround and defeat Tang's force. Tang quickly recognized the futility of his situation and on January 8 sent a representative to Wuhan to formally surrender to He Yingqin, who guaranteed Tang's safety if he came to Wuhan. He Yingqin then disarmed Tang's 10,000-odd troops and sent a telegram to Chiang with news of the successful completion of the campaign.[60]

During the military revolts of Li Zongren, Feng Yuxiang, Zhang Fakui, and Tang Shengzhi over the course of 1929 and early 1930, He Yingqin

[57] *HYQJJ*, I, 224–26.
[58] *HYQJJ*, I, 226; Xiong Zongren, *He Yingqin: xuanwozhong de lishi*, I, 252–53.
[59] He Yingqin, "Jinhou nuli de fangxiang" [The Direction for Future Hard Work], January 1, 1929, in *HZZYQYLXJ*, 94–97.
[60] Li Zhongming, *He Yingqin dazhuan*, 66–67; *HYQJJ*, I, 227–28.

served as a forceful advocate in word and deed, supporting Nanjing's essential message of the need to eliminate those who defied central authority and to carry out demobilization and centralization. Visiting Changsha in late January, He Yingqin gave a speech in which he noted that the suppression of recent revolts meant that the enemies of the Nanjing government had been weakened to the point at which issues could now be resolved through political means rather than military campaigns.[61] A few days later in Nanjing, he repeated these themes when he took questions from reporters about the recent military action against Tang and the continuing trouble with Feng Yuxiang in the northwest. While giving credit to his subordinate Liu Zhi for the successful execution of the military campaign despite adverse weather conditions, He Yingqin downplayed the significance of the revolt, claiming that most of Tang Shengzhi's troops did not support his actions. The campaign ended quickly in part, he told reporters, because Tang's cold and hungry soldiers had little heart for the fight and most of them simply wanted to lay down their arms and go home. When asked about Feng Yuxiang and the situation in the northwest, He Yingqin claimed that the fighting in Henan the previous year had dramatically weakened Feng's force, with casualties and prisoners (defectors) amounting to the loss of more than two-thirds of his total force. As a result, He Yingqin saw "no cause for concern" in the northwest. He went on to argue that the most pressing issue remained alleviating the suffering of the common people and protecting the nation, which he believed could be accomplished only through national unification and complete support for the central government. "From my perspective," He Yingqin concluded, "those who support unification are revolutionary, while those who oppose it are counterrevolutionary."[62]

Over the course of 1929 and early 1930, He Yingqin played a critical role in helping Chiang strengthen his position. Whether leading troops as commander of the field headquarters in Wuhan, Guangzhou, or Kaifeng, visiting regional leaders to win support and neutralize other potential opponents, or simply spreading Chiang's central message in speeches and editorials, He Yingqin helped lead the new government through some of its most dire challenges of the period. As evidence of Chiang's trust in He Yingqin, on March 10, 1930, Chiang appointed him minister of military administration, a position he would hold until 1944. In his remarks upon assuming office, He Yingqin opened with a statement of his unequivocal belief that "military strength is the only guarantee of the nation's existence and development." Addressing his subordinates in the ministry, he explained that military strength served

[61] *HYQJJ*, I, 229.   [62] *HYQJJ*, I, 230.

as the basis for the nation's independence and as the key to its ability to rise in status in the international community, as well as enhancing its prestige, so therefore those who worked for the ministry must take their responsibility seriously.[63]

## The Central Plains War of 1930

The revolts of 1929 turned out to serve as warmups for the largest and most serious challenge that the Nanjing government faced in the early years of its existence. Often overlooked, the Central Plains War of 1930 matched the combined forces of Feng Yuxiang, Yan Xishan, Li Zongren, and Zhang Fakui, totaling more than 700,000 soldiers, against Chiang's 300,000-odd central army and allied provincial forces in a major conflict that lasted five months and resulted in hundreds of thousands of casualties.[64] There are two points to make about the Central Plains War. First, historians have tended to see political alliances as more important than battlefield success in determining the outcome. Zhang Xueliang's September announcement of support for Chiang Kai-shek and the Nanjing government, in particular, emerges as a turning point, tilting the balance of power in favor of Chiang and against the other major northern regional military commanders, Feng and Yan. Yet Michael Richard Gibson has argued that Zhang's decision to support Chiang did not determine the outcome of the war, which came instead through a series of military battles that had already ensured victory. Gibson cites as the decisive battle the capture of Xuchang, Henan – which opened the road to Zhengzhou and Luoyang – on September 18, just about the same time as Zhang's announcement.[65] Second, while the most intense combat took place along the Long–Hai and Ping–Han railroads, the most important victory of the war came in Hunan where He Yingqin led a smaller force against Li Zongren's 30,000–40,000 troops and prevented Li from uniting with Feng and Yan.[66] As he had during the Eastern and Northern Expeditions and the various regional revolts of 1929, He Yingqin played a central role in this war and made a significant contribution to the survival of the Nanjing government and Chiang Kai-shek as commander.

---

[63] He Yingqin, "Jiuren junzheng buzhang dui quanti zhiyuan xunhua" [Exhortation to the Staff Upon Assuming the Post of Minister of Military Administration], in *HZZYQYLXJ*, 113.

[64] Liu Zhi, *Wode huiyi*, 87; van de Ven, *War and Nationalism*, 138.

[65] Gibson, "Chiang Kai-shek's Central Army," 202–05.

[66] Lu Ping, *He Yingqin jiangjun yinxiang ji* [A Record of Impressions of General He Yingqin] (Taipei: Minben chuban gongsi, 1946), 14–15. Lu Ping is a pseudonym for Liu Jianqun, who served as He Yingqin's secretary in the early 1930s.

Throughout 1929, Yan Xishan had remained cautious and avoided an open rupture with Chiang Kai-shek and Nanjing, but in February 1930 he presided over the formation of a new coalition that would launch a large-scale revolt that dwarfed those of the previous year. With the support of Feng Yuxiang, the Guangxi Clique, Zhang Fakui, and a host of Chiang's political rivals such as Wang Jingwei, Yan sent out a circular telegram calling on Chiang to resign and offering to do the same. This triggered a brief "telegram war" in which other regional military figures and their subordinates openly denounced Chiang, accusing him of using military force to eliminate his rivals.[67] In early April, Feng, Yan, and Li all announced their resignations and declared opposition to the Nanjing government, with Yan Xishan serving as commander in chief of the combined anti-Chiang military forces.

The War of the Central Plains posed a particularly dangerous challenge for Nanjing because it forced Chiang to deploy his forces across multiple fronts, a situation he had sought to avoid whenever possible. In 1930, the largest regional forces had come together in a united effort to defeat Chiang, forcing him to fight on three fronts. In the northwest, where Chiang commanded his forces from Xuzhou, Feng Yuxiang's units moved east along the Long–Hai railroad. At the same time, Yan Xishan's forces moved into Shandong, threatening central army units in north China from the east. In Guangxi, Li Zongren had returned from Hong Kong and sent forces under the command of Bai Chongxi and Zhang Fakui north into Hunan and threatening Hubei. The southern front played a central role in the combat, as Li Zongren envisioned advancing to Wuhan within two weeks and connecting with Feng and Yan in order to crush Chiang's central army.[68] Chiang again sent He Yingqin to Wuhan to command the field headquarters, with responsibility for all of Nanjing's forces in Hunan, Hubei, Guangdong, and Jiangxi, and charged him with protecting Wuhan and preventing Li Zongren's southern force from uniting with Feng and Yan in the north. If He Yingqin failed in Hunan and Hubei, Li's Guangxi troops could either move north to attack Chiang's rear area in Henan and Anhui or even launch an attack downriver on Nanjing itself.[69]

The invading Guangxi force encountered little resistance as it crossed into Hunan, and Bai and Zhang captured Changsha on June 4. Knowing that the Guangxi forces had greater numbers, Chiang ordered He

---

[67] For a brief review of these telegrams, see *FRUS, 1930*, vol. II, 4–5.
[68] Furuya, *Chiang Kai-shek*, 284; van de Ven, *War and Nationalism*, 138; Tsung-jen Li, *Memoirs*, 279; Liu Zhi, *Wode huiyi*, 83–97; Gibson, "Chiang Kai-shek's Central Army," 196–99.
[69] *HYQJJ*, I, 232.

Yingqin to "lure the enemy in deep and then look for an opportunity to annihilate them."[70] He Yingqin commanded a small force at Wuhan and could expect no reinforcements from neighboring Henan, where central army units had their hands full with Feng Yuxiang. He Jian commanded the largest contingent of troops at He Yingqin's disposal but could not match the invading force. The obvious course of action for He Yingqin would be to order He Jian to fall back on Wuhan and prepare to defend the city against assault from the larger Guangxi force. He Yingqin had little confidence that his smaller force could successfully defend Wuhan, yet if he failed it would possibly mean the end of the Nanjing regime, the revolution, and his career. He pored over maps of the region, thinking long and hard about an alternative approach before he finally settled on an "empty-fortress strategy," designed to delay and confuse the advancing force. In a letter to He Jian, He Yingqin instructed him not to fall back on Wuhan from Changsha, as Bai and Zhang undoubtedly expected he would, but to move northwest to Changde. This simple yet effective strategy accomplished multiple goals. First, it preserved He Jian's force for the time being, which might have been crushed had it engaged the Guangxi force at Changsha or been isolated at Wuhan. Second, it confused Bai Chongxi and Zhang Fakui, who had expected He Yingqin to pull all available forces back to Wuhan to defend the city. Instead, He Yingqin left the road to Wuhan wide open, seemingly unconcerned about an attack. Bai and Zhang not only suspected a trap in Wuhan, but they also had to prepare for the possibility of ambush as He Jian's forces might launch a surprise attack against the Guangxi force as it moved toward Wuhan. This meant they had to slow their advance and move cautiously. This bought He Yingqin some time, which he used to order two divisions under Cai Tingkai and Jiang Guangnai to move from Guangdong into southern Hunan and to reinforce Wuhan with additional troops from Guangdong, which arrived on ships via Shanghai.[71]

Cai Tingkai and Jiang Guangnai took up position at Hengyang, south of Changsha, cutting off the enemy's path of retreat back to Guangxi and severing its supply line. Seeing trouble both ahead and behind, Bai and Zhang concluded that they had now lost the opportunity to capture Wuhan and decided it would be better to turn south to attack Cai and Jiang and return to Guangxi. As they departed from Changsha, Chiang Kai-shek instructed He Yingqin to attack the Guangxi force, so in the

---

[70] *HYQJJ*, I, 232.

[71] Wang Zhiping, ed., "He Yingqin (1889–1987)," *Zhongwai mingren zhuan*, 64, 10 (October 1997), 75–76; Wang Chengsheng, "He Yingqin Zhuanqi (yi)" [The Legend of He Yingqin (Part I)], *Zhongwai zazhi*, 44, 1 (July 1988), 16; Wu Xiangxiang, "He Yingqin dajiang caineng fujiang mingyun," 104.

last days of June the latter ordered all his forces to converge on the enemy. He Jian attacked Changsha from the northwest, Cai Tingkai and Jiang Guangnai attacked from Hengyang, other units attacked from the Jiangxi–Hubei border, and naval units arrived to provide additional support from the river. Under assault from multiple directions, Bai and Zhang managed to work their way back across the border into Guangxi, but their force suffered heavy casualties, depleted though not defeated.[72]

The victory on the southern front provided Nanjing's forces with a much-needed boost and changed the nature of the conflict. The fighting in the north had raged for months with Chiang's troops achieving at best a stalemate on the Long–Hai railroad and losing control of Jinan, which Yan Xishan's troops occupied on June 25.[73] With the victory over Li Zongren's force in Hunan, Chiang's central army now concentrated its forces against Feng and Yan, where a series of defeats compelled them to retreat into their home bases. Some of He Yingqin's units pursued the Guangxi force as it left Hunan, but others shifted to the northern front to help defeat Feng and Yan.[74] Zhang Xueliang's September announcement of support for Nanjing left the anti-Chiang forces with no hope of reversing their fortunes and brought the fighting to a close.

In his assessment of the Central Plains War, Hans van de Ven has pointed out that Chiang Kai-shek came close to defeat at the hands of Feng's forces along the Long–Hai railroad and even narrowly escaped capture in June. Yet Feng halted his advance when he learned that Li Zongren's forces had stopped moving north at Hunan and returned to Guangxi, in essence turning the tide of the war.[75] Ray Huang has also remarked upon the importance of preventing Li Zongren from connecting with the Feng–Yan coalition.[76] He Yingqin's victory in Hunan proved critical to Chiang's and the central army's ultimate success by eliminating the southern front and altering the balance of power on the northern front. Returning to Gibson's argument, Chiang's forces had indeed achieved a military victory on the northern front before Zhang Xueliang threw his support behind Nanjing.[77] Yet this victory on the northern front depended heavily on He Yingqin's victory on the southern front. Had Chiang lost this war, along with control of the Nanjing government and military forces, his career as a commander might have

[72] *HYQJJ*, I, 234–36.
[73] "The Minister in China (Johnson) to the Secretary of State," June 11 and July 10, 1930, *FRUS, 1930*, vol. II, 17, 20.
[74] Lu Ping, *He Yingqin jiangjun yinxiang ji*, 17.
[75] Van de Ven, *War and Nationalism*, 139.
[76] Huang, "Chiang Kai-shek and His Diary," 61.
[77] Gibson, "Chiang Kai-shek's Central Army," 204–05.

come to an abrupt end. Chiang Kai-shek biographer Jay Taylor argues
that the Central Plains War established Chiang's reputation as an accomplished military commander. With few resources and equipment, Taylor
points out, Chiang "successfully maneuvered multiple army corps over
fronts that could stretch as long as a thousand miles."[78] If this is so, then
it also underscores He Yingqin's value to Chiang Kai-shek as a military
commander and his central role in meeting the challenges of the period.

The end of the War of the Central Plains, the bloodiest of a series
of internal revolts in 1929, brought an end to military challenges from
within the Nationalist camp, drove Feng, Yan, and Li back into their
regional bases, and marked the expansion of Chiang's power base to
include Anhui, Henan, and Hubei. These victories stabilized the young
Nanjing regime and allowed the Nationalist military to move on to concentrate on external enemies. He Yingqin began 1928 with a humiliating
loss of command, but he played a central role in these victories and within
a matter of eighteen months had returned to his prized position as Chiang's top subordinate and "right-hand man." He again demonstrated
his value to Chiang, advocating reorganization and demobilization of
the Nationalist army, making speeches and penning editorials to promote Chiang's agenda, commanding the field headquarters in Wuhan,
Guangzhou, and Kaifeng, providing both military and political support
for Chiang against Li, Feng, and Yan, and winning a critical victory in
Hunan during the War of the Central Plains. His assumption of command of the field headquarters and then the office of minister of military administration marked his place among the top tier of leadership
in the Nationalist regime and the resumption of his close professional
relationship with Chiang Kai-shek. Over the next decade, Chiang would
continue to assign He Yingqin primary responsibility for dealing with the
Nationalists' most pressing challenges.

This proved something of a turning point in He Yingqin's career. Up
until 1930, he had enjoyed his greatest successes as a combat commander, but afterwards he faced a series of new challenges, not all of which he
could resolve with a decisive battle. As a minister of military administration, he took on new and complex assignments and left a more ambiguous
record, which rendered him vulnerable to criticism.

[78] Taylor, *Generalissimo*, 89.

# 6    Trading reputation for time

In May 1933, Liu Kan, commander of the Chinese central army's eighty-third division, stormed into He Yingqin's office in Beiping's Zhongnanhai complex. As chair of the Beiping Branch of the Military Affairs Commission (*Beiping fenhui junshi weiyuanhui*) and the Nanjing government's highest-ranking military officer in north China, He Yingqin had assigned two engineer battalions to Liu Kan and ordered him to construct defensive fortifications to protect Beiping against attack from the Japanese. He Yingqin had been pursuing negotiations with the Japanese in the hope of securing a ceasefire but, in the event of an attack on Beiping or Tianjin, he wanted his forces prepared to defend these major cities. An irate Liu Kan reported that, as he began work on the fortifications, a Japanese military police officer stationed in Beiping had appeared and demanded to observe the construction. Liu had refused and threatened to shoot any Japanese who tried to observe the work, vowing that he would rather die than suffer this insult. He Yingqin explained that at this critical time, with the nation hovering between war and peace, they all had to be careful to avoid anything that might provoke the Japanese to further aggressive action. The construction of the fortifications had to proceed quickly, so Liu must allow the Japanese officer to observe, regardless of how insulting or humiliating he might find it. When Liu Kan stalked out of the office without acknowledging the order, He Yingqin turned to another officer present and snapped, "if you want to resist the Japanese then you must first obey orders! This is not the case in north China right now so how can we talk about resistance? This is why I am suffering condemnation from all around for negotiating a ceasefire with the Japanese!"[1]

The ceasefire to which he referred is better known as the Tanggu Truce of May 1933, an unpopular agreement that led to the creation

---

[1] Zhang Xingzhi, "He Yingqin zai beiping fenhui" [He Yingqin at the Beiping Branch of the Military Affairs Commission], in Tu Yueseng, ed., *Xingyi Liu, Wang, He sanda jiazu*, 184–85.

of a demilitarized zone south of the Great Wall and sparked significant criticism of the Nanjing government and of those officials who had concluded the agreement. During the period between the end of the Central Plains War in the fall of 1930 and the outbreak of the Sino-Japanese War in the summer of 1937, He Yingqin worked diligently to carry out Chiang Kai-shek's policy of "internal pacification before external resistance" (*rangwai bixu xian annei*). In essence, this meant dealing with internal divisions before mounting a military defense against Japanese aggression in north and northeast China. He Yingqin believed in the necessity of this policy, yet the broader public and numerous civil and military officials called for immediate resistance and military action against Japan. In his efforts to carry out this policy, He Yingqin confronted three major challenges: eradicating the CCP's rural base in Jiangxi province, forestalling Japanese military aggression in north China, and resolving the crisis of Chiang's kidnapping during the Xi'an Incident of 1936. After several years of commanding troops in successful battles to establish and secure the new government in Nanjing, he now entered a phase of his career during which he faced new enemies and challenges of a different sort. While he worked just as hard on these issues as he had on earlier assignments, this time his efforts produced more ambiguous and controversial results.

### Encirclement and suppression in Jiangxi

He Yingqin's victory on the southern front of the Central Plains War helped Chiang Kai-shek fend off the greatest challenge to the Nanjing regime since its establishment. Feng Yuxiang, Yan Xishan, Li Zongren, and other opponents returned to their home bases or otherwise withdrew and began to reconcile with Nanjing. Even before the end of the fighting in September 1930, Chiang and He planned for the next step in the process of unifying the country under Nanjing's authority, a campaign against the CCP base in southern Jiangxi province. By this time Mao Zedong and Zhu De had established a small but resilient military force that had created an autonomous "Soviet Republic." After defeating the combined forces of Feng, Yan, and Li, the Nationalist leadership looked forward to a quick campaign to "encircle and suppress" the modest Red Army forces in Jiangxi. He Yingqin presided over a series of meetings in which the Nationalists assembled a plan to send approximately 100,000 troops under Lu Diping on what would become the first encirclement campaign. Chiang Kai-shek ordered Lu to have his troops "drive straight through" and "advance separately, attack together," envisioning a successful destruction of the Red Army in Jiangxi within six months.[2] Instead, the first encirclement campaign ended in failure within two months. Mao and Zhu employed a scorched-earth policy to deny the Nationalists supplies and moved their forces around the base, forcing the Nationalists to disperse their troops over a broad area and making communication difficult. After "luring the enemy in deep," Red Army forces attacked individual Nationalist units with overwhelming force, bringing the campaign to a rapid close.[3]

The results of the first encirclement campaign indicated that the task would not be as easy as he had imagined, so Chiang ordered He Yingqin to organize and command a second encirclement campaign for the spring of 1931. After establishing a field headquarters in Nanchang in February 1931, He Yingqin met with other officers and carefully analyzed the experience of the first campaign against the CCP base in Jiangxi. He concluded that the Nationalists had made critical mistakes in planning and execution that caused its failure. First, troop strength had proved inadequate for an attack on a mobile enemy in such a large territory. In organizing the second campaign, He Yingqin assembled a larger force of 200,000 troops, double the number of the first campaign. Second, the units involved had not prepared adequately for the attack and did not coordinate their movements. Some units pushed forward too quickly, which made it easier for the Red Army to cut them off from support and attack them on unfavorable terrain. While employing the same basic strategy of a multicolumned attack targeting southern Jiangxi, He Yingqin adopted the principle of "proceeding steadily, step by step" (*wenza, wenda*). That meant that the four route armies, three divisions, and one independent brigade deployed for the operation would advance into Jiangxi in carefully coordinated movements to encircle the CCP base. He gave strict instructions that each unit must not advance more than 20 *li* (about 8 miles) per day, in order to maintain position in the encirclement formation. Before advancing, commanders must send out battalions or a regiment to conduct reconnaissance in order to avoid ambushes. Finally, in order to weaken the Red Army in advance, He Yingqin ordered a blockade of the CCP base area in southern Jiangxi, preventing the movement of people, food, money, and supplies in or out.[4]

[2]  Chen and Zhang, *Jiang Jieshi he huangpu xi*, 159–60; Li Zhongming, *He Yingqin dazhuan*, 70–71.
[3]  William Wei, *Counterrevolution in China: The Nationalists in Jiangxi During the Soviet Period* (Ann Arbor: University of Michigan Press, 1985), 36–37.
[4]  *HYQJJ*, I, 238–41; Li Zhongming, *He Yingqin dazhuan*, 71–72; Xiong Zongren, *He Yingqin: xuanwozhong de lishi*, I, 261–62; Li Yuan, *Jiang Jieshi he He Yingqin*, 104–05.

Despite the careful planning, slow and steady troop movements, and doubling the force's numbers, the second campaign fared no better for the Nationalists. The highly mobile Red Army forces again managed to lure Nationalist units deep into the base area and attack them individually. In April and May of 1931, the Fifth, Sixth, and Twenty-Sixth Route Armies all suffered defeats, and He Yingqin ordered them to pull back to their initial positions. Chiang Kai-shek traveled to Nanchang to supervise personally a third encirclement campaign that featured 300,000 troops, mostly under central army commanders such as Chen Cheng, Wei Lihuang, and Jiang Dingwen. He Yingqin helped plan the third campaign and commanded the Left Wing Group Army on the eastern flank. Starting from Nanfeng, He's force drove south through Jiangxi toward Ningdu county, seeking out elusive Red Army units that constantly moved about and seldom stood still long enough for the Nationalists to locate them and attack.[5]

At the time, He Yingqin viewed the CCP as the greatest threat to the nation and believed that the government and military must use all resources at their disposal to destroy it, just as had been the case with the old warlords and regional militarists within the Nationalist camp. His concerns about the CCP stemmed not so much from ideological or political disagreements, but rather from his view that the CCP had close connections to the Soviet Union and the forces of foreign imperialism. He took the same position against the CCP that he had taken against the old-style warlords, who he believed threatened China's internal unity, rendered it vulnerable to external attack, and at times formed alliances with or accepted funding from imperialist states that sought political, legal, and economic privileges in return. Since his early days back in Guizhou when he organized the Young Guizhou Association, He Yingqin had opposed foreign imperialism in China regardless of the country in question or the Chinese group that allied with the imperialists. In the early 1930s, despite the fact that the Nationalists had defeated or coopted many of the warlords, he still regarded foreign imperialism as the greatest threat to China and warned against the activities of both "Red" and "White" imperialists. The Red imperialists of the Soviet Union, he argued, used the CCP as a tool and sought to foment chaos, financial disruption, and civil war in China in order to gain control of territory and railroads in Mongolia and Manchuria. At the same time, the more traditional White imperialists continued to cause economic problems and unemployment

---

[5] *HYQJJ*, I, 257–60; Li Yuan, *Jiang Jieshi he He Yingqin*, 108–09; Gibson, "Chiang Kai-shek's Central Army," 231–32. Gibson blames He Yingqin's overly cautious approach for the failure of the second campaign.

through the privileges gained in unequal treaties. The CCP exploited such conditions in order to win more adherents.[6]

Historians looking back on the encirclement and suppression campaigns have tended to point to internal divisions within the Nationalist camp to explain the early failures, noting that the first two campaigns in particular featured large numbers of regional troops rather than central army units.[7] He Yingqin acknowledged such problems, but took a broader view in his own analysis. Unaccustomed to military failure, he again analyzed the reasons behind the Nationalist defeats in a June 1931 report. First, he acknowledged the Red Army's successful strategy and tactics. Rather than confront attacking Nationalist columns on the periphery of the base area and defending territory, the Red Army lured them in deep, took advantage of the terrain, and attacked isolated and vulnerable units with overwhelming force. Second, the CCP enjoyed the support of the local people in the base area, which made things exceedingly difficult for Nationalist forces. The local population provided the CCP with intelligence and supplies, and assisted with communications and logistics, all while denying this same support to the Nationalists. In some cases, they found that local inhabitants fled and took with them all food and supplies, leaving the Nationalist forces unable to purchase even rice. Unable to procure anything locally, the Nationalists had to bring all supplies in via truck, which complicated resupply of forward units. Third, the continuous internal revolts of the previous few years had obstructed military operations against the CCP. He Yingqin maintained that, had it not been for the revolts of Feng Yuxiang, Yan Xishan, Tang Shengzhi, and others, the Nanjing government could have dealt with the CCP problem much earlier and destroyed the bases in Hunan and Jiangxi. The distraction of the 1929 revolts and the Central Plains War had cost the government opportunities to nip the problem in the bud and allowed the CCP to expand its territory and increase the size of its military forces. Finally, He Yingqin argued that local defense organizations remained weak and did not provide effective protection for the local population. Local officials feared the CCP and refused to help Nationalists in the field.[8]

In order to overcome these problems and mount a successful campaign against the CCP, He Yingqin advocated a combination of military, political, and economic measures that would weaken the CCP and its appeal to

---

[6] See He Yingqin's remarks in a report on the campaigns against the Jiangxi Soviet on May 12, 1931, in *HYQJJ*, I, 247–50.

[7] Wei, *Counterrevolution in China*, 156; Gibson, "Chiang Kai-shek's Central Army," 226.

[8] "He Yingqin baogao jiaochi" [He Yingqin's Report on Suppressing the Reds], *Guanhai*, June (1931), 199–201.

the people, while galvanizing support for the Nanjing government. Militarily, He Yingqin reiterated that the Nationalists must maintain a strict blockade of the Jiangxi Soviet to prevent the Red Army from replenishing its stores of weapons, ammunition, medical supplies, and winter clothing. Nationalist forces must also show greater discipline and coordination, and must follow the same logic as the Red Army in only attacking smaller enemy forces. To address the problem of popular support for the CCP in Jiangxi, he urged local government to do more to help Nationalist efforts. County- and village-level officials should organize local people to provide supplies and offer service as guides to the Nationalists, help combat CCP propaganda, and do a better job of training militia and strengthening local defense. Most importantly, He Yingqin believed that local officials must explain to the people exactly what the Nationalist forces stood for and sought to do for them. This, he argued, would help rouse the local population to support the Nanjing government and oppose the CCP. Military blockades and attacks played an important role in this overall strategy, but he understood that local officials served as a critical component in the process of winning the hearts and minds of the people and eradicating the CCP. With such a military, economic, and political strategy, He Yingqin foresaw a dramatic weakening of the CCP and the Red Army, and a Nationalist victory in Jiangxi.[9] Such views reflect the Nanjing government's shift toward a policy of "three parts military, seven parts political" after the third encirclement and suppression campaign in June 1932.[10] He Yingqin had already taken steps in this direction during the second campaign when he ordered his commanders to work with *baojia* leaders – village chiefs and rural administrators – to strengthen local defense. As He Yingqin would see later in his career when he addressed problems at the grassroots level relating to conscription, understanding the problem is one thing. Correcting it is often quite another.

Before He Yingqin and Chiang Kai-shek could do much to address these problems, two events in 1931 interrupted the campaigns against the CCP. First, a secessionist movement based in Guangdong and involving Li Zongren, Bai Chongxi, Chen Jitang, and Wang Jingwei diverted attention and resources from the Jiangxi campaign. Chiang ordered He Yingqin to leave one unit of his Left Wing Group Army in Jiangxi to guard against CCP expansion and organize the rest for action against the rebellious Guangdong and Guangxi forces.[11] This revolt, more political than military, proved strong enough to force Chiang to step down as chair

[9] He Yingqin, "Jiaomie chifei xu junzheng hezuo" [Destroying the Red Bandits Will Require Military and Political Cooperation], *Zhongyang zhoubao*, 226 (1932), 32–33.

[10] Wei, *Counterrevolution in China*, 50–51.

[11] *HYQJJ*, I, 258–62; Wei, *Counterrevolution in China*, 45–47; Tsung-jen Li, *Memoirs*, 284–86.

of the national government on December 15, but he returned to duty as chair of the Military Affairs Commission in January 1932.[12] Second, on September 18, agents of the Japanese Guandong Army (GDA) blew up a section of the South Manchurian Railroad near the city of Shenyang, sometimes known by its Manchu name Mukden, in the infamous Mukden or Manchurian Incident. The GDA blamed Chinese saboteurs for the "attack" and seized first Shenyang and then all of Manchuria. In 1932, the Japanese established a new state called Manchukuo, with the former Qing dynasty emperor Puyi as its sovereign.

Japanese actions in China after September 1931 pulled He Yingqin away from the encirclement and suppression campaigns and marked the start of a new phase in which he would take on responsibility for dealing with the Japanese military in north China. For the next several years, He Yingqin worked to implement Chiang's central policy of the 1930s, working for "internal pacification before external resistance." Essentially, Chiang and He argued that, in its current state of weakness and disunity, China could not stand up to a militarily powerful enemy like Japan. The proper course of action remained pursuit of national unification, meaning continuing the encirclement and suppression campaigns against the CCP, before turning to confront the Japanese in the northeast. As Parks Coble has demonstrated, Chiang consistently advocated this policy dating back to 1927 and the Jinan Incident, stressing that nonresistance to Japanese aggression at this time did not amount to cowardice, but rather reflected a deeper understanding of national priorities. Chiang understood that pursuing campaigns against the CCP while refusing to defend Manchuria would anger many Chinese, and he gave numerous speeches explaining why he saw it as necessary.[13] At the same time, Chiang wanted to demonstrate to the world that China was prepared to defend itself, so he also talked of all-out resistance and boycotts of Japanese goods, and discussed general mobilization.[14] As minister of military administration, He Yingqin understood that the Nationalist military had yet to reach a level of unity and proficiency that would offer a chance of success against the technologically superior Japanese Imperial Army, and he agreed with Chiang's position wholeheartedly. On September 28, just ten days after the explosion outside Shenyang, He Yingqin distributed a copy of a speech to officers and enlisted men in which he explained what had happened and what they needed to do. His remarks

---

[12] *HYQJJ*, I, 264. There is a misprint in the text where it states that Chiang stepped down on February (*eryue*) 15 when it should read December (*shi'eryue*) 15; Tsung-jen Li, *Memoirs*, 284–87; Taylor, *Generalissimo*, 96–98.

[13] Parks Coble, *Facing Japan: Chinese Politics and Japanese Imperialism, 1931–1937* (Cambridge, MA: Council on East Asian Studies, Harvard University Press, 1991), 54–59.

[14] Taylor, *Generalissimo*, 93–94.

linked the Japanese attack to what Chiang identified as the principal problem China faced, internal division, arguing that the Japanese knew that China remained divided and had deliberately taken advantage of the situation to violate China's sovereignty and seize its territory. The Japanese attack had put the military in an extremely difficult position, he told them, but they must resist the urge to react with military force and "endure this heavy burden of bitter humiliation" in order to "carry out their duty to defend the nation and protect the people."[15]

It would take more than speeches to restrain some Nationalist army officers. When Chiang Kai-shek returned to Nanjing as chair of the MAC in January 1932, with Wang Jingwei serving as president of the Executive Yuan, Chiang sent He Yingqin to Shanghai where the Nineteenth Route Army was squaring off against Japanese forces and threatened to derail Chiang's policy of avoiding a major conflict at this time. Commander of the Nineteenth Route Army General Cai Tingkai reported to his superiors in Nanjing that his force was prepared to resist the Japanese invaders at all costs.[16] He Yingqin sent Cai Tingkai multiple telegrams on January 27 ordering him to take all precautions not to provoke a clash with the Japanese and pointing out that to do so would be to obstruct broader, national policy. The next day Japanese marines attacked Zhabei, a section of northern Shanghai, initiating the 1932 Shanghai War. He Yingqin again ordered the Nineteenth Route Army commanders to stand down, avoid expanding the conflict, and accept international mediation, but the hostilities continued for more than a month. The fighting proved costly for China, but perhaps the greatest cost to the Nanjing government came with the rising tide of public opinion, which reacted strongly against the policy of "internal pacification before external resistance."[17] The national focus now shifted toward relations with Japan, though the Guangzhou separatist movement and the CCP's Jiangxi Soviet remained thorns in Nanjing's side.

### The Tanggu Truce of 1933

The next crisis for He Yingqin and the Nanjing government erupted in January 1933 when Japanese forces attacked Shanhaiguan, the pass

---

[15] *HYQJJ*, I, 262–63.

[16] Donald Jordan, *China's Trial by Fire: The Shanghai War of 1932* (Ann Arbor: University of Michigan Press, 2001), 15–16. The Nationalist government was composed of five branches of "Yuan." The Executive Yuan was the equivalent of a cabinet, with a president and the heads of various ministries. Other branches included the Control Yuan, Legislative Yuan, Judicial Yuan, and Examination Yuan.

[17] Coble, *Facing Japan*, 55.

at the eastern end of the Great Wall, which historically gave access to north China from Manchuria. Unhappy with what they interpreted as Chinese insults and desirous of creating a buffer zone between north China and Manchukuo, the GDA inflicted hundreds of casualties on Chinese defenders. Knowing this might expand into a major conflict for which China was still not ready, Chiang Kai-shek sent He Yingqin north to become the new chair of the Beiping Branch of the Military Affairs Commission (BMAC) and deal with the Japanese.

The BMAC had come into existence in the wake of the Japanese seizure of Manchuria when Chiang needed to create a new position for Zhang Xueliang, the Nationalist commander of the Northeast Army, whose troops had withdrawn to north China. As this new round of fighting broke out in Rehe province in January 1933, Chiang decided to remove Zhang and replace him with He Yingqin. In early March, Chiang ordered He Yingqin to leave Nanchang, where he was planning a fourth encirclement and suppression campaign against the CCP, and proceed to Beiping. Chiang also chose Minister of the Interior Huang Shaohong to accompany He as his chief of staff. Huang had a good relationship with He Yingqin, and Chiang felt that he would provide good support on this important and delicate mission of defending north China while avoiding an expansion of the conflict.[18]

As they made their way north, things took a turn for the worse when Japanese forces occupied Chengde with a small force, as mayor Tang Yulin fled and yielded the city with no resistance. When He Yingqin and Huang Shaohong arrived in Tianjin on the morning of March 5, they met with reporters who questioned them about the situation. He Yingqin declined to comment, stating that he had just arrived and needed to meet with Zhang Xueliang, still chair of the BMAC, to formulate a plan.[19] That same day they took a train to Beiping, where He Yingqin set up his office in Jurentang, a part of the Zhongnanhai complex in central Beiping. His initial actions concentrated on preparations for armed resistance, as he convened an emergency meeting of military officers, dispatched three divisions north to support Chinese forces in Rehe, and ordered an investigation into Tang Yulin's failure to defend Chengde.[20] Zhang Xueliang did not meet them at the train station, claiming poor health, and did not attend the emergency meeting, but He Yingqin and Huang Shaohong later called on him at his residence to get an update on the situation. While he expressed great anger at Tang Yulin's withdrawal from Chengde and proclaimed his desire to lead a campaign to drive the Japanese out of

---

[18] Zhang Xingzhi, "He Yingqin zai beiping fenhui," 180.
[19] *HYQJJ*, I, 279.    [20] *HYQJJ*, I, 282.

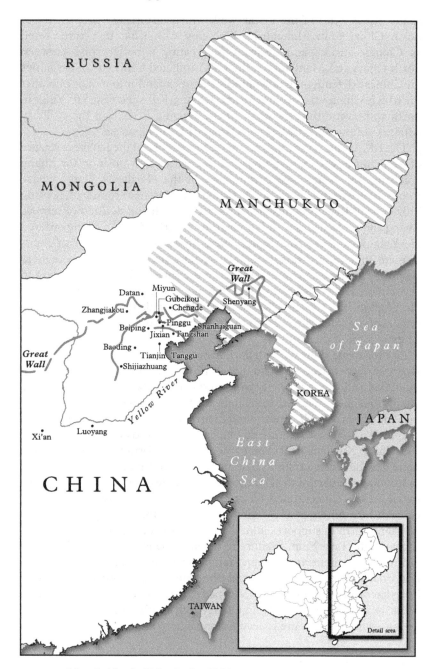

Map 6: North China in the 1930s

Rehe, Zhang appeared thin and sickly. He had to excuse himself during the course of their conversation to take a morphine injection, part of his attempt to kick an opium habit. Despite his enthusiasm for action against the Japanese, Zhang himself realized that he could not lead any attack and told them of his intention to resign as chair of the BMAC.[21]

When Chiang Kai-shek learned that the Japanese had captured Chengde and that Zhang had tendered his resignation, he left his head-quarters at Nanchang and took a train north. Arriving in Shijiazhuang on March 7, he first met privately with He Yingqin and Huang Shao-hong to discuss the situation. Zhang wanted to meet with him as well, but Chiang put him off until he had had a chance to confer with He and Huang and assess the situation and attitude of Zhang's troops. Chiang worried that removing Zhang from his position as chair of the BMAC and from his north China command might trigger a revolt among offi-cers and soldiers of the Northeast Army. At their private meeting, He Yingqin and Huang Shaohong urged Chiang to accept Zhang's resig-nation for several reasons. First, despite his genuine desire to lead a counterattack against the Japanese, his poor health rendered him unfit for this command. If he did remain in command, they reported to Chiang, it would not have a good outcome. Second, considering that Zhang had already yielded to the Japanese in Manchuria in 1931, albeit with Chiang's support, they believed that, if Chiang allowed Zhang to remain in his position as chair of the BMAC after this second withdrawal in the face of Japanese aggression, it would upset the entire country and especially anger other northern commanders such as Yan Xishan, Shang Zhen, and Song Zheyuan. They might then reject Nanjing's authority or decide to launch their own attacks on the Japanese and expand the fighting. With central army forces tied up in operations against the CCP in Jiangxi, they relied heavily on these regional commanders and needed them to adhere to central authority. Finally, they assured Chiang that the Northeast Army would not revolt. Chiang agreed and proceeded to Baoding, where he met with Zhang and accepted his resignation. On March 13, 1933, Chiang appointed He Yingqin chair of the BMAC.[22]

In this new position, He Yingqin's specific goal was to prevent fur-ther Japanese encroachment on Chinese territory while avoiding provo-cations that might incite a larger conflict. He had command over seven group armies, totaling 250,000 troops, which he positioned at Gubeikou, Lengkou, and other passes of the Great Wall. He focused first on

---

[21] Zhang Xingzhi, "He Yingqin zai beiping fenhui," 181.
[22] *HYQJJ*, I, 283; Zhang Xingzhi, "He Yingqin zai beiping fenhui," 181–82; Li Yuan, *Jiang Jieshi he He Yingqin*, 113–14.

stabilizing the situation without expanding the fighting and then pursuing a negotiated settlement with the Japanese, perhaps with international mediation. In mid March, he met with diplomats from the United
States, Belgium, and Italy, seeking support from their governments in
negotiating with the Japanese. At the same time, he took further steps
to defend north China, ordering the destruction of a bridge to delay a
Japanese advance toward the Great Wall. Newspaper articles criticized
the move as passive and defensive rather than offensive, suggesting that
the Chinese government intended to again cede territory to the Japanese
without a fight. He Yingqin countered that the destruction of the bridge
amounted to a strategic necessity and in no way implied a political agreement or concession of territory to Japan. Despite his attempts at securing
international mediation, he told reporters that there would be no accord
with Japan and that China would resist to the end.[23]

He Yingqin clearly prevaricated with the press on this issue, not for
the last time in his career, but his remarks reflect the general policy
that Chiang Kai-shek and president of the Executive Yuan Wang Jingwei
had settled upon. They believed that the central government must show
a willingness to resist at every step, yet at the same time remain open
to a negotiated settlement.[24] In late March, Chiang made a secret visit
to Beiping, where he consulted with various officers in the north and
convened a meeting of top officials at He Yingqin's office. Some present
argued for all-out resistance, asserting that Chinese forces should lure
the Japanese further south in order to wipe them out in a counterattack.
Chiang and He Yingqin disagreed and pointed out that, with the central
army units occupied with the encirclement and suppression campaign in
Jiangxi, few additional troops could move north for such an operation,
not to speak of any operations that followed. He Yingqin argued that
diplomatic action offered the only viable solution to the problem. Chiang
agreed and informed the assembled officers that they must resist only with
those forces present in the north and could expect no reinforcements.[25]
A few weeks later, He Yingqin reiterated this point in a report to Chiang
and Wang in which he described the dire military situation. The Japanese,
he told them, now stood within striking distance of Beiping and Tianjin
and might occupy these cities, establishing a "puppet government" as
they had in Manchuria. In his opinion, at this time the Japanese did not
intend to attack either city, but rather wanted to threaten them in order
to intimidate the Chinese. He recommended directing additional forces

23  *HYQJJ*, I, 284; Zhang Xingzhi, "He Yingqin zai beiping fenhui," 183.
24  So Wai Chor, "The Making of the Guomindang's Japan Policy, 1932–1937: The Roles
    of Chiang Kai-shek and Wang Jingwei," *Modern China*, 28, 2 (April 2002), 222.
25  Zhang Xingzhi, "He Yingqin zai beiping fenhui," 183.

to north China not to resist so much as to strengthen China's bargaining position in negotiations. Of one thing he was sure. Genuine resistance at this point, he argued, would be disastrous.[26] This plan fully adhered to Chiang and Wang's policy of putting up a show of resistance while continuing to solicit international support for a diplomatic resolution.

He Yingqin continued to explore the possibility of international mediation, and on April 12 he went hunting with the British minister to China and discussed a diplomatic solution over lunch at Yihe Yuan. He also met with chancellor of Peking University Jiang Menglin, asking him to approach both the American and British ministers on the question of mediating the Sino-Japanese dispute. The British showed an initial willingness to get involved, but backed out in part because the Japanese government in Tokyo objected and in part because the Chinese government spoke with divided voices on the issue. Foreign Minister Luo Wengan, for example, broke with Chiang and Wang and adamantly opposed any negotiated settlement.[27] He Yingqin also had one of his subordinates in the Ministry of Military Administration open confidential contacts with Japanese officers of the GDA in Shanghai. Through this channel he learned that the Japanese military sought only to protect Manchuria and would agree to a ceasefire provided that Chinese troops withdrew to the south of the Great Wall. These GDA officers in Shanghai expressed understanding of the difficult position of the Chinese government with regard to unpopular agreements with Japan and stated that they would not insist upon a written agreement, but instead would settle for a mutual understanding. He Yingqin knew that his government might agree to these conditions, but he could not ascertain whether these officers in Shanghai had the authority to arrange such an understanding, so it did little to help.[28]

In order to assess reaction to another negotiated settlement with the Japanese military, Chiang Kai-shek instructed He Yingqin to meet with Chinese officers in north China and survey their attitudes. He had been in constant contact with other officers and officials since his arrival in Beiping, but on April 26 He Yingqin convened a special meeting to discuss the possibility of a ceasefire agreement. Chair of the Hebei provincial government General Yu Xuezhong spoke up, explaining his view that most of the officers in north China would go along with the orders of the central government regardless of whether it decided on war or peace. Having said that, he continued, they generally favored a ceasefire

[26] *HYQJJ*, I, 285.
[27] *HYQJJ*, I, 284–87; Li Yuan, *Jiang Jieshi he He Yingqin*, 117; Coble, *Facing Japan*, 105.
[28] *HYQJJ*, I, 289.

agreement over a war of resistance as long as it did not harm or adversely impact any other part of China, meaning no recognition of Japanese control of Manchuria or north China. A number of others voiced support for this view and the meeting concluded with general agreement that the primary goal should be to preserve Beiping and Tianjin as bases for long-term resistance to Japanese aggression. At the same time, they recommended diplomatic measures and international support to secure a settlement, which would give the Chinese time to prepare for a possible larger war.[29] He Yingqin reported the results of the meeting to Chiang and then continued his attempts to bring in the British as meditators. The Japanese continued to reject this as interference in what they saw as essentially a Sino-Japanese affair, so the attempts came to naught.[30]

As a ceasefire emerged as the most desirable outcome, Chiang Kai-shek created a new organ in north China, the Beiping Branch of the Political Affairs Council (*Beiping zhengwu zhengli weiyuanhui*) or BPAC. Huang Fu, a longtime friend and supporter of Chiang Kai-shek who had studied in Japan and enjoyed extensive contacts with Japanese officials, chaired the committee. The BPAC, like the BMAC, served to bolster the central government's authority in north China and facilitate a negotiated settlement with the Japanese military. Moreover, as a semi-autonomous committee of the Executive Yuan, it could serve as a buffer between Chiang and the Nanjing government and any settlement, limiting the political damage that might result.[31] Regardless, He Yingqin sensed that Chiang and Wang had not yet made a clear decision on whether to seek a ceasefire agreement or to begin a war of all-out resistance against Japan. He Yingqin plainly favored the former, but the Japanese continued to advance and posed a direct threat to Beiping and Tianjin, critical cities that he believed the Chinese must defend at all costs. On May 6, He Yingqin sent an urgent message to Chiang and Wang asking for a decision: would it be war or peace? All-out resistance or a negotiated ceasefire? Either way, he urged them to make a decision and have a plan in place as soon as possible. While acknowledging that resistance remained an alternative, He Yingqin made no bones about his own view of the situation. A ceasefire, he argued in the same message, would clearly benefit the central government, provided its representatives could survive the

---

[29] *HYQJJ*, I, 290–91.    [30] *HYQJJ*, I, 292–93.

[31] *HYQJJ*, I, 297; Coble, *Facing Japan*, 109–10; Marjorie Dryburgh, *North China and Japanese Expansion, 1933–1937: Regional Power and the National Interest* (Richmond, UK: Curzon, 2000), 3–4; He Yingqin shangjiang jiuwu shoudan congshu bianji weiyuanhui, *Beiping junfenhui sannian* [Three Years as Chair of the Beiping Branch of the Military Affairs Commission] (hereafter *BPJFHSN*) (Taipei: Liming wenhua shiye youxian gongsi, 1984), 17.

criticism and shame that would be sure to follow. It would provide an opportunity to regroup, acquire foreign financial support, develop national strength, and revive or rouse the population. Was that not why, he asked, Chiang had created the BPAC and appointed Huang Fu as chair? On the other hand, he continued, if it is to be resistance and war, they must consider larger issues of resources. He predicted the rapid fall of Beiping and Tianjin, a Japanese occupation of all of Hebei, and the loss of important financial resources. Under these circumstances, soldiers would complain, the people would experience great hardships, and the CCP would run wild. It was hard to see, He Yingqin concluded, how anything good could come from this choice.[32] In response, Chiang gave no indication that he had made a decision on war or peace; indeed, he stated that it might be either. He explained to He Yingqin that the most important thing at this time was to ease the current tension and avoid any actions that might adversely influence the situation in north China, and this was the nature of Huang Fu's role. Chiang urged He Yingqin to make all efforts to keep things calm to avoid anything that might provoke the Japanese.[33]

Chiang's reluctance to rule out either course of action and make a decision left He Yingqin in an increasingly difficult position in which he could not adequately prepare for either option. As for keeping everyone in line, he knew he could not ensure that no Chinese carried out provocative actions as Chiang insisted. One such potentially disruptive act took place the very next day, when an assassin murdered Zhang Jingyao at his hotel residence in Beiping. A former Hunan militarist, Zhang had accepted GDA chief of intelligence Itagaki Seishiro's offer to help the Japanese establish a new political authority in north China. Zhang claimed to have wide-ranging connections with Chinese military commanders in north China and sought to enlist them in the plan.[34] Concerned that this murder of a prominent "friend" of the GDA might serve as a pretext for further Japanese military action, Chiang sent a query to He Yingqin asking how this might influence the situation. He Yingqin felt that conflict between various groups in north China – Guomindang authorities, northern regional commanders, and pro-Japanese elements – would only grow worse after Zhang's murder and worried that he could do nothing to ease the tension. He eventually suggested to Chiang that he should consider offering Yan Xishan unified command of all forces in

---

[32] *HYQJJ*, I, 303.    [33] *HYQJJ*, I, 304.
[34] Furuya, *Chiang Kai-shek*, 410–11. Frederic Wakeman claims that He Yingqin arranged the murder of Zhang Jingyao in order to discourage others from collaborating with the Japanese: Frederic Wakeman, *Spymaster: Dai Li and the Chinese Secret Service* (Berkeley: University of California Press, 2003), 118.

north China, thinking that this might reduce some of the tension between central authorities and the other groups based in north China and help unify disparate elements. Though a northern regional commander, Yan Xishan, he pointed out, had a national outlook on affairs and was "relatively reliable," and central authorities could control him. He Yingqin also believed that bringing in a regional commander to help defend Beiping and Tianjin, rather than depending solely on central army troops, would be a smart move. If the central government tried to go it alone in defending the north, it would likely result in large sacrifices of central army forces, leaving the government's base area in Nanjing and Shanghai vulnerable. Chiang acknowledged some merit in this idea, but rejected the suggestion. He doubted that Yan Xishan would accept the position, but more importantly he told He Yingqin that at this critical time central authorities must not shirk their responsibilities and must handle things on their own.[35]

He Yingqin's discomfort grew as he saw signs that the Japanese might indeed attack Beiping and Tianjin. Chen Yi, He Yingqin's subordinate at the Ministry of Military Administration, had learned from a Japanese military officer in Nanjing that authorities in Tokyo intended to break off negotiations.[36] Two days after that, on May 10, Japanese forces attacked at Gubeikou, inflicting heavy losses on the Chinese with artillery and air power.[37] He Yingqin contacted Huang Fu to ask if any possibility remained for a negotiated settlement, but Huang could only recommend that He Yingqin pull Chinese forces back out of artillery range. He agreed and ordered a fallback to a line running through Miyun, Pinggu, Yutian, and Tangshan, then sent a message to Wang Jingwei urging an all-out effort to secure a ceasefire agreement. As the Chinese forces fell back to the new line, He Yingqin again heard from Chen Yi, who now claimed that his Japanese contacts had told him that, if the Chinese fell back to this exact line, then the Japanese would agree to a ceasefire. Meanwhile, Japanese forces occupied Luanzhou and Tangshan and pushed on to capture Miyun, Sanhe, and Jixian, taking them within 50 miles of Beiping.[38]

Despite Chen's report that the Japanese would agree to a negotiated settlement, He Yingqin now believed an attack on Beiping and Tianjin would come at any moment and the central government had still not determined a clear course of action. He sent a series of messages to Wang and Chiang on May 20–21, describing the deteriorating situation in the north and explaining that his intelligence sources indicated that

[35] *HYQJJ*, I, 304–08.    [36] *HYQJJ*, I, 304.    [37] *HYQJJ*, I, 304–05.
[38] *HYQJJ*, I, 310; Coble, *Facing Japan*, 105–06; Furuya, *Chiang Kai-shek*, 413.

the Japanese intended to attack Beiping and Tianjin. He reported that contacts with Japanese officers of the GDA in Beiping revealed a hardening of the Japanese demands and little hope remained for a negotiated ceasefire. He Yingqin saw two possible courses of action at this point. Plan A involved a "fight to the death" (*jueyi sizhan*) in north China, with Chinese forces organizing a defense at the Bai River (the modern-day Hai River) for an all-out defense of Beiping and Tianjin. Plan B called for the forces to fall back on the northern bank of the Yongding River to the south of Beiping, where they would prepare for a long-term standoff that might result in a political or diplomatic resolution. If they chose Plan A, he told Chiang and Wang, the Chinese could expect exceedingly difficult conditions, substantial casualties, and the loss of north China. Plan B promised little better, and there was no guarantee the Chinese could organize a sufficient force at the Yongding River in time. Even if they did succeed in holding this position, it would only mean increased Japanese military pressure on the north, and the people of China would never forgive the government for yielding territory. While asking Chiang and Wang for a decision, He Yingqin expressed his view that the only recourse under these conditions was to fight to defend Beiping and Tianjin, even though he remained pessimistic about the ability of the Chinese forces to hold the cities and suggested that it was simply a matter of time before they fell under Japanese occupation.[39] In all of his plans for dealing with the Japanese in north China during this period, He Yingqin deemed the defense of Beiping and Tianjin essential, a line which if crossed would necessitate an all-out war of resistance.

Just as a major battle for Beiping and Tianjin appeared inevitable, the Japanese softened their position and offered the possibility of a negotiated ceasefire. On the evening of May 22, Huang Fu met with Lieutenant Colonel Nagatsu Sahie and other GDA officers in Beiping, who offered a ceasefire in return for the creation of a neutral or demilitarized zone in eastern Hebei. Wang Jingwei had given He Yingqin and Huang Fu freedom to use their own discretion in negotiations, but warned against any agreement that recognized Japanese control over Manchuria. Except for this restriction, Huang and He could agree to any settlement as they saw fit.[40] Fully aware of the dire military situation and seeing the opportunity to arrange a ceasefire without formally recognizing Japanese control over Chinese territory, He Yingqin accepted the terms and informed the Japanese that he would send a representative to Miyun to formalize the agreement.[41] The National Defense Council in Nanjing supported He Yingqin's view and agreed on May 23 that, if the Japanese attacked

---

[39] *HYQJJ*, I, 314–16.     [40] *HYQJJ*, I, 317–18.     [41] *HYQJJ*, I, 320–21.

Beiping and Tianjin, Chinese forces had no choice but to defend the cities and engage in all-out resistance. Otherwise, they must agree to a cease-fire under the terms offered.[42] Having accepted the deal, He Yingqin composed a message to all frontline commanders informing them of the details of the agreement, ordering withdrawals to designated positions, and emphasizing that they should no longer fire upon Japanese forces.[43]

The two sides had reached an agreement on conditions for a cease-fire, but there remained several tense days before the completion of the truce. When details of the agreement appeared in the pages of a Tianjin newspaper along with a story that Chiang Kai-shek had ordered the murder of a Japanese soldier guarding Tokyo's embassy in Beiping, Japanese officers expressed anger at what they described as Chinese insincerity and threatened to break off the talks. He Yingqin had to send one of his subordinates to apologize and explain that the killing of the soldier had been an individual act, with no connection to the Chinese government or Chiang Kai-shek. Regardless, he feared that the agreement might collapse at any time and ordered troops to spend the night preparing to defend Beiping in the event that the Japanese resumed their attacks.[44] The Japanese did not attack, and He Yingqin's chief of staff Xu Yanmou traveled to Miyun to meet with Japanese officers, where they worked out the details and agreed to meet again at Tanggu to sign the final agreement. Wang Jingwei reminded He Yingqin and Huang Fu that the agreement must not recognize Japanese control of Manchuria, but also stressed that they should not put anything at all in writing. Chiang Kai-shek agreed and told He and Huang to restrict themselves to an oral agreement. He Yingqin did not believe the Japanese would accept an oral agreement and predicted that they would insist on a written document, but Wang and Chiang continued to urge him to avoid putting anything in writing. Eventually, they conceded that, should this prove impossible, it must take the form of a purely military agreement, not a political agreement subject to approval of the Legislative Yuan.[45] On May 31, BMAC representative General Xiong Bin signed what became known as the Tanggu Truce (*Tanggu xieding*), which created a demilitarized zone between the Great Wall and a line running just north of Beiping and Tianjin.

Knowing that this truce would meet with widespread criticism from those who favored a stronger stand against Japanese encroachments

---

[42] *BPJFHSN*, 25.    [43] *HYQJJ*, I, 320–21.
[44] Zhang Xingzhi, "He Yingqin zai beiping fenhui," 186; *HYQJJ*, I, 323.
[45] *HYQJJ*, I, 329–30.

on Chinese territory, He Yingqin sent a message to provincial governors, mayors, pacification force commanders, and all frontline officers in north China, explaining that to reject the truce would have been disastrous. He pointed out that given China's military weakness it would have been tremendously difficult to defend Beiping and Tianjin, both of which would have fallen under Japanese occupation. The Japanese would then establish pro-Japanese governments, which would pressure Chinese forces near the Yellow River, the Central Plains, and then the Yangzi River region. Finally, the loss of Beiping and Tianjin would mean surrendering the tax revenue from these two cities, which provided the funds to maintain military forces in the north.[46] He sent a special telegram to Chen Jitang, leader of the Guangzhou separatist government, asking him not to react to this agreement with pure emotion. He urged Chen to look at the situation from a national perspective and to understand the realities of both the Chinese and Japanese militaries, in order contribute to a united and long-term response to the problem of Japanese aggression.[47]

As He Yingqin had predicted, the reaction from across the country brought loud criticism of Chiang Kai-shek, He Yingqin, Huang Fu, and Wang Jingwei, the principal architects of this agreement.[48] In later years, He Yingqin pointed out that, throughout the process of negotiating the Tanggu Truce, his office had maintained constant contact with all ranking military officers in north China, but not one of them offered a viable alternative to the ceasefire agreement. He also stressed that the BMAC had strictly adhered to the orders of the central government, which in the end acceded to all Japanese demands, including insistence on a written agreement.[49] At the time, He Yingqin accepted responsibility for the truce, but argued that it amounted to a purely military agreement and denied that it contained any secret clauses or stipulations as rumors suggested. He defended the basic policy of "internal pacification before external resistance" and suggested to critics that everyone must focus on meaningful preparations for the future and avoid "pointless empty talk."[50] As an individual, He Yingqin felt the sting of the criticism to such an extent that in June 1934 he submitted a request that the Executive Yuan demote him to the rank of lieutenant general for his role in accepting the ceasefire, though that body rejected his request.[51] Not all observers criticized his handling of the situation. An American military attaché in Beiping reported that He Yingqin's "position in North China the past year and one half has been the most difficult one in China," but that he "has stood up against constant and vicious political attacks during the

[46] *HYQJJ*, I, 336–37.     [47] *HYQJJ*, I, 342–43.     [48] Coble, *Facing Japan*, 14–19.
[49] *BPJFHSN*, 29–30.     [50] *HYQJJ*, I, 350–51.     [51] *HYQJJ*, I, 370.

past two years showing him to be a man of moral courage."[52] Historian
Ray Huang also offered praise, arguing that, while the Chinese public and
pundits branded Huang Fu and He Yingqin as traitors for negotiating
agreements with the Japanese military, the two deliberately sacrificed
their reputations to acquire additional time for Chiang and China to
work toward unification and to prepare for an all-out war of resistance
against Japan.[53] In this sense, He Yingqin had successfully traded his
reputation for additional time to prepare for such a war.

### The so-called He–Umezu Agreement of 1935

The stipulations of the Tanggu Truce and the creation of a demilitarized zone in Hebei north of Beiping and Tianjin did not long satisfy
the Japanese military, which soon sought a greater buffer zone between
north China and Manchukuo. In January 1935, the GDA went on the
offensive again, citing alleged Chinese insults and failure to respond to
Japanese demands for an apology as pretext. Having recently returned
to Beiping after two months in Nanjing and Shanghai, He Yingqin again
took up the cause of "internal pacification before external resistance" and
approached Japanese officials about settling the issue peacefully. On January 19, Major Takahashi Tan, a military attaché at the Japanese embassy
in Beiping, declared to He Yingqin that Chinese forces in Chaha'er
province actually occupied territory within the boundaries of the state
of Manchukuo and accused the governor of Chaha'er, General Song
Zheyuan, of violating that state's sovereignty. He demanded that the
Chinese government pull all armed forces in Chaha'er back to the east
of Datan and remove Song from his position as governor.[54]

He Yingqin reported these demands to Nanjing along with a recommendation that the government deal with this issue within the larger context of Sino-Japanese relations. Clearly, he did not want to take responsibility for negotiating another unpopular agreement in north China.
Unfortunately, he found that officials in Nanjing preferred that any settlement take the form of a local, military agreement, and rejected his
recommendation. As had been the case in 1933, He Yingqin sought
to avoid any action that might provoke a Japanese military response or
expand the conflict, so he quickly ordered Song Zheyuan to pull his forces
away from the disputed area, leaving only military police to maintain law
and order.[55] Japanese forces continued to push west into Chaha'er and

[52] See Lieutenant Colonel W. S. Drysdale's October 9, 1934, report on He Yingqin (Ho
Ying-chin), *US Military Intelligence Reports: China, 1911–1941*, Reel XII, 0813.
[53] Huang, "Chiang Kai-shek and His Diary," 75.
[54] *HYQJJ*, I, 380.    [55] *BPJFHSN*, 34.

then sought to engage Song Zheyuan in separate negotiations at Datan. He Yingqin opposed this idea and insisted that any negotiations must take place in Beiping or at least Zhangjiakou. Nanjing authorities, on the other hand, preferred an informal understanding among local parties and agreed to hold talks at Datan, giving detailed instructions to local officials of the Twenty-Ninth Corps and the Chaha'er provincial government. The talks produced an ambiguous understanding that settled the matter for the moment, but made no progress toward solving the larger issue of Japanese aggression against north China. He Yingqin again protested to Nanjing that these ad hoc solutions and sporadic talks with various Japanese military officials had to stop and urged the government to put together a comprehensive policy for dealing with Japan and engaging authorities in Tokyo right away.[56] Nanjing officials attempted to initiate higher-level discussions with the Japanese government but, when Chinese ambassador to Japan Zhang Zuobin tried to raise the issue with the foreign office in Tokyo, officials there simply referred Zhang to the Japanese military.[57]

The situation remained relatively stable until early May 1935 when two incidents prompted Japanese military officers to demand additional concessions. First, on May 2 two prominent Chinese editors of pro-Japanese newspapers in Tianjin turned up dead, murdered at the hands of unknown assassins. Second, an irregular military force under the command of Sun Yongqin operated in the demilitarized zone created through the Tanggu Truce and north of the Great Wall. He Yingqin had traveled to Taiyuan to discuss suppressing elements of the CCP with Yan Xishan, where he learned that in his absence Takahashi Tan had visited the office of the BMAC in order to lodge complaints about these incidents. Takahashi blamed Chinese authorities for the two murders and asserted the right to send Japanese forces into the demilitarized zone to root out Sun Yongqin's force. He Yingqin quickly returned to Beiping and informed the Japanese that he had been in touch with Hebei governor Yu Xuezhong about these matters. The Chinese had their own concerns about Sun Yongqin, who had caused trouble for Chinese civilians as well as the Japanese. Within days of Takahashi's complaint, a Japanese force located and attacked Sun Yongqin's irregulars, killing 300 including Sun himself.[58]

Takahashi called on He Yingqin at his office on May 29, arguing that these acts threatened the stability of the area and would force the

---

[56] Dryburgh, *North China and Japanese Expansion*, 29–31.     [57] *BPJFHSN*, 41.

[58] *HYQJJ*, I, 390–95; *BPJFHSN*, 37–38; He Yingqin, "Hebei shibian zhong juewu suowei 'Hemei xieding,'" [There Was Absolutely No So-Called "He–Umezu Agreement" During the Hebei Incident], in He Yingqin, ed., *Weibang bainian ji*, 113–14.

Japanese to take certain steps to impose order and defend themselves. He demanded an end to all anti-Japanese activities, for which he specifically blamed Hebei provincial authorities, including supporting Sun Yongqin's irregular forces and arranging the murder of the two editors. He offered nothing in writing, but suggested to He Yingqin that the Hebei government should move its offices to Baoding, about 150 km southwest of Beiping, and that Nanjing authorities should remove governor Yu Xuezhong. He accused specific offices of engaging in anti-Japanese activities, such as the third regiment of military police and the political training section of the BMAC, both of which had ties to the ultra-nationalist Blue Shirt organization. On top of these demands, Takahashi called for the removal of all central army troops from Hebei.[59]

When He Yingqin reported on this conversation to Wang Jingwei in Nanjing, he included a recent intelligence report that indicated several ominous signs of impending Japanese military action in Hebei. First, the Japanese planned to reinforce their position in Tianjin with an additional 1,000 troops sent via the land route from Manchukuo. Second, the Japanese force that had moved though the passes into the demilitarized zone south of the Great Wall to attack Sun Yongqin had not yet withdrawn back to the north of the wall and remained in Hebei. Third, Japanese planes flew over Beiping each day, conducting reconnaissance and inspecting the city's defenses. Finally, He Yingqin reported that Japanese officers talked openly about the GDA's willingness to act, claiming that if the Chinese did not take steps to ensure order the GDA would do it through military force. Whether they intended take action or simply intimidate the Chinese he could not say, but He Yingqin perceived a serious threat to both Beiping and Tianjin.[60]

Wang responded to this information by stressing that the murders of the two editors had taken place in the Japanese concession in Tianjin, an area in which Chinese authorities had no legal jurisdiction. He denied any connection between the Chinese government and Sun Yongqin's force, but with Sun now dead this issue had been settled. Regardless, Wang believed in the need to avoid further conflict and suggested a transfer to another position for Yu Xuezhong. He stressed to He Yingqin that they must not embarrass or humiliate Yu and that it would be best if he agreed to this on his own, resigning the governor's position and turning it over

---

[59] *BPJFHSN*, 39; *HYQJJ*, I, 396–97; He Yingqin, "Hebei shibian zhong juewu suowei 'Hemei xieding,'" 115–16.

[60] *HYQJJ*, I, 398–99. Zeng Kuoqing later confirmed the presence of Blue Shirt activists in this organization. See Zeng Kuoqing, "Hemei xieding qian fuxingshe zai huabei de huodong" [Activities of the Fuxingshe in North China Prior to the He–Umezu Agreement], *Wenshi ziliao xuanji*, 14 (n.d.), 132–33.

to his deputy, Zhang Houwan. Perhaps, Wang suggested, He Yingqin could talk to Yu and convince him that this course of action would best serve the interests of the nation as a whole.[61] He Yingqin had in fact already invited Yu Xuezhong and Huang Fu to Beiping to discuss the situation. When he pitched the idea that Yu should resign of his own accord, Yu refused, stating that he would follow whatever orders central authorities issued, but since he had done nothing wrong he would not resign his position. As for shifting government offices to Baoding, he asked, "what will we do if the Japanese threaten us again? Move them out of the province?"[62] He Yingqin followed up with telephone calls urging Yu to resign, but he still refused. On June 1, Chiang Kai-shek gave the order for Yu Xuezhong to move his office to Baoding.[63] The government also announced the transfer of Zeng Kuoqing, head of the political training section of the BMAC, and Zhang Xiaoxian, commander of the third regiment of military police.[64] Days later the government announced that Yu Xuezhong would leave the Hebei government to take up a new position as commander in charge of suppressing CCP forces in Shaanxi province.

The question of who would take Yu's place as Hebei governor proved contentious. He Yingqin and Wang Jingwei had discussed the issue and decided that the job should go to Yu's deputy, Zhang Houwan, at least temporarily until they could name an appropriate permanent governor. Chiang Kai-shek recommended that He Yingqin replace Yu as governor of Hebei. Why go to the trouble of bringing in someone else, he asked, when He Yingqin was already in north China and as well equipped as any other officer to handle the job? He Yingqin had a different view and believed that Yu's replacement must be a northerner, which would prove more acceptable to other northern officers and would avoid arousing suspicions that the "southerners" from the Nanjing government sought to use this crisis as an excuse to extend their control over north China. Given Nanjing's tenuous relations with northern officers such as Feng Yuxiang, Yan Xishan, and Zhang Xueliang, not to mention the secessionist government in Guangzhou under Li Zongren, Bai Chongxi, and Chen Jitang, He Yingqin's plan made sense. Moreover, taking up this political position would simply add to his responsibilities and occupy valuable time that

---

[61] *HYQJJ*, I, 398–400.

[62] Yu Xuezhong, "Wo shi zenyang bei rikou bichu huabei de" [How the Japanese Bandits Forced Me out of North China], *Wenshi ziliao xuanji*, 14 (n.d.), 174.

[63] Qin Xiaoyi, ed., *Zhonghua minguo zhongyao shiliao chubian: duiri kangzhan shiqi* [Important Historical Materials of the Republic of China: The Period of the War of Resistance Against Japan] (hereafter *ZHMGZYSL*), diyi bian, *Xubian*, 3 vols. (Taipei: Zhongguo guomindang zhongyang weiyuanhui dangshi weiyuanhui, 1981), 1, 675.

[64] *BPJFHSN*, 40.

he needed to concentrate on military matters.[65] Wang Jingwei agreed
with He Yingqin's view and temporarily appointed Zhang Houwan to
the job, then replaced him with another senior northern officer, General
Shang Zhen, in June. As this demonstrates, with Chiang away in Sichuan
concentrating on suppression of the CCP and Red Army, Wang Jingwei,
He Yingqin, and Huang Fu took primary responsibility for dealing with
matters in north China.[66]

Takahashi Tan returned to He Yingqin's office on June 4, along with
Sakai Takashi, chief of staff of the Japanese Garrison Army in Tianjin.
He Yingqin explained to them that his government would cooperate
in the investigation of the murder of the two newspaper editors, but
since it had taken place in the Japanese concession at Tianjin Chinese
authorities lacked jurisdiction. With regard to Sun Yongqin, Japanese
forces had advanced south of the Great Wall, killed Sun, and scattered
his force, so there would be no further problems. On a more constructive
note, he reported that Nanjing had decided to transfer Yu Xuezhong to
another position, to shift all Hebei government and Guomindang offices
to Baoding, and to reassign the heads of the BMAC political training
section and the third regiment of military police. Takahashi ignored these
gestures and insisted on the removal of all central army units, an end
to all anti-Japanese activities in China, and the removal of Yu's Fifty-
First Corps from Hebei.[67] As He Yingqin attempted to arrange full
compliance with Takahashi's demands, all the while making them appear
as voluntary actions on the part of the Chinese government, another
incident threatened to increase the tension in north China and precipitate
another round of Japanese demands.

On June 5, authorities in Chaha'er province detained a group of
Japanese soldiers for lacking proper documentation. Major General Doihara Kenji, an intelligence officer with the GDA with long experience
in China, protested the detention as a deliberate insult to Japan, insisted
that provincial governor Song Zheyuan apologize, and demanded that the
Chinese government remove him as governor. Unless the Chinese met
these demands, Doihara threatened a military occupation of Chaha'er.
Song Zheyuan ordered the release of the detained soldiers the next day,
but refused to apologize. Having just gone through the Hebei Incident
and the transfer of Yu Xuezhong, He Yingqin now had to deal with this

[65] *HYQJJ*, I, 400–01; He Yingqin, "Hebei shibian zhong juewu suowei 'Hemei xieding,'"
118–19.
[66] So, "Making of the Guomindang's Japan Policy," 225.
[67] *BPJFHSN*, 40; *HYQJJ*, I, 402.

North Chaha'er Incident and arrange for the transfer of Song Zheyuan as well.[68]

He Yingqin had expressed a willingness to address Sakai and Taka-hashi's concerns, but on June 6 Sakai again visited the BMAC office to deliver a series of demands in writing, reiterating those presented orally two days before. The list included the dismissal of Yu Xuezhong as gov-ernor of Hebei, the withdrawal of all GMD and government offices, the transfer of the third regiment of military police and the BMAC political training section, the removal of all Blue Shirt and anti-Japanese organi-zations in Hebei, and the withdrawal of Yu Xuezhong's Fifty-First Corps from the province. He Yingqin reacted to this with a reminder that the Chinese government had already agreed to transfer Yu and withdraw the Blue Shirt organizations, but he would contact officials in Nanjing about the other issues.[69] Over the next few days, He Yingqin's intelligence sources indicated that the commander of the Japanese Garrison Army in China, Lieutenant General Umezu Yoshijiro, had called a meeting of GDA officers in Tianjin, at which they had discussed a plan to attack and occupy Chaha'er and threaten Beiping and Tianjin in the event that the Nanjing government did not agree to the demands before a certain deadline. He Yingqin therefore recommended pulling all central army forces back to the south of Baoding or Changxindian, in order to reduce the immediate tension. Chiang Kai-shek disagreed, as he did not feel that this would relieve the tension, and insisted that they keep these units in place in preparation to defend Beiping and Tianjin. He agreed to meet all other demands, but remained strongly opposed to removing central army troops from Hebei.[70]

This issue came to a head when Takahashi and Sakai made their third visit to He Yingqin's office in a little over two weeks. As he had at their last meeting, He Yingqin reported his government's acceptance of most of the demands. Sakai and Takahashi now demanded that the Chinese provide specific dates for the completion of these changes and added new demands, including the removal of all GMD offices from Hebei province, the transfer of the second and twenty-fifth divisions (central army) from Hebei, and an end to all anti-Japanese activities across China. They handed He Yingqin a three-page document that spelled out these demands and gave a deadline of June 12 for a Chinese response. Other-wise, they informed him, the Japanese military would take action. At

[68] Dryburgh, *North China and Japanese Expansion*, 40.
[69] He Yingqin, "Hebei shibian zhong juewu suowei 'Hemei xieding,'" 120.
[70] *ZHMGZYSL, Xubian*, 1, 677–78.

roughly the same time, Japanese forces advanced on Gubeikou and Shan-haiguan.[71]

He Yingqin relayed these latest details to Wang Jingwei in Nanjing and Chiang Kai-shek in Sichuan, and they exchanged opinions via telegram. Wang felt that they must agree to the demands and called a meeting of Nanjing officials for the next morning to discuss the situation and get government approval. He urged He Yingqin to order the removal of the various military units, which did not require government approval and which he could authorize as chair of the BMAC.[72] Chiang Kai-shek still adamantly opposed the removal of central army units from Hebei. To agree to this, he argued, would be tantamount to abandoning Beiping, Tianjin, and all of north China. Having given in to every other demand, Chiang believed that they must stand their ground and resist on this final issue. Even if the Chinese agreed to this demand, he believed the Japanese military would simply continue to pick a fight with the Chinese, and nothing would change. He saw this as the key to the situation in north China and absolutely refused to accept this last demand.[73]

With Wang and Chiang split over the issue of removing central army forces from Hebei, He Yingqin attempted to persuade Chiang to accept Wang's view. Late on the evening of June 9, He Yingqin sent a message to Chiang explaining why he believed they must accept all the Japanese demands and transfer these troops out of Hebei. He pointed out that the Japanese sought a confrontation in north China that would allow them to attack Nanjing, Shanghai, and the Yangzi area at the same time. The Nationalists simply had not made the military, economic, or diplomatic preparations for such an attack and there was no way to do so on such short notice. The only viable course of action at this point, he stressed, was to follow Wang Jingwei's plan and voluntarily move central army units from Hebei into Henan. He Yingqin saw this as the only way to protect Beiping and Tianjin, which they must retain as the foundation for a protracted war of resistance.[74] The next morning Wang reported that an emergency meeting of central government officials had agreed to accept the Japanese demands, including the withdrawal of central army units from Hebei.[75] Wang and He prepared to accept the Japanese demands despite Chiang's continued objections.

Takahashi and Sakai did not wait for the deadline, but showed up at He Yingqin's office in the late afternoon on June 10. He Yingqin gave

[71] *HYQJJ*, I, 407–08; He Yingqin, "Hebei shibian zhong juewu suowei 'Hemei xieding,'" 123–26.
[72] *HYQJJ*, I, 410.     [73] *ZHMGZYSL, Xubian*, 1, 679–80.
[74] *ZHMGZYSL, Xubian*, 1, 681.
[75] He Yingqin, "Hebei shibian zhong juewu suowei 'Hemei xieding,'" 127.

them verbal assurance that the Chinese military and government would meet all their demands and pointed out that on that very day the government had addressed the issue of improving relations with Japan with a "Goodwill Mandate" that prohibited anti-Japanese activities.[76] The Japanese representatives expressed satisfaction, but unexpectedly one of Takahashi's staff officers appeared at the BMAC office the next day with a formal document that listed nine individual demands, which He Yingqin had accepted orally the day before. It also included additional points that they had not discussed, including the removal of all Chinese officers or officials whom the Japanese felt might harm Sino-Japanese relations, Japanese authority to approve all new appointments, and the right of the Japanese military to oversee and verify the implementation of all changes associated with these demands. He Yingqin not only refused to sign the document but immediately dispatched one of his staff officers to return it to Takahashi's office with a message that he would not acknowledge it as the Chinese government had already indicated its intention to make these changes of its own accord without a written agreement.[77]

Though Chiang had disagreed with Wang and He over the issue of removing central army units from Hebei, they all agreed that under no circumstances should He Yingqin sign this document and that he must avoid a written agreement at all costs.[78] In the following days, the Japanese repeatedly visited He's office, pressuring him to sign the document, which he refused to do. Eventually, he concluded that, as long as he remained in Beiping, the Japanese would target him as the only Chinese military officer in north China with sufficient rank and title to authorize such an agreement. On June 12, he sent a message to Chiang explaining that he had been under constant pressure from Japanese officials and that he had learned that the Japanese also planned to resurrect the demand for the removal of Chaha'er provincial governor Song Zheyuan. He concluded that it would be better to leave Beiping and return to Nanjing, where not only would he avoid the pressure but he could also make a full report on the situation to the government. He left that day, leaving his chief of staff Bao Wenyue in charge of the BMAC office.[79]

Some scholars have cast a critical eye on He Yingqin's departure and interpreted his decision to leave Beiping as fleeing his post. Marjorie Dryburgh described He Yingqin as "losing his courage" at this critical moment, while Youli Sun suggested that "He Yingqin's nerve appeared

[76] Dryburgh, *North China and Japanese Expansion*, 39–40; Coble, *Facing Japan*, 204.
[77] *HYQJJ*, I, 412–13; He Yingqin, "Hebei shibian zhong juewu suowei 'Hemei xieding,'" 128–29.
[78] *HYQJJ*, I, 413–14; *ZHMGZYSL, Xubian*, 1, 682.
[79] *ZHMGZYSL, Xubian*, 1, 683–84.

to fail" and referred to his departure from Beiping as "desertion."[80] This interpretation may stem in part from the fact that Chiang Kai-shek still believed that He Yingqin should take over as governor of Hebei, and sent several messages urging him to reconsider in the weeks after He Yingqin left Beiping. He Yingqin refused to change his mind on this issue and, like Wang Jingwei, continued to believe that a northern officer must take that position.[81] He Yingqin's rejection of Chiang's appeals to "return to the north" to serve as governor of Hebei have been misunderstood as He's unwillingness to return to the north to negotiate with the Japanese. Indeed, Youli Sun argues that the Nanjing government could not find an "official of high position and courage to face the Japanese in north China."[82] Others have recognized that He Yingqin's trip to Nanjing did not reflect a lack of courage – he had after all been "facing the Japanese" since March 1933 – but was rather a tactical move to avoid signing a document that all agreed would cause further uproar among the Chinese public.[83] Reaction to the Tanggu Truce had been swift and severe, and He Yingqin, Chiang Kai-shek, and Wang Jingwei did not want a repeat. They were especially sensitive to the impact this would have on the secessionist government in Guangzhou. Despite He Yingqin's refusal to take over as Hebei governor, Chiang Kai-shek certainly did not fault He for leaving Beiping or interpret it as dereliction of duty. He received He's telegram message only after He Yingqin had already departed from Beiping, but Chiang responded with a strong expression of sympathy for the difficult situation He Yingqin faced there and supported his decision to return to the capital.[84]

When He Yingqin arrived in Nanjing on June 15, he met with reporters and offered some remarks on the "diplomatic issues in Hebei." There had been a great deal of reporting, he told them, so he saw no need to repeat the details. Instead, he simply stated that on May 29 Japanese officials had orally proposed some "improvements" (*gaishan gedian*). After getting guidance from the government in Nanjing, He Yingqin had given his agreement to the Japanese orally on June 10, which had peacefully resolved the Hebei issue. He then proceeded to Nanjing, where he reported to the government in detail on the process of the negotiations.[85] Back in Beiping, Takahashi Tan called on the BMAC office to again press

[80] Dryburgh, *North China and Japanese Expansion*, 39; Youli Sun, *China and the Origins of the Pacific War, 1931–1941* (New York: St. Martin's Press, 1993), 55.
[81] *ZHMGZYSL, Xubian*, 1, 686–89.
[82] Sun, *China and the Origins of the Pacific War*, 55.
[83] Xiong Zongren, *He Yingqin: xuanwozhong de lishi*, I, 320–21; Coble, *Facing Japan*, 205.
[84] *ZHMGZYSL, Xubian*, 1, 685.    [85] *HYQJJ*, I, 415.

for a signature on the document. Bao Wenyue greeted him cordially, but claimed that he had no authority to act on such an important issue and that Takahashi would have to wait for He Yingqin's return.[86] Takahashi searched for another officer or diplomat who might sign, but came up empty-handed. Huang Fu had already left north China, and the government had disbanded the BPAC in late 1933. This meant He Yingqin was the only official who carried sufficient rank and authority to sign such a document, and he showed no sign of a prompt return to Beiping. Takahashi made threats, then offered to drop some of the demands, all to no avail.[87]

He Yingqin's absence from Beiping allowed him to avoid signing the document over the Hebei Incident, but negotiations continued over the North Chaha'er Incident. Doihara Kenji presented the Chinese with a set of demands that included an apology from and punishment for Chaha'er governor Song Zheyuan, removal of Song's Twenty-Ninth Corps from Chaha'er, elimination of all "anti-Japanese organs," and an extension of the demilitarized zone. From Nanjing, He Yingqin arranged for the transfer of Song Zheyuan to another command and the removal of the Twenty-Ninth Corps, and Qin Dechun, chief of civil affairs bureau and a BMAC committee member, took over as acting governor of Chaha'er.[88] Before his departure, He Yingqin and Qin Dechun had discussed the situation and the two kept in constant communication via telegram after He arrived in Nanjing. He directed Qin to follow the same process He Yingqin had used in negotiations over the Hebei Incident, essentially accepting all demands but avoiding a written agreement. The BMAC could handle issues such as an apology or moving troops and the central government could deal with the removal of political offices, all of which must appear as though the Chinese side had made the changes of its own accord. He Yingqin understood that the tactic he had used to avoid signing a document over the Hebei Incident would not work again, so he devised a new strategy for Qin Dechun in dealing with the North Chaha'er Incident. He Yingqin instructed Qin not to sign a formal written agreement or pact, but he suggested that a personal reply in writing would do no harm. If the Japanese insisted on putting something in writing, then Qin should use a common letter (*putong xinhan*) rather than a formal document. Finally, He Yingqin told Qin not to address all demands in a single letter, but rather to use two different letters to separate the demands so that they would not all appear in a single document.[89] Two days later, Qin Dechun

[86] *ZHMGZYSL*, *Xubian*, 1, 686.
[87] He Yingqin, "Hebei shibian zhong juewu suowei 'Hemei xieding,'" 130.
[88] *HYQJJ*, I, 417–18; *ZHMGZYSL*, *Xubian*, 1, 687–88.     [89] *HYQJJ*, I, 430–31.

did just as instructed, accepting all Japanese demands on June 27 in two separate, personal letters addressed to Doihara Kenji.[90]

The "common-letter formula" appeared to satisfy the Japanese insistence on a written agreement without committing the Chinese government to anything that others might construe as a treaty or formal agreement. If this had worked in the case of the North Chaha'er Incident, then why not follow the same formula to put the Hebei Incident to rest? After discussions with Wang Jingwei and others, the Executive Yuan authorized He Yingqin to send a written message to General Umezu Yoshijiro, commander of the Japanese China Garrison Army. The brief, typewritten message, dated July 6, 1935, included no signature or official stamp, and simply stated "Notice is hereby given that all matters raised by Chief of Staff Sakai on June 9 have been agreed to and will be voluntarily carried out."[91] Informed of the content, Chiang Kai-shek asked for revisions, but his request came too late.[92] These written communications served as the basis for what many later described as the He–Umezu (*Hemei xieding*) and Qin–Doihara (*Qintu xieding*) Agreements of 1935.

Thereafter He Yingqin argued that these two "so-called agreements" never existed, but the Chinese had clearly acceded to Japanese demands for a second time in two years. Moreover, He Yingqin had played a central role arranging them, in the case of 1935 over Chiang Kai-shek's objections. He did so because he believed these agreements preserved Chinese authority in Beiping and Tianjin, put off a larger military conflict with Japan, and provided time for the Nationalists to continue their pursuit of internal unity and military development. At the time, this view put him in the minority and, in the wake of the Tanggu Truce and the so-called He–Umezu and Qin–Doihara agreements, the policy of "internal pacification before external resistance" grew increasingly unpopular.[93] Chiang Kai-shek, Huang Fu, Wang Jingwei, and He Yingqin all found themselves targets of critics, some of whom branded them as "pro-Japanese" for their alleged willingness to accommodate the Japanese demands at the expense of territory in northern and northeastern China. In describing the "Northern China Incident of 1935" in particular, Mao Zedong and the CCP criticized the He–Umezu Agreement in which "China forfeited much of her sovereignty in the provinces of Hopei and Chahar [*sic*]."[94]

[90] *HYQJJ*, I, 431–32.

[91] He Yingqin, "Hebei shibian zhong juewu suowei 'Hemei xieding,'" 131.

[92] *ZHMGZYSL, Xubian*, 1, 692–93.     [93] Coble, *Facing Japan*, 211–215.

[94] Mao Tse-tung [Zedong], "Tasks of the Chinese Communist Party in the Period of Resistance to Japan," in *The Selected Works of Mao Tse-tung*, 4 vols. (Beijing: Foreign Languages Press, 1961), vol. I, 276 n. 1.

Ironically, while some criticized He Yingqin as "pro-Japan" for his willingness to yield to Japanese demands, others claim that some Japanese viewed him as an obstacle to their goals and tried twice to assassinate him in 1935.[95]

## The Xi'an Incident

With the situation in north China temporarily calm, He Yingqin spent most of 1936 addressing the same problems and issues that had occupied him since the start of the decade: improving the Nationalist military, promoting internal unity behind Chiang Kai-shek's policies, and eliminating regional rivals to Nanjing's authority. Japanese actions in the north had distracted the Nationalist leadership from these core goals, and much work remained in order to prepare for a future war with Japan. At a political work conference in April, He Yingqin gave a speech that highlighted the weaknesses that still plagued the Nationalist army and pointed out ways to address these problems. The extensive list of areas in which he saw a need for improvement included material concerns, such as the lack of preparations for war, failure to care for weapons and equipment, and poor training. It also touched on issues such as the general lack of revolutionary zeal, poor discipline, and weak adherence to central authority. All of these areas required strengthening and improvement through more diligent work, greater discipline, closer attention to individual responsibilities, and stronger obedience to central authority. His remarks left no room to doubt his conviction that the Chinese military in its present shape could not stand up to the Japanese Imperial Army in a war of resistance. They also reaffirmed his commitment to the policy of "internal pacification before external resistance," despite its growing unpopularity.[96]

After He Yingqin traveled north to take on new duties as chair of the BMAC, Chiang Kai-shek had continued the campaigns against the CCP base in Jiangxi. Beginning in the fall of 1933, he employed a blockhouse strategy, building thousands of fortified pillboxes in ever-tightening rings, designed to isolate the CCP base and limit the movements of the Red Army. Changes in CCP defensive strategy, favoring defense of territory over mobility, also contributed to a more successful outcome from

[95] Wu Tong, "Rijun mouci He Yingqin" [The Japanese Army's Plot to Assassinate He Yingqin], *Chuban cankao*, 2 (2006), 23–25; Liu Jianming, "Rijun yinsha He Yingqin de qianqian houhou" [The Whole Story of the Japanese Army's Secret Plan to Assassinate He Yingqin], *Wenshi chunqiu*, 3 (2001), 66–67.
[96] *HYQJJ*, I, 473.

the Nationalist perspective. In October 1934, Mao Zedong and approximately 85,000 CCP members broke through the blockade, entering southeastern Hunan and beginning the Long March, which took them on a 6,000-mile trek to a new base area in rural Shaanxi province. In addition to continuing experiments with land reform and rebuilding its military forces, CCP leaders also made contact with Nationalist commanders Zhang Xueliang and Yang Hucheng, both of whom expressed a desire to convince Chiang Kai-shek to abandon his campaigns against the communists and adopt a policy of military resistance to Japanese aggression in north China. In December 1936, Chiang traveled to Xi'an to check on Zhang and to supervise another campaign against the CCP base.[97]

The news that came out of Xi'an on December 12 struck like a thunderclap. Zhang Xueliang, commander in charge of "bandit suppression" in Hebei, Henan, and Anhui, and Yang Hucheng, commander of the Xi'an pacification force, had detained Chiang Kai-shek at Xi'an. They sent a telegram to Nanjing with series of demands that included the adoption of a policy of active resistance against Japan, an end to the civil war against the CCP, a reorganization of the Nationalist government, and the release of political prisoners.[98] By afternoon, He Yingqin had learned of Zhang and Yang's telegram and immediately contacted Nationalist officials at Luoyang, 233 miles to the east of Xi'an, attempting to get additional details on the situation. Just before midnight, he attended a joint meeting of the standing committee of the GMD Central Executive Council and the government's Central Political Council, at which top officials of the army, party, and government discussed how to deal with this crisis. After hours of heated exchanges, the group agreed on a few preliminary actions to establish effective leadership in Chiang's absence. First, Kong Xiangxi, Chiang's brother-in-law and vice-president of the Executive Yuan, would assume the acting presidency of that body. They also agreed to reorganize the Military Affairs Commission with five members, including He Yingqin, under the authority of vice-chair Feng Yuxiang. Finally, already anticipating the need for a military campaign against Xi'an, the group appointed He Yingqin to direct all military operations. Feng Yuxiang briefly disputed the decision to give He Yingqin control of

[97] S. C. M. Paine, *The Wars for Asia 1911–1949* (Cambridge: Cambridge University Press, 2012), 74; Wei, *Counterrevolution in China*, 157–60; Taylor, *Generalissimo*, 114; Alexander V. Pantsov with Steven Levine, *Mao: The Real Story* (New York: Simon & Schuster, 2012), 275–87.

[98] He Yingqin shangjiang jiuwu shouyan congshu bianji weiyuanhui, *Xi'an shibian de chuli yu shanhou* [The Handling and Aftermath of the Xi'an Incident] (hereafter *XSBCLSH*) (Taipei: Liming wenhua shiye youxian gongsi, 1984), 26.

the military campaign, believing that it should fall to himself as head of the MAC, but did not press the issue.[99]

The next morning Kong Xiangxi and Song Meiling arrived from Shanghai and met with He Yingqin for a report on the situation. From the outset, Kong and Song stressed the need for a negotiated settlement to this incident, fearing that a military conflict between Nanjing and Xi'an would result in Chiang's death. Song Meiling in particular urged Nanjing's leaders to hear Zhang Xueliang out and consider his demands, some of which she argued might have legitimacy.[100] This essentially drew a line between those who favored negotiations with Zhang and Yang to resolve the crisis, the "Peace Faction" (*zhuhepai*), and those who believed that the situation required military action, the "Punitive Faction" (*taofapai*). A number of authors who have written about the Xi'an Incident have identified Song Meiling and He Yingqin as the leaders of these two factions, respectively, and pointed to some sharp exchanges between them in the early days of the crisis. Wu Tien-wei claimed that He Yingqin infuriated Song Meiling with his insistence on a military campaign against Xi'an and his alleged remarks that as a woman she had no business interfering in affairs of state.[101] In her memoir of the Xi'an Incident, Song described the "unhealthy obsession on the part of leading military officers who felt it was their inexorable duty to mobilize the military machine forthwith and launch an immediate punitive expedition to attack Sian [sic]."[102] She did not attribute this "obsession" to a specific individual, but many have argued that she was referring to He Yingqin.[103] Rumors began to circulate in Nanjing, which some attribute to Song Meiling, that He Yingqin had pushed hard for a military campaign and aerial bombing of Xi'an because he hoped it would result in Chiang's death and create an opportunity for He Yingqin to take his place as paramount leader of the Nanjing regime.[104] Mao Zedong also embraced this view, describing He Yingqin as "pro-Japanese" and claiming that he "planned

---

[99] *HYQJJ*, I, 493; *XSBCLSH*, 34–35; Tien-wei Wu, *The Sian Incident: A Pivotal Turning Point in Modern Chinese History* (Ann Arbor: Center for Chinese Studies, University of Michigan, 1976), 89; Li Zhongming, "JiuJiang haishi haiJiang? He Yingqin zai xi'an shibian zhong" [To Save Chiang or Harm Chiang? He Yingqin in the Xi'an Incident], *Wenshi jinghua*, 2 (1997), 12–13.

[100] Mayling Soong Chiang, *Sian: A Coup d'Etat* (Shanghai: China Publishing Company, 1937), 5–6.

[101] Tien-Wei Wu, *The Sian Incident*, 90–91.

[102] Mayling Soong Chiang, *Sian: A Coup d'Etat*, 5.

[103] Taylor, *Generalissimo*, 130–32; Li Zhongming, "JiuJiang haishi haiJiang?," 13.

[104] Zuo Shuangwen, "Xi'an shibian hou de nanjing taofapai: yi Dai Jitao, He Yingqin wei zhongxin de zai tansuo" [The Nanjing "Punitive Faction" After the Xi'an Incident: A Reexamination Centering on Dai Jitao and He Yingqin], *Jindai zhongguo yanjiu*, 6 (2006), 67.

to kill Chiang Kai-shek by bombing Sian [*sic*], in order to take over Chiang's position."[105] This later appeared in his *Selected Works*, which made it a standard interpretation in the People's Republic for decades. Such accusations spread widely and found their way into numerous Western accounts of the Xi'an Incident.[106]

He Yingqin no doubt felt tremendous pressure to take decisive action against Zhang and Yang in the first days of Chiang's detention, since the general mood of the military and public favored an attack. On December 13, General Hu Zongnan, a former student of both Chiang and He at the Whampoa Military Academy, sent a message to He Yingqin on behalf of 178 other officers requesting authorization to attack Xi'an. Liu Zhi and forty-one other officers sent a similar message, and the newspaper *Zhongyang ribao* carried an editorial calling for strong military action.[107] Though consistently identified as one of the leading members of the Punitive Faction during the Xi'an Incident, from the start He Yingqin advocated a combination of military pressure and negotiations to secure Chiang's release. As Hu Zongnan, Liu Zhi, and others pressed him to order an attack, he sent a message to unit commanders who remained loyal to Nanjing in which he outlined a careful and measured response. Insisting on the need for unity and calm, he argued against rash and emotional responses to the situation, warning against both hasty attacks and rushing into negotiations with Zhang and Yang. Rather, he planned to deploy loyal military forces against Xi'an before Zhang and Yang could put their own limited military forces in place to defend themselves. Once central army units had applied sufficient military pressure, He Yingqin believed that other figures from the party and government could open negotiations from a position of strength. Rather than advocating an immediate attack, as Song Meiling believed, He Yingqin ordered his commanders to prepare for action, but to wait and see how the situation developed. This combination of military pressure and negotiations, he believed, would secure Chiang's release.[108]

---

[105] Mao Zedong, "Statement on Chiang Kai-shek's Statement," in *Selected Works*, I, 258 n. 5.

[106] Fenby, *Generalissimo*, 284; Sterling Seagrave, *The Soong Dynasty* (New York: Harper & Row, 1985), 351; Donald G. Gillin, "Problems of Centralization in Republican China: The Case of Ch'en Ch'eng and the Kuomintang," *Journal of Asian Studies*, 29, 4 (August 1970), 841; Laura Tyson Li, *Madame Chiang Kai-shek: China's Eternal First Lady* (New York: Atlantic Monthly Press, 2006), 123.

[107] *XSBCLSH*, 55–57; Chen Jianxing and Qin Chengjie, "Lun xi'an shibian zhong He Yingqin de zhuzhan yitu" [On He Yingqin's Intentions in Advocating Military Action in the Xi'an Incident], *Huanghe keji daxue xuebao*, 10, 1 (January 2008), 51.

[108] *HYQJJ*, I, 496–98; Yang Huanpeng and Wang Runhu, "Xi'an shibian qijian He Yingqin 'wuli taofa' celue jianxi" [A Brief Analysis of He Yingqin's "Punitive Expedition" Strategy in the Xi'an Incident], *Xibei di'er minzu xueyuan xuebao*, 5, 83 (2008), 86.

Accordingly, He Yingqin first ordered reliable forces to take control of Tongguan, the strategic pass between the Qin Mountains and the Yellow River, which gives access to Xi'an from the east, and alerted air force units at Luoyang to prepare for aerial attacks. Nearly all of Zhang's and Yang's forces had joined in the revolt, but some units under their command had not. This included an artillery unit near Luoyang, which might have threatened the Nationalist air base there.[109] He Yingqin's next concern revolved around regional commanders in north China who had opposed Chiang in the past and might lend their support to Zhang and Yang. A number of these regional commanders sent messages to Nanjing declaring their support for the central government, but in reality most of them preferred to wait and see how things developed before committing to one side.[110] At least it seemed that none had immediately thrown in their lot with Zhang and Yang. Some in Nanjing even believed that the government might convince some regional commanders to take a positive role in rescuing Chiang. President of the Control Yuan Yu Youren put forward a plan to invite Yan Xishan to serve as a mediator between Xi'an and Nanjing, with the provision that Zhang and Yang allow Chiang to travel to Taiyuan and remain with Yan during the talks. He Yingqin supported this idea, and he sent Huang Shaohong to Taiyuan to make contact with Yan Xishan. He also dispatched his brother He Jiwu to Jinan to meet with Shandong commander Han Fuju to shore up his support. The plan to have Yan mediate never came to fruition as Zhang rejected the idea, but He Yingqin's support for it contradicts claims that he pushed for military action in order to kill Chiang and replace him.[111]

Nanjing authorities felt keen pressure to resolve the crisis quickly before Zhang and Yang picked up more support, perhaps from the CCP. Although Zhou Enlai and the Chinese communists played a significant role in the Xi'an Incident, He Yingqin and others in Nanjing did not fully understand this until December 19 when the CCP revealed some of its correspondence with Zhang and Yang.[112] In fact, they did not know that Chiang Kai-shek had been in secret talks with CCP leaders about a united front agreement for some time prior to his kidnapping. Negotiations between Zhou Enlai and Zhang Qun had produced a draft agreement that only needed final approval from Mao and Chiang. When CCP leaders learned that Zhang and Yang had detained Chiang, they followed Moscow's directive to find a peaceful solution. Moscow feared that, if Zhang and Yang killed Chiang, He Yingqin might step in and

[109] *HYQJJ*, I, 505–06; Mayling Soong Chiang, *Sian: A Coup d'Etat*, 7.
[110] *HYQJJ*, I, 500–02; Tien-wei Wu, *The Sian Incident*, 93.
[111] Chen and Qin, "Lun xi'an shibian zhong He Yingqin de zhuzhan yitu," 52; Yang and Wang, "Xi'an shibian qijian He Yingqin 'wuli taofa' celue jianxi," 87.
[112] *XSBCLSH*, 63–64.

lead the Nanjing government into an alliance with Japan. Zhou Enlai met with Zhang and Yang and began discussions directly with Chiang on the topic of a united front between the CCP and the Nationalists.[113]

After making contact with Chiang through old advisor and family friend W. H. Donald, and ascertaining that he had come to no harm, Nanjing authorities took more formal steps to apply military pressure against Zhang and Yang. On December 16, the GMD Central Committee appointed He Yingqin commander of a Punitive Expeditionary Force and authorized a military campaign against Xi'an. He Yingqin dispatched several divisions to the west via rail, ordered air force planes to fly over Xi'an proper, and authorized bombing of locations to its east, including Weinan, Huaxian, and Huayang counties and the train station at Chishui. The next day he appointed Liu Zhi and Gu Zhutong as commanders of the Eastern and Western Route Group Armies (*dong/xi lu jituan jun*), respectively, which would surround Xi'an and prevent Zhang and Yang from spiriting Chiang Kai-shek off to another location.[114] Such signs of intent to attack Xi'an added to the sense of urgency on the part of Zhang Xueliang and Zhou Enlai to negotiate an end to the incident. Zhang Xueliang sent a telelgram directly to He Yingqin asking him to refrain from military action, pointing out that his own forces had not advanced against those of the government. Since He Yingqin had already sent troops to surround Xi'an and had ordered bombing strikes, "Who is it," Zhang asked, "who is initiating civil war?" He urged He Yingqin to pull his forces back to the east of Lintong in return for Zhang's promise not to advance his troops from their current positions. He Yingqin rejected the offer.[115]

From the start of the Xi'an Incident, He Yingqin faced a dilemma over how to respond to the crisis. On one hand, he felt considerable pressure from central army officers to take aggressive action. In fact, those who supported the Punitive Faction outnumbered those identified with the Peace Faction by a substantial margin and were calling loudly for a military operation. If he did not respond promptly with military force, he risked incurring the anger of numerous central army officers who

[113] Taylor, *Generalissimo*, 125–30.
[114] *HYQJJ*, I, 508–09; *XSBCLSH*, 73; Yang and Wang, "Xi'an shibian qijian He Yingqin 'wuli taofa' celue jianxi," 86; Chen Jiuru, "He Yingqin chubing xi'an de dongyin guanjian" [An Opinion on He Yingqin's Motives for Sending Troops Against Xi'an], *Lishi jiaoxue wenti*, 1 (1999), 34.
[115] *HYQJJ*, I, 509–12; Xiong Zongren, "Xi'an shibian yanjiu zhong de zhongda queshi: lun He Yingqin zhu 'taofa' zhi dongji ji 'qinripai' wenti" [An Important Missing Part in Research on the Xi'an Incident: On the Questions of He Yingqin's Motivations for Advocating "Punitive Action" and the "Pro-Japan Faction"], *Guizhou shehui kexue*, 220, 4 (April 2008), 120.

might accuse him of sympathizing with Zhang Xueliang and even launch attacks on their own. On the other hand, He Yingqin had to worry about provoking the Japanese, who strongly opposed any change in Nanjing's foreign policy with regard to Japan. If he delayed and negotiated with Zhang and Yang, he risked antagonizing the Japanese military, which might begin another set of aggressive actions in north China.[116]

Perhaps fortunately, after the initial bombing of targets to the east of Xi'an, Chiang Kai-shek managed to send word to He Yingqin to postpone any planned attack. Zhang Xueliang had detained several members of Chiang's staff, including Jiang Dingwen, whom he allowed to meet with Chiang Kai-shek before sending him back to the capital. Jiang left Xi'an and flew to Luoyang where he telephoned Nanjing with the news that he carried a handwritten order from Chiang to delay all military action against Xi'an for three days. When He Yingqin first learned of this order he refused to accept it, concerned that Chiang might have written it under duress. Only when Jiang Dingwen arrived in Nanjing on December 18, presented the handwritten *shouling* – personal directive – with Chiang's signature, and vouched for its authenticity did He Yingqin acknowledge its validity. The message directed He to postpone any attacks until Saturday (December 19), by which time Chiang indicated that he might return to Nanjing.[117] Song Meiling fumed over "some government officials" who refused to accept Chiang's written orders, but as soon as He Yingqin confirmed the authenticity of the order he complied immediately, ordering all frontline forces to stay put and halting all bombing around Xi'an.[118] Knowing that he must keep the threat of military force alive, He Yingqin's orders made it clear that, if Chiang Kai-shek did not secure his release and safe return to Nanjing by December 19, the original plan for a punitive military campaign would go forward.[119]

Meanwhile, Zhang Xueliang sent another telegram to Nanjing, this time inviting Chiang's brother-in-law and former minister of finance Song Ziwen to Xi'an to discuss the situation. He Yingqin did not support this proposal to send a private citizen to conduct the negotiations, but he did nothing to block the move once it won the support of other leading officials. He went along with the plan and even extended the bombing

---

[116] Yang and Wang, "Xi'an shibian qijian He Yingqin 'wuli taofa' celue jianxi," 86.

[117] *HYQJJ*, I, 513–14.

[118] Mayling Soong Chiang, *Sian: A Coup d'Etat*, 22. Curiously, though she refers to countless individuals on both sides of the Xi'an Incident by name and even courtesy names (she refers to Zhang Xueliang as "Han Ching"), in her memoir she never uses He Yingqin's name. The text refers only to his title, the "minister of war." This is an indication of the animosity Song Meiling bore against He Yingqin.

[119] *HYQJJ*, I, 514; Xiong Zongren, "Xi'an shibian yanjiu zhong de zhongda queshi," 119–20.

pause to allow the negotiations to continue beyond December 19.[120]
The ensuing days saw a series of visitors to Xi'an, including Song Ziwen,
Kong Xiangxi, Song Meiling, W. H. Donald, and Dai Li, to negotiate for
Chiang's release. As the discussion between Zhang, Chiang, Zhou
Enlai, and others continued in Xi'an, the Nanjing government publicly
announced details of a plan for an attack on Xi'an from both east and
west.[121] Rather than being the leader of the Punitive Faction which was
demanding military action, it would be more accurate to say that He
Yingqin remained true to his plan for a two-sided approach to the problem. He held off on military action in order to allow the two sides to work
out a solution, keeping troops ready for action at any time but allowing
the efforts at personal diplomacy time to work. This combination of CCP
influence, military pressure, and personal diplomacy eventually produced
a settlement. Chiang refused to agree to anything under duress, but discussions with Zhou Enlai produced a general agreement on the basic
principles of the earlier draft agreement. On December 24, Jiang Dingwen sent He Yingqin a telegram informing him that Zhang Xueliang
had agreed to release Chiang Kai-shek. Shortly thereafter, Chiang himself sent a message ordering He to withdraw the forces deployed against
Xi'an. Reluctant to do so until Chiang arrived safely in Nanjing, He
Yingqin ordered his forces to pull back 1,000 meters from their current
positions in order to avoid unintentional clashes, but to remain ready in
the event that things went awry.[122] By the early evening of Christmas
day, word of Chiang's return to the capital had spread across China.

In recent years, He Yingqin's role in the Xi'an Incident has garnered
the interest of a number of historians in the People's Republic of China,
who have closely examined his actions during this crisis. They reject the
view commonly associated with Song Meiling that He Yingqin sought
to bring about Chiang Kai-shek's death in order to take his place in the
Nanjing regime, pointing to several pieces of evidence that contradict
this theory. First, if He Yingqin had truly wanted to kill Chiang, he
could easily have ordered a military attack on Xi'an that would have
garnered significant support from the military and public. He Yingqin
deployed troops to surround Xi'an, but never ordered an attack. He sent
air force planes over Xi'an, but bombed only to the east of the city, far
from Chiang's location. Second, He Yingqin supported the attempt to
use Yan Xishan as a mediator and have Chiang transferred to Taiyuan
and out of harm's way. He also agreed to send a telegram to Wang

---

[120] *HYQJJ*, I, 515–16; *XSBCLSH*, 95; Chen and Qin, "Lun xi'an shibian zhong He
Yingqin de zhuzhan yitu," 52.
[121] *HYQJJ*, I, 523; *XSBCLSH*, 84–85.    [122] *HYQJJ*, I, 527.

Jingwei, a more senior political figure who had greater seniority within the GMD and the government than He Yingqin, asking Wang to return to China from Europe in order to lend stability to the Nanjing government. Neither action supports the argument that He Yingqin sought to kill or replace Chiang. Finally, after his release, Chiang Kai-shek continued to work closely with He Yingqin and made no move to punish him or remove him from his position as minister of military administration. To the contrary, he continued to place great trust in He Yingqin and even designated him to speak on his behalf at a mass rally to welcome Chiang back to Nanjing on December 27.[123] Contrary to the enduring myth that He Yingqin had tried to take advantage of the Xi'an Incident to take Chiang's place, the reality was that both He and Chiang understood that they needed each other and the events at Xi'an did nothing to erode the trust and strong relationship between them.

He Yingqin's appointment as minister of military administration in 1930 marked a change in the nature of his work. He would have opportunities to command troops in the future, but for most of the 1930s he concentrated on using the military to achieve Chiang Kai-shek's political and diplomatic objectives. Prior to 1930, he had commanded regiments, divisions, corps, and group armies to help Chiang establish a new government and defend it against internal opponents. His contributions to the military victories during this period had been clear and unequivocal. From 1930 until the start of the Sino-Japanese War in 1937, he faced difficult challenges in rooting out the CCP from Jiangxi, holding the Japanese military at bay in north China, and dealing with the crisis of Chiang's kidnapping at the hands of his own generals. His work on these issues left a more ambiguous record and gave his detractors ample opportunity to criticize his work. From his own perspective, he had taken a careful and correct approach in dealing with the Red Army in Jiangxi, preserved Chinese authority in the key cities of Beiping and Tianjin against the predatory Japanese military, and contributed to the

---

[123] See Chen Jiuru, "He Yingqin chubing xi'an de dongyin guanjian"; Zuo Shuangwen, "Xi'an shibian hou de Nanjing taofapai"; Yang and Wang, "Xi'an shibian qijian He Yingqin 'wuli taofa' celue jianxi"; Xiong Zongren, "Xi'an shibian zhong de He Yingqin zhuzhan dongji zhi bianxi: dui 'qujiang er daizhi' lun de zhiyi" [An Analysis of He Yingqin's Motives for Advocating Military Action During the Xi'an Incident: Calling into Question the Theory that He Sought to Replace Chiang], *Junshi lishi*, 4 (1993), 38–43; Xiong Zongren, "Xi'an shibian yanjiu zhong de zhongda queshi"; Li Zhongming, "He Yingqin yu xi'an shibian" [He Yingqin and the Xi'an Incident], *Lishi jiaoxue*, 2 (1994), 8–11; and Chen and Qin, "Lun xi'an shibian zhong He Yingqin de zhuzhuan yitu." T'ien-wei Wu wrote that during the negotiations for Chiang's release Zhang Xueliang and Chiang Kai-shek discussed replacing He Yingqin as minister of military affairs, with Chiang considering Chen Cheng for the position. Chiang did appoint Chen to replace He Yingqin, but not until 1944.

successful peaceful resolution of the crisis at Xi'an. Regardless, in other circles these events planted the seeds of accusations that He Yingqin had failed miserably in the early campaigns against the Red Army, committed tacit recognition of Japan's control over Manchuria and parts of north China, and contemplated murdering Chiang Kai-shek during the Xi'an Incident. He had little time to ponder these developments as the greatest challenges of his career lay just ahead.

# 7    "A force for a hundred-year war of resistance"

In January 1942, Chiang Kai-shek sent a *shouling* to He Yingqin on the subject of conscription. By this point, five years into the war, Nationalist officials had encountered significant problems recruiting and training new soldiers, and Chiang had heard reports that conscription officials sometimes bound recruits with ropes or otherwise abused them on their way to training centers. Chiang demanded that He Yingqin do something to improve conscription and insisted that any official guilty of such abusive practices should face the same punishment as a military officer who disobeyed direct orders. At the very least, Chiang declared, the Conscription Bureau, which operated under the Ministry of Military Administration, should transfer officials who did not follow the rules and regulations of the conscription policy and get them away from new recruits.[1] Chiang's directive added to He Yingqin's sense of urgency in resolving these problems, but he had long known about them and had already devoted significant time and effort to improving conscription work.

When China and Japan went to war in the summer of 1937, He Yingqin had a long list of responsibilities as he prepared for a war of undetermined length against a formidable and determined enemy. While he had a voice in guiding many aspects of the war including strategy, operations, and supply, his most important responsibilities revolved around conscription and training of new soldiers. Given the eventual Chinese strategy of protracted war, designed to avoid a rapid defeat, disperse Japanese forces, and drain enemy resources through a prolonged conflict, conscription played a critical part in the war effort. Indeed, He Yingqin repeatedly stated his view that the key question that would determine victory or defeat for the Nationalists would be whether China could procure a sufficient number of men to serve over the course of a brutal war of long duration. His work on wartime conscription not only had a strong impact on the war, but also had a profound influence on future assessments of

---

[1] *SLGB*, XLVIII, January 17, 1942, 104.

both the Nationalist military and He Yingqin. The enormous task of conscripting, training, and supplying new troops eventually presented numerous problems for the Nationalists, many of which lay beyond He Yingqin's control. Regardless, as these conscription problems grew more apparent to observers, they exposed him to criticism both in China and abroad and for many came to represent the shortcomings of both He Yingqin and the Nationalist regime as a whole.

## Preparing for war

As Chinese and Japanese forces clashed at Wanping in July 1937, He Yingqin wrapped up a conference to reorganize the military forces in Sichuan and Xikang. He had completed a draft plan to reorganize the armies and streamline the budget and expenses, and had laid out a timetable for the changes, when Chiang Kai-shek sent him an urgent telegram alerting him to the clash and ordering him back to Nanjing. He Yingqin left immediately and arrived in the capital on the evening of July 10 to begin mobilizing the nation for war.[2] He Yingqin and Chiang Kai-shek had worked for several years to avoid a full-scale military conflict against the Japanese Imperial Army, pursuing the policy of "internal pacification before external resistance" for most of the decade. For various reasons they now decided to stand firm in north China. Jay Taylor has shown that even before the Xi'an Incident Chiang was seriously considering a policy of accommodation with the CCP and greater resistance to Japanese aggression. After his release, he allocated funds for the CCP, pushed for new forms of cooperation between Nationalist and communist military forces, and halted the campaigns against the Red Army.[3] Chiang's German advisor Alexander von Faulkenhausen offered optimistic assessments of China's capabilities in a larger Sino-Japanese conflict, which might also have influenced Chiang to adjust his view.[4] Most of all, Chiang believed that the Chinese public had reached the limit of its willingness to accept Japanese territorial encroachments and that, if he lost control of Beiping or Tianjin, he could not expect continued popular support. Moreover, from a strategic perspective the loss of sections of the Ping–Han railroad to the Japanese would endanger large parts of north

---

[2] *ZHMGZYSL*, di'er bian, *Zuozhan jingguo*, 4 vols. (Taipei: Zhongguo guomindang zhongyang weiyuanhui dangshi weiyuanhui) 2, 35–36; *HYQJJ*, I, 567–70.

[3] Taylor, *Generalissimo*, 142–44.

[4] Donald Sutton, "German Advice and Residual Warlordism in the Nanking Decade: Influences on Nationalist Military Training and Strategy," *China Quarterly*, 9, 91 (September 1982), 401.

China. As Marjorie Dryburgh put it, in mid 1937 Chiang had to either "resist [the Japanese] or lose Hebei–Chaha'er altogether."[5]

As the fighting erupted in Hebei, Chiang sent central army units to north China to support local forces and declared a policy of all-out resistance. Nationalist officials debated how to handle the crisis, but Chiang Kai-shek made clear his intention to bolster the Nationalist position in north China. Even as he held a series of meetings to discuss the situation in mid July at the Lushan mountain retreat in Jiangxi, Chiang sent a steady stream of orders to He Yingqin directing him to prepare for an active defense of north China. These included sending anti-aircraft artillery to Baoding for use in various areas as needed, procuring 500,000 yuan for the construction of defensive fortifications in Hebei and Chaha'er, distributing 3 million rounds of ammunition to Song Zheyuan's Twenty-Ninth Corps, and preparing a military headquarters at Shijiazhuang, approximately 200 miles southwest of Beiping.[6]

He Yingqin clearly understood the change in Chiang's position with regard to Japan and promptly accepted the decision to stand firm in the face of Japanese aggression. Up to this point, He Yingqin had believed in the policy of "internal pacification before external resistance" and had arranged agreements with the Japanese in 1933 and 1935 to avoid war. In each case, he made it clear that maintaining control of Beiping and Tianjin was essential and that, if the Japanese attacked either city, China would have no choice but to engage in an all-out war of resistance. His earlier negotiations had preserved control over Beiping and Tianjin, but in 1937 fighting took place just miles from Beiping, and another negotiated settlement would undoubtedly require yielding control of all of Hebei. Unlike previous incidents in north China, this situation left little room for negotiation. Several Japanese diplomats and military officers contacted the Ministry of Military Administration requesting meetings with He Yingqin, undoubtedly hoping that he would help arrange yet another accommodation that would avoid a larger conflict. He refused all such requests save one. On July 19, he made an exception and agreed to meet with Japanese military attaché Kita Seiichi, whom He Yingqin had met while serving as chair of the BMAC. It is not clear why he accepted this meeting, but he listened as Kita expressed a desire to localize the incident and avoid a larger conflict. Why, Kita wanted to know, would the Chinese government not accept a negotiated settlement? He Yingqin dismissed the question and showed no inclination to negotiate or to accept Kita's view of the situation. Instead he told Kita that blame for

[5] Dryburgh, *North China and Japanese Expansion*, 148–49.
[6] *ZHMGZYSL, Zuozhan jingguo*, 2, 39, 44, 69.

the clash rested squarely with the Japanese military. Reminding him that the Chinese government had all along desired a peaceful resolution and had no intention of expanding the conflict, he told Kita that, since the Japanese had moved such a large infantry force into Hebei, the Chinese had no choice but to prepare for a war of self-defense and would not back down. If the Japanese genuinely desired peace, he stressed, then it was up to them to take steps to avoid war, not the Chinese government. If the Japanese removed the ground forces it had recently deployed in Hebei, the Chinese government might consider pulling its own forces back as well. At the end of the conversation, He Yingqin perhaps played to Japanese anti-communist sentiment by suggesting to Kita that a larger Sino-Japanese war would prove devastating for both countries and predicting that "the only winner in such an unfortunate event would be the Chinese Communist Party."[7] He Yingqin knew better than to take Kita's professions of a Japanese desire for peace at face value. Just a few months later in December 1937, Kita Seiichi would help create a North China Provisional Government under Wang Kemin, which collaborated with Japan and later joined Wang Jingwei's pro-Japan Nanjing government.[8]

Some authors have suggested that He Yingqin had a difficult time adjusting to the change from the earlier policy of accommodating the Japanese to preparing for a major conflict.[9] In fact, the new policy of resistance represented not so much a reversal as the realization that the long-anticipated time for war had finally arrived. Moreover, the evidence suggests that He Yingqin had carefully considered the situation and arrived at certain optimistic conclusions about China's chances for ultimate victory. In June 1937, just prior to the outbreak of hostilities at the Marco Polo Bridge, he met with Wu Xingye, an old friend and official in the Ministry of Communication. Wu later wrote about their conversation in which He Yingqin described his view of how China would deal with a military conflict with Japan. Referring to Sun Zi's well-known adage to "Know oneself, know one's enemy, in one hundred battles you will not know defeat" (*zhiyi zhibi, baizhan buyi*), He Yingqin acknowledged the strength of the modernized Japanese Imperial Army, which enjoyed superior firepower and a technological advantage. Yet he emphasized three factors that he believed would offset these Japanese advantages and eventually determine the outcome of such a war. First and foremost,

[7] *HYQJJ*, I, 571.

[8] T'ien-wei Wu, "Contending Political Forces During the War of Resistance," in James C. Hsiung and Steven I. Levine, *China's Bitter Victory: The War with Japan, 1937–1945* (Armonk, NY: M. E. Sharpe, 1992), 65.

[9] Li Yuan, *Jiang Jieshi he He Yingqin*, 150; Li Zhongming, *He Yingqin dazhuan*, 195.

he considered China's great territorial expanse and large population distinct advantages, clearly envisioning a strategy of protracted war in which the Japanese would find themselves bogged down in a war of attrition. Under these circumstances, China enjoyed greater manpower and a large territory over which to disperse the smaller Japanese force. Second, he pointed out that the Japanese had invaded China, which made it a just war and gave the Chinese the moral high ground in the conflict. As he had in earlier conflicts, He Yingqin valued morale and "spirit" among soldiers and civilians alike, and believed that this gave the Chinese a critical advantage in this kind of war of aggression. Finally, He Yingqin pointed out that in the future China could likely count on moral and material support from the international community, implying that Japan would have to go it alone for the duration of the conflict.[10] These factors led He Yingqin to believe that in a protracted war China would ultimately defeat Japan, both materially and spiritually. He repeated this basic message in numerous speeches and reports throughout the war.

In July and August, preparations and development of a general war plan continued at a furious pace. He Yingqin held nightly meetings in his office at the Ministry of Military Administration, conferring with senior officers on strategy, tactics, logistics, and other aspects of the war. On August 6, Chiang chaired a National Defense Council meeting at which he announced a general strategy of protracted war to an audience of leading military officers and political officials. He created five war zones in order to defend against possible Japanese operations in north China and along the coastline. He Yingqin assumed command of the Fourth War Zone, which encompassed Fujian and Guangdong, with responsibility for guarding against an attack on China's southeastern coast.[11] In the course of this meeting, He Yingqin discussed the military situation with Yan Xishan, commander of the Second War Zone, trading views on appropriate strategy and tactics. Yan agreed with He's view that the Japanese enjoyed a significant edge in terms of firepower and mobility, but also faced some serious disadvantages fighting in China. In order to achieve victory, Chinese forces had to find ways to offset this advantage in firepower by choosing terrain that made it difficult for the Japanese to employ their airpower, armored vehicles, and artillery effectively. If

---

[10]  He Yingqin's remarks to Wu are reproduced in Li Zhongming, "Zhanhe paihuaizhong gensui Jiang Zhongzheng weiyuanzhang zou: qiqi shibian qianhou de He Yingqin" [Following Chairman Chiang Kai-shek in Wavering Between War and Peace: He Yingqin Before and After the Marco Polo Bridge Incident], *Jindai zhongguo*, 1, 132 (August 1999), 41–42.

[11]  *HYQJJ*, I, 572–73.

caught in open areas in which the Japanese could apply their superior firepower, Chinese forces would not fare well. Both men agreed that protracted war provided the only reasonable long-term strategy, but also felt it important to engage in a potentially decisive battle at the outset. Because the Japanese underestimated the Chinese, He and Yan felt that the Nationalist military must demonstrate that it would not collapse in the face of the Japanese threat. As a result, they favored a strong stand in the initial fighting to show Chinese resolve, humble the enemy, and attract the attention of the wider world.[12]

Concerns about the unity of Chinese military forces tempered He Yingqin's optimism with regard to the Nationalist army's ability to deal with the Japanese. In the several years before the clash at Marco Polo Bridge, Chiang Kai-shek and He Yingqin had argued that the Chinese military had no chance of victory against the Japanese until it had achieved internal unity, referring specifically to the Chinese Communist Party and regional military forces. This had been a goal from the beginning, and He Yingqin had worked for years to ensure that regional commanders adhered to central authority, but it remained a concern. On August 9 he addressed the issue in a speech, warning that the Japanese would use "the trick of provocative rumors" to try to divide the Chinese people. The Japanese would use newspapers to spread stories that some areas were unstable in order to sow seeds of division between local areas and the central authorities, he argued, but the truth was that China was united under a single leadership and government. In order to survive this "time of national peril," he urged everyone to rally behind the central government and obey its orders.[13]

Leaders of the Nationalist government and military met in Nanjing on August 12 to reorganize the political and military structure, essentially combining the National Defense Council and the Central Political Council to create a Supreme National Defense Council (SNDC). This body, divided into five subordinate units, the Ministry of Military Orders, Ministry of Military Administration, Ministry of Military Training, Ministry of Political Affairs, and Department of the Navy, presided over the war effort throughout the conflict. As minister of military administration and chief of staff of the Military Affairs Commission (as of January 1938), He Yingqin had a hand in all aspects of the Chinese war effort. As such he took responsibility for a wide variety of issues relating to national defense, and the August 12 meeting produced a clear set of issues that would dominate He Yingqin's time in the initial stages of the war.[14]

---

[12] Li Zhongming, *He Yingqin dazhuan*, 198.    [13] *HYQJJ*, I, 573–74.

[14] He Yingqin's responsibilities in the initial phase of the war as discussed during the August 12 meeting are delineated in *HYQJJ*, I, 575–80.

At the top of his list of responsibilities lay the fundamental task of building and maintaining an armed force that would serve the Nationalist government in a protracted war of undetermined length. He placed greatest emphasis on the army, which stood at 182 divisions in 1937, yet he continued with plans to develop the air force. In order to produce enough officers and technical specialists, He Yingqin established additional training institutes for various branches of the army, such as infantry, engineers, cavalry, transport, and communications, all critical to the war effort. With regard to the air force, He Yingqin launched plans to create new branch campuses of the Central Air Force Academy, established in Hangzhou in 1931, and develop the existing branch academies at Luoyang, Nanchang, and Guangzhou. He had initially hoped to produce as many as 400 graduates per year to staff the air force, but the rigorous standards and demanding examinations meant that fewer than 250 men graduated per year. During the course of the war, He Yingqin would frequently point to the low educational level of the Chinese population as an impediment to building a modern, professional military.[15]

Among the more immediate tasks He Yingqin faced at the start of the war was to preside over a vast array of projects designed to strengthen China's infrastructure in support of its national defense needs. The SNDC eventually divided the nation into nine strategic regions, each of which required the construction of defensive fortifications, including updating and modernizing the defensive fortifications along the Yangzi River and China's eastern and southern coasts. Existing river and coastal installations at Nanjing, Zhenjiang, Jiangyin, Wusong, Fuzhou, and Xiamen dated back to the late Qing period and badly needed improvement. Since 1934, the Ministry of Military Administration had been updating these fortifications, replacing the guns and adding anti-aircraft artillery to some installations, but much work remained. Artillery pieces in these forts lacked adequate range and accuracy and suffered from a slow rate of fire, far behind the capabilities of the Japanese navy. With regard to air defense, at the start of the war the Nationalists had only six anti-aircraft companies, so He Yingqin planned to purchase anti-aircraft weaponry and to establish a school to train officers in the principles of air defense. He also called for a network of communications between large cities and the creation of numerous monitoring teams which would travel and supervise air defense in various locations. These teams would assist local officials with preparations for fighting fires, dealing with poison gas attacks, establishing warning systems, conducting air raid drills, creating refugee centers, constructing trenches, caves, and underground

[15] *HYQJJ*, I, 575–76.

shelters, and imposing blackouts on urban areas.[16] A final area of his responsibility involved developing war-related industry. Modern warfare required an industrial support base, which China had only recently begun to build. He Yingqin called for new facilities in Hunan, Jiangxi, and Shaanxi to increase China's production of steel, coal, and oil. He also called for increases in production in industrial chemicals, electricity, and telecommunications equipment.[17]

In planning for war with Japan, the Nationalists had long envisioned a protracted struggle and possible retreat to the interior in the event of a major conflict but, as He Yingqin helped prepare for a protracted war, it is unlikely that he anticipated the eight-year conflict that ensued. In the initial phase of the war, the Nationalists hoped to blunt the Japanese offensive with a strong stand in the east designed to demonstrate Chinese resolve to resist and then, if necessary, withdraw into the interior until the Japanese exhausted their resources or the threat of an attack from the Soviet Union forced them to withdraw from north China. This might prove costly, but both Chiang and He believed in the importance of taking the initiative and favored committing Nationalist forces to a major battle at the start of the war. As a part of this plan, Chiang Kai-shek decided to move the battle from north China to Shanghai, where he believed the Nationalists had a better chance against the Japanese, with the urban setting providing better cover against Japanese superior fire-power. He believed the Nationalists needed to make a stand at Shanghai in order to deny the Japanese a quick victory and demonstrate that further operations in China would come only at a significant cost. Some have criticized this decision, concluding that the Nationalists had little chance of defeating the Japanese, whose modern army and impressive firepower clearly outmatched the Chinese forces in training and technology, if not in numbers. Yang Tianshi argued that the horrific casualties suffered in the Shanghai campaign, perhaps as much as 60 percent of Chiang's central army, could have been avoided if Chiang had withdrawn Nationalist forces earlier and engaged in a protracted war from the very start of hostilities.[18] Others have claimed that He Yingqin did not agree with Chiang's decision to mount a defense at Shanghai, but dared not speak out for fear of incurring Chiang's wrath and thereby risking his position.[19]

---

[16] *HYQJJ*, I, 577–78.    [17] *HYQJJ*, I, 579–80.

[18] See Tianshi Yang, "Chiang Kai-shek and the Battles of Shanghai and Nanjing," in Peattie, Drea, and van de Ven, eds., *The Battle for China*, 152–54. See also Li Zongren's remarks in Tsung-jen Li, *Memoirs*, 425–26.

[19] Xiong Zongren, *He Yingqin: xuanwozhong de lishi*, I, 397–98; Li Zhongming, *He Yingqin dazhuan*, 200; Cheng and Zhang, *Jiang Jieshi he huangpu xi*, 266.

There is little evidence to support the latter view, which casts He Yingqin as a "yes man" who told Chiang only what he wanted to hear and attributes He's continued presence at the top of the Nationalist military to his willingness to keep quiet and always support Chiang's views. To accept this interpretation of He's position in the Nationalist military is to ignore his capabilities as a military officer and those occasions on which he opposed Chiang on important issues, as he had done in 1927 and 1935. A more logical argument is that He Yingqin and Chiang Kai-shek held similar perspectives on the appropriate strategy and tactics to employ in the war against Japan. It should be no surprise that these two men who had worked together so closely for more than a decade should have a common view of what the situation required. He Yingqin agreed with Chiang and believed that the Nationalists must make a strong stand at Shanghai, in part because his own experience as a combat commander in earlier campaigns dating back to the Eastern Expeditions of 1925 told him that speed, mobility, and the aggressive "Whampoa spirit" could help Nationalist forces overcome their disadvantages in firepower and mechanization. Looking back on important battles at Danshui, Mianhu, and Longtan, and in the Central Plains War, He Yingqin saw the value of bold action against the enemy in the initial phase of combat, even if it resulted in high casualties and did not produce an immediate victory. He took great pride in these battles, all of which came against numerically superior and better-equipped opponents. He Yingqin later claimed that the early battles, in which the "Whampoa spirit" of attacking aggressively despite unfavorable odds, served as the foundational experience which prepared Nationalist officers for the Sino-Japanese War.[20] Chiang Kai-shek also drew on the experiences of the Nationalist forces' early battles, stressing the importance of taking the initiative in battle and declaring that "spirit" would be more important than weapons.[21] In his analysis of the Sino-Japanese War, Hsi-sheng Ch'i argued that Chiang's early experiences had "conditioned him to think that any odds could be overcome with will power" and pointed out that during the war against Japan Chiang consistently recalled how his "small revolutionary army had defeated more numerous and better-armed warlord armies" in the Nationalists' early campaigns.[22]

[20] Liu Bingcui, *Gemingjun diyici dongzheng shizhanji fu: mianhu dajie wushi zhounian jinian tekan* [A Record of the Revolutionary Army's First Eastern Expedition with a Special Publication on the Fiftieth Anniversary of the Great Victory in the Battle at Mianhu] (Taipei: Wenhai chubanshe, 1981), 7.

[21] Wu Hsiang-hsiang, "Total Strategy Used by China and Some Major Engagements in the Sino-Japanese War of 1937–1945," in Paul K. T. Sih, ed., *Nationalist China During the Sino-Japanese War, 1937–1945* (Hicksville, NY: Exposition Press, 1977), 41.

[22] Ch'i, *Nationalist China at War*, 60.

The specific conditions of the larger Sino-Japanese conflict in 1937 also led He Yingqin to favor committing forces to a major battle at Shanghai. Looking back to the Japanese seizure of Manchuria several years earlier, he believed that the Chinese must demonstrate to the Japanese military that this attempt to take control of large parts of China south of the Great Wall would not be as easy as such efforts had been in the past. He Yingqin later wrote that the origins of the Marco Polo Bridge Incident of July 1937 lay in the Manchurian Incident of 1931, when the Japanese military "without losing a single soldier, and without firing a single shot" (*bufei yibing, buzhe yishi*) took control of three provinces of China.[23] In contrast, when the fighting spread to Shanghai in early 1932, Nationalist forces demonstrated an ability to resist Japanese firepower, which led some to believe that a similar feat might be possible in 1937.[24] He Yingqin believed that China could no longer put off a major military conflict with Japan and, unlike in 1931, Chinese forces had to demonstrate that further seizure of Chinese territory would be neither quick nor easy. The strong Nationalist defense at Shanghai, though tremendously costly, caught the Japanese unprepared and delivered this message in no uncertain terms. Despite the substantial casualties incurred in defending the lower Yangzi, He Yingqin subsequently pointed out the importance of the first phase of the war, from the August 1937 battle at Shanghai to the November 1938 loss of Wuhan, during which the Japanese planned to "destroy China's ability to wage war in three to six months." According to his view, the Nationalist stand in the Yangzi region had dashed this plan and subjected the Japanese to "losses far beyond expectations," which sowed "doubt and fear among Japanese soldiers and civilians alike."[25]

After the first phase of the war ended with the fall of Shanghai, Nanjing, and Wuhan, and the move of the government upriver to Chongqing, the Nationalist military leadership announced the start of a new phase of the war, which called for changes in strategy and tactics. He Yingqin helped articulate these changes with a report to the GMD Central Executive Committee in Chongqing in January 1939. While the first phase of the war had included strong defensive stands in areas in which the enemy had advantages in mechanization and firepower, the second phase of the war marked a change in which Nationalist forces had to shift

[23] He Yingqin, "Qiqi shibian yu banian kangzhan shilüe" [A Brief History of the Marco Polo Bridge Incident and the Eight-Year War of Resistance], *Yiwenzhi*, 166 (July 1979), 24.
[24] Donald Jordan describes the Nationalist action against the Japanese military at Shanghai in 1932 as China's "first modern victory": Jordan, *Trial by Fire*, 235–36.
[25] See He Yingqin's January 1939 remarks in "Jianding kangzhan bisheng jianguo bicheng de xinnian" [Have Faith that a Resolute War of Resistance Will Be Victorious and the Nation Will Succeed], in *HYQJJJCXJ*, 58–59.

focus to attacks on the enemy's many weak points. Rather than stand against the Japanese in defense of strategic areas or important cities, the Nationalists now planned to bog the enemy down in a prolonged war of attrition in an attempt to sap Japanese resources and will. In order to halt the enemy's western advance, He Yingqin argued, Chinese forces must "make occupied areas part of the battlefield" by organizing guerrilla attacks, thereby "turning the rear areas into the front lines."[26] In a protracted war in which the Nationalists would surely continue to suffer significant losses, their survival would depend upon a reliable supply of new recruits to replace losses at the front. He Yingqin's task, perhaps the most important of the entire war, was to ensure China's ability to procure enough soldiers to keep the war effort going for an undetermined period.

## Conscription and military service

In the nineteenth and early twentieth centuries, Chinese militaries had largely relied on volunteers, but many viewed this as hindering national unity and contributing to the rise of private military forces under regional commanders of the "era of warlords." From the earliest days of his military career, He Yingqin believed deeply in the need for a strong military to protect China against internal and external threats and to guarantee the continued existence of the nation. At the same time he believed that this called for a new kind of military which differed substantially from traditional forces. With the establishment of the Nanjing government in 1928, He Yingqin drew up a "Proposal to Change the Conscription System," which laid out a system of conscription that he believed would yield such a national military force.[27]

From He Yingqin's perspective, the old system of volunteers produced a military full of those who sought only a payment and joined simply to sustain their livelihood, with no thought for the larger good of the nation. Many of the volunteers procured through this system were local toughs or ne'er-do-wells who lacked discipline and had no understanding of the larger role of the military in Chinese society. This not only resulted in generally poor military forces but also contributed to the suffering of the Chinese people whose crops and tax money supported these unpredictable forces. Indeed, He Yingqin saw this as one of the root causes of China's problems: rather than supporting and protecting the nation, the traditional armies had served as a burden on society. The new system

[26] *HYQJJ*, I, 603.
[27] "Gaixing zhengbing zhidu zhi ti'an" [Proposal to Change the Conscription System], in Zhu Huilin, ed., *Yizheng shiliao* [Materials on Conscription], vol. I (Taipei: Guoshiguan, 1990), 1–48.

had to ensure that all the military units served the nation rather than a single individual or region and must be made up of high-quality recruits who would become educated, properly trained, and professional soldiers. In order to reduce expenses, He Yingqin planned for a relatively small standing army, but with a large group of trained reservists who could return to service in time of war.[28] The 1928 preparatory plan called for a standing army of approximately 800,000, but the ever growing body of reservists who exited the standing army meant that in ten years China would have a pool of 2.8 million soldiers to draw upon.[29]

This plan for a new national conscription system went beyond the goals of defending the state and people, as He Yingqin intended it to have a positive influence on Chinese society and contribute to the building of the nation. Not surprisingly, he saw great value in military training for young Chinese and felt that military service and the professionalization of large numbers of young men would ultimately help turn China's citizens into "Samaritans" (jianyi yongwei) with a strong sense of duty and commitment to the nation.[30] Conscription into military service and the discipline that came along with it would improve societal order, strengthen patriotism, and bring local areas into the national fold. It would also provide rural youths with education and training that they could not otherwise obtain in their home villages. Most would take this education and newfound "common sense" (changshi) back to their villages once their period of service ended, which would have a good influence on these rural areas.[31] The new conscription system, which in some respects attempted to militarize Chinese society through the spread of martial values, had strong ties to state-building and modernization.

To help prepare young men for military service, He Yingqin also advocated including military training as part of the regular curriculum for high school and university students. This training would take several different forms, including having teachers and administrators implement military-style discipline in the schools to teach students respect for authority. He recommended that schools devote more time to military training, such as physical education and military drill, the latter to take place on a daily basis in the morning or evening. He also suggested that teachers could easily adjust the regular curriculum to support military training, for example by emphasizing practical military skills such as map-reading

[28] "Gaixing zhengbing zhidu zhi ti'an," 3; He Zhihao, "He jingong dui bingyi zhidu zhi jianli" [Mr. He Yingqin and the Establishment of the Conscription System], Zhongguo yu riben, 107 (March 1969), 17. He Zhihao worked on conscription for the Ministry of Military Administration.
[29] "Gaixing zhengbing zhidu zhi ti'an," 23–24.
[30] "Gaixing zhengbing zhidu zhi ti'an," 6.    [31] "Gaixing zhengbing zhidu zhi ti'an," 22.

when teaching geography, major military conflicts when teaching history, and stories of patriotism and heroism when teaching literature. In order to support these programs, schools could request that the government provide a military advisor to guide teachers and administrators in providing sound military training.[32]

In practical terms, He Yingqin envisioned a three-step process to put the conscription system into effect, starting with the survey and registration of each household, which would serve as the foundation for the system. This proved an enormous task, but he optimistically estimated that within one year each province would have complete registration information on all of its inhabitants, including names, birthdates, addresses, occupations, criminal record (if any), and ethnicity. Once the household registration process wrapped up, local officials could begin to draw up lists of young men (*zhuangding*) eligible for military service and select individuals for conscription into the army. This process, again, would take approximately one year, after which officials would transport the new recruits to training centers to begin their military service. This meant approximately two years from the start of registration to the beginning of training of the first group of conscript soldiers.[33] The Nationalist government unveiled the plan as the Conscription Law in 1933 and established a conscription section (*bingyike*) within the Ministry of Military Administration in November 1935. Due to continued internal and external conflicts, the law did not go into effect until March 1, 1936. Essentially based on the Japanese model, it also bore some marks of the conscription system employed in Guangxi.[34] According to the law, eligible males between the ages of eighteen and forty-five would serve in either the standing army (*changbei jun*) or the national guard (*guomin bingyi*). Active service in the standing army featured three years of full-time military service followed by a six-year period of "inactive service" with part-time training. After completing the six years of inactive service, the soldier remained on reserve status until age forty. All such terms of service remained subject to extension in times of war. The 1936 Conscription Law called for the creation of division (*shi*) and regiment (*tuan*) district offices to handle conscription matters. Technically, the Ministry of Military Administration and the Ministry of the Interior had joint responsibility for conscription, but the former took most direct action through its conscription section. It planned to open division district offices in all provinces,

---

[32] He Zhihao, "He jingong dui bingyi zhidu zhi jianli," 16.

[33] "Gaixing zhengbing zhidu zhi ti'an," 9–11, 14.

[34] Fang Qiuwei, "Kangzhan shiqi de 'Bingyi fa' he bingyi shu" [The Conscription Department and the "Conscription Law" During the War of Resistance], *Minguo dang'an*, 1 (1996), 123. Fang was a journalist who wrote about conscription during the war.

beginning with Jiangsu, Zhejiang, Anhui, Jiangxi, Hubei, and Hunan. The Ministry of Military Administration staffed them down to the county or township level, but at the grassroots level village officials supervised the registration of eligible males and the selection of conscripts. By the end of 1936, the Nationalists had brought in some 50,000 new recruits.[35]

Once the war began in 1937, the Ministry of Military Administration rushed to establish division district offices in more provinces. By early 1938, following the loss of Shanghai and Nanjing, and with an imminent threat to Xuzhou and the northwest, Chiang Kai-shek ordered two changes in conscription. First, in February at a meeting of military leaders at the Wuhan field headquarters, Chiang expanded the conscription section (*bingyike*) into a conscription department (*bingyisi*), retaining Zhu Weiling as section, now department, head. As the war expanded and more of the central provinces fell under Japanese occupation, the need for replacement soldiers intensified, but many interior provinces had not yet set up division district offices and had few conscription officials at work. At this time Hunan and Fujian each had only eight division district offices open and Guangdong had only five.[36] The expansion of the conscription administration and the need for a faster rate of recruitment resulted in revisions to conscription practice known as the "Principle of the Three Equals in Conscription" (*bingyi sanping yuanze*). The Three Equals, *pingdeng*, *pingjun*, and *pingchong*, all roughly translated as "equal," attempted to ensure equal application of the conscription law to all individuals and to spread the burden of military service in an equitable manner. *Pingdeng* meant equal application of the conscription law to all men of appropriate draft age, regardless of their wealth, status, or class. Sons of the rich and influential had the same obligation for military service as the poor and unconnected. *Pingjun* meant that the burden of providing conscript soldiers should fall equally on individual provinces, with each contributing equally in proportion to its population. *Pingchong* implied that officials would adhere strictly to the stipulations of the Conscription Law and only those with legitimate reasons would get exemptions or deferments, all handled according to established policy.[37]

---

[35] "Conscription Law," in *US Military Intelligence Reports: China, 1911–1941*, Reel VI, 0193; He Zhihao, "He jingong dui bingyi zhidu zhi jianli," 13. See also Guofangbu shizheng bianzeju, *Junzheng shiwu nian* [Fifteen Years in Military Administration] (hereafter *JZSWN*) (Taipei: Guofangbu shizheng bianzeju, 1984), 74. F. F. Liu puts the number of 1937 recruits at 500,000: F. F. Liu, *Military History of Modern China*, 137.

[36] He Zhihao, "He jingong dui bingyi zhidu zhi jianli," 13.

[37] *JZSWN*, 74; Fang Qiuwei, "Kangzhan shiqi de 'Bingyi fa' he bingyi shu," 13; Xia Jing, "Guomindang zhengfu bingyi zhidu yanjiu" [A Study of the Guomindang Government's Conscription System], master's thesis, Shandong shifan daxue, Jinan, Shandong, 2009, 22–24.

These adjustments clearly reflect the shift in strategic thinking taking place in Nationalist military circles, as many now envisioned a protracted war of considerable length.

A second change came in May 1938 when, on the recommendation of the Ministry of Military Administration, Chiang Kai-shek authorized He Yingqin to investigate the possibility of reorganizing local militia and other self-defense forces into the regular Nationalist Army. He Yingqin developed a general plan to fold such units into the national guard, joining the pool of trained soldiers from which to draw upon as replacements. The quality of local defense units varied, with some provinces such as Yunnan and Guangxi possessing fully trained militia forces, but in many other areas training mechanisms for local defense units remained inadequate. Other such forces demonstrated an unwillingness to obey directives from the central military authorities. He Yingqin made the relevant organizational changes, asserting control over all such units through the division district offices and assigning them responsibility for providing training and support for these local units. Eventually, perhaps within three years, they would serve as replacement troops for regular Nationalist units, take up local security duty, or conduct operations behind enemy lines.[38]

In order to meet the ongoing need for replacement troops, in February 1939 the Ministry of Military Administration, now relocated with the government to Chongqing, again expanded its conscription administration with the establishment of the conscription bureau (*bingyishu*). Cheng Zerun and Zhu Weiling served as director and deputy director, respectively. By this time He Yingqin was clearly devoting most of his efforts to this issue, which he believed would determine victory or defeat. As he pointed out to his colleagues, in the current war the Nationalists had enough weapons, ammunition, food, and equipment but, "without soldiers, these things are useless."[39]

Conscription officials performed their work rather well in the early years of the war, bringing in more than 2.7 million new recruits, but the experience also revealed a number of problems that required immediate attention. In a speech marking the establishment of the conscription bureau in 1939, He Yingqin emphasized the need for greater attention to certain aspects of conscription work in order for the bureau to complete its mission. First, he explained that poor record-keeping and inaccurate reporting meant that there was at times little relationship between the numbers local conscription officials sent forward and the actual number

[38] *HYQJJ*, I, 595–96; *JZSWN*, 82.
[39] He Yingqin, "Dui bingyishu quanti zhiyuan xunhua" [Lecture to the Employees of the Conscription Department], in *HZZYQYLXJ*, 330–31.

of new soldiers brought in for training or arriving at new units. At times he found it impossible to determine the status of recruits in a given location. How many men had arrived for induction or training? Had they received uniforms and equipment? Had conscription officials distributed funds for food and housing as the recruits moved from their home villages to training centers or from there to their assigned units? The consequences of these problems had already begun to show. At the end of 1938, Chiang asked He Yingqin to make another 1 million new soldiers ready for action by the end of February 1939. As of February 1, He Yingqin noted that only 300,000 new soldiers stood ready for action, less than one-third of the requested number.[40]

Another perhaps more important problem that came to He Yingqin's attention involved the treatment of recruits. Addressing this issue, he pointed out to conscription officials that they must make recruits comfortable as they left their homes to go through induction and training, which required having food, shelter, and uniforms arranged in advance. In fact, He Yingqin argued that the recruits must feel that their lives would improve after they left home to join the army; otherwise they would avoid military service. If conscription officials took the time to arrange everything carefully in advance, they would avoid many of the problems associated with conscription. He Yingqin also warned against favoritism and discrimination, believing it essential that conscription officials follow the Principle of the Three Equals and treat all draft-eligible men the same. He read numerous reports that indicated that sons of wealthy families or those who worked for the government managed to get deferments or exemptions, regardless of the stipulations of the 1936 Conscription Law.[41] As the war progressed, he found it increasingly difficult to correct these problems.

The Nationalists' conscription problems eventually caught the attention of numerous observers, both Chinese and foreign, and became a lens through which to assess the entire Chinese war effort. In his postwar memoir Li Zongren criticized the "conscription authorities of the central government" who "simply grabbed men from all over the country," a practice he likened to "driving sheep to feed tigers."[42] In his 1984 book *Seeds of Destruction*, Lloyd Eastman detailed some of the major deficiencies of the Nationalist conscription system, which he understood as indicative of the gradual decay of the Nationalist military. Citing general problems of poor leadership, slack discipline, and an absence of fighting spirit, Eastman pointed to an array of abusive practices which Chinese conscripts endured. Eastman described these conscripts – seized

---

[40] *HYQJJ*, I, 605–06.    [41] *HYQJJ*, I, 607.    [42] Tsung-jen Li, *Memoirs*, 417.

in their own fields or villages and roughly delivered to a training center – as "so ill-treated and ill-fed that they lacked both the ability and the morale to fight effectively."[43] Over the course of the war, Eastman concluded, conditions proved so bad for those unfortunate enough to fall into the hands of conscription officials that 10 percent died before reaching the battlefield.[44]

As minister of military administration, He Yingqin took much of the blame for the failings of the conscription system. Referring to problems in conscription and supply, Theodore White and Annalee Jacoby accused He Yingqin of presiding over the "gradual rotting away of the Chinese armies in the field" and directly attributed what they saw as "the starving of Chinese troops" and "the extortion and slaughter of conscription" to He Yingqin's work.[45] Brooks Atkinson of the *New York Times* specifically blamed He Yingqin for treating Chinese soldiers with "callousness and inhumanity," and for permitting "the Chinese armies to disintegrate."[46] This reputation followed He Yingqin after the war, especially in the works of Western historians of China who described him in almost wholly negative terms.[47]

While criticisms of He Yingqin and Nationalist conscription practices are common, a number of scholars have noted that over the long course of the war the Chinese succeeded in the vital task of providing replacements for losses at the front. Despite pointing out numerous problems with the conscription system, Eastman credited the Nationalists with surviving for an extended period against a superior enemy with a minimum of external support.[48] Van de Ven has argued that the Nationalists handled conscription well in the first four years of the war, but after 1941 economic problems, the Japanese embargo of the China coast, and the gradual drying up of the pool of recruits posed significant problems for conscription officials, forcing them to rely more on coercion.[49] Needless to say, the conscription problems during the war against Japan extended far beyond the capabilities, or deficiencies, of any one man. Yet far from sitting idly by as Chinese armies disintegrated, He Yingqin devoted significant time and energy to conscription, and he came to understand the problems that plagued the system all too well. If one reviews his remarks

---

[43] Eastman, *Seeds of Destruction*, 147.     [44] Eastman, *Seeds of Destruction*, 152.

[45] White and Jacoby, *Thunder out of China*, 105.

[46] Brooks Atkinson, "Realism Is Urged in Judging China," *New York Times*, November 21, 1944.

[47] Eastman, *Seeds of Destruction*, 143; Eastman, "Nationalist China During the Sino-Japanese War," 571; Lattimore, *China Memoirs*, 115; John Garver, "China's Wartime Diplomacy," in Hsiung and Levine, eds., *China's Bitter Victory*, 9; McLynn, *Burma Campaign*, 168.

[48] Eastman, *Seeds of Destruction*, 131.     [49] Van de Ven, *War and Nationalism*, 252–53.

on the subject over the course of the war years, it is clear that he made consistent references to the same problems over and over again, but made little headway in solving them.

As a result of his analysis of numerous reports, investigations, and conversations with officers at various levels, He Yingqin identified several critical problems that made conscription difficult. For example, in many areas household registers remained incomplete, despite efforts since the mid 1930s to log the names, birthdates, addresses, and occupations of all citizens. Without this information, it proved difficult to identify and locate young men eligible for military service. China's chronic poverty and underdevelopment proved to be another problem as many recruits came from poor families who could ill afford to lose the labor of a young adult male. Under these conditions, recruits constantly worried about the fate of their families and avoided military service or deserted upon being conscripted.[50] He Yingqin also noted the general poor health of many Chinese men, especially in the southwest, where he claimed people tended to be "short and skinny" and unprepared for the rigors of military service.[51] In many rural areas where people had no access to proper medical care, young men who reported for service sometimes had such poor health that they did not pass the physical requirements. According to Gong Xilin, in 1938 in Dazu county, Sichuan province, of the 327 recruits who arrived for training, 147 had to be dismissed for bad health. In Yongchuan county in 1944, of 155 who arrived for training, 75 failed the physical. Poor health among recruits stemmed from China's poverty and lack of adequate medical care more than from any shortcomings in the conscription system.[52]

Beyond these issues, He Yingqin also saw problems in conscription personnel, especially at the grassroots level. Even in the earliest stages of planning, He Yingqin pointed out the essential relationship between central military officials who would devise and oversee the system and the local officials who would actually identify eligible young men and see them off to the induction and training centers.[53] His investigations revealed that a certain number of officials simply did not do their jobs properly and refused to adhere to central policy. He found this the most

[50] He Yingqin's speech at the Conscription Conference, February 24, 1939, in *JZSWN*, 90.

[51] He Yingqin's remarks on Conscription, July 10, 1939, in *JZSWN*, 97; He Yingqin, "Zhengbing zhengce zhi jiantao" [A Review of Conscription Policy], *Bingyi yuekan*, 4, 7–8 (1942), 4–6.

[52] Gong Xilin, "Kangzhan shiqi jiceng baojia zhengbing de zhidu yuexing yinsu tanxi" [An Analysis of the Facts Regarding the Grassroots-Level *Baojia* in the Conscription System During the War of Resistance], *Lishi jiaoxue*, 16 (2011), 23.

[53] "Gaixing zhengbing zhidu zhi ti'an," 12.

troublesome aspect of conscription. The conscription bureau employed hundreds of thousands of officials who staffed various levels of offices, and sometimes relied on army unit commanders to handle conscription in their areas of operation. Yet when it came to the task of going into the villages and identifying young men eligible for military service and delivering them to the training centers, the conscription bureau had to rely on local *baojia* officials who held authority in the countryside. *Baojia* served as the traditional system of mutual responsibility and rural organization, which the Nationalist government revived in 1934. According to this system, each family had a head of household, with ten families making a *jia*. One of the ten heads of households in this group served as *jiazhang*, with responsibility for the conduct of the members of the ten families and for serving as a liaison with government. A group of ten *jia*, or one hundred families, made up a *bao*, with one of the heads of household serving as *baozhang*. The *baozhang* and *jiazhang* had responsibility for collecting taxes, organizing public works, and dealing with conscription.[54] After reviewing hundreds of reports from county-level conscription officials, He Yingqin identified these *baojia* officials as the weakest link in the conscription chain. He concluded that, in 80 to 90 percent of the cases in which he found conscription problems, the local *baojia* officials proved "unsound" (*bujianquan*).[55] Although critical of central government officials, Eastman also identified the local authorities as the most important problem in the conscription system, rather than central authorities working directly under the conscription bureau.[56]

As a result of his investigations of local conditions, He Yingqin understood the reasons why some *baojia* officials often failed to follow through on their duties with regard to conscription. Certainly, some might be corrupt, lazy, or incapable of doing their jobs effectively. Some openly took payments in exchange for exemptions or deferments while others pocketed funds designated for uniforms or food for new recruits, leaving the unfortunate conscripts to provide for themselves. Yet, even if a local *baojia* official intended to do his job properly, he might find himself overwhelmed with responsibilities during wartime, of which identifying local men eligible for military service was only one. Many found themselves subject to pressures from all around, including relatives, friends, wealthy families, and local toughs who sought to avoid military service or who wanted to protect someone else. Their work in conscription made them targets of criticism, intimidation, and sometimes even violence when

---

[54] Yang Zhong, *Local Government and Politics in China: Challenges from Below* (Armonk, NY: M. E. Sharpe, 2003), 35–36.
[55] *JZSWN*, 97.    [56] Eastman, *Seeds of Destruction*, 147.

they went to villages to check on the status of the young men. A 1944 investigation of conscription in Sichuan province uncovered cases in which bands of young men carried swords and knives and beat or stabbed *baojia* officials who tried to conscript them.[57] This undoubtedly explains why some described conscription as the "most detested function" of the local *baojia* officials.[58] If unable to withstand these pressures, local officials might allow some men to avoid conscription or knowingly take paid substitutes in their place, both violations of the conscription law.

At the same time, higher-level conscription officials pressured the same *baojia* leaders to meet their quotas for conscripts or face punishment. As a result, they sometimes resorted to coercion, forcing the old, young, sick, or lame into service. They sometimes bound conscripts with ropes, locked them in rooms, or took their clothes away to prevent them from fleeing, all in clear violation of the conscription policy. Such practices did little to encourage peasants give up their sons to conscription or their grain to support the army. As the saying went in some parts of the countryside, "If you have sons, they belong to old Chiang [Kai-shek]; if you have gold, it belongs to the *baozhang*."[59] Ironically, *baojia* leaders might also find themselves in a difficult position, caught between the Scylla of the central government's conscription officials and the Charybdis of resentful villagers. Whether callous and corrupt or simply seeking to avoid the pressure from above or below, the situation made abusive treatment of newly recruited soldiers at the hands of officials at the grassroots level increasingly common. This gave young men even less incentive to enter military service and made it even more difficult for officials to meet their quotas, exacerbating an already dire situation. He Yingqin, at the apex of this system, knew well its problems and shortcomings. He once described the conscripts' predicament to a group of officials from the conscription bureau, saying "cold and hungry, beaten and cursed at: why not run away?"[60] Western and Chinese observers blamed Nationalist officers such as He Yingqin for ignoring the situation and allowing the "gradual rotting away of Chinese armies." Yet it is clear that he understood only too well the problems in conscription and remained painfully

---

[57] Gong Xilin, "Kangzhan shiqi jiceng baojia zhengbing de zhidu yuexing yinsu tanxi," 25.

[58] *JZSWN*, 85; William Rowe, *Crimson Rain: Seven Centuries of Violence in a Chinese County* (Stanford: Stanford University Press, 2007), 297–98.

[59] Cai Hailin, "Kangzhan shiqi guomin zhengfu bingyi zhidu yanjiu zongshu" [A Review of Studies on Nationalist Government Conscription During the Sino-Japanese War], *Junshi lishi yanjiu*, 1 (2008), 186.

[60] "Guoqu yizheng zhi jiantao yu jinhou yingyou zhi gaishan" [A Review of Past Conscription Policy and Improvements for the Future], in *HYQJJJCXJ*, 80.

aware that in far too many cases local officials ignored central policy, and too many recruits arrived for training in poor condition.[61]

Important changes in village leadership in the early twentieth century contributed to the problem, as many capable individuals eschewed local leadership positions. In his study of north China villages in this period, Prasenjit Duara marked a significant shift away from traditional village leaders as "protective brokers," who played a key role in negotiating between the village and the state and looked after the interests of the collective village. In their place Duara described the emergence of a new breed of "predatory" or "entrepreneurial brokers" who accepted village leadership positions largely for personal gain. In many cases, these new local leaders tended to be "young, had little education, and were unable to bear any financial responsibility."[62] William Rowe studied local leaders in Macheng county, Hubei, and like Duara found clear evidence of the declining quality of *baojia* officials during the war, citing provincial surveys which indicated widespread discontent with local authorities, whom some described as "illiterate and unable to keep simple accounts."[63] Such officials proved unable or unwilling to manage the complicated and demanding task of presiding over conscription according to central policy and ignored the Principle of the Three Equals in Conscription. He Yingqin and Chiang Kai-shek knew of these problems, and in April 1944 Chiang ordered He to provide data on the connection between the current conscription system and the *baojia* system of local self-governance.[64] These conditions, not to mention the other dislocations and disruptions the war brought, exacerbated the problems He Yingqin faced in trying to ensure that the Nationalists maintained a steady stream of new recruits in order to support the strategy of protracted war.

In addition to these problems in personnel, He Yingqin believed that Chinese culture played a role in conscription problems. He felt that many rural Chinese, common people and authority figures alike, held antiquated views based in a local context and lacked a "national perspective." As a result, they operated according their own limited experience and local interest and did not fully appreciate the importance of conscription work and the role it played in the war effort.[65] Moreover, among the common people the traditional view that "good men do not make

[61] See He Yingqin's remarks at the Third Conscription Conference, March 1940, in *HYQJJJCXJ*, 78–79.

[62] Prasenjit Duara, *Culture, Power, and the State: Rural North China, 1900–1942* (Stanford: Stanford University Press, 1988), 169.

[63] Rowe, *Crimson Rain*, 298.

[64] *SLGB*, vol. LVI, April 17, 1944, 664.         [65] *JZSWN*, 84–85.

soldiers" (*haonan bu dangbing*) continued to hold sway in many areas, causing He Yingqin to decry the lack of patriotism in rural China.[66] In his more pessimistic moments, He Yingqin blamed a cultural "shortcoming" that led the Chinese people as a whole to refuse to take responsibility and to leave important tasks for someone else.[67]

In fact, whether they had a national perspective or not, most rural men saw military service during the war as akin to a death sentence and devised numerous ways to avoid it. Some fled to cities where they could evade local draft officials or enrolled in private schools if they had the means. American general Joseph Stilwell, Chiang Kai-shek's Allied chief of staff from 1942 to 1944, cynically noted an encounter with a married, 26-year-old father of three children who had avoided the draft because of his status as a "middle-school student."[68] One of the more common methods of avoiding conscription involved attempts to take advantage of the rule that provided exemptions from military service for sons of families with only one child. In his research on conscription, Gong Xilin noted numerous complaints against *baojia* officials who allegedly ignored the policy that granted only children an exemption from military service and seized these men for conscription. These complaints, Gong Xilin notes, must be seen in light of the fact that many villagers concealed the true number of children in their families to shield a son from military service. In Fujian province, Gong uncovered a village in which thirteen of a total fourteen families claimed to have only one child.[69]

With many rural families unwilling to cooperate with local officials in charge of conscription, it grew increasingly difficult for these officials to meet their quotas. In practice, this meant that many ceased to care whether or not conscripts met the physical requirements, fell within the designated age range, or even acquired the appropriate training before being sent into battle. They sought only to fulfill their quotas with whatever recruits they could find, regardless of age, health, or suitability for military service. "These officials understand only numbers, but not quality," an exasperated He Yingqin complained in 1940, declaring that, "if we go to war with the old, weak, and sick, there is no way we can win!'[70]

---

[66] *JZSWN*, 90.

[67] "Dui bingyishu quanti zhiyuan xunhua" [Lecture to Staff of the Conscription Department], February 1, 1939, in *HZZYQYLXJ*, 335.

[68] Theodore H. White, ed., *The Stilwell Papers: General Joseph Stilwell's Iconoclastic Account of America's Adventures in China* (New York: Schocken Books, 1972), 159.

[69] Gong Xilin, "Kangzhan shiqi jiceng baojia zhengbing de zhidu yuexing yinsu tanxi," 24.

[70] "Guoqu yizheng zhi jiantao yu jinhou yingyou zhi gaishan," 86.

## Attempts to improve conscription

Not only did He Yingqin understand these problems, he and his colleagues in the Ministry of Military Administration made numerous attempts to address them and to improve conscription work. Over the course of the war, the government issued some 240 new rules, changes, and adjustments to conscription law.[71] For example, the government issued identification cards to make it easier to identify potential recruits and harder to avoid conscription, though the lack of photos on the cards limited the effect.[72] With regard to personnel, the government made a determined effort to punish officials caught violating conscription policy. In 1942, He Yingqin reported that dozens of conscription officials had been sentenced to prison for various offenses.[73] In order to make *baojia* positions more attractive to encourage capable candidates, the government exempted them from military service and labor duties and offered tax reductions, expense reimbursements, and free education for their children.[74] In order to address the lack of "national perspective," the conscription bureau sent propaganda teams to distribute films to movie theaters across China, all designed to make people understand and appreciate the importance of conscription.[75] The Nationalists even put some 32,000 prisoners in uniform between 1939 and 1944 to help make up for shortages of new recruits.[76]

He Yingqin convened a series of conscription conferences in Chongqing in order to rectify these problems with a top-down campaign to encourage conscription officials to do their jobs more effectively. At the first such conference in February 1939, the discussion ranged over a variety of topics with special emphasis on the need for conscription officials at all levels to understand the importance of their work and to take it seriously. In his remarks to assembled officials, He Yingqin stressed the critical role of conscription in the war effort, repeatedly pointing out that victory depended on a sound conscription system that could procure a constant supply of replacement troops. As he told his colleagues, "the

---

[71] Cai Hailin, "Kangzhan shiqi guomin zhengfu bingyi zhidu yanjiu zongshu," 182.

[72] Xia Jing, "Guomindang zhengfu bingyi zhidu yanjiu," 49.

[73] He Yingqin, "Dui sichuan bingyi huiyi xunci" [Instructions to the Sichuan Conscription Conference], *Bingyi yuekan*, 4, 3 (1942), 8–10.

[74] Van de Ven, *War and Nationalism*, 258.

[75] Wang Dongmei, "Kangzhan shiqi guomindang bingyi fubai de yuanyin tanxi" [An Analysis of the Corruption in Guomindang Conscription During the War of Resistance Against the Japanese], *Wenshi bolan (lilun)*, 10 (October 2010), 10; Xia Jing, "Guomindang zhengfu bingyi zhidu yanjiu," 55.

[76] Wang Xuezhen, "Dahoufang kangzhan wenxue de bingyi ticai" [The Theme of Conscription in Literature of the Rear Areas During the War of Resistance], *Zhongguo xiandai wenxue yanjiu zongkan*, 7 (2011), 17.

long-term war of resistance depends upon an endless supply of replacement soldiers. Our country is large and our people are many, so all we need is a good conscription system and procuring supplemental troops will not be a problem. If we do this, we will show the world that we have a force for a hundred-year war of resistance."[77] Although it flew in the face of his own combat experience and he typically emphasized spirit and discipline as more important that numerical superiority, He Yingqin now argued that the history of warfare over the previous two centuries indicated that the force that was able to muster greater numbers of soldiers would triumph. He cited examples of conscription in Western warfare, such as the French *levée en masse* of 1793, the Prussian conscription system of the late nineteenth century, and the American involvement in World War I.[78]

In order to reach the mid- and lower-level officials, He Yingqin dispatched numerous teams to investigate the work of division district offices and to make sure that these officials understood the policy properly, closely supervised those working under them, and observed strict accounting and record-keeping. He sent out repeated warnings against abusing recruits and orders to ensure that new soldiers received adequate food and shelter as they left their homes, uniforms and clothing appropriate to the season, and thorough training before entering battle. When addressing a group of conscription officials, he asked them to consider whether or not they were guilty of poor work and how they might improve. Conscription officials, he emphasized, should take great pride in their work and serve as role models for others. He criticized those who did not take their work seriously and urged those who discovered crimes or abuses to severely punish the guilty.[79]

As a practical measure, He Yingqin stressed that conscription officials must engage in careful planning in order to solve some of the problems that occurred repeatedly. If everything was carefully planned and organized in advance, he reasoned, the results would be much better. For example, if an official knew how many men he was to procure, he then knew how many beds he would need to accommodate them, how much food he would need to feed them, and how many uniforms he would need to clothe them. All of this had to be carefully arranged in advance so that

---

[77] He Yingqin's remarks on the establishment of the Conscription Department, February 1, 1939, in *JZSWN*, 95–96; *HYQJJ*, I, 609.

[78] He Yingqin, "Nianlai yizheng zhi qianzhan ji jinhou zhi gaijin" [A View of Conscription Policy and Future Improvements], *Bingyi yuekan*, 2 (1941), 10–12.

[79] He Yingqin's remarks to Conscription Department staff, February 1, 1939, in *HZZYQYLXJ*, 336.

things moved smoothly and efficiently. He Yingqin employed an eight-character couplet to express to conscription officials what they must do: "Quickly and ably, we can get it done" (*xunsu queshi, nenggou zuodao*).[80]

Beyond raising the issue in conferences with conscription officials in attendance, He Yingqin also tried to address these problems with the Chinese public. Reaching the large population of rural, sometimes illiterate villagers proved difficult, but He Yingqin periodically used speeches and radio broadcasts to encourage the Chinese people as a whole to support conscription. In a January 1939 speech entitled "Resolute Faith in Victory and National Construction," He Yingqin reminded his audience that everyone must be willing to sacrifice their lives to oppose the enemy and that everyone had responsibility in this struggle. In these extraordinary times, he stated, everyone should contribute to the cause and, "rather than avoid military service, they should eagerly accept conscription."[81] In a February 1940 radio broadcast, He Yingqin tied conscription to the New Life Movement, pointing out that everyone had a responsibility to the nation and must give their full support to military service.[82] He did not limit his appeals to those under the administration of the Chongqing government but also reached out to those who lived under Japanese occupation. In an April 1942 radio broadcast to occupied areas of China, He Yingqin repeated his argument that modern war was about national strength (*guoli*), measured in terms of people and materials. In both cases, China enjoyed a distinct advantage over Japan. This did not mean, He Yingqin warned, that the average Chinese could just sit back and wait for victory. Rather, it was time for everyone to increase the spirit of self-sacrifice, and those in the rear or in occupied areas must unite with those at the front to attack the enemy.[83] He had no guarantee, however, that these speeches reached the appropriate ears or had the desired effect.

Despite his efforts to eliminate abusive practices and to rally the Chinese people to support conscription, the same problems continued to plague the process throughout the war. His conferences and radio broadcasts in all likelihood reached only a limited audience and could not compensate for the strains on the conscription system. Speaking on the subject in August 1942, five years into the war, he identified the same problems – incomplete household registers, unsound officials at the

---

[80] He Yingqin's remarks to Conscription Department staff, February 1, 1939, in *HZZYQYLXJ*, 335.

[81] He Yingqin, "Jianding kangzhan bisheng jianguo bicheng de xinnian" [Resolute Faith in Victory and National Construction], in *HZZYQYLXJ*, 327–28.

[82] *HYQJJ*, I, 621.

[83] He Yingqin, "Zhongguo bisheng" [China Will Be Victorious], *Bingyi yuekan*, 4, 4 (1942), 5–7.

local level, an underdeveloped national economy, the common people's low educational levels, and traditional aversion to military service – that he had pointed to in 1939.[84] During the last years of the war, Chiang Kai-shek viewed conscription as increasingly problematic. Over the course of 1942 and 1943, he sent numerous *shouling* to He Yingqin, reacting to reports of abuses and cruel treatment of new recruits and the continuing problem of paid substitutes. In early April and mid June of 1942, Chiang wrote to He Yingqin repeating his demand for stronger punishments for those who violated policy, abused new recruits, or knowingly accepted paid substitutes for those who did not want to serve. He stressed the importance of providing new soldiers with proper training and ordered He Yingqin to find out why these problems continued and to report his findings.[85] Chiang offered no advice as to how to correct these problems, but he did suggest that the conscription bureau must make sure that all frontline units that sent officers to division-level conscription district offices to pick up and transfer new recruits back to their units for training should use the most capable men and the highest-quality officers available. Chiang now viewed this as a critical assignment for which units must designate their best and most morally upstanding officers.[86] A year later, in May 1943, Chiang again sent He Yingqin a *shouling* demanding that all recruits receive proper food, treatment, and training, and that only the most capable officers should take on this responsibility. He also stressed the need to change the way the common people thought about military service. Again, he offered He Yingqin no guidance on how to do this, but stated that it was important to do so quickly.[87] He Yingqin had been hard at work trying to do just this for years, but it proved far easier said than done.

According to some, internal struggles within the Nationalist military led He Yingqin's rivals, primarily Chen Cheng, to target the conscription bureau for public criticism, hoping to drive a wedge between He and Chiang.[88] The issue came to a head in late August 1944, when Chiang Kai-shek personally witnessed the deplorable condition of some new recruits in Chongqing and decided things had to change. At that time, Chiang's son Jiang Weiguo came across a group of new army recruits occupying some rooms off a small alley in Chongqing, near the Luohan Temple. Some exhibited signs of serious illness, and all appeared

---

[84] He Yingqin, "Zhengbing zhengce zhi jiantao."

[85] *SLGB*, XLIX, June 13, 1942, 607–08.

[86] *SLGB*, L, June 30, 1942, 135–36.    [87] *SLGB*, LIII, May 17, 1943, 451.

[88] Keyun Liyang, "Jiang Jiashi qinzhan Cheng Zerun de zhenshi neimu" [The True Inside Story of How Chiang Kai-shek Personally Cut Down Cheng Zerun], *Zhongshan fengyu*, 6 (2009), 51–52.

emaciated and malnourished, thin as sticks. Without proper beds, the ill sprawled on the floor with no medical care and two corpses lay outside the rooms, evidently having been there long enough to fill the area with a foul odor. Jiang Weiguo sought out the officer in charge to ask the reason for their poor condition, but found no one. When he reported this scene to his father, Chiang Kai-shek flew into a fit of rage and demanded to see He Yingqin, conscription bureau chief Cheng Zerun, and a few other prominent conscription officials the next morning.

At 8 a.m. the next day, Chiang Kai-shek had cars pick up He Yingqin, Cheng Zerun, and others and proceed to the site Jiang Weiguo had visited the day before. When the caravan arrived at the recruitment office in question, Chiang went inside the rooms to see for himself what his son had reported. He Yingqin and the others lined up outside where they could hear Chiang cursing from inside. When he emerged in a rage, he gestured to the miserable recruits and the dead bodies and demanded to know if this was "how the officials of the Ministry of Military Administration handled conscription!"[89] When Cheng Zerun stepped forward, attempting to explain that this was not his responsibility, Chiang raised his walking stick and began to beat Cheng about the head as a group of civilians gathered to watch the scene. Cheng remained upright and would have been subjected to more blows had Jiang Weiguo not stayed his father's hand. Chiang Kai-shek ordered his guards to place Cheng Zerun under arrest and stripped him of his official position. As his rage boiled over, Chiang demanded an execution on the spot for both Cheng and the local district office chief responsible for this group of recruits. At this point, He Yingqin stepped forward, stated that according to military law officers could not be summarily executed or subjected to corporal punishment, and requested that Chiang turn them over for a proper court martial.[90] Chiang relented and left the scene, later noting in his diary that the pitiful sight of these recruits who suffered from illness and abusive treatment left him with "unbearable pain and anger."[91]

Cheng Zerun's court martial took place in closed session and resulted in a death sentence. In December, He Yingqin appealed to Chiang Kai-shek for leniency, pointing out that Cheng had been a disciplined official and arguing that it would be better to allow him to redeem himself

---

[89]  Fang Qiuwei, "Kangzhan shiqi de 'Bingyi fa' he bingyi shu," 130; Keyun Liyang, "Jiang Jiashi qinzhan Cheng Zerun de zhenshi neimu," 52.
[90]  Fang Qiuwei, "Kangzhan shiqi de 'Bingyi fa' he bingyi shu," 130–31. F. F. Liu refers to this incident, which he claims began when Jiang Jingguo, Chiang Kai-shek's oldest son, reported that a number of recruits had committed suicide in their barracks. See F. F. Liu, *Military History of Modern China*, 137–38. See also Li Zhongming, *He Yingqin da zhuan*, 232–33.
[91]  *SLGB*, LVIII, August 30, 1944, 240.

through service in some other capacity. Chiang rejected He's appeal, and a firing squad carried out the sentence in the spring of 1945.[92] By this time complaints about conscription had reached a fever pitch. A *Dagong bao* editorial on September 11, 1944, highlighted the poor state of the Chinese army and disorganized conscription administration. While it did not name He Yingqin specifically, observers noted it as an open "attack on General Ho Ying-ch'in ... the individual whom most Chinese critical of the present situation appear to hold responsible for the maladministration of the Chinese army."[93] Not long afterwards, Chiang took responsibility for conscription away from the Ministry of Military Administration and created a new Ministry of Conscription (*bingyibu*). By this time, He Yingqin had already resigned as minister of military administration, a position he had held for fourteen years, though the reasons for his resignation went far beyond problems with conscription.

There were no short-term solutions to these conscription problems, even under optimal conditions. There is sporadic evidence that the situation improved near the end of the war, which might suggest that He Yingqin and the Ministry of Military Administration saw some success in improving conscription. Wang Dongmei cites a review of 547 conscription cases between November 1944 and February 1945. Of the 547 individual cases investigated, 49 percent reported no problems in their experience, 13.5 percent reported that local officials had seized or coerced them into service, 10.7 percent reported that they had received payment to serve as a substitute for another draftee, and a mere 8 percent reported abusive treatment at the hands of conscription officials.[94] The final figure is perhaps an indication that the conscription bureau had some success in reducing the abusive treatment of new recruits. Still, one must recognize that over the course of the war the Ministry of Military Administration conscripted and trained 11 million men and sent more than 9 million to the front lines as replacements.[95] As Hans van de Ven has pointed out, from 1937 to 1945 the Nationalists recruited 2 million men annually, "something they could, of course, not have done by force alone."[96] Despite all of its flaws, abuses, and weaknesses, He Yingqin clearly understood the problems in conscription policy and practice and

[92] *SLGB*, LIX, December 7, 1944, 254–55.
[93] *FRUS, 1944*, vol. VI, 160–61. "Ho Ying-ch'in," or sometimes "Ho Ying-chin," conforms to the older Wade–Giles system of transliteration for Chinese-language terms, which was in wide use for most of the twentieth century. "He Yingqin" follows the Pinyin system of transliteration, which is more common today.
[94] Wang Dongmei, "Kangzhan shiqi guomindang bingyi fubai de yuanyin tanxi," 10.
[95] He Yingqin, "Zhengbing zhengce zhi jiantao."
[96] Hans van de Ven, "The Sino-Japanese War in History," in Peattie, Drea, and van de Ven, eds., *The Battle for China*, 456.

actively sought to improve the situation. Public criticisms of his work notwithstanding, he regarded the Nationalists' conscription work during the war as a successful effort and described it as the "bedrock" of the ultimate victory over Japan.[97]

[97] He Yingqin, "Zhengbing zhengce zhi jiantao."

# 8 "Maybe now the fire is hot enough to fry Ho Ying-ch'in!!!!"

In October 1944, General Joseph Stilwell departed from Chongqing after more than two years as Chiang Kai-shek's Allied chief of staff. President Franklin Roosevelt had sent Stilwell to China hoping to improve Sino-American cooperation and more effectively prosecute the war against Japan. Instead, his constant clashes with Chiang and He Yingqin drove a wedge between the wartime allies and eventually forced Stilwell's recall. As Stilwell boarded his plane, his aide Colonel Frank Dorn stood beside He Yingqin on the tarmac. Dorn later wrote that he remarked to He that the recall was a terrible mistake on the part of the Chinese. According to Dorn, He Yingqin agreed and frankly expressed "his fears for the future without Stilwell at the helm and his hope that somehow the general could return."[1] Ironically, after years of complaining about what Stilwell and Dorn had regarded as He Yingqin's "meaningless words" and "blank wall of courtesy," on this final occasion when there is little doubt that He Yingqin was simply trying to be polite, Dorn chose to accept his words at face value.

As minister of military administration, He Yingqin's most difficult problems revolved around conscription and keeping Chinese armies in the field. As chief of staff to Chiang Kai-shek, his greatest challenge came in managing relations with China's allies, the British and American officials who arrived in China after the Japanese attack on Pearl Harbor in December 1941, when the Sino-Japanese War developed into the Pacific War. As he continued to try to manage conscription and other aspects of the war, he now had to coordinate war plans and operations with his British and American counterparts. Nothing did more to hurt He Yingqin's reputation in the West than his work with Joseph Stilwell, which helped make He a prime target for critics of China's war effort. One month after Stilwell's departure, He Yingqin also lost his position as minister of military administration, not because of his work

[1] Frank Dorn, *Walkout with Stilwell in Burma* (New York: Crowell, 1971), 81.

against the Japanese enemy, but due to his work with China's American allies.

## New allies and the first Burma campaign

Even before the Japanese attack on Pearl Harbor and the start of the Pacific War, Nationalist officials had been talking to the British about a military operation in Burma. While Chiang Kai-shek did not consider it a central part of the war in China, he welcomed discussion of an Allied operation to defend Burma, which provided a critical link between China and the outside world. In February 1941, a Chinese preparatory committee under General Shang Zhen traveled to Burma, India, and Malaya, spending three months inspecting supply routes and military fortifications. The committee reported to He Yingqin, who then began planning for a Chinese force to enter Burma in order to protect supply routes.[2] With the passage of the Lend-Lease Act in March and the promise of American material aid for China's war effort, protecting the land route from India to southwest China took on a higher priority. He Yingqin addressed the issue in an international radio broadcast, describing the war situation and inviting China's "friend nations" to provide generous amounts of material for the Chinese to employ against the Japanese. In doing so, he noted, they would not only support China's struggle but also assist in the establishment of a "united, free, and democratic world."[3] In May, the Chinese and British established a committee for the management of the Yunnan–Burma Road, which He Yingqin argued should be opened quickly in order to accommodate the upcoming flow of American Lend-Lease aid to China.[4] In early October, Brigadier General John Magruder arrived in Chongqing with a small team of US military representatives who would assist in Sino-American military cooperation.[5] Nationalist leaders called a meeting on December 8, the day after the Pearl Harbor attack, to discuss how the new international situation would influence the war in China. The meeting produced a decision to shift to a more offensive strategy designed to tie up Japanese troops to prevent Tokyo from committing them to the war in the Pacific. The leadership also agreed to commit Chinese ground forces to operations outside China if necessary, in order to protect important lines of communication and transportation. After four years of bitter military conflict, the Nationalist government finally declared formal war

[2]  Xiong Zongren, *He Yingqin: xuanwozhong de lishi*, II, 466–68.
[3]  *HYQJJ*, I, 648.     [4]  *HYQJJ*, I, 649.
[5]  Xiong Zongren, *He Yingqin: xuanwozhong de lishi*, II, 468.

on the empire of Japan, bringing the Chinese together with Britain and the United States in a common cause.[6] While it had not been part of their original plan, the Japanese high command now came to see Burma as a critical part of the embargo on China and in January 1942 sent forces to occupy Burma, severing the road connecting India and Kunming, which served as the primary route for war supplies into China's southwest.

He Yingqin had already been prepared to send Chinese forces outside China's borders to cooperate with British forces, and he now began planning for coordinated action with American forces as well. The new alliance with the United States and Britain elevated Chiang and the Chinese to a new international level, ostensibly equal to these allies, but He Yingqin quickly sensed that the British did not view the Chinese as equals. He intended for General Magruder, Major General L. E. Dennys (a British military attaché), and himself to form a Joint Military Council in Chongqing to coordinate Allied military operations. Since the council would meet and operate in China, He Yingqin insisted that the Chinese representative, himself, chair the committee. Dennys hesitated, giving the impression that he did not believe He Yingqin up to the task. An angry He shot back that, if the Allies would not accept a Chinese chair for the council, the Chinese government would have to reconsider its participation. Magruder intervened and Dennys yielded.[7] On December 16, they met again to discuss the defense of Burma. The British had requested only two divisions of Chinese troops for support, which He Yingqin and Chiang Kai-shek believed insufficient for the job. Not only did He Yingqin feel that the operation called for more Chinese troops – he offered two corps or roughly three times what the British had requested – but he also stated that these troops should operate independently in cooperation with British forces, rather than under formal British command. At the end of the conference, Dennys asked He Yingqin to agree to allow the British to take possession of some American Lend-Lease materials in Burma, originally bound for China. He Yingqin made no comment on this request at this time.[8] These disagreements over the number, role, and command of Chinese troops in Burma along with attempts to redirect Lend-Lease supplies badly needed in China foreshadowed future disagreements among the new allies.

[6] *HYQJJ*, I, 658.
[7] Chen Yanzhen, "Zai He Yingqin de canmou zongzhang bangongshi sannian" [Three Years in He Yingqin's Chief of Staff Office], *Guiyang wenshi ziliao*, 3 (n.d.), 157–58.
[8] Memorandum of Conference with Minister of War on December 16, 1941, United States National Archives (USNA), Record Group 165 M1513, Roll 35.

He Yingqin and Chiang Kai-shek met with Magruder, Dennys, and British commander in chief in India, Archibald Wavell, on December 23, 1941, to produce a "Preliminary Plan for Allied Military Activities in the Far East."[9] Referring to Dennys' request to take control of Lend-Lease materials bound for China, He Yingqin told them that, while the Nationalists stood ready to undertake a campaign in Burma to support the British, China needed material aid. He pointed out that China had been fighting alone for four years and now needed the support of its allies more than ever. Wavell's response shocked and angered the Chinese as he now downplayed the need for Chinese involvement in Burma at all, perhaps doubting that the Japanese would actually invade Burma. He might also have been concerned about the impact of significant numbers of Nationalist Chinese troops occupying parts of Burma and spreading nationalist sentiment among the Burmese population.[10] Whatever his intent, the Chinese interpreted Wavell as suggesting that it would be humiliating for the British in Burma to have to rely on the Chinese for rescue. According to Owen Lattimore, who sat in on the meeting as an advisor to the Chinese, Chiang Kai-shek took this as an insult. Chiang angrily pointed out that the Chinese had significant experience fighting the Japanese and that it would not be as simple for the British as "suppressing colonial rebellions."[11] Following this meeting, a report from Chinese minister of transportation Yu Feipeng added to the Chinese sense of irritation with their new allies. Even though He Yingqin had not given his approval to Dennys' request, Yu informed Chongqing that British officials had already taken control of a shipment of American Lend-Lease military supplies, including 150 trucks that had arrived at Rangoon aboard the USS *Tulsa* for ultimate delivery to China. For the second time in the month of December, He Yingqin angrily threatened to reject all aid from the Allies and to end all cooperation with regard to Burma.[12]

Despite these early disagreements, Chiang Kai-shek again pledged to dispatch forces to cooperate with the British army in an operation in Burma in order to protect India and reopen the Burma Road. He Yingqin flew to Burma to consult with British officers and began preparing a Chinese Expeditionary Force (*zhongguo yuanzheng jun*), or CEF, which would cooperate with British forces in Burma. In order to more effectively

---

[9] *HYQJJ*, I, 656.    [10] McLynn, *Burma Campaign*, 21.
[11] Lattimore, *China Memoirs*, 469.
[12] Chin-tung Liang, *General Stilwell in China, 1942–1944: The Full Story* (New York: St. John's University Press, 1972), 27 n. 16; Maochun Yu, *The Dragon's War: Allied Operations and the Fate of China, 1937–1947* (Annapolis, MD: Naval Institute Press, 2006), 59, 165.

coordinate Allied planning, He Yingqin preferred to work through a committee composed of military officers from China, the United States, and Britain, but this did not materialize.[13] The Joint Military Council established in December got off to a rocky start and did not last long in any event. Dennys died in a plane crash at Kunming in March 1942, and Magruder fell ill and returned to the United States in June of the same year.[14] In the end, rather than a committee representing each of the Allied militaries, He Yingqin got a committee of two, an American officer and himself. Chiang Kai-shek had requested that Franklin Roosevelt send an experienced, high-ranking officer to command American forces in China and to serve as Chiang's American chief of staff in the China theater. Roosevelt consulted with General George Marshall, who selected General Joseph Warren "Vinegar Joe" Stilwell for the job. Stilwell arrived in early March 1942, setting in motion a chain of events that would have a dramatic impact on He Yingqin's career and reputation, not to mention Sino-American relations.

In their initial meetings, the two chiefs of staff seemed to work together cooperatively. Before agreeing to accept the position, Stilwell had expressed concern that Chinese officers might remember him from his earlier posting as a military attaché in China in the 1930s, a "small fry colonel," as he put it, who marched in the mud, consorted with "coolies," and rode trains with common soldiers.[15] Indeed, He Yingqin did not make the connection between the newly promoted General Stilwell and the American colonel he had met briefly years before in Hankou. When he greeted Stilwell in person in Chongqing, he quickly recognized him and exclaimed "It's you!" According to He Yingqin's staff officer and interpreter, Chen Yanzhen, the two men got on quite well at this initial meeting and talked warmly about old times.[16] Stilwell noted in his diary that the two spoke in Chinese and described He Yingqin as "very pleasant."[17] Western writers often emphasize Stilwell's prior experience in China and language skills, but not all Chinese who met him acknowledged his expertise. Chen Yanzhen claimed that, whenever He Yingqin and Stilwell met, they spoke in their native languages with Chen interpreting. In fact, Chen wrote that in his entire time serving under He Yingqin he never heard Stilwell speak Chinese and that he had no idea that some considered Stilwell a "China expert." He recalled that

[13] Xiong Zongren, *He Yingqin: xuanwozhong de lishi*, II, 470.
[14] Chen Yanzhen, "Zai He Yingqin de canmou zongzhang bangongshi sannian," 158; Yu, *The Dragon's War*, 40.
[15] *The Stilwell Papers*, January 1, 1942, 19, and March 5, 1942, 50.
[16] Chen Yanzhen, "Zai He Yingqin de canmou zongzhang bangongshi sannian," 160.
[17] *The Stilwell Papers*, 50.

Stilwell had two American officers with him who spoke Chinese, one an American citizen of Chinese ancestry who had graduated from Yanjing University.[18]

In early March, Chiang hosted He Yingqin, Stilwell, General Claire Chennault, commander of the Fourteenth Air Force, Bai Chongxi, and Li Zongren at his Chongqing residence at Huangshan, where they discussed a Burma operation. By that time, the Fifth, Sixth, and Sixty-Sixth Corps had all assembled in Yunnan and stood ready for action in Burma under Stilwell's command.[19] The Japanese had captured Rangoon, the major port in southern Burma, and Chiang advocated a defensive strategy focused on Mandalay in central Burma. With British support on the western flank, he believed the CEF could defend Mandalay and northern Burma. Given the lack of air and naval support for the Burma operation, Chiang argued that this cautious and defensive strategy made sense. Stilwell disagreed and pushed for a more aggressive approach that featured an attack on southern Burma, designed to drive the Japanese out of Rangoon and Burma altogether. Though Chiang viewed Stilwell's plan as overly ambitious and optimistic, and he worried about the security of China's southwest if the Fifth and Sixth Corps met disaster in Burma, he reluctantly agreed to Stilwell's aggressive plan.[20]

In February 1942, the Fifth and Sixth Corps moved from Yunnan into Burma, crossing the Salween River to support British positions. When Japanese forces attacked the CEF at Toungoo on March 19, the Chinese units fought well, but faced a series of problems relating to the climate, terrain, and poor coordination between Chinese and British forces. As the Japanese surrounded the Chinese, the British and Indian forces on the western flank withdrew, leaving the CEF vulnerable. Moreover, Stilwell discovered that, while he commanded the Chinese forces in Burma, the corps commanders did not always accept his direction and kept in contact with Chongqing and Chiang Kai-shek throughout. General Du Yuming, the commander of the Fifth Corps, went so far as to describe Stilwell to British officials as an "advisor," rather than commander of the CEF.[21] Frustrated with what he viewed as insubordination on the part of the Chinese commanders, on April 1 Stilwell left the battlefield and flew to Chongqing to confront Chiang Kai-shek and He Yingqin

---

[18]  Chen Yanzhen, "Zai He Yingqin de canmou zongzhang bangongshi sannian," 162.
[19]  Xiong Zongren, "He Yingqin yu Shidiwei" [He Yingqin and Joseph Stilwell], *Wenshi jinghua*, 12 (1998), 36; Taylor, *Generalissimo*, 197–99.
[20]  Rana Mitter, *Forgotten Ally: China's World War II 1937–1945* (New York: Houghton Mifflin Harcourt, 2013), 254–55.
[21]  Xiong Zongren, *He Yingqin: xuanwozhong de lishi*, II, 475–76.

on this matter. The fact that Stilwell had left the front at a critical time did not ease Chiang's doubts about Stilwell and the Burma operation, but He Yingqin and others persuaded him to continue to support Stilwell's plan.[22] Moreover, Chiang did not want to damage Sino-American relations and risk losing promised material aid, so he assured Stilwell that he would make it clear to Chinese officers that they must follow his orders. He assigned General Luo Zhuoying to accompany Stilwell back to Burma and to communicate all Stilwell's orders to Chinese corps and division commanders. Moreover, Chiang himself traveled with Stilwell to Burma and publicly ordered his officers to carry out Stilwell's commands.[23]

Chiang's assurances that Chinese commanders would obey Stilwell's orders did little to improve the situation in Burma when Stilwell returned to the front. In early May, as the Japanese continued their aggressive attacks on the Chinese forces in central Burma and threatened to encircle and destroy both the Fifth and Sixth Corps, Stilwell gave orders to withdraw, eventually opting for a northwesterly route that would take them to India. Du Yuming reported this order to Chiang, who overruled Stilwell's orders and instructed Du to return to Yunnan. After a harrowing journey, getting lost along the way and suffering more casualties on the retreat than in the actual fighting, Du's forces managed to limp back to the Chinese border and cross into Yunnan. Others under General Sun Liren followed to the south of Stilwell's small group and arrived in India. The CEF suffered more than 25,000 casualties in the operation, a substantial material and psychological blow.[24] With this debacle, the cooperative phase of Stilwell's relationship with He Yingqin came to an abrupt end. From this point on Stilwell expressed considerable contempt for He, whom he came to regard as obstructionist, a simple "yes man" who told Chiang only what he wanted to hear, and a failure as minister of military administration.[25] He Yingqin left little record of his personal views of Stilwell, but it is clear that by the summer of 1942 Chiang Kai-shek did not trust the American and questioned his abilities as an officer and commander. Chiang believed that, in withdrawing to India, Stilwell had essentially abandoned his Chinese troops in Burma.[26]

[22] Xiong Zongren, "He Yingqin yu Shidiwei," 242.
[23] Mitter, *Forgotten Ally*, 256–57.
[24] Taylor, *Generalissimo*, 204–08; Li Chen, "The Chinese Army in the First Burma Campaign," *Journal of Chinese Military History*, 2, 1 (2013), 44.
[25] See remarks in Stilwell's diary, *The Stilwell Papers*, June 19, 1942, 115; June 16, 1943, 206–07; and June 28, 1943, 209.
[26] Taylor, *Generalissimo*, 205.

### The two chiefs of staff

While his relationship with Stilwell suffered as a result of the first Burma campaign, He Yingqin still sought to work constructively with his American allies and continued to ask for increased amounts of Lend-Lease aid. He met regularly with Stilwell and others on Thursday afternoons to discuss supply, training, and another joint operation in Burma. Stilwell's attitude toward He Yingqin varied, perhaps depending on his mood, sometimes noting constructive meetings while at other times displaying utter contempt. For example, on September 23, 1942, Stilwell wrote in his diary with a certain sense of satisfaction that meeting with He Yingqin had "borne fruit" on several points, suggesting that the two men had found some room to work constructively toward common goals. The next day, Stilwell dismissed He as a mere "blocking back" who deflected attempts at reform, and derided his military education and ability as a "joke."[27] Stilwell's complaints generally revolved around the slow pace at which the Chinese administrative wheels turned and as minister of military administration He Yingqin served as a frequent target. After the war, Stilwell's subordinate Colonel Frank Dorn described his experiences in China and identified He as representative of all that was wrong with the Chinese military:

There were hours of talk and countless cups of tea: the whole performance a minuet of meaningless words always followed by more tea. Ho Ying-ch'in, the Minister of War and top man in the military setup, was obviously behind the stumbling blocks and do nothing attitude. He was jealous of his [Stilwell's] rank and position. And we soon ran up against a blank wall of courtesy, delay and protocol. Inclined to fat, he had a round shiny face and wore round glasses. His round little mouth was always smiling. A pleasant, polite man, he said little at military conferences, his mind apparently retiring safely behind his double chins and half-closed, sleepy-looking eyes.[28]

From He Yingqin's perspective, the greatest problems revolved around the small amount of American material aid reaching China and American control over its distribution. With the closure of the Burma Road in early 1942, American supplies came via air transport across the Himalayas, known as the "Hump," a complicated and dangerous transport route by which only much smaller amounts of aid reached Kunming compared to the land route. While grateful for American material support, which Stilwell controlled and distributed, He Yingqin noted that most of the materials flown into China from India went to support the US forces in China, including the Fourteenth Air Force. This left little for Chinese

---

[27] *The Stilwell Papers*, September 23 and 24, 1942, 149–51.
[28] Dorn, *Walkout with Stilwell*, 36.

forces, which had already been fighting alone for five years and badly needed the equipment.[29]

While this situation irritated He Yingqin and served as the main source of tension with Stilwell, it also undoubtedly made the Chinese more amenable to a second Burma operation in the hope of reopening the land passage to Kunming. In October 1942, construction began on an alternative land route from India to southwest China, known as the Ledo Road, which would increase the flow of supplies for Nationalist troops. The second Burma operation took longer to plan and prepare for, in part because it involved deploying Chinese troops from both India and Yunnan. Stilwell intended to take the Chinese troops that had withdrawn to India after the first Burma operation, add reinforcements from China to bring this force up to nearly three divisions, and then equip and retrain them at the training center in Ramgarh in India's Bihar province. Meanwhile, the Nationalists would prepare a second force in Yunnan, which would participate in a two-pronged attack on Japanese forces in Burma planned for 1943. Stilwell had plans to equip and train another thirty Chinese Nationalist divisions as a part of a larger plan to reorganize the Chinese army and more effectively engage Japanese forces in China. He Yingqin cooperated with Stilwell, providing additional troops for the Chinese units in India, but it did not proceed fast or effectively enough for Stilwell. Multiple flights carrying as many as 400 to 600 men per day made the dangerous and uncomfortable three-hour flight from Kunming to India. Many of the 23,000 soldiers He Yingqin dispatched to India suffered from poor health and made the trip in shorts, since they would get American uniforms when they landed. Over the course of nearly two years, approximately 40 percent had to return to China because poor health precluded them from military service.[30] Barbara Tuchman noted one particular month in which American doctors rejected 89 percent of the Chinese recruits sent to Ramgarh as unfit for service.[31] Stilwell no doubt concluded that He Yingqin was deliberately dragging his feet on supplying troops for training and sent only the dregs of China's military conscripts for service in India. For He Yingqin, finding the 50,000 recruits Stilwell demanded for training in India proved no small feat. It is likely that He Yingqin preferred to keep his best military forces within China's own borders where they could deploy against the Japanese in central China, but over the summer of 1942 he worked diligently to send some 23,000 soldiers to Ramgarh.[32] Given the realities of China's

---

[29] *HYQJJ*, I, 669.    [30] Xiong Zongren, "He Yingqin yu Shidiwei," 36.

[31] Tuchman, *Stilwell and the American Experience in China*, 418.

[32] Liang, *General Stilwell in China*, 83.

conscription problems in 1942, it is not surprising that Stilwell found a high percentage of Chinese soldiers in poor physical condition, as was the case with many Chinese units at this point in the war.

While Stilwell fumed over what he perceived as Chinese failure to follow through on promises, He Yingqin also found that Stilwell did not always live up to his word. According to a verbal agreement between them, since Stilwell commanded Chinese soldiers, he promised to appoint a Chinese officer as his deputy chief of staff in India. Stilwell did so but, when he learned that this officer had been in direct contact with the Ministry of Military Administration in Chongqing, Stilwell removed him and appointed one of his own American subordinates, Brigadier General William Bergin, to take his place. Chinese officers in India resented such arbitrary and insulting actions.[33] In a memo to the US ambassador to China reporting on Stilwell's work in India, foreign service officer John Paton Davies remarked that Stilwell "has not concealed from the Chinese what he thinks of their incompetence and corruption. Naturally, many of them have thereby been offended."[34] When He Yingqin visited the Ramgarh training center in February 1943, he heard Chinese officers express a number of complaints about Stilwell. He Yingqin told them that he did not want to deal with Stilwell either, but asked them to put up with the situation as the price they must pay to get American aid.[35] He Yingqin also could not help noticing that Stilwell had stockpiled far more equipment, weapons, and trucks than He Yingqin believed he required to equip the Chinese forces training at Ramgarh, all at a time when the Chinese badly needed such materials in China.[36]

During his visit to India, He Yingqin discussed the second Burma operation with Stilwell and a host of other Allied officers including Lieutenant General John Somervell, head of Army Force Services, Lieutenant General Henry "Hap" Arnold, chief of the Air Corps, Field Marshal Archibald Wavell, and Sir John Dill, British representative to the combined chiefs of staff. He Yingqin went over the plan for the operation, stating that he would commit ten divisions of the Yunnan force (Y Force) to attack across the Yunnan–Burma border at Myitkina and Bhamo. The Chinese force in India (X Force) would push through the Hukawng valley to the west and drive toward Myitkina. With the reconquest of northern Burma, the united forces would push south toward Mandalay. The British would assist with an additional force also driving toward Mandalay from the west. He Yingqin insisted, as had Chiang Kai-shek

[33] Liang, *General Stilwell in China*, 87 n. 68.
[34] "The Stilwell Mission," USNA, RG 165, M1513, Reel 35.
[35] Xiong Zongren, "He Yingqin yu Shidiwei," 38.
[36] Xiong Zongren, *He Yingqin: xuanwozhong de lishi*, II, 481.

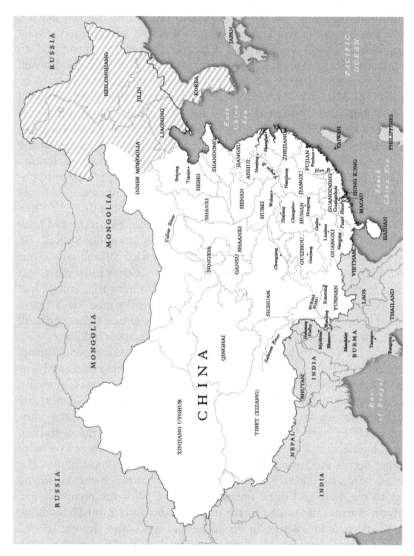

Map 7: China during the Sino-Japanese War

with regard to the first Burma operation, that the campaign required air and naval support along with secure control of the Bay of Bengal. Moreover, in preparation for the attack, scheduled for the end of October 1943, the United States must increase the amount of supplies delivered to China to 10,000 tons per month.[37] All parties generally agreed with the plan. In May, Stilwell made the long journey to Washington, DC, where American and British officials again discussed and agreed upon the plans for the second Burma operation. On May 25, President Roosevelt informed Song Ziwen, Chiang Kai-shek's special representative, that the United States would increase its material aid to China to 10,000 tons per month as requested.[38] More precisely, Roosevelt agreed to increase the amount of supplies flown into China to 7,000 tons per month as of July 1 and to 10,000 tons by September. He also insisted that, with this initial increase, 5,000 tons must go to the Fourteenth Air Force, leaving only 2,000 tons of supplies for all remaining Chinese forces.[39]

Upon his return to Chongqing, Stilwell joined He Yingqin in a meeting that revealed the fundamental differences in their perspectives on the war and their missions. According to He's interpreter, Chen Yanzhen, only the three of them were present for this meeting on June 15, 1943, with Chen interpreting. After Stilwell brought He Yingqin up to date on his discussions with Roosevelt, Marshall, and others in Washington, DC, they went over the preparations for the second Burma campaign and talked about the training center at Ramgarh. The stockpile of American Lend-Lease supplies in India, which He Yingqin had noted on his February trip to Ramgarh, would serve to outfit the Chinese forces currently training there. Stilwell reported that he had requested Roosevelt to provide equipment and arms, including artillery, for three more Chinese divisions that could help with the Burma operation and reopen the land route for supplies. While they could not transport the artillery pieces via air, they would first send the essentials over the Hump and then ship the artillery over land once the Allied forces reopened the road to Yunnan. Stilwell also told He Yingqin that as a part of his larger plan to reorganize Chinese military forces he had already requested equipment to outfit thirty divisions of Chinese troops, which would go through training at soon-to-be-established new training centers at Kunming and Guilin, based on the model of Ramgarh. In preparation, Stilwell asked He Yingqin for a chart showing all military units in China.[40]

[37] Liang, *General Stilwell in China*, 101.     [38] *HYQJJ*, I, 679.
[39] Tuchman, *Stilwell and the American Experience in China*, 476.
[40] Chen Yanzhen, "Zai He Yingqin de canmou zongzhang bangongshi sannian," 164–65.

He Yingqin appreciated the promises of increased American aid, but some aspects of the relationship troubled him greatly. First, the fact that Americans controlled the distribution of Lend-Lease supplies in China angered and insulted the Chinese, who interpreted this as a sign of American arrogance and condescension toward the Chinese government and military. Other countries receiving American aid, such as Britain and the Soviet Union, controlled distribution once the materials arrived. As a consequence, much of the aid that made it through to China went to American forces, especially the Fourteenth Air Force, rather than Chinese units. Stilwell and other Americans complained that Lend-Lease supplies ended up on for sale on the black market and therefore asked to verify Chinese unit rolls, along with equipment and food supply information. From the Chinese perspective, the meager amounts of aid the Americans provided did not justify this kind of intrusive behavior, causing He Yingqin to complain that, "if the Americans give something, they want to act as a 'supervisor' of the army."[41] Second, the request for the chart showing all Chinese military units implied that Stilwell and the Americans would choose which Chinese units received American arms and equipment. What if Stilwell decided to supply arms to a regional force that did not always adhere to Chongqing's directives, such as Long Yun's forces in Yunnan province? What if he wanted to arm CCP units, such as the Eighteenth Group Army? At this point, no one had suggested this, but it loomed as a distinct possibility. From He Yingqin's perspective, the goal of the Nationalist revolution, for which he had been working his entire career, had been to eliminate regional military forces and to unite China under a single government. Stilwell's distribution of Lend-Lease supplies threatened this core goal and led to He's strong objection. These divergent views served as a major source of tension between Stilwell and He Yingqin throughout their period of work together.[42]

Concerns about Lend-Lease aside, He Yingqin agreed with most of Stilwell's report, stating that some items required "further study and discussion" and needed Chiang Kai-shek's approval. Still, He Yingqin took the opportunity to remind Stilwell that, while he was able to focus exclusively on Burma, the Chinese had a broad swath of territory to protect, stretching across nine war zones, the Kunming field headquarters, and the substantial rear area around Chongqing. This reflects the fundamental perspective of each of these two chiefs of staff. Stilwell worked day and night with a singular focus on the reconquest of Burma and the

---

[41]  Chen Yanzhen, "Zai He Yingqin de canmou zongzhang bangongshi sannian," 166.
[42]  Chen Yanzhen, "Zai He Yingqin de canmou zongzhang bangongshi sannian," 163.

reestablishment of a land-based supply route from India to southwestern China. During his time in the China theater from 1942 to 1944, he devoted all of his energy and attention to this campaign outside China's borders. He Yingqin welcomed the idea of a campaign in Burma and the prospect of increasing the flow of American material aid from India, but he took a broader view of the war, which included dealing with Japanese offensives in other parts of China. Between early 1942 and late 1943, the Japanese launched major attacks against Nationalist forces in Zhejiang, Shaanxi, Yunnan, Guangdong, Hunan, and Hubei. From his perspective, Burma remained a secondary concern throughout the war. In the aftermath of the June 15 meeting, Stilwell's diary shows that he interpreted He Yingqin's remarks as pessimistic and opposed to the operation in Burma. "Ho's argument that nothing should be done to make it possible to win," Stilwell wrote on June 16, "because we will probably fail with things as they are, is typically Chinese."[43]

Later that month, the two men again clashed over priorities in the war effort. As Japanese forces pushed into Hunan, He Yingqin wanted to transfer some Yunnan forces and weapons that had been prepared for action in Burma to Hunan to help defend the Sixth War Zone. He Yingqin also requested that Stilwell send anti-tank weapons designated for the Yunnan force to units defending Hubei and Hunan against the Japanese. Stilwell ridiculed the request, which he interpreted as a deliberate attempt to obstruct his own efforts to build up a force for the Burma campaign and evidence of He's utter failure to execute his role as minister of military administration.[44] Stilwell tended to see He Yingqin as the major obstacle to his work in assembling a force for the Burma campaign and reorganizing the Chinese army. The different priorities of the two men produced strong tensions in their relationship, and it seems clear that the two chiefs of staff spent as much time talking past each other as they did talking to each other.

This contentious relationship generated attempts among the Chongqing elite to oust both Stilwell and He Yingqin from their respective positions. Stilwell's diary and letters reflect his growing contempt for He Yingqin, and he found a sympathetic ear in Chiang's wife, Song Meiling, and sister-in-law, Song Ailing. In meetings in September 1943, China's first lady confided to Stilwell that she too believed He Yingqin incompetent and that she was seeking to replace him as minister of military administration. She had long borne a grudge against He, in part because she felt that he did not take her seriously and in part because

---

[43] *The Stilwell Papers*, June 16, 1943, 207.
[44] *The Stilwell Papers*, June 21, 1943, 208, and June 28, 1943, 209.

she believed that he had attempted to have her husband killed during the Xi'an Incident. Over the course of several private conversations with Song Meiling and Song Ailing, Stilwell learned of the sisters' intense hatred of He Yingqin, refusing to even use his name, referring to him as the "unmentionable" and describing him as "a terribly conceited little monkey."[45] At the same time, Stilwell had his own critics working to remove him from his position and replace him with another American officer. In Washington, DC, Song Ziwen lobbied for Stilwell's removal based on the miserable performance in the Burma campaign and Stilwell's difficult personality. Song met with Franklin Roosevelt in August and requested Stilwell's recall. Roosevelt agreed, noting that General George Marshall had lost confidence in Stilwell, and informed Song that, if Chiang Kai-shek requested a change, Roosevelt would comply. Song relayed this to Chiang, who formally requested Stilwell's recall on October 15.[46]

Despite his growing conviction that Stilwell lacked the necessary skills to lead Chinese military forces effectively, Chiang almost immediately changed his mind and instead expressed to Roosevelt strong confidence in his American chief of staff. Most historians attribute this change of mind to a combination of factors, including Chiang's concern that insisting on Stilwell's removal would damage Sino-American relations and weaken China's overall war effort. Stilwell had been a strong advocate for more material aid for China and, as Hans van de Ven points out, Chiang may have seen retaining him as "the best way to secure a greater effort from the USA."[47] Others have suggested that strong support from Song Meiling and Song Ailing helped persuade Chiang to change his mind.[48] Interestingly, He Yingqin also lobbied Chiang to retain Stilwell. General Somervell reported to Stilwell that, when Chiang made the formal request for Stilwell's recall, He Yingqin went to Chiang to inquire why. By way of explanation, Chiang raised an old incident in which Stilwell had referred to Minister of Transportation Yu Feipeng as a "bandit," but He Yingqin remarked that he did not see this as sufficient reason to remove Stilwell.[49] Jay Taylor has suggested that He Yingqin opposed the recall in the hope that keeping Stilwell on might weaken Chiang's domestic position and allow He to take his place. At the same time, Taylor also suggests that Chiang reversed his decision because he feared that it would provoke a "squabble" with the United States, which might embolden his domestic enemies.[50] Putting aside the fact that there is no

[45] *The Stilwell Papers*, September 28, 1943, 228–29.
[46] Mitter, *Forgotten Ally*, 303.      [47] Van de Ven, *War and Nationalism*, 39.
[48] Yu, *The Dragon's War*, 170.      [49] *The Stilwell Papers*, October 15, 1943, 232.
[50] Taylor, *Generalissimo*, 237–38.

evidence to support claims that He Yingqin sought to replace Chiang, even if He was so inclined, as Taylor suggests, then logically he would have supported the recall and hoped for the domestic political backlash that Chiang feared. A more likely explanation is that He Yingqin understood the need for American Lend-Lease equipment as well as anyone. Like Chiang, he balked at the idea of requesting Stilwell's recall, fearing that it might send the wrong message to their American allies, especially with the important Cairo Conference just weeks away.

This might have been an opportunity for both sides to start again and find more effective ways to cooperate on the war effort. As Chiang prepared to depart for Cairo to meet with Roosevelt and Churchill, he directed He Yingqin to take steps to address Stilwell's complaints and to make sure the Chinese forces in India got the replacements they needed.[51] For his part, Stilwell promised Chiang that he would give his full cooperation going forward and would avoid "any superiority complex," though he privately described this as "balderdash."[52] Regardless, the development of the Chinese army in India and preparations for the second Burma operation continued to move at a pace that Stilwell found unacceptable. He continually complained that He Yingqin was dragging his feet on fulfilling Chiang's promise to provide 50,000 men for training in India. He also expressed disappointment with the change in commander of the India-based X Force as his preferred option Chen Cheng fell ill and gave way to Wei Lihuang, whom Stilwell did not believe up to the job.[53] The Song sisters continued to meet with Stilwell, with Meiling reminding him of her earlier promise to oust the "unmentionable" from his positions as minister of military administration and chief of staff.[54] On November 14, Stilwell learned with great satisfaction that Chiang had called in He Yingqin and angrily criticized him for not moving quickly enough in providing replacement troops to Ramgarh. Sensing that Song Meiling had been right and that Chiang might well sack He, Stilwell gleefully noted in his dairy: "Wonderful. Maybe now the fire is hot enough to fry Ho Ying-ch'in!!!!"[55]

Stilwell and Song Meiling may have had other reasons for anticipating He Yingqin's downfall. In late 1943 and early 1944, rumors circulated in Chongqing that Dai Li, head of the Bureau of Investigation and Statistics, had uncovered a group of military officers who had plotted a coup that some believed targeted He Yingqin. According to initial reports, the

[51] Liang, *General Stilwell in China*, 147.
[52] *The Stilwell Papers*, October 17, 1943, 232–33.
[53] *The Stilwell Papers*, November 7, 1943, 238.
[54] *The Stilwell Papers*, November 13, 1943, 240.
[55] *The Stilwell Papers*, November 14, 1943, 241.

plotting officers intended to seize Chiang upon his return from Cairo and demand that he dismiss several of his top officers, including He Yingqin, whom they blamed for the poor condition of the Chinese army. These reports also linked He's rival and Stilwell favorite General Chen Cheng to the group of plotters. In the wake of this discovery, Chiang ordered the execution of sixteen division commanders and the arrest of numerous lower-ranking officers.[56] Shortly thereafter, investigating journalists reported a different version of this "Young Officers Plot" that did not target He Yingqin at all. According to this version, the plot had grown out of He's attempt to implement a staff system based on the model of the German army. This involved placing graduates of the Military Staff College (*lujun daxue*) in all division commands of the army, which angered a number of division commanders who resented what they saw as an infringement on their authority. In this scenario, the graduates of the Staff College, not the unit commanders, hatched the plot and rather than target He Yingqin they may have believed their actions would win his support. This version credits Chen Cheng with uncovering the plot, rather than participating, and all sixteen officers executed in the end came from the ninth class of the Military Staff College. The exact details of this plot remain unclear, but it suggests widespread dissatisfaction and rivalry within the ranks of the Chinese military. Reporting on the issue from Chongqing, John Service noted that everyone he approached had some knowledge of this plot and the arrests.[57]

While Joseph Stilwell and Frank Dorn had long believed that He Yingqin stood to blame for the generally poor condition of the Chinese army and the lack of progress on the second Burma campaign, by early 1944 other American officials began to pay greater attention to him and report critically on his work. In late February, General Thomas Hearn, Stilwell's chief of staff, wrote to General Shang Zhen, director of the Foreign Affairs Bureau of the National Military Council, asking permission to send an "observer mission" to Yan'an to evaluate the CCP military force for potential cooperation with Americans in operations against the Japanese. In response, on April 12 He Yingqin penned a letter to Hearn rejecting the request, pointing out his view that the CCP amounted to an independent, armed entity with the long-range goals of seizing political power in China and fomenting world revolution. As such, the Nationalist government had to remain prepared for a possible CCP armed revolt and perhaps an attack on the Eighth War Zone, which would prove devastating to the Nationalists and benefit the Japanese. He explained that the central government had deployed Nationalist troops in

---

[56] *FRUS, 1944*, vol. VI, 312–13, 319–26.    [57] *FRUS, 1944*, vol. VI, 335–36.

the area around the CCP base to defend against this threat and described CCP military forces as engaging in unlawful activities. Prior to 1940, He Yingqin wrote, the central government had welcomed CCP forces into the Nationalist military and encouraged them to join the war of resistance. Instead, they instigated insubordination and advocated revolt against the government.[58] Given the experiences of the CCP attack on Nationalist forces at Huangqiao in 1940, of which the Americans remained unaware, and the Nationalist attack on the CCP's New Fourth Army in January 1941, He Yingqin did not see much chance for cooperation between the two forces. US ambassador to China Clarence Gauss took note of the letter, reporting to US Secretary of State Cordell Hull on some of He's "obvious untruths," and describing his views as "hardly credible" and even "slightly ludicrous."[59] The point here is not the accuracy of He's views, as he naturally had a different perspective on the CCP than his American allies, but rather the tone and terminology American officials now employed when they spoke of him. Stilwell's complaints, combined with domestic criticism of his work on conscription and supply, had now created a sharper focus on He Yingqin as a major problem within the Chinese government and military.

Some of the dissatisfaction with He Yingqin that Stilwell, Gauss, and other American officials expressed stemmed not so much from his actions as his words, which struck them as ungrateful. In early May, Ambassador Gauss alerted Secretary Hull to remarks He Yingqin had made on the issue of American aid to China while addressing the standing committee of the People's Political Council a few weeks earlier. According to Gauss, He Yingqin complained that most of the material aid designated for China went to Stilwell's forces in India and the Fourteenth Air Force, leaving next to nothing for other Chinese units. What aid they did receive consisted primarily of communications equipment and medical supplies. Noting that the Americans allowed the Soviets to use Lend-Lease aid as they saw fit, He Yingqin concluded that the Americans sought to both determine Chinese needs and control Chinese troops through liaison officers. Gauss described this to Hull as an example of what the "less friendly and [more] chauvinistic Chinese" are saying about American aid to China, clearly positioning He as anti-American. Gauss had to concede that many Chinese officials shared this view, but complained that "even usually reasonable Chinese friends of the United States are apt to display an unreasonable attitude" on this issue.[60] A few weeks later He Yingqin

[58] *FRUS, 1944*, vol. VI, 335–36.
[59] A translation of the letters and Gauss' comments are found in *FRUS, 1944*, vol. VI, 401–05.
[60] *FRUS, 1944*, vol. VI, 85–86.

hit many of the same points while delivering a military report at the Twelfth Plenum of the Fifth GMD National Congress in Chongqing. He Yingqin told his colleagues that, up to this point in the war, Allied material support to China had been minimal and that the weapons and ammunition that Chinese forces had used in the previous two years of combat operations had come primarily from domestic sources. He noted that, had the Allies provided greater amounts of material aid, Chinese forces could have launched more counterattacks against the Japanese. In the end, he told his audience, while China now stood as an equal member of the Allied war effort, its forces had essentially fought alone and the "final victory, without a doubt, belongs to China."[61] Such remarks angered American officials and no doubt sharpened their criticisms of He Yingqin.

## The Stilwell Incident and aftermath

The issue of American aid and its distribution came to a head in the spring and summer of 1944, with the famous Stilwell Incident.[62] As the Sino-American relationship deteriorated, the Japanese launched the largest operation of the war, designed to destroy airbases and create a corridor through central China that would allow direct communication and transport of Japanese forces in Manchuria, China, and Indochina. Operation Ichigo began in mid April with a thrust south along railroad lines into Henan, Hunan, and Hubei, followed by a two-pronged attack into Guangdong, Guangxi, and Guizhou.[63] In order to deal with this attack, He Yingqin appealed to American officials for increased aid and air support, describing China's current military situation as "desperate." He informed them that the Japanese had been moving troops and planes from Manchuria for use in central China and asked if the United States could persuade the Soviet government to take steps to prevent the Japanese from executing these transfers.[64] The response came from Cordell Hull in mid June, rejecting each one of He Yingqin's requests.

---

[61] *HYQJJ*, I, 697–98.

[62] Most works on the subject have told the story of the Stilwell Incident from the American perspective, such as Barbara Tuchman's *Stilwell and the American Experience in China* and Frank Dorn's *Walkout with Stilwell*, both of which amount to sympathetic portrayals of Stilwell. Frank McLynn's *Burma Campaign* continues this tradition. More recently, Hans van de Ven and Rana Mitter have done excellent work in examining the issue from the Nationalist Chinese perspective. See van de Ven, *War and Nationalism*, 19–63; and Mitter, *Forgotten Ally*, 239–62 and 335–44.

[63] Hara Takeshi, "The Ichigo Offensive," in Peattie, Drea, and van de Ven, eds., *The Battle for China*, 392–93.

[64] *FRUS, 1944*, vol. VI, 91.

In his explanation, Hull expressed doubts about the veracity of He Yingqin's characterization of the situation, noting cynically that Chinese claims to be in "grave danger" accompanied by requests for more aid amounted to nothing new and had been a regular part of conversations between American and Chinese officials since the start of the Pacific War. Even when he went on to acknowledge that the current situation indeed appeared dire and that the Japanese offensive might even threaten the capital at Chongqing, he insisted that American military officials had not been able to confirm He Yingqin's claims of Japanese troop transfers from Manchuria to central China, which served as the basis for the request. With regard to the Soviet government, Hull wrote, "it is not opportune at the present time to request the Soviets to carry out any diversionary movements in eastern Siberia." As for increased material aid, Hull directed Ambassador Gauss to explain to He Yingqin and Chinese officials that, while the United States desired to help, its military operations in the European theater made it impossible to increase aid to China. He closed with some advice for Chinese officials that he believed might improve the military situation: reconciliation between the GMD and the CCP, better utilization of material and manpower at hand, and better military intelligence and coordination with the help of American staff officers.[65] With 500,000 Japanese troops pushing south through Hunan and threatening the entire southwest of China, He Yingqin no doubt found these suggestions unhelpful and insulting.

As Operation Ichigo unfolded, the Nationalists' inability to defend central China confirmed the views of American officials who had come to believe Chiang Kai-shek and He Yingqin incapable of providing effective leadership. In July 1944, Franklin Roosevelt began sending a series of messages to Chiang Kai-shek that triggered a crisis in Sino-American relations. Though Stilwell had his detractors, by mid 1944 both US Army chief of staff General George Marshall and President Roosevelt had concluded that to reverse the deteriorating military situation in China they must remove Stilwell from Burma and send him to Chongqing to take command of all Chinese military forces. When Marshall consulted with Stilwell to ask if he thought such a change would improve the situation in China, Stilwell replied in the affirmative and laid down the precondition that "Ho Ying-ch'in would have to step out as Chief of Staff."[66] With the support of Marshall and the Joint Chiefs of Staff, Roosevelt sent Chiang Kai-shek a formal message on July 6, 1944, requesting that he

[65] *FRUS, 1944*, vol. VI, 105–06.
[66] Charles F. Romanus and Riley Sunderland, *China-Burma-India Theater: Stilwell's Command Problems* (Washington, DC: Office of the Chief of Military History, 1955), 380.

put Stilwell "directly under you and in command of Chinese and American forces." He urged Chiang to "charge him with the full responsibility and authority for the coordination and direction of operations required to stem the tide of the enemy's advances."[67]

Though deeply insulted, Chiang understood that an outright refusal might mean the end of the Sino-American alliance and material aid from the United States. Instead, he decided to agree in principle with this request, but to delay its execution.[68] His response to Roosevelt on July 8 expressed willingness to accept Stilwell as commander of all Chinese forces, but warned that a hasty implementation might only make things worse. He therefore requested a "preparatory period" of undetermined length before Stilwell took the new position.[69] Chiang then assembled his top officers to discuss the situation. As one might expect, He Yingqin strongly opposed the change and counseled Chiang to reject Roosevelt's request even if it meant the loss of all American Lend-Lease aid.[70] This is not surprising, as most Chinese officers found the idea of placing a foreigner in control of Chinese military forces an affront to Chinese sovereignty and an insult to China's leadership. He Yingqin had on more than one occasion expressed his view that in the grand scope of the war American aid had made little difference to China's war effort and that, given the circumstances, China must be prepared to go it alone. On a personal level, he could not help but see this as a direct attack on himself. Regardless, he accepted Chiang's decision and then offered a plan for mitigating the impact of the change.

On July 17, He Yingqin proposed to Chiang Kai-shek a plan to reorganize the Chinese military as a way to limit the number of Chinese units that would fall under Stilwell's command. According to this plan, Chiang would divide the Nationalist army into two categories, a "field" army (yezhanjun) and a "garrison" (shoubeijun) army. The "field" army would include only those units currently engaged in combat against the Japanese in parts of China or in Burma. These units, probably a total of three to five corps, would fall under Stilwell's command, and the United States would be obligated to equip and arm them while the Chinese would take care of replacements and appoint personnel. The "garrison" army, composed of all remaining military forces, would remain under the command of Chiang and his Chinese officers. He Yingqin believed that this would meet the letter of Chiang's promise, limit the scope of

[67] Romanus and Sunderland, *Stilwell's Command Problems*, 383.
[68] Taylor, *Generalissimo*, 278.
[69] Romanus and Sunderland, *Stilwell's Command Problems*, 385–86.
[70] Xiong Zongren, "He Yingqin yu Shidiwei," 39.

Stilwell's control, and, perhaps most importantly, allow Stilwell to experi-ence the complexity of the larger Chinese military and lead him to realize that he could not command it effectively. This agreement excluded all CCP forces, which He Yingqin regarded as a deal-breaker.[71] Chiang accepted the basic outline of this plan and established a set of param-eters for Stilwell's new position. As "Chief of Staff and concurrently Commander in Chief of the Sino-American Allied Field Forces," Stilwell would have complete control of the designated field army. The United States would provide weapons, military and communications equipment, and vehicles to support the field army, but the Chinese government would take responsibility for distribution of this material. Chiang sent this plan to his new special representative in Washington, his brother-in-law Kong Xiangxi, who passed it on to Roosevelt on July 23.

In the summer of 1944, the Americans kept a watch on operations in Burma and waited to see if Chiang would follow through on his general agreement to put Stilwell in command of Chinese forces. The National-ists focused on the situation in central and southwestern China, where Japanese forces pushed into southern Hunan, capturing Hengyang on August 8, and prepared to advance into Guangxi and Guizhou. In early September, He Yingqin flew to Guiyang to direct the defense of Guilin and Liuzhou, which lay directly in the path between the Japanese and the temporary capital at Chongqing. To defend against approximately 150,000 advancing Japanese, He Yingqin had only 120,000 National-ist troops.[72] He perhaps understandably felt that many of the Nation-alists' best troops now engaged in Burma would have come in handy in the defense of Guilin and Liuzhou, as would the Lend-Lease mate-rials devoted to that battlefield. Meanwhile, Stilwell visited Guilin to examine the plan to defend the city and found what he described as 50,000 "demoralized" Chinese troops preparing to face 9 Japanese divi-sions and complained that He Yingqin had done nothing to bring in reinforcements. His advice to improve the situation, noted in his diary, included putting He Yingqin and Chiang Kai-shek in front of a firing squad.[73]

Returning to Chongqing in early September, He Yingqin met with Stilwell and Patrick Hurley, Franklin Roosevelt's special representative to China. In a series of discussions on September 12 and 13, they argued over Lend-Lease materials, which He Yingqin maintained he badly needed for the defense of southwestern China. They also discussed

[71] Liang, *General Stilwell in China*, 244–45; *SLGB*, LVIII, September 13, 1944, 346. Liang uses the terms "Offensive" and "Defensive" units rather than "Field" and "Garrison" units.
[72] *HYQJJ*, I, 700.    [73] *The Stilwell Papers*, September 9, 1944, 327.

the details of the plan to put Stilwell in command of Chinese forces, such as whether he would have the authority to appoint or dismiss Chinese officers and implement discipline as he saw fit, and whether to include Chinese communist forces under Stilwell's command.[74] With the negotiations deadlocked, Stilwell received Roosevelt's famous September 19 message to Chiang Kai-shek, which in frank language demanded for the final time that Chiang put Stilwell in "unrestricted command of all your [Chiang's] forces."[75] Chiang had been willing to accept Stilwell's command in some modified form, but with this final insult he refused to consider the matter further. A few days later, He Yingqin met privately with Stilwell, urging him to drop the demand for control of distribution of Lend-Lease materials, which He saw as a key sticking point. Stilwell acknowledged the legitimacy of this point, noting, as He Yingqin had on a number of occasions, that the British and Soviets suffered no such restrictions on their aid. As a result, Stilwell dropped his demand for control of Lend-Lease materials in an attempt to break the deadlock.[76] It proved too late to salvage the relationship, and on September 25 Chiang Kai-shek notified Hurley that he could not accept Stilwell as a commander because to do so would "do irreparable injury to the vital Chinese–American military cooperation" and asked that the United States replace Stilwell with another officer.[77]

In the wake of Chiang's decision to refuse Roosevelt's request and his demand for Stilwell's recall, on October 3, 1944, He Yingqin made a public speech intending to clarify some "misunderstandings" in the international community about China's war effort, the Stilwell affair, and questions about Lend-Lease aid. Ostensibly, He gave this speech to refute statements by British prime minister Winston Churchill, who in addressing the lower house of Parliament had criticized the Chinese war effort, but there is no doubt that he also aimed his remarks at Joseph Stilwell and other American officials. Speaking on behalf of the Military Affairs Commission, He Yingqin claimed first that General Stilwell had spent the previous two years trying to wipe away the memory of his initial defeat in Burma. His attempts to take control of Chinese forces served as a way to help him redress his own personal failure in the first Burma campaign. Second, he described Stilwell as a victim of CCP propaganda, which falsely claimed that Nationalist forces could not adequately make use of Lend-Lease material aid. He Yingqin stated that this had made a deep impression on American and British views of the Nationalists and

[74]  Liang, *General Stilwell in China*, 250.
[75]  Romanus and Sunderland, *Stilwell's Command Problems*, 446.
[76]  Liang, *General Stilwell in China*, 258; *The Stilwell Papers*, September 23, 1944, 335.
[77]  Romanus and Sunderland, *Stilwell's Command Problems*, 452–53.

had contributed to Churchill's willingness to find fault with China's war effort. Defending his government against accusations that it had misused material aid from its allies, He Yingqin asserted that the problem lay not in Chinese mishandling of aid but in the meager amounts that actually reached forces under Chinese command. According to his statistics, by the end of June 1944, the United States had distributed a total of US$28.2 billion in Lend-Lease aid. Of this, US$9.3 billion went to Britain, while only US$150 million went to China. This represents a little more than 0.5 percent of all Lend-Lease aid. Moreover, most of this US$150 million in aid went to the Fourteenth Air Force and Chinese forces under American command and was destined for the campaigns in Burma, leaving little for troops inside China.[78] He Yingqin's remarks amounted to a public expression of the view Chiang privately expressed to Franklin Roosevelt a week later on October 9. As Chiang put it, Stilwell's insistence on giving priority to the Burma operation had endangered China's very existence, pointing out that the Japanese offensive in Hunan and Guangxi involved six times as many troops as those Stilwell faced in Burma and represented a much more serious threat. Exhibiting complete indifference to the situation in China, Chiang complained, Stilwell refused to redirect Lend-Lease material in Yunnan, designated for use in Burma, to the east China front. "In short," Chiang summed up, "we have taken Myitkina but we have lost almost all of east China."[79]

On October 19, as Japanese forces pushed deeper into Guangxi and the threat against Chongqing intensified, Roosevelt recalled Stilwell. As he prepared to leave China, Stilwell learned that Chiang Kai-shek had decided to award him a military decoration as a conciliatory gesture, but Stilwell declined the honor. The conclusion of the Stilwell Incident might have relieved some of the immediate tension in the Sino-American relationship, but it did nothing to change American views of He Yingqin, whom US officials continued to identify as a central obstacle to effective military operations in China. A September report from Augustus Chase of the State Department's division of Chinese affairs referred to He Yingqin's "violent prejudice and utterly unscrupulous disregard of the truth." Relying on reports of an "off the record" conversation between He Yingqin and a British journalist, Chase argued that He had made a number of "ridiculous assertions" about the Chinese communists.[80] As Roosevelt and Marshall considered their options for replacing

---

[78] *HYQJJ*, I, 701.
[79] Romanus and Sunderland, *Stilwell's Command Problems*, 461–62.
[80] *FRUS, 1944*, vol. VI, 582–83.

Stilwell, John Carter Vincent, Chase's division chief, offered his view on the situation in a memorandum to the president. Any American officer who took over as Chiang's Allied chief of staff, Vincent argued, would find it difficult to operate effectively unless Chiang was willing to make changes to his Chinese staff. Singling out only one individual, Vincent emphasized, "It is understood that much of General Stilwell's difficulty can be traced to the uncooperative attitude of General Ho Ying-ch'in, Minister of War and Chief of Staff. Furthermore, General Ho's inefficiency and military incompetence have undermined the morale of the Chinese Army and prevented its organization into an effective military force." Vincent went on to recommend General Chen Cheng, an officer whom Stilwell had praised, as a replacement for He Yingqin and advised that Roosevelt make this suggestion to Chiang Kai-shek directly.[81]

Some American journalists offered similar assessments, echoing the criticisms of US diplomats and military officers. Brooks Atkinson of the *New York Times* wrote articles praising Stilwell for his "constantly frustrated attempt to help China stay in the war and to improve the combat efficiency of the Chinese forces." With regard to He Yingqin, Atkinson described Stilwell as "more intimately acquainted with the needs and capacities of the Chinese Army than the Generalissimo and Gen. Ho Ying-chin, Minister of War and Chief of Staff."[82] Beyond the conflict with Stilwell, Atkinson pointed specifically to problems in conscription, blaming He Yingqin for treating Chinese soldiers with "callousness and inhumanity," for permitting "the Chinese armies to disintegrate," and for causing the "military disasters of Honan and Hunan" earlier in the year.[83]

The fallout from the Stilwell Incident precipitated changes on both sides of the Sino-American alliance. On October 27, General George Marshall informed General Albert Wedemeyer that President Roosevelt had appointed him as Stilwell's replacement as commander of American forces in the China theater and Allied chief of staff to Chiang Kai-shek.[84] One week later, He Yingqin resigned as minister of military administration, and Chiang Kai-shek appointed General Chen Cheng to replace

---

[81] *FRUS, 1944*, vol. VI, 181–82.

[82] Brooks Atkinson, "Long Schism Seen, Stilwell Break Stems from Chiang Refusal to Press War Fully," *New York Times*, October 31, 1944. Western reporters often referred to Chiang as "Generalissimo."

[83] Brooks Atkinson, "Realism Is Urged in Judging China," *New York Times*, November 21, 1944.

[84] Albert C. Wedemeyer, *Wedemeyer Reports!* (New York: Henry Holt and Company, 1958), 267–68.

him. News reports at the time suggested significant American pressure on Chiang to reorganize the government.[85]

Ostensibly, He Yingqin tendered his resignation because he had accepted an appointment as commander of the Chinese army in late November 1944, taking on responsibility for the defense of the southwest. With this new responsibility, he claimed he could not continue his work as minister of military administration and therefore resigned from this position, but few have accepted this official explanation.[86] Some have suggested that Chiang Kai-shek demanded He Yingqin's resignation due to his poor performance as a military administrator or his frustration with problems in conscription and supply, or because the results of the Ichigo Offensive "discredited" He Yingqin as minister of military administration.[87] Others have interpreted it as part of a longstanding rivalry between He Yingqin and Chen Cheng, with Chen lobbying Chiang to remove He so that Chen could replace him.[88] Another theory holds that one of Chiang's war goals involved the intentional destruction of regional units and the preservation of central army units. According to this view, Chiang removed He Yingqin because he had not done enough to weaken these regional forces.[89] A common thread in all of these theories is that Chiang removed He Yingqin against his wishes and that this represented a fall or demotion for He.

There is reason to doubt He Yingqin's claim that his new duties made it impossible for him to continue as minister of military administration. He submitted his letter of resignation on November 3, almost three weeks before his appointment as commander of the Chinese army, which came on November 20. Perhaps Chiang and He discussed the matter and agreed to these changes privately, well before the official announcements in order to provide He with a "face-saving" way out. It is clear, however, that He Yingqin had tried to resign before, but Chiang had refused to allow him to do so. Chiang Kai-shek left a detailed description of He's letter of resignation in his personal papers, which reflects He's desire to give up his position as minister of military administration. In his November 3 letter, He Yingqin wrote that he "*again* [emphasis added] seeks your Excellency's [Chiang's] approval of my earlier request to resign as minister of military administration" (*chongshen qianqing rengken junzuo*

---

[85] Associated Press, "Chiang Drops Ho as War Minister," *New York Times*, November 21, 1944; "Chungking Changes," *New York Times*, November 26, 1944.

[86] *HYQJJ*, I, 703.

[87] Chen and Zhang, *Jiang Jieshi he huangpu xi*, 270; Gillin, "Problems of Centralization in Republican China," 847.

[88] Xiong Zongren, *He Yingqin: xuanwozhong de lishi*, II, 494; Li Zhongming, *He Yingqin dazhuan*, 278–82.

[89] Tsung-jen Li, *Memoirs*, 436.

*zhunzhi jiechu junzheng buzhang jianzhi*), clearly implying that this was not his first attempt to resign.[90] In fact, one of He's secretaries, Xie Boyuan, claimed that he tried to resign several times over the course of the war, but each time Chiang either ignored the request or asked him to stay on as minister of military administration.[91] The resignation letter also makes it clear that He Yingqin believed that the minister of military administration carried too much responsibility and had far too many duties to be effective. He pointed out that each day he had to attend at least 2 meetings and give reports, to meet with more than 10 visitors or guests, review more than 200 documents, and cooperate with relevant Allied officials on military affairs. In fact, he recommended that Chiang reduce the responsibilities of the next minister of military administration, which would allow him more time to do more important work such as visit the front lines and inspect and improve the work of various military offices.[92] Perhaps most importantly, He Yingqin's letter makes reference to public opinion both in China and abroad which blamed him for recent problems. He not only wrote that he felt a weariness of mind and body as a result of the burdens of the job and the sting of criticisms, but also expressed a concern that these criticisms might have an adverse effect on the central government.[93]

He Yingqin's resignation came as a result of a combination of factors, but the existing evidence suggests that it is best understood as a consequence of the Stilwell Incident. It is certainly true that Chiang Kai-shek expressed frustration at problems in conscription and other areas of military administration under He's purview but, though he had multiple opportunities to accept He's resignation, he chose not to do so. Moreover, when Chiang finally did accept it, he appointed He Yingqin commander of the Chinese army and gave him responsibility for stopping the Japanese advance into the southwest. This does not support the argument that Chiang had lost faith in He Yingqin or that Chiang forced him to resign for poor performance, but rather suggests continuing confidence and trust. It is also true that He Yingqin had a longstanding rivalry with Chen Cheng, dating back to the Northern Expedition. If this was a key factor in the change, why did it take place at this time? He Yingqin had offered to resign on several occasions and Chiang could have taken advantage of any one of them to promote Chen Cheng. T'ien-wei Wu claims that Chiang had discussed this change as far back as 1936 during the Xi'an Incident.[94] More compelling is the connection between

[90] *SLGB*, LIX, November 3, 1944, 14.
[91] Xie Boyuan, "Wosuo liaojie de He Yingqin," 149.
[92] *SLGB*, LIX, November 3, 1944, 15.
[93] *SLGB*, LIX, November 3, 1944, 13.    [94] T'ien-wei Wu, *The Sian Incident*, 91.

American criticisms of He Yingqin and his resignation. Without pressure from the United States, it is not at all clear that Chiang would have removed He as minister of military administration. In the wake of Stilwell's recall, Chiang needed to restart Sino-American relations, to ensure that the Americans would continue to provide material support for China's war effort, and to find a way to begin working constructively with the Allies. With the Sino-American relationship at its lowest point of the war, He Yingqin stood out as a prominent target for critics on both sides. Franklin Roosevelt had accepted his demand for Stilwell's recall, so Chiang reciprocated by accepting He's resignation in order to start again with a clean slate. In the end, Stilwell's prediction about frying He Yingqin in the fire came true.

The change had immediate effect as Americans in Chongqing quickly reported an improvement in the Sino-American relationship. On the very same day that the Chinese government announced that Chen Cheng would replace He Yingqin as minister of military administration, John Carter Vincent reported this as an encouraging step, tempered only by the fact that He Yingqin retained his position as Chiang's chief of staff.[95] Three days later, US chargé d'affaires George Atcheson described the change as "a concrete improvement" and claimed that with this stumbling block out of the way Americans now enjoyed "excellent" relationships with Chinese officials at the highest level.[96]

### Commander of the Chinese army

Since most observers interpreted He Yingqin's resignation as coerced or a punishment for poor performance, it no doubt caused him a certain degree of pain and humiliation. On the other hand, his new assignment as commander of the Chinese army meant a shift away from the tiresome administrative duties that had occupied him during the preceding fourteen years and a return to command of troops and direct responsibility for major operations. It came at a critical time as Japanese forces continued the attacks associated with Operation Ichigo, which began in the spring of 1944, but in the fall targeted the southwestern provinces of Guangxi and Guizhou, and threatened Sichuan. He Yingqin had twenty-eight corps, eighty-six divisions, and a number of specialty units at his disposal for the defense of the southwest.[97] By late November and early December 1944, as He Yingqin took up his new post, the Japanese had

[95] *FRUS, 1944*, vol. VI, 705.     [96] *FRUS, 1944*, vol. VI, 197.
[97] *HYQJJ*, I, 704. American sources indicate that He Yingqin had twelve corps comprising thirty-six divisions, but this represents only those Chinese units that had American arms and equipment. See *FRUS, 1945*, vol. VII, 84–85.

pushed deep into Guangxi, capturing airbases at Guilin and Liuzhou, and now stood poised to strike north toward Guiyang. From there, the Japanese could either continue north to threaten the wartime capital at Chongqing or, perhaps more importantly, move west to capture Kunming and shut off the flow of American Lend-Lease supplies to China. Either would prove disastrous for the war effort. The civilian populations of both cities had begun to panic, and the American embassy advised Americans in Yunnan, Guizhou, and Guangxi to leave immediately.[98]

At this crucial moment, American officials expressed deep concerns about He Yingqin's ability to direct major operations in the southwest. In mid November 1944, when Wedemeyer and Chiang first conferred on Operation Alpha, the plan for the defense of Kunming, Wedemeyer recommended that Chen Cheng take command of Chinese troops involved. Chiang demurred, informing his new American chief of staff that he preferred to keep Chen as minister of military administration. Stressing the importance of the mission, Wedemeyer urged Chiang to give the assignment to his most capable general. Chiang agreed and then informed him on November 21 that he had appointed He Yingqin to the position. Stunned and disappointed, Wedemeyer could not help but ask if Chiang realized that this was the most important position in China and if he was sure that He Yingqin was the best man for the job. Other American officials raised the same question, and in each case Chiang defended his choice. Wedemeyer did not take this decision well, describing it as a "decisive blow," and "forcefully" raised the matter with Chiang again. Chiang repeatedly supported He, describing him as "China's outstanding general."[99]

With Chiang's strong support, though not Wedemeyer's, He Yingqin traveled to Guiyang in early December to meet with his commanders and local officials to discuss the defense of the city. The discussion revealed a variety of views, with some advocating a withdrawal and a scorched-earth policy, perhaps even setting fire to the city as had been the case at Changsha in 1938. He Yingqin remained quiet and listened to the discussion, but did not support such drastic action. Among those present at the meeting, Zhang Zhizhong, governor of Hunan at the time of the Changsha fire, spoke against a repeat of this tactic. Though unwilling to torch the city, He Yingqin left the meeting convinced of the likelihood that he could not hold Guiyang and of the need to take measures to ensure that the Japanese could not make use of any military or industrial

[98] "Americans Urged to Leave Kunming," *New York Times*, December 3, 1944.
[99] Charles F. Romanus and Riley Sunderland. *China-Burma-India Theater: Time Runs Out in CBI* (Washington, DC: Office of the Chief of Military History, 1959), 63.

facilities. He then met with the Guiyang garrison commander Song Siyi to develop a plan to destroy twenty-eight installations across the city, including power plants, textile factories, communications facilities, and military bases. Song expressed his concern that this would be a difficult task and worried about a mistake, which could lead to greater-than-expected damage. With He Yingqin's permission, Song passed the job along to another officer.[100]

The plan proved unnecessary as the Japanese halted their operations in Guizhou and wrapped up Operation Ichigo, concentrating on completing the overland route through to Indochina and abandoning the push to the west. With the pressure on the southwest abating, He Yingqin established a new headquarters at Kunming and began planning a counterattack. He organized his forces into four front armies, with Generals Lu Han, Zhang Fakui, Tang Enbo, and Wang Shengwu commanding the First, Second, Third, and Fourth Front Armies, respectively. By this time, most and perhaps all of these units had American weapons and equipment.[101] In his remarks at the ceremony marking the formal establishment of the Chinese army headquarters at Kunming, he returned to familiar themes to instill pride in his troops. He reminded them that, while other countries had sympathized with China during the past four and a half years of war, they had provided only minimal amounts of material aid. The Allies had conducted naval and air operations in the Pacific theater, but in China the Chinese soldier had fought alone, for which he should be proud. At the same time, he stressed the need to modernize the Chinese army with up-to-date equipment and training. He pointed to Chinese soldiers trained in India to fight in the second Burma operation as an example of what Chinese troops could accomplish if properly armed and trained. He concluded with the optimistic view that the combination of manpower and revolutionary spirit of the Chinese and the weapons and material supplies of the Allied countries that would flow through the reopened road in Burma would lead to the destruction of the enemy.[102]

The end of Operation Ichigo and Allied success in the Pacific took the immediate pressure off the Chinese army in early 1945, allowing He Yingqin to prepare for an attack on Guangxi in the spring and summer of 1945. The Chinese force in Burma captured Wanding in late January, reopening the China–India land route, which Chiang Kai-shek officially

---

[100]  Xia Lumei, "He Yingqin zai lujun zongbu" [He Yingqin as Commander of the Army], in Tu Yueseng, ed., *Xingyi Wang, Liu, He sanda jiazu*, 194–95.

[101]  *HYQJJ*, I, 704–05.

[102]  He Yingqin, "Zhongguo lujun zongsilingbu chengli de yiyi yu renwu" [Remarks on the Importance and Mission of the Chinese Army Headquarters at Its Establishment], in He Yingqin, ed., *Weibang bainian ji*, 386–87.

named the "Stilwell Road" in honor of his former American chief of staff.[103] He Yingqin spent much of the spring of 1945 traveling with an American officer, Major General Robert B. McClure, chief of staff to General Wedemeyer. The two men inspected troops in Burma and Yunnan, which now had greater access to American weapons, ammunition, and supplies and were preparing for the Guangxi and Hunan campaign. The counterattack McClure and He organized on Guangxi gradually pushed the Japanese back over the course of May, June, and July, recapturing Nanning, Liuzhou, and Guilin in succession.[104] In June, He Yingqin directed the final major campaign of the war, which took place in western Hunan, where Japanese forces were planning an attack on the American airbase at Zhijiang. The attack went smoothly with a victory for the Chinese forces, despite significant casualties.[105]

McClure and He Yingqin worked closely together, but many Americans still perceived He as a problem for US policy in China, and the mention of his name continued to invoke a stream of criticism. In a February 1945 telegram to the acting Secretary of State, director of the Office of Far Eastern Affairs Joseph Ballantine repeated well-worn criticisms of He Yingqin, describing him as "uncooperative" and so ardently anti-communist that he stood as "the principal stumbling block to a settlement between the Chinese government and the Chinese communists." He also reported that the Soviets viewed He as "pro-Japanese." Still, mindful of the need to tread softly in the wake of Stilwell's stormy relationship with Chinese authorities, Ballantine advised his superiors that, if journalists inquired about He Yingqin, it would be best to restrict themselves to noncommittal remarks, such as that he had long served as a trusted military advisor and associate of Chiang Kai-shek.[106] That same week, General Wedemeyer, careful to present a façade of confidence and optimism, went far beyond noncommittal remarks in referring to He Yingqin as "the General Eisenhower of this Theater."[107]

He Yingqin knew well that many Americans held him in contempt and took a dim view of the Chinese military as a whole. One particular rumor that bothered him involved accusations that the Nationalists had hoarded American Lend-Lease supplies in order to use them in a later civil war against the CCP. When the opportunity presented itself, He Yingqin attempted to refute these accusations and bring American observers around to what he considered a more accurate understanding of the Chinese military and its situation. On June 25, following the

---

[103] *HYQJJ*, I, 706.    [104] *HYQJJ*, I, 714–15.
[105] Xia Lumei, "He Yingqin zai lujun zongbu," 196–97; Romanus and Sunderland, *Stilwell's Command Problems*, 288–89.
[106] *FRUS, 1945*, vol. VII, 47–48.
[107] "China Announces 500,000 Draft Call," *New York Times*, February 16, 1945.

victory over Japanese forces in western Hunan, He found himself in front of an audience of American journalists. He gave them a typical report on the situation in each war zone, but then launched into extensive remarks on Sino-American relations during the war. He acknowledged American contributions to the Chinese war effort, in terms of both material through the Lend-Lease Act and the work of American officers in China such as Stilwell, Chennault, and McClure. At the same time, he addressed what he called widespread "misunderstandings" between the Chinese and American people. For example, he told the journalists that he had heard that many Americans thought that US officers had direct command over Chinese forces in the China theater. With the exception of General Stilwell and the Chinese Expeditionary Force in Burma, he explained, this was false. American officers in the China theater served as advisors to Chinese commanders. He Yingqin then addressed the frequent rumor that the Chinese government and military had secretly hoarded American Lend-Lease supplies. He referred to a report from a joint Sino-American Committee formed the previous year to look into such claims, which found no evidence of any such hoarding or misuse of Lend-Lease supplies. He also pointed out that the allocation and distribution of Lend-Lease supplies were determined with cooperation between American and Chinese officers, and that the supplies were delivered with the assistance of American service of supply officers, who staff each Chinese corps and division. In fact, He Yingqin stressed, the supplies were never in the sole possession of the Chinese government or army. In concluding, he guaranteed the reporters that "each rifle and each bullet" would be used against the Japanese.[108]

Perhaps realizing that he needed to take steps to improve his relations with American officials, during the summer of 1945 He Yingqin began to change his tone when speaking about the American role in the Chinese war effort. At least some observers took note and began to change their views of He. After Stilwell's departure from China, He Yingqin had on a number of occasions downplayed the American role in the China theater and pointed out the meager amounts of Lend-Lease supplies that had found their way into the hands of Chinese soldiers. Yet Consul General William R. Langdon's July 23 report to the newly appointed secretary of state James Byrnes noted a change in He's attitude, as evidenced in recent remarks which Langdon believed gave "credit where credit is due as far as American participation" in the China theater was concerned. Langdon also reported on remarks from a "fairly high placed" American officer who commented favorably on He Yingqin's recent work as commander of the Chinese army. The officer concluded that perhaps the

[108] *HYQJJ*, I, 723–26.

administrative and political duties in He's earlier position as minister of military administration had kept him "held in" and not allowed him to exercise his strengths. The new position as commander of the Chinese army returned him to "field work," where his "qualities of initiative and capability" served him well.[109]

The success of the western Hunan campaign marked the end of major combat operations in China and, together with the American campaign in the Pacific, the bombing of Japan's home islands, the Soviet entry into the war, and the two atomic bombings, brought the war to a close. When the Chinese Foreign Ministry received a message from the Japanese government on August 14 announcing its surrender, Chiang Kai-shek informed He Yingqin that he would serve as the representative of Chinese Supreme Command in the China Theater in the formal surrender ceremony.[110] Continuing to work with General McClure, He Yingqin took over the task of managing the surrender of the more than 2 million Japanese troops in China and the northern portion of French Indochina. This involved creating fifteen surrender zones, appointing Chinese commanders in each zone to supervise the disarming and concentrating of Japanese troops for repatriation, coordinating with the Japanese to identify officers responsible for organizing their troops for surrender in each zone, and making sure that troops on both sides understood the procedure and adhered to it.[111] He Yingqin disseminated a set of rules or "admonitions" for Chinese forces taking the surrender of Japanese troops, including warnings to maintain order and discipline, to protect civilians in the reoccupied areas, and to turn over all Japanese documents and materials, and a prohibition against harming or humiliating prisoners.[112]

The high point of the surrender process, and perhaps of He Yingqin's military career, came with the formal surrender ceremony in Nanjing on September 9, 1945. He Yingqin arrived in Nanjing the day before where a substantial crowd of well-wishers met his plane at the airport and flag-waving schoolchildren lined the road. The ceremony took place in the main hall of the Central Military Academy, which had been badly damaged during the war. White bedsheets and screens covered the worst of it. Tables for the Chinese and Japanese delegations sat on a north–south axis, with a section for dignitaries, including representatives of the United States, Britain, France, the Soviet Union, Canada, the Netherlands, and Australia, along with journalists and other observers to the side. At exactly 9 a.m. martial music filled the hall as He Yingqin entered and took

---

[109] *FRUS, 1945*, vol. VII, 140.     [110] *HYQJJ*, I, 737.
[111] Xia Lumei, "He Yingqin zai lujun zongbu," 199; *HYQJJ*, I, 754.
[112] *HYQJJ*, I, 774.

up his place at the main table along with Admiral Chen Shaokuan, General Gu Zhutong, and General Zhang Tingmeng, representing China's naval, ground, and air forces respectively. He Yingqin gestured for everyone to sit, then the Japanese delegation filed in. General Okamura Yasuji, the commander of the China Expeditionary Army, and six other Japanese officers then sat at the table opposite the Chinese delegation. Okamura signed copies of the document of surrender, giving them to his subordinate Kobayashi Arasaburo to return to He. Photographers captured the moment in one of the most famous images of the war, Kobayashi leaning forward to return the signed document to He, who accepted it with both hands. He Yingqin then passed Okamura a copy of Supreme Commander Allied Powers General Douglas MacArthur's General Order Number One, which called for the cessation of hostilities of all Japanese forces in China, Taiwan, and Indochina north of the sixteenth parallel. Okamura signed the order and, again through Kobayashi, returned it to He Yingqin. Guards then escorted the Japanese from the hall and the Chinese dignitaries exited. The entire ceremony took only 20 minutes.[113]

In his radio broadcast remarks after the ceremony, He Yingqin took the opportunity to express his feelings, describing the surrender ceremony as marking one of the most significant days in China's long history. Not only did it conclude the "bitter struggle of the eight-year war of resistance," but it also "marked the start of a new era of peace and prosperity for the people of East Asia and all humankind."[114] Gracious and perhaps pragmatic in victory, in the days that followed He Yingqin displayed a greater willingness to share credit for China's achievement, openly acknowledging the contribution of his American allies to the victory over Japan. At a banquet for General Wedemeyer shortly after the surrender ceremony, He Yingqin described the victory not as China's alone, as he had done on many occasions, but as the result of collective action with the Allies, especially the Americans who made great sacrifices in the cause. "Without American participation in the Pacific theater," He Yingqin asked those assembled, "who knows how long the war might have lasted?" In expressing his gratitude, he made specific reference to Presidents Franklin Roosevelt and Harry Truman, to General Wedemeyer, and to the American people. He made no mention of Stilwell.[115]

---

[113] Xia Lumei presided over the preparations for the ceremony: Xia Lumei, "He Yingqin zai lujun zongbu," 202–06; *HYQJJ*, I, 776–77; "Japan's Troops Surrender in China; Nanking Signing Covers 1,000,000," *New York Times*, September 9, 1945; "Nanking Acclaims Japanese Surrender," *New York Times*, September 10, 1945.
[114] *HYQJJ*, I, 777.     [115] *HYQJJ*, I, 801.

# 9    "A tall building on shifting sands"

The May 2, 1948, edition of the *New York Times* carried a letter to the editor from He Yingqin in which he articulated his views on the democratization of China and asked his American audience for continued support for his government. In doing so, he highlighted certain values he had observed since his arrival in the United States, specifically a sense of civic duty and respect for the rule of law, which he believed would benefit China. He stressed the enormity of the task and the need for more time, reminding readers that the process of building democracy took many years in places such as England and France. "The democratization of China involves nothing less than a radical reconstruction of the Chinese people's social and ethical values," he argued, which required patience and understanding. "The infant of democracy is at last walking on two legs in China," he wrote, pointing out how far China had progressed in the previous few decades, despite the trauma of the war of resistance against Japan. "True, it is still a little wobbly," he admitted, "but nonetheless it stays on its feet, and that alone is enough to justify our faith in the future of China." He closed with an assessment of the consequences for the rest of the world should the communists triumph in the civil war in China, warning, "as goes Asia, so will Europe and so will the world."[1] His letter to the *Times*, which appeared after a two-year assignment in the United States, represented his desire to help Americans see the situation in China as he did, in order to understand better the stakes in the unfolding civil war.

As the war with Japan concluded, signs of impending conflict between the Nationalists and CCP began to appear. Even as Chiang Kai-shek

---

[1] "Democracy in China," *New York Times*, May 2, 1948. He Yingqin's letter drew a response from a young associate professor of Chinese history at Harvard University named John K. Fairbank. His letter to the *Times* appeared on May 9, 1948 and, while he granted many of He Yingqin's points, Fairbank criticized the Nationalist government for its totalitarian nature and for organizing violent attacks on students and faculty at Peking University: "Our Policy in China: Uncritical Support of National Government Held Hazardous," *New York Times*, May 9, 1948.

and Mao Zedong met in Chongqing for talks aimed at settling their long-simmering dispute, each side accused the other of sabotaging opportunities for a rapprochement. Chiang ordered He Yingqin to move Chinese Nationalist forces as quickly as possible into areas that had been under Japanese occupation.[2] In order to facilitate this transition, He Yingqin allowed some Japanese troops to retain their arms and used them to maintain order in certain areas, especially around Nanjing and Shanghai. He also used some of the "puppet" Chinese troops that had served the Japanese-sponsored government of Wang Jingwei for this same purpose.[3] These decisions stemmed as much from the desire to prevent CCP forces from taking control of these areas as from the need to preserve order and facilitate the restoration of the administrative authority of the Nanjing government. Such actions drew criticism from the CCP, which claimed on a number of occasions not only that He Yingqin had refused to disarm the defeated Japanese enemy and its "puppet troops," but also that he had ordered them to attack CCP forces.[4] He Yingqin responded with accusations that CCP sabotage had hindered the process of surrender and the recovery of occupied territories. In particular, he told international journalists that the CCP had destroyed sections of the Long–Hai, Ping–Han, and Jin–Pu railroads, which had obstructed the work of those attempting to disarm Japanese forces and added to the suffering of the people.[5]

The reemerging conflict with the CCP caused He Yingqin concern because he viewed the end of the war as an opportunity to begin a new era in East Asia and he did not want to see China again cast into internal dissent and civil war. He had long believed that, in order to avoid repeats of past problems and suffering, China required national unity and a restoration of traditional values above all else. In a speech at a celebration commemorating both the victory over Japan and the anniversary of the 1911 Revolution, He Yingqin noted that throughout China's long history, and in his lifetime in particular, foreign invasion had been a constant threat and would continue to pose the greatest danger in the future. Knowing that China and its people had suffered through several wars in the previous century and had just emerged from eight years of brutal warfare against Japan, He Yingqin advocated three essential steps to protect China and help it move forward toward peace and stability. First, China must have genuine unity and solidarity among its people. The preceding two decades had shown that only when the people were united

---

[2] *HYQJJ*, I, 751.      [3] Xia Lumei, "He Yingqin zai lujun zongbu," 200.
[4] "Chungking Parleys Hold Peace Prospect in China," *New York Times*, October 7, 1945; "US Force in China Cautioned by Reds," *New York Times*, October 8, 1945.
[5] *HYQJJ*, I, 810–12.

could China successfully defend against outside aggressors. Division and regionalism only rendered the state and people vulnerable to foreign imperialism. Second, he stated that the people must revive their sense of ethics and morality, referring to the Confucian virtues of loyalty (*zhong*), filial piety (*xiao*), benevolence (*ren*), sincerity (*xin*), righteousness (*yi*), and peace (*heping*). Reviving these traditional values would unite the people in a common goal of state-building and encourage individuals to "put the public before self, put the state before family" (*gonger wangsi, guoer wangjia*). Third, China needed a modernized army, which would serve as the foundation of a new state. In order to do this, China needed to raise the educational level of its people, improve communications and transportation systems, and develop heavy industry. These were heavy burdens but essential tasks, he told his audience, and all Chinese must work hard together in order to complete them.[6] At a celebration marking the return of the government to Nanjing on May 5, 1946, He Yingqin repeated these themes in a national radio broadcast. Beyond the material objectives of improving China's infrastructure, he stressed the importance of "spirit-building" (*jingshen jianshe*), which meant restoring the people's morality and ethics, based on traditional Confucian values. This stage of national construction required everyone to be loyal, filial, and sincere, and to sacrifice everything to contribute to the nation.[7] Within this context, he viewed the CCP as an obstacle to the most important goal of the day, the drive for national unity and the restoration of traditional values that he believed essential to China's future development and security.

As he traveled to different parts of the country at the turn of the new year, supervising the surrender and repatriation of Japanese troops, He Yingqin continued to express his concerns about CCP activities that disrupted this process and threatened the stability and unity of China.[8] CCP leaders in turn consistently identified He Yingqin as a reactionary and die-hard anti-communist, describing him as the principal obstacle to the peace talks. Reports from Nanjing indicated that the CCP had demanded his removal from the position of chief of staff as a prerequisite to offering a peace proposal. He Yingqin publicly rejected accusations that he had obstructed peace talks, boldly declaring himself among "China's leading liberals and supporters of democracy."[9] Evidently, some Americans who hoped to facilitate an agreement for a coalition government agreed that He Yingqin posed a problem. Acting Secretary of State Dean Acheson described He to George Marshall, who had been

[6] *HYQJJ*, I, 808–09.    [7] *HYQJJ*, I, 840–41.    [8] *HYQJJ*, I, 811, 823, 833.
[9] "US Aide in China Sees Early Truce," *New York Times*, May 1, 1946.

working to bring the GMD and CCP together since December 1945, as one of Chiang's reactionary political cronies, implying that he owed his position more to his relationship with Chiang Kai-shek than to his own abilities. He advised Marshall that it would be particularly helpful to the peace process if Chiang would send He off on "some innocuous tour or mission abroad."[10] There is no evidence that Marshall raised this with Chiang, but there is little doubt that Chiang knew the prevailing American attitudes toward his chief of staff. Reports at the time suggested that Chiang, who had seen Nationalist forces capture several cities in Manchuria over the course of the spring of 1946, considered sending He Yingqin out of the country.[11] When the Nanjing government announced plans to unveil a new constitution and reorganize the military establishment under a newly created Ministry of National Defense (*guofangbu*), Chiang decided to remove He Yingqin as chief of staff, replacing him with Chen Cheng.

In early May 1946, He Yingqin told reporters that he intended to resign his current position as chief of staff, but had no interest in taking over as the new minister of national defense. Having spent fourteen years as minister of military administration and eight years as chief of staff, He Yingqin explained, made him reluctant to continue in either capacity. Instead, he indicated that he had requested a new position as China's military representative to the United Nations in New York.[12] Denying that this had anything to do with accusations that he formed part of a "reactionary clique" within the GMD, or CCP accusations that he was seeking to foment civil war, He Yingqin described the move as a retirement of sorts that would allow younger officers to advance their careers.[13] On June 1, as most observers paid attention to the establishment of the new Ministry of National Defense and its head Bai Chongxi, He Yingqin quietly resigned as both chief of staff and commander of the Chinese army.[14] Before he left China for his new post, reporters pressed him for his views on the prospects for the GMD–CCP peace negotiations. He declined to comment, claiming he did not know the details.[15] For the second time in two years, He Yingqin lost a long-held position due to pressure from external forces. For the second time, he accepted it and took up a new assignment without comment or complaint.

[10]  *FRUS, 1946*, vol. IX, 1295–96.
[11]  "Chinese Reds Take 3D Manchuria City," *New York Times*, April 29, 1946.
[12]  "China Government Moves to Nanking," *New York Times*, May 2, 1946.
[13]  "Ho Quits as Chief of Chinese Army," *New York Times*, May 14, 1946.
[14]  *HYQJJ*, I, 850–51.     [15]  *HYQJJ*, I, 856.

## The United Nations Military Staff Committee

Less than one week after his resignation, He Yingqin accepted appointment as head of a Chinese military mission to the United States and the Chinese delegation to the newly formed United Nations Military Staff Committee (MSC). These duties took him to New York and other American cities and occupied his time for the next two years. Many saw this position as a demotion to a sinecure, intended primarily to remove him from China and the peace negotiations, but his work with the MSC proved both challenging and important, as he worked on general principles for the use of military force under the auspices of this new multilateral organization. He Yingqin regarded it as a major step forward in avoiding future wars and described this effort as "without precedent in human history."[16] His experience in the United States also had a strong influence on him, and some aspects of American society shaped his views on postwar China.

After a brief stay in Tokyo, where he met with General Douglas MacArthur, He Yingqin arrived in San Francisco on July 15, 1946. Two days later, refreshed after the long trip across the Pacific, he met with reporters at the Fairmont Hotel, offering remarks on the situation in China and answering questions. He Yingqin believed that his responsibilities as a representative of the Chinese military and government included trying to correct what he felt were mistaken views of China, its government, and its people. He also knew that, in his new position, anything he said might influence American views on China, so he chose his words carefully when talking about Sino-American cooperation during the war and in postwar China. Six months earlier in Kunming, he had virtually ignored the American role in the China theater and emphasized the meager percentage of overall Lend-Lease aid that went to China. In San Francisco, he praised the close cooperation between China and the United States during the war and thanked the Americans for their "spiritual and material support." When asked specifically what had forced the Japanese to surrender, rather than emphasize the impact of the slow, grinding war of attrition that Chinese forces had carried out since 1937, he replied that American air power had destroyed Japan's cities, the American navy had ravaged Japanese shipping, and the American army had prepared to invade the Japanese home islands. Now that the war had ended, he encouraged reporters to visit China in order to understand better its history, culture, and customs. No simple words

---

[16] He Yingqin, "Lianheguo junshi canmoutuan de renwu ji chengjiu" [The Mission and Accomplishments of the United Nations Military Staff Committee], in He Yingqin, ed., *Weibang bainian ji*, 407.

of courtesy, this reflected the fact that He Yingqin had little confidence that the American press and public had any realistic understanding of the situation in his homeland. He also suggested that they should take a longer view of developments in China because, if one looked back on the situation in 1925, the start of the Nationalist revolution, one could see that great progress had taken place.[17]

He Yingqin understood that Americans differed in their views of the Chinese government, and he rather quickly found that as a high-ranking member of the Chinese military he became the a target for both praise and criticism. Upon his arrival he received a warm welcome from the San Francisco Chinese community. A periodical called the *Young China Morning News* ran a flattering profile of him in which he stood out as Chiang Kai-shek's right-hand man. After listing his accomplishments over the past three decades, the article described him as the most appropriate individual to serve as head of the Chinese delegation to the UN Military Staff Committee, particularly because of his personal relationships with Wedemeyer, Stilwell, and Marshall. Another article in a different Chinese-language newspaper described his work during the war in glowing terms, but acknowledged that many saw his dispatch to the United States as a demotion or punishment. The article defended He Yingqin, pointing out that, though he had been unjustly criticized both inside and outside China, he had accepted his new assignment without a word of complaint.[18] Less than a week later, he arrived in New York City to a very different experience when he encountered protestors demonstrating against his presence on American soil. On July 23, as he attended a banquet at the Waldorf Astoria Hotel, approximately twenty-seven members of an organization called the Chinese Veterans Committee participated in a protest carrying signs reading "Ho Wants War!" "China Vets for Peace!" and "No Seat on UN Military Staff for Warmonger Ho." The organization's leader, Jack Edelman of the Bronx, told reporters that his group consisted of American and Chinese veterans of the China theater and that "the Chinese people do not want Ho in their country and it is a bad thing for the American people and the hope of peace" that he had come the United States.[19] When asked for comment, He Yingqin joked that when he arrived in the United States only a few officers at the Pentagon knew his name but, thanks to the protestors and the media, it seemed that everyone would now know it.[20]

[17] *HYQJJ*, II, 871–72.    [18] *HYQJJ*, II, 872–73.
[19] "New and Retiring Chinese in UN Post," *New York Times*, July 24, 1946.
[20] *HYQJJ*, II, 934–36.

It is unlikely that this modest demonstration surprised him, as he had become accustomed to criticism from Americans. He might have been surprised, however, to learn that he had also become a focal point of debate in the pages of one of the most prominent American newspapers. In the fall of 1946, He Yingqin's name appeared repeatedly in a series of letters to the editors of the *New York Times* as part of a growing national debate on China policy. The exchange began on August 20, 1946, when the *Times* published a letter to the editors from a Herman B. Gerringer of New York. The letter expressed strong objection to an editorial of a few days before, which Gerringer felt inappropriately lauded Chiang's government and criticized CCP leaders who "broke all of their pledges" and had created "a state within a state and in revolt against the National government."[21] In Gerringer's view, responsibility for the failure of the peace negotiations in China fell entirely on the shoulders of the dictatorial and anti-democratic Chiang Kai-shek and his reactionary regime.[22] This provoked a response from Alfred Kohlberg, a businessman with long experience in China and strong connections to the pro-Chiang "China Lobby." Kohlberg took exception to Gerringer's description of the Chinese leadership as "reactionary" and specifically mentioned He Yingqin as a frequent target of such unjust criticisms. Claiming to know He personally, Kohlberg described him as a "leftist" and "semi-socialist" since the 1920s and compared his political leanings to those of the British Labour Party.[23]

Kohlberg's singling out of He Yingqin caught the attention of J. Spencer Kennard, an academic and missionary who had taught at a Chinese university in Chengdu. Kennard's letter to the editors of the *Times* expressed astonishment that Kohlberg could have such a view of He Yingqin and recommended that readers consider He's "record." In a reference to the May 1935 He–Umezu Agreement, Kennard reminded readers of He's betrayal of the Chinese people when he "handed over to Japan" control over a substantial portion of north China. In December 1936, the letter continued, He Yingqin had ordered the air force to bomb Xi'an in a deliberate attempt to kill Chiang Kai-shek, his own superior officer. In 1937 He Yingqin had opposed war with Japan, and after February 1941 until the end of the war he had organized civil war "upon a scale that narrowly missed bringing the Nationalist Government into the Axis camp." Kennard credited Joseph Stilwell with preventing He from aligning with the Japanese in 1943. In a word, He Yingqin

---

[21] "Chiang Kai-shek's Program," *New York Times*, August 15, 1946.
[22] "For Democracy in China," *New York Times*, August 20, 1946.
[23] "Our Ally the Kuomintang," *New York Times*, September 2, 1946.

personified the weakness and corruption of the Nationalist government.[24] A week later Freda Utley joined the chain of letters. A scholar-activist and one-time member of the British Communist Party, Utley had lived in the Soviet Union but had moved to the United States to become an ardent anti-communist writer. As a *Reader's Digest* correspondent in China in 1945, she had taken up the cause of the Nationalist government and now came to He Yingqin's defense, refuting Kennard's assertions. She cast the He–Umezu Agreement not as a betrayal but as the Chinese government's attempt to maintain some control over north China in the face of Japanese military aggression. If He Yingqin had organized civil war in China, she asked, how was it that the CCP forces had acquired so much territory between the end of the war in August and December 1945? Utley claimed to "hold no brief" for He, but reminded readers of the fact that his government and country had been under attack from Japan since 1931 and that the current civil war "masked" Soviet aggression against China.[25] A final letter from a Michael Lindsey accused He of encouraging Chinese armies in north China to desert to the Japanese in order to keep a Nationalist presence there to oppose the communists.[26] Evidently, the editors felt the conversation had run its course and moved on to other topics, but this prominent exchange clearly demonstrated the differing views of both He Yingqin and his government among American observers.

The MSC first convened in February 1946, but did not began its real work of creating guidelines for the use of military forces of member states under UN command until August. General Shang Zhen, a Chinese military attaché in Washington, DC, served as temporary head of the Chinese delegation until He Yingqin's arrival in July. Article 47 of the UN Charter established the MSC and dictated that the chiefs of staff of each of the five permanent members of the Security Council should head a delegation to serve on the committee, with the position of chair rotating among the delegation leaders on a monthly basis. He Yingqin believed in the mission and took his role seriously, but found the actual work of the committee tedious and torturously slow. Rules mandated that meetings take place at least every two weeks, though they often met more frequently, especially in small subgroups of two or three members of the various delegations. Each meeting, be it large or small, required significant preparation. All speeches and oral remarks had to go through interpreters, and all written reports and documents required translation. Afterwards, all such materials had to undergo careful scrutiny and discussion among delegation

---

[24] "Struggle in China," *New York Times*, September 11, 1946.
[25] "Communism in China," *New York Times*, September 20, 1946.
[26] "New Order in China," *New York Times*, October 2, 1946.

members, a process that typically took several days. During the meetings, the atmosphere often grew tense, with participants spending entire sessions arguing over one sentence or a single word. Because the chair of the MSC rotated among the head delegates, when He Yingqin chaired the committee's sessions he took on even more responsibility. The fact that the Chinese delegation had lodgings in Long Island but conducted its work in Manhattan simply complicated matters.[27]

Before beginning his work on the committee, He Yingqin visited Washington, DC, for meetings with President Harry Truman, General Dwight Eisenhower, and Chinese ambassador to the US Gu Weijun. After returning to New York, he laid down some general principles to guide the work of the Chinese delegation, which involved close cooperation with the United States, Britain, and other democratic countries against the "imperialist" countries such as the Soviet Union. He Yingqin viewed external interference or invasion as the greatest threat to China, and he believed the Soviet Union was working through the CCP to achieve its own imperialist goals in China.[28] His work on the MSC only deepened his suspicions as he noted that the Soviet delegation typically opposed any proposal that had the support of the American, British, French, and Chinese delegations. The Soviets, he complained, refused to participate in many sessions, which meant that only informal discussion between the other delegations could take place. Among other things, the Soviet representative, Lieutenant General Aleksandr Vasiliev, disagreed with leaders of the other four delegations on the size of the UN military force and the contribution of each member state. The UN Security Council eventually set a deadline for the committee to submit its report on basic principles, and the committee did so on April 30, 1947. The final report included forty-one articles, of which only twenty-five had the unanimous support of the five delegations. Lengthy appendices explained the points of disagreement over the remaining sixteen articles.[29] His experience in dealing with Soviet representatives to the MSC only confirmed He Yingqin's view that the Soviet Union stood as a major obstacle to peace in China and across the world.

If He Yingqin found his work at the MSC tedious and frustrating, he found American society interesting and instructive. He traveled widely during his time in the United States, visiting Washington, DC, Detroit, Philadelphia, Pittsburgh, Atlanta, Norfolk, Louisville, and other cities. In many cases he went to observe American military bases and training

---

[27] *HYQJJ*, II, 935–36.    [28] *HYQJJ*, II, 875–76.
[29] *HYQJJ*, II, 935–36; *SLGB*, LXX, July 31, 1947, 469–73; Captain William G. Wheeler, "The United Nations Security Council Military Staff Committee: Relic or Revival?," unpublished paper, National War College, Washington, DC, 1994, 3–9.

centers such as Fort Benning, Fort Meade, the Military Academy at West Point, the Naval Academy at Annapolis, and the Brooklyn Naval Yard. In other cities he visited steel-manufacturing plants and petrochemical factories. From these visits he developed ideas for the reform and modernization of the Chinese military, yet he paid greatest attention to the more fundamental aspects of American society that caught his eye and which he described at length to his colleagues back in China. He Yingqin had long believed in the importance of the human element of military operations and talked often of the importance of the "Whampoa spirit" to the Chinese army. During his time as minister of military administration he had frequently focused on personnel, admonishing his subordinates to improve their work habits. His observations of American society served to deepen his belief that the task of modernizing China and its military must begin with profound individual and societal change.

Apart from his work at the MSC, his job as the head of the Chinese military delegation to the United States required him to observe and report on those things he felt might benefit China. In early August 1946, after less than one month in the United States, he wrote down his initial impressions of the country and its people, sending copies to several officers and officials back home. He found two aspects of American society particularly noteworthy and remarked on them numerous times over the next two years. First, he noted the spirit of public service among government officials and those in positions of authority. He found it remarkable that he had not encountered a single official who did not take his job seriously or who sought only personal gain from his position. Second, he found the general respect for the rule of law admirable, citing the examples of traffic lights and the subway. More impressive than the fact that he saw automated traffic lights everywhere he went, he marveled at the fact that car drivers waited patiently at red lights. Even with no other car or pedestrian within sight and no police supervision, drivers remained in place until the light turned green before proceeding. At the subways, again with no police or official on duty, passengers willingly placed five-cent coins in the "box" before entering the station and boarding the train. He Yingqin came to believe that these two facets of American society, a spirit of public service and a respect for rule of law, served as the foundation of the prosperous and ordered society he saw all around him and that he must work to cultivate these traits among his own people and society.[30] A few months later, he repeated these observations when explaining to several colleagues why the United States had such strength and wealth. When ranking the factors that accounted for this, he placed the spirit of

[30] *HYQJJ*, II, 881–82.

public service and respect for rule of law at the top of the list, ahead of a developed industrial sector, good transportation and communication systems, and an educated public.[31]

These observations had an influence on his view of the situation back in China, where Nationalist and communist forces had squared off in a military conflict. Prior to leaving China to take up his new post in New York, He Yingqin had often talked of the need to modernize the Chinese army in terms of weapons and training. After his arrival in the United States he dwelt almost exclusively on socioeconomic issues as the key to defeating the CCP and building a strong state. In February 1947, he wrote to Chen Cheng, Chen Guofu, Chen Lifu, and Wu Tiecheng, responding to a report from them on the deteriorating situation in China. He explained his view that "to use only military force to try to resolve the current communist problem is to simply treat a symptom." He believed that the CCP was using a variety of methods to conduct its struggle and that the Nationalists needed to do the same. For example, he argued that skillful propaganda on the part of the CCP and its supporters had led many Americans to believe that the communists had the best interests of the Chinese peasant at heart. He cited Theodore White's book *Thunder out of China* as an example.[32]

Rather than continue to push for a military solution, He Yingqin advocated the adoption of effective political and economic policies that would address the needs of the people who found the CCP an appealing alternative. In particular, he stressed the importance of the land question, on which the CCP had capitalized to win the support of large numbers of peasants. He argued that the government should call together experts to study the problem and create policies to address them. These policies, he stressed, must be flexible in order to allow for differences between provinces, but the most important factor was that the government must fully implement them. He reminded Chen Cheng and the others that the Nationalists had at one time discussed land reform and developed new policies, but had never fully carried them out.[33] Now that the CCP had capitalized on the land question, it was more important than ever to address this issue quickly and effectively. He Yingqin also suggested studying foreign governments that had developed policies that restricted the growth of communist movements. He pointed to social- and wealth-equalization policies in Britain and the Netherlands as examples of ways both to serve the best interests of the people and to

[31] *HYQJJ*, II, 888–89.    [32] *HYQJJ*, II, 913.

[33] He Yingqin was perhaps referring to discussions of land reform and rent reduction in 1930, 1937, and 1946. See Suzanne Pepper, *Civil War in China: The Political Struggle, 1945–1949*, 2nd edn. (Lanham, MD: Rowman & Littlefield, 1999), 230–31.

weaken internal communist movements. Beyond developing appropriate policies to address the land issue, He Yingqin believed it essential to fully implement the new constitution, adopted in December 1946, in order to combat CCP characterizations of the GMD as a "one-party dictatorship" and "undemocratic."[34]

His observations of American society and the policies of other Western states influenced He Yingqin's views on what China needed to do to fend off the Communist challenge, but he also drew inspiration from another source he encountered during his stay in the United States. At the invitation of Frank Buchman, He Yingqin agreed to attend and give a speech at the Moral Re-Armament (MRA) meeting at Mackinac Island, Michigan, on January 3–4, 1947. Buchman's organization, sometimes known as the "Oxford Group," originated as a self-proclaimed Christian "revolution" in the years after World War I, which took as its goal the restoration of basic moral values among members of all faiths and nationalities. Buchman believed that the answer to the world's most difficult problems, including the challenge of international communism, must come from individuals and then extend to governments and nations. Not only did the MRA message appeal to He Yingqin as a Christian, but also he found its message compatible with his own belief in the importance of traditional Chinese values of sincerity, uprightness, self-cultivation, and moral government. He saw this spiritual movement as a way to combat the "materialism" of the communists.[35] In a radio speech in June 1947, Frank Buchman remarked that He Yingqin had long used military force to combat "materialism in China," but after joining the MRA he had decided to fight "an idea with an idea." He quoted He as saying that "there is no use in trying to reform the Communists by naked force alone," but rather by "moral force" that would come through economic reform and a revival of traditional ethics and morals.[36] He Yingqin remained fundamentally opposed to the Chinese communists and the Soviet Union, but his views on how to deal with them had undergone a substantial change.

These opinions, which He Yingqin shared in letters to friends and colleagues in early 1947, would have surprised many American officials, who continued to view him as a die-hard reactionary who remained fixated on using military force to deal with the CCP. In January 1947,

---

[34]  *HYQJJ*, II, 913–14.
[35]  *HYQJJ*, II, 909–10. He Yingqin wrote to colleagues on January 12, 1947, praising the MRA and its approach. *HYQJJ* mistakenly places the meeting in Canada. It took place within the United States at MRA headquarters on Mackinac Island in Lake Huron, close to the US–Canadian border.
[36]  Frank Buchman, *Remaking the World: The Speeches of Frank Buchman* (London: Blandford Press, 1961), 152–53.

when rumors circulated that He Yingqin would return to China, American officials including George Marshall, recently returned from his mission in China and now serving as secretary of state, took this to mean that Chiang Kai-shek had rejected Marshall's advice to negotiate with the CCP and instead intended to pursue a military solution.[37] In April, when Chiang appointed He as chair of a new president's strategic advisory committee, American officials again interpreted the move as a sign that the Nationalists had given up on negotiations in favor of military force. In a report to Ambassador John Leighton Stuart and George Marshall, W. Walton Butterworth, a counselor at the American embassy in Nanjing, pointed out that He's appointment meant that, despite "repeated warnings from enlightened Chinese and unbiased foreigners that social and economic problems cannot be permanently resolved by force," the Chinese government gave every indication of intending to do so.[38] From the perspective of American officials, He's appointment to chair this committee could only mean an inflexible and unilateral reliance on military force. High-profile journalists such as Joseph Alsop reinforced such views, labeling He Yingqin as one of the most prominent reactionaries in the Chinese government and lamenting that "mediation of China's internal conflict has always been impossible so long as the Kuomintang reactionaries had a large influence on the government."[39]

These observers of China's internal affairs had no idea that He Yingqin had recently urged his own government to engage in serious land reform and explore policies aimed at social and material equalization. Had they paid close attention, they might have seen signs that alerted them to the fact that they had misunderstood He's views on the current situation. In June, the same W. Walton Butterworth met with Luo Longji, a leader of the Democratic League and frequent critic of the Nationalist government. Luo told Butterworth that many Chinese army officers, including many from the "Whampoa Clique," now favored compromise with the communists and a political solution rather than continued military conflict. Chiang Kai-shek stood in the way of this approach, according to Luo, and no solution would be possible unless Chiang stepped down or a coup removed him from power. He went so far as to speculate that, if such a coup took place under the direction of more liberal-minded army officers, He Yingqin might be the logical leader.[40] This might have been

[37] R. H. Shackford, "Marshall Will Watch Return of Gen. Ho Ying-chin," *Evening Observer* (Dunkirk, NY), February 6, 1947.
[38] *FRUS, 1947*, vol. VII, 127–30.
[39] Joseph Alsop and Stewart Alsop, "Marshall the Statesman," *Los Angeles Times*, January 17, 1947.
[40] *FRUS, 1947*, vol. VII, 194–95.

not only an indication that the Americans had misjudged He, but also the first hint of a possible wedge between He Yingqin and Chiang Kai-shek.

Rumors that He Yingqin would soon return to China continued to circulate throughout 1947. In September, reports of an imminent "shake-up" of the Nationalist military leadership predicted that He Yingqin would return to take over the post of minister of national defense from Bai Chongxi.[41] He Yingqin wrote to Zhang Junmai (Carson Chang), a prominent liberal and leader of the China Democratic Socialist Party, denying these rumors. He admitted a strong desire to work toward China's restoration, wealth, and strength, and hoped that the Chinese people would "wake up and work hard," but claimed that he still had important work to do at the United Nations and intended to meet the responsibilities of his current assignment.[42] In truth, most of his work with the MSC had concluded now that the committee had delivered its report to the Security Council, and there were some indications that his mission might be coming to an end. For example, Chiang Kai-shek pressed He Yingqin to cut back on the delegation's expenses and complained about reports that some Chinese officers in the United States had engaged in excessive spending and lavish entertaining. Chiang inquired specifically about Mao Bangchu, chair of the Chinese air force acquisitions commission in the United States, who had allegedly hosted a banquet that cost US$4,000. Claims of such spending reached Nanjing at a time when the financially strapped Nationalist government could ill afford it. He Yingqin investigated and reported back that Mao had not hosted such a banquet and had not misused public funds. Still, he followed orders and implemented some cost-cutting measures, including moving the delegation from Long Island to the first floor of a hotel on Fifty-Seventh Street, cutting down on the commute in order to both save money and work more effectively.[43]

Meanwhile, He Yingqin continued to address publicly the issue of the civil war in China, mostly through speeches at MRA meetings. In June 1947, he attended an MRA conference in Detroit, in October he attended a meeting on Mackinac Island, Michigan, and in December he spoke at his fourth MRA event of the year, this time in Richmond, Virginia. In each case, he referred to the civil war, but cast it as a part of a larger struggle between democratic and communist states or, in the language of the MRA, the struggle against "materialism." He Yingqin had always viewed the problem of the CCP as a part of China's longstanding conflict

[41] "Big Army 'Shake-Up' Reported in China," *New York Times*, September 8, 1947.
[42] *HYQJJ*, II, 939.
[43] *SLGB*, LXX, July 11, 1947, 326–27; *HYQJJ*, II, 940.

with external imperialist powers, yet he now began to speak in terms of global ideological conflict with far-reaching consequences. In his address at the MRA meeting in Richmond on New Year's Day 1948, he warned the audience that the civil war in China "is not one of those Gilbert and Sullivan opera wars but a full-dress war." "If China fails in its struggle," he continued, "we can reasonably be assured that all of Asia will fall. As Asia goes, so goes Europe and the rest of the world."[44] His public remarks bear out what he told his friends and associates in more private correspondence. In February 1948, he wrote to General Ji Yiqiao, explaining his views on the need for a restoration of morality and ethics among people across the world, referring in particular to the importance of traditional Chinese values in pursuit of the MRA goal of world peace. These moral values were essential, he stressed, because they served as the foundation of a strong, prosperous, and democratic world. Trying to build a new and prosperous China "without this foundation," he wrote, "is like constructing a tall building on shifting sands."[45]

Back in China, the government had unveiled a new constitution and prepared for elections for the new positions of president and vice-president. On March 5, 1948, three weeks before the scheduled convening of more than 2,900 delegates in Nanjing for the formal end of the period of "political tutelage" and the start of constitutional rule, Chiang Kai-shek sent a telegram to He asking him to come back to China. As He Yingqin prepared for his departure, a second, more urgent message ordered him to return right away. He rushed back to China and on April 1, 1948, He Yingqin met with Chiang Kai-shek in Nanjing.[46] In one of his last acts as military representative to the United Nations, He Yingqin penned his letter to the editors of the *New York Times*, making a final effort to communicate to an American audience his view on the situation in China. Throughout his stay in the United States, he had complained that the CCP was doing a much better job of getting its message across to the American public and that the Nationalists needed to find ways to win this propaganda struggle. He wrote to colleagues that they needed to find a way to place written pieces in American newspapers and magazines that would refute the claims of the CCP and its supporters in the United States.[47] In early 1948, upon learning of the upcoming publication of a book about Joseph Stilwell which included numerous criticisms of Chinese military officers and government officials, he asked a colleague to have people go through the documentary record in China

[44] "Gen. Ho Warns of Reds," *New York Times*, January 2, 1948.
[45] *HYQJJ*, II, 962.    [46] *HYQJJ*, II, 963–64.    [47] *HYQJJ*, II, 927–28.

in order to counter these claims and point out Stilwell's "unreasonable demands."[48]

## Return to China

The situation at home had changed a great deal in the time He Yingqin had been away. George Marshall had left China in January 1947, giving up on his mediation mission as both Nationalists and communists seemed intent upon settling the conflict on the battlefield. The Nationalist government had reinstituted conscription and mobilized for war to suppress the CCP "rebellion," but communist victories in Manchuria had dramatically shifted the military situation, and inflation and economic instability had eroded public confidence in the Nanjing government. Critics and university students demonstrated against a demoralized GMD, accusing its members of corruption, ineptitude, and authoritarian rule.[49] After his two-year sojourn in the United States, He Yingqin returned to a war-weary military, a demoralized party, and a government that was teetering on the brink of collapse.

The situation in China had changed in He Yingqin's absence, but he had also changed his views on what the government must do to retrieve the situation. This had consequences for his relationship with Chiang Kai-shek. The National Assembly convened at the end of March and, to the surprise of none, elected Chiang president. The election of Li Zongren, a longtime rival who had aligned himself with many of Chiang's critics, as vice-president, however, surprised many. Chiang had supported General Zhang Qun for vice-president, and the election of Li Zongren suggested that the president's control over the party and government had waned considerably.[50] The next order of business in implementing the new constitutional system involved electing a president of the Executive Yuan, or premier, and forming a cabinet of ministers. Chiang called He Yingqin back from New York not only to consult on the military situation but also with an eye toward appointing He, a staunch Chiang loyalist, as premier. Yet, when Chiang approached him about taking the position, He Yingqin demurred and first consulted with a number of groups and experts before giving his answer. He then demonstrated his new attitude toward the conflict, telling Chiang that he would accept only if he had free rein to design and implement policies he

---

[48] *HYQJJ*, II, 960–61.
[49] See Pepper, *Civil War in China*, ch. 5, "A Summary of the Indictment," for an overview of domestic criticism of the Nationalists.
[50] Odd Arne Westad, *Decisive Encounters: The Chinese Civil War, 1946–1950* (Stanford: Stanford University Press, 2003), 182.

believed necessary, including land redistribution and a progressive tax system.[51]

Chiang refused to agree to these conditions and ordered Zhang Qun, who had been serving as acting premier since April 23, to take on the job of forming a cabinet. Zhang did not relish this position as the premier inevitably found himself caught between Chiang, accustomed to having things his own way, and the Legislative Yuan, increasingly determined to curb Chiang's authority. Claiming illness, Zhang boarded a plane for Chongqing, leaving his deputy with instructions to turn things over to whomever should assume office after him. Zhang's flight from Nanjing helped convince Chiang Kai-shek that his chosen candidate did not possess the necessary "forcefulness" to serve as premier, so he again turned to He with a second request that he take the job. At the same time, members of the Legislative Yuan conducted a straw vote to determine which candidate had greater support, He Yingqin or Zhang Qun. He Yingqin won an overwhelming majority, 259 votes to 94.[52] Chiang believed that He would now accept, even expressing his confidence that his longtime comrade would rally around in a meeting with American ambassador John Leighton Stuart. He Yingqin told others that he had by no means made up his mind. If he took the job, he would focus primarily on important socioeconomic reforms and would need the right people around him to do so successfully. One of his major concerns involved the appointment of a minister of finance, since he considered the economic situation the most critical problem at the moment. Returning to Chiang, he again asked for a free hand in designing policy and assembling the cabinet.[53] Chiang refused to agree to his conditions for a second time, so on May 23 He Yingqin announced that he would not accept the position, explaining that his recent time out of the country had left him "out of touch" with the situation in China and that he lacked experience in economic affairs. Finding no one of his liking willing to take the position, Chiang quickly offered up a compromise candidate, Dr. Weng Wenhao, a geologist who had served in several government ministries. Lacking viable alternatives, the Legislative Yuan confirmed him with a vote of 489 to 94.[54]

He Yingqin's refusal to take the position of premier reflected a developing rift with Chiang Kai-shek, after many years of close collaboration. It did not, however, mean an end to their relationship. Weng consulted with

---

[51] *FRUS, 1948*, vol. VII, 223; "Gen. Ho Groomed for Premiership," *New York Times*, May 6, 1948.

[52] "Chinese Premier Leaves for 'Rest,'" *New York Times*, May 22, 1948.

[53] *FRUS, 1948*, vol. VII, 255–56.

[54] *FRUS, 1948*, vol. VII, 256; "Wong Is Confirmed as China's Premier," *New York Times*, May 25, 1948.

Chiang, who then appointed He as minister of national defense in the new cabinet, with the understanding that he would have complete control over military administration.[55] Upon assuming office, He Yingqin gave a speech that again reflected the influence of his stay in the United States, pointing out that in his time working at the United Nations he had had opportunities to discuss issues with many military experts from around the world. He favored following the practice of the major democracies of the world in which a civilian official held the position of minister of defense. While he still held rank in the Chinese military, he expressed the wish that in the future China would adopt this policy and place unified command of the ground, air, and naval forces in the hands of a civilian official. In the meantime, he promised to do his utmost to use the resources at hand to effectively prosecute the war, as the Nationalists prepared to attack CCP forces along the Yellow River. In what might be construed as a criticism of his predecessor, He Yingqin stated that the most important mission of the ministry would be to ensure that no men, money, or material went to waste.[56]

He Yingqin's return to China as a part of the new cabinet provoked mixed reactions from American observers. Some interpreted this as an indication that nothing would really change despite the new constitution and cabinet, continuing to see He as one of Chiang's corrupt and incompetent cronies. Now back in Washington, DC, W. Walton Butterworth, who had long attributed the Nationalist government's problems to poor leadership from individuals like He Yingqin, reported that his appointment as minister of national defense marked a continuation of earlier failed policies. He wrote to a colleague that the new cabinet featured "no new changes except possibly for the worse in the person of Ho Yingchin."[57] Another diplomatic officer drew a similar conclusion, reporting that the new cabinet showed no improvement and that the inclusion of He Yingqin reflected a turn in an even more conservative direction.[58] Others took note of his interest in economic reform and willingness to disagree with Chiang Kai-shek, which suggested a change in his views. Shortly after the establishment of the new cabinet, Ambassador Stuart had conversations with He Yingqin and others that led him to speak of the new minister of national defense in more positive terms. In June the two conferred on the situation and found broad agreement on the need to adopt an overall strategic plan, to embrace an offensive military strategy in place of passive defense, and to focus on training centers to produce high-quality replacement troops for combat units. Perhaps more

[55] "New Cabinet Is Formed by Wong," *New York Times*, June 1, 1948.
[56] *HYQJJ*, II, 969.  [57] *FRUS, 1948*, vol. VII, 268.  [58] *FRUS, 1948*, vol. VII, 278.

importantly, the ambassador noted that He Yingqin remarked on his current difficulties in dealing with Chiang Kai-shek.[59] This new divide between Chiang and He led Stuart to hope that He Yingqin would take over authority for military operations from Chiang Kai-shek and work constructively with General David Barr, head of the US Military Mission to the Nationalist government. He Yingqin agreed that this would be best and promised to collaborate closely with General Barr, but Chiang continued to send orders directly to subordinates without going through the Ministry of National Defense.[60] Zhang Junmai lent support to Stuart's hopes a few weeks later when he told an American official that He Yingqin had been "enlightened" as a result of his stay in the United States.[61]

In reality, He Yingqin's responsibilities as minister of national defense revolved primarily around military administration and training, though he had a voice in planning and operations. The reorganization of the Nationalist military in 1946, which abolished the National Military Council and created the Ministry of National Defense, made its minister a cabinet appointee, subject to approval of the Legislative Yuan and subordinate to the premier and president. Technically speaking, his responsibilities involved the military budget, conscription and training, civil affairs, and public relations. His long service record and close relationship to Chiang Kai-shek meant that He Yingqin had significant status within the Nationalist military, but did not mean that he would play a strong role in developing and executing military strategy and operations. In May 1948, Chiang Kai-shek articulated a general principle that held that, with regard to military operations, the chief of staff Gu Zhutong would take his orders from the president. With regard to matters of military administration, the chief of staff would take his orders from the minister of national defense.[62] Indeed, Chiang continued to personally direct military operations and sometimes did not even include the minister of national defense when he held briefings with the chief of staff and a few others.[63]

He Yingqin's term as minister of national defense, which lasted less than five months, began at an inauspicious time as the Nationalist military position in the civil war had just taken a dramatic turn for the worse. Armed conflict between the Nationalists and the CCP's People's Liberation Army (PLA) resumed within months of the Japanese surrender and continued despite a brief ceasefire agreement in 1946 arranged through the mediation of General George Marshall. Chiang Kai-shek

---

[59]  *FRUS, 1948*, vol. VII, 291.     [60]  *FRUS, 1948*, vol. VII, 298.
[61]  *FRUS, 1948*, vol. VII, 326.     [62]  *HYQJJ*, II, 969.
[63]  F. F. Liu, *Military History of Modern China*, 258.

made the critical decision to deploy substantial numbers of troops to north and northeast China, determined to take back Manchuria, which had been under Japanese occupation since 1931 and more recently Soviet postwar occupation. The Nationalist forces enjoyed some success in 1946, but over the course of the next one and a half years found their positions in Manchuria increasingly tenuous as PLA forces cut off rail connections and compressed the Nationalists into isolated positions centered on the three cities of Shenyang, Changchun, and Jinzhou.

In June 1948, He Yingqin did not like what he saw of the Nationalist military situation, but found little he could do about it. As he observed the conflict from the United States, he had devoted a great deal of thought to its political and economic aspects. Now that he had returned and taken up his new post, he concentrated more on the military facets of the situation. He estimated that the Nationalists still enjoyed a numerical superiority with approximately 2.7 million troops to the CCP's 1.5 million (not including militia), but he saw clearly that the initiative had passed to the enemy. The Nationalist forces had spread out over a vast amount of territory, defending cities and strategic locations, and the railroads that connected them, but this required a dispersal of forces that left them vulnerable to attack. To defend everywhere is to be weak everywhere, He Yingqin believed, noting that the PLA could mass its forces against any number of Nationalist weak points. Even if they could secure the lines of transportation, the Nationalists could not move troops around quickly enough to defend against swift attacks from PLA forces. As a result, the enemy had now taken an active or attacking position, while the Nationalist forces now took a passive or defensive stance.[64]

As he had not been in China during the previous two years, He Yingqin did not share in the blame for the military failures and dramatic reverses that had taken place. Perhaps for this reason, he did not shy away from listing them in his military reports. In one session of a series of meetings held at the Ministry of National Defense in early August, He Yingqin recounted for an audience of top military officers the numbers of men, weapons, and material lost over the course of the preceding two years. This included more than 300,000 men, 100,000 rifles, 70,000 light and heavy machine guns, 1,000 pieces of artillery, and an assortment of ammunition, trucks, and armored vehicles. Though not present for He's remarks, Chiang heard about them and flew into a rage over what he deemed a defeatist and demoralizing attitude. Chiang took the podium the next day and admitted that there had been mistakes and losses, but the important task ahead required that everyone, especially high-ranking

[64] *HYQJJ*, II, 970–71.

officers, work together and be prepared to sacrifice all to achieve victory. As He Yingqin listened to Chiang's animated speech, his expression betrayed no sign that he felt singled out or that his own remarks had prompted this response from the president.[65]

In subsequent remarks and writings, He Yingqin refrained from mentioning past failures and instead concentrated on mobilizing the army and people by contextualizing the conflict as a continuation of the war of resistance against foreign aggression. Commemorating the third anniversary of the victory over Japan, in early September 1948 He Yingqin penned a report to all officers and enlisted men in the Chinese army in which he reviewed the recent history of Japanese aggression against China and the struggle to abolish the unequal treaties of the previous century, before linking them to the current conflict. In his view, the struggle to preserve China's independence had triumphed over foreign imperialism, defeating its traitorous minions such as Puyi, the last Qing emperor and ruler of Manchukuo, and Wang Jingwei, former head of the pro-Japan regime in Nanjing. He described the CCP, which he argued had used the war of resistance to expand its power, as the next "fifth-column traitor," which served a foreign enemy. Understood in this light, the current conflict was no simple political or ideological disagreement, but rather an "extension of the war of resistance" in order to preserve China's independence and freedom. He called on everyone in the armed forces to help destroy the CCP and achieve victory in this latest battle.[66] He repeated this theme in a national radio speech a week later, emphasizing that everyone must understand that the current "disorder" in China originated not from inside the country but from outside. Never mentioning the Soviet Union specifically, he referred to the forces of international communism, again describing the war against the CCP as an extension or continuation of the war of resistance.[67]

While He Yingqin worked on preparing the military and the people to continue the struggle, the CCP prepared to launch the first of three military campaigns that would drive the Nationalists from the capital and bring the war to a close. The Liao–Shen campaign began in mid September with the goal of cutting off and annihilating the remaining Nationalist forces in Changchun, Shenyang, and Jinzhou. The campaign took two months and resulted in the complete CCP conquest of Manchuria and the loss of perhaps as many as 400,000 of the Nationalists' best troops.[68]

[65] Li Zhongming, *He Yingqin dazhuan*, 297–99.
[66] *HYQJJ*, II, 973.    [67] *HYQJJ*, II, 974.
[68] Harold Tanner, *The Battle for Manchuria and the Fate of China* (Bloomington: Indiana University Press, 2013), 206; Westad, *Decisive Encounters*, 192–97; Paine, *The Wars for Asia*, 256.

With the Nationalist position collapsing in the northeast, the battlefield shifted to the Central Plains for the Huai–Hai campaign, where PLA forces utilized the same tactics that had brought success in Manchuria. From mid November to early December, they isolated, attacked, and captured Xuzhou, the gateway to Nanjing. In the process, the PLA captured or killed 550,000 Nationalist troops.[69] In the Ping–Jin campaign of November 1948 to January 1949, PLA forces again inflicted tremendous casualties on the Nationalists, captured Beiping and Tianjin, and secured control of north China.[70]

With the military situation worsening daily, inflation increasing unchecked, and the social order of China's cities unraveling, Premier Weng Wenhao delivered his resignation. Chiang nominated Sun Ke, Sun Yat-sen's son, as his replacement, and the Legislative Yuan approved his choice. With the collapse of Weng's cabinet, He Yingqin also tendered his resignation and checked into a military hospital in Shanghai for treatment of a longstanding minor medical condition. A prominent surgeon, Colonel Zhang Xianlin of the Jiangwan Army Hospital, performed the operation. He Yingqin spent nearly two months recovering, as the Nationalist army and government struggled to maintain control of China south of the Yangzi River with PLA forces reaching its northern bank and on the verge of attacking Nanjing and Shanghai. While still in the hospital, He Yingqin received a letter from Chiang Kai-shek wishing him a speedy recovery. With regard to the larger situation, Chiang confessed that the military effort had failed and that the only possibility he could envision would be for all parties to unite and create a reasonable settlement to the conflict. He expressed the hope that He Yingqin would return to assist him in this important cause, whether as a public servant or private citizen.[71]

While Chiang expressed to He Yingqin his hopes for a negotiated settlement, other Nationalist leaders began pushing Chiang to achieve just that. As had been the case in August 1927, the leaders of the Guangxi Clique, Li Zongren and Bai Chongxi, concluded that the time had come for Chiang Kai-shek to step aside for the good of the state and the people. On December 24, Bai Chongxi, commander of the anti-CCP headquarters in central China, contacted Chiang and recommended that

[69] Gary J. Bjorge, "Move the Enemy: Operational Art in the Chinese PLA's Huai Hai Campaign," Leavenworth Paper Number 22 (Fort Leavenworth, KS: Combat Studies Institute Press, 2003), 67; Westad, *Decisive Encounters*, 199–210.

[70] On the Ping–Jin campaign, see Larry M. Wortzel, "The Beiping–Tianjin Campaign of 1948–1949: The Strategic and Operational Thinking of the People's Liberation Army," in Mark A. Ryan, David M. Finkelstein, and Michael A. McDevitt, eds., *Chinese Warfighting: The PLA Experience Since 1949* (Armonk, NY: M. E. Sharpe, 2003), 56–72.

[71] *HYQJJ*, II, 979.

he initiate peace talks with communist leaders. Chiang understood the realities of the situation and responded with a proposal that involved a ceasefire and resumption of peace talks with American, British, and Soviet mediation. Li Zongren offered a different and more detailed set of proposals that called for Chiang's resignation as president, the release of political prisoners, preservation of freedoms of speech and association, a withdrawal of all military forces 30 *li* from their current positions, and the establishment of Shanghai as a "free city" that would host talks with the CCP. Bai followed this proposal with a direct request to Chiang to resign.[72]

Chiang took no immediate steps, but in a 1949 New Year's address he indicated that, while he would remain in office, he planned to consider peace proposals as long as the agreement did not endanger the sovereignty or independence of the country, harm the welfare of the people, or jeopardize the constitution.[73] Mao Zedong ridiculed the address, remarking that "Chiang Kai-shek has lost his soul, is merely a corpse, and no one believes him any more."[74] On January 14, Mao offered a more formal response in which he laid down eight points as the basis for peace talks, including the punishment of war criminals, the abolition of the constitution, land reform, and the confiscation of "bureaucratic capital."[75] The reference to punishment of war criminals carried an ominous threat as the CCP had recently issued a list of Nationalist military officers and government officials it considered war criminals, including Chiang Kai-shek, He Yingqin, and Li Zongren.[76] After meeting with the Executive Yuan and determining that the vast majority favored a ceasefire and a resumption of peace talks, on January 21, 1949, Chiang announced that he would "step down" from his position as president, leaving the government and military in the hands of Acting President Li Zongren. The widespread belief that the United States government would be more likely to increase material aid to China if Chiang stepped aside no doubt encouraged Chiang to do so.[77]

Li Zongren quickly took steps to begin peace negotiations, appointing a five-man team to represent the Nationalist government and ordering

[72] He Yingqin, "Zuge yu huxian" [Organizing a Cabinet and Protecting the Constitution], in He Yingqin, ed., *Weibang bainian ji*, 94–95.
[73] Furuya, *Chiang Kai-shek*, 901–02.
[74] Mao Zedong, "On the War Criminal's Suing for Peace," in *Selected Works*, IV, 313.
[75] Mao Zedong, "Statement on the Present Situation," in *Selected Works*, IV, 318.
[76] *FRUS, 1948*, vol. VII, 718–20.
[77] Li-fu Chen, *The Storm Clouds Clear over China: The Memoir of Ch'en Li-fu, 1900–1993*, edited and compiled with an Introduction and notes by Sidney H. Chang and Ramon H. Myers (Stanford: Stanford University Press, 1994), 210; Taylor, *Generalissimo*, 398–400.

the release of prisoners held for their association with the communists. He responded to Mao's eight points in vague terms, acknowledging the need to release political prisoners and ensure freedoms of speech and association, while remaining silent on the punishment of "war criminals." When the CCP asked for the arrest of these war criminals as a show of good faith, Li refused, but proposed a ceasefire with a resumption of talks aimed at solving the nation's problems through political means, rather than military conflict. CCP forces bided their time, consolidating newly controlled areas north of the Yangzi River. Meanwhile, the situation grew increasingly difficult for the Nanjing leadership.[78]

While Chiang Kai-shek had stepped down, as had been the case in late 1927 he continued to wield tremendous influence through the officers of the central army or "Whampoa Clique." Indeed, he did not formally resign but rather stepped aside in what most perceived as another temporary withdrawal. After returning to his home in Xikou, he still directed military operations without consulting with the Ministry of National Defense or the chief of staff. Many unit commanders still accepted his personal directives or simply would not make a move without Chiang's approval. Chiang had deep reservations about the peace negotiations and tried to block them, working through General Tang Enbo, Air Force Commander Zhou Zhirou, and others on preparations to withdraw from Nanjing in order to defend Shanghai.[79] He Yingqin held no official position but tried to bring some kind of order and unity to the Nationalist military and government. He understood that Chiang Kai-shek and Li Zongren might work at cross-purposes and therefore sought help from the United States in trying to persuade Chiang to cease his interference so as to allow the government to pursue its military and political policies.

He Yingqin first sent one of his subordinates, General Cai Wenzhi, to see Ambassador Stuart to ask if the Americans might help dissuade Chiang from his "present stupidly disastrous course." Cai explained that he had confidence that the Nationalists could hold the line at the Yangzi River and defend the capital if American officials could help prevent Chiang from drawing troops away from Nanjing. The ambassador promised nothing, other than to pass this report on to Washington.[80] Two weeks later, He Yingqin made his own call on Ambassador Stuart, repeating complaints that Chiang had been obstructing the peace negotiations and interfering in military affairs. He Yingqin claimed to

---

[78] He Yingqin, "Zuge yu huxian," 406–07; Tsung-jen Li, *Memoirs*, 491–95.
[79] Westad, *Decisive Encounters*, 219; *FRUS, 1949*, vol. VIII, 290.
[80] *FRUS, 1949*, vol. VIII, 113–14.

be at a loss to explain Chiang's behavior, but indicated that many of his closest supporters agreed that the only way to retrieve the situation and block the communist advance would be to remove Chiang from China. Specifically, He asked if the American government might invite Chiang to visit the United States. He Yingqin viewed this as the most important factor in determining whether there would be peace in China or continued warfare. With just three months free from Chiang's interference, he assured the ambassador, he could turn the situation around and prevent CCP forces from crossing the Yangzi River. After expressing deep appreciation for all that the Americans had done for China over the years, He Yingqin predicted that "this one thing would do more for the national welfare than anything else."[81] These appeals produced no results, and the Nationalist government continued to struggle to overcome its divisions and formulate a coherent policy.

### Into the "fire pit"

The government suffered another crisis in early March when Premier Sun Ke resigned, causing the cabinet to fall. Sun Ke had taken over as premier in November 1948, after Weng Wenhao's resignation, and remained close to Chiang Kai-shek. He had aroused the animosity of Li Zongren and members of the Legislative Yuan when he moved the offices of the Executive Yuan to Guangzhou in February. Sun had tried to persuade He to support this move, but He refused.[82] Li persuaded Sun to return, but the Legislative Yuan soon thereafter prepared a vote of no confidence against Sun, which precipitated his resignation.[83] This triggered a frantic search for another capable candidate willing to take on the job at this desperate moment. Li Zongren quickly set his sights on He Yingqin, one of the few elites in Nanjing who might help Li win the support of the Whampoa officers and execute his military and political plans. Without military support, negotiations had no hope of success.

Li sent General Zhang Zhizhong to Xikou and telephoned Chiang Kai-shek personally to discuss possible candidates for the position, as he knew that unless Chiang approved of the choice there was little chance that the new premier could work effectively. Yet when Li raised He Yingqin's name as a candidate, Chiang did not agree. He claimed that, if the Nationalists intended to pursue peace talks with the CCP, He Yingqin

[81] *FRUS, 1949*, vol. VIII, 142. Li Zongren made similar remarks to other American diplomats in China: *FRUS, 1949*, vol. VIII, 143.
[82] "Gen. Ho Arrives in Nanking," *New York Times*, February 16, 1949.
[83] "Sun Fo Quits Post as China's Premier," *New York Times*, March 8, 1949; Tsung-jen Li, *Memoirs*, 496.

might have a negative influence. Moreover, he should be busy with military preparations, and this would simply distract him from that important task. Besides, Chiang knew that He Yingqin had reservations about the job and he did not want Li to pressure him into it. Beyond these reasons, it is also likely that Chiang did not want someone so close to him working with Li Zongren, a man he did not trust.[84] Convinced that he needed He to win support among the Whampoa officers, Li persisted, arguing with Chiang that, if He did not take the position, it would be nearly impossible to get another viable candidate. Chiang finally relented and agreed to support He Yingqin for premier.

Li Zongren then sent Generals Bai Chongxi and Wu Zhongxin to Shanghai to invite He Yingqin to succeed Sun Ke as premier, but He Yingqin flatly refused. Li then went to Shanghai to meet with him personally, reminding him of how they had worked together in 1927 when Chiang had stepped down as commander of the NRA, winning an important victory in the battle at Longtan, but He Yingqin again refused. While He generally supported Li's plan for peace negotiations, it is not hard to understand why he harbored deep concerns about serving as premier. Politics had never been his strength and the prospect of trying to assemble a cabinet and assert authority over an unruly Legislative Yuan did not appeal to him. Moreover, while Li might have hoped that this would help garner support among Whampoa Academy graduates who remained ultimately loyal to Chiang, He Yingqin understood the limits of his ability to command these officers. Perhaps the biggest concern on He's part was the fact that Chiang Kai-shek had only reluctantly agreed to his appointment, which meant he had little chance of commanding the obedience of the Whampoa Clique. Chiang certainly did not trust Li Zongren, who had opposed him on a number of occasions, and the two had been at odds for long stretches despite cooperation during the war against Japan. When Li brought up their cooperation during Chiang's 1927 "retirement," He Yingqin indeed remembered Longtan, but also recalled Chiang's anger over his collaboration with the leaders of the Guangxi Clique, Li Zongren and Bai Chongxi.

After rejecting Li Zongren's request for a second time, He Yingqin took his family on a trip to Hangzhou to celebrate his impending sixtieth birthday, staying at a house Tang Enbo owned near the famous West Lake. Desperate to get He to take the position, Li dispatched Zhang

---

[84] According to Zhang Zhizhong, when Chiang first learned that He Yingqin might be a candidate for the premiership, he exclaimed, "Why must it be someone with such a close relationship to me to serve as premier? Someone else should do it." See Zhang Zhizhong, "He Yingqin zuge" [He Yingqin Forms a Cabinet], in Tu Yueseng, ed., *Xingyi Wang, Liu, He sanda jiazu*, 209.

Zhizhong, Wu Zhongxin, Bai Chongxi, and Gu Zhutong to Hangzhou to persuade He to change his mind and accept the responsibility of leading the Executive Yuan. Only when they gave him a handwritten letter from Chiang Kai-shek, in which Chiang explained that they must put aside personal desires and continue to work to protect the revolution, did He Yingqin change his mind, finally concluding that he had no choice but to help prepare for whatever lay ahead. If the government pursued a peace settlement with the CCP, then he must work to ensure its viability. If not, then he must help prepare for a final battle to settle the issue once and for all.[85] Before accepting, He Yingqin first asked Li to agree to a set of seven principles, which included assurances that he would agree to abide by the constitution, implement necessary economic reforms, reorganize the military, and work constructively with the Legislative Yuan. Li agreed with these principles and formally nominated He Yingqin as the next premier. The Legislative Yuan voted in favor of his nomination, 209 to 30 with 1 abstention.[86]

News that He Yingqin had accepted the premiership suggested to some that Li Zongren would have a much better chance of winning over the commanders of the 300,000 Nationalist troops in the Yangzi River area to support his "peace or war" policy.[87] Others believed it would help, but would not offset the fact that Chiang Kai-shek still controlled large segments of the military and likely would not lend wholehearted support to the efforts of Li Zongren's government.[88] Returning to Nanjing on March 15, He Yingqin set about the business of forming his cabinet of ministers. He met with journalists, telling them that he had not yet decided upon all cabinet members, but the names of candidates would be available in a few days. In more private remarks the next day, he told members of the Control Yuan that due to the heavy responsibility of the premier's job at this critical time he felt as though he had "jumped into a pit of fire."[89] Evidently others hesitated to take the leap with him, as He Yingqin and Li Zongren had difficulty finding appropriate individuals willing to serve in the cabinet. After several days, they unveiled the new government portfolio, which included mostly newcomers to this level of service. It lacked influential figures who might command the respect of veteran officers and officials, not to mention those who remained

---

[85] *HYQJJ*, II, 990; He Yingqin, "Zuge yu huxian," 98; "4 Envoys Press Premiership on Ho," *New York Times*, March 12, 1949.

[86] He Yingqin, "Zuge yu huxian," 99–100. He Yingqin claimed that he prevented Li Zongren from accepting all eight of Mao's demands of January 14: *ibid.*, 107.

[87] "Nanking Assembly Names Ho Premier," *New York Times*, March 13, 1949; "China's Reds Make Claim to Formosa," *New York Times*, March 16, 1949.

[88] *FRUS, 1949*, vol. VIII, 199–200.    [89] *HYQJJ*, II, 993–94.

loyal and obedient to Chiang Kai-shek.[90] On his first day in office, He Yingqin listed his priorities, which included protecting the constitution, reforming the military, calming the public, and stabilizing social and economic order. He indicated that the government would pursue peace talks with the CCP while at the same time making military preparations for continuing the conflict. The latter task involved preparing the southwest or Taiwan as a base for retreat and counterattack.[91] With regard to stabilizing the socioeconomic situation, he met again with John Leighton Stuart to ask for a "stabilizing loan" of US$200 million to $300 million to support the Chinese currency. Without such a loan, he stressed, the government could not survive to engage in peace talks with the CCP. He Yingqin even offered a "lien" on the island of Taiwan or its products as security. Stuart made no comment, but promised to pass it on to his Department of State.[92] With regard to military preparations, at a meeting of top military commanders on March 31, the new premier read from a letter from Chiang Kai-shek. Knowing that many officers would not act without Chiang's approval, He Yingqin tried to unify the group by informing them of Chiang's wish that they should prepare a strong military defense. After reading the letter, He Yingqin told the assembled officers that, though Chiang had withdrawn, he still supported them and every one of them must be prepared to fight. The third great war was about to begin, he told them, and they must defend the Nanjing–Shanghai region as a base for counterattack.[93]

Both Li Zongren and He Yingqin hoped that at best the peace talks would yield a few months of time in which to regroup and organize a better military plan. In preparing for peace talks, Li Zongren selected five delegates to represent the Nationalist government, Zhang Zhizhong, Shao Lizi, Huang Shaohong, Zhang Shizhao, and Li Zheng. Li Zongren later added Liu Fei to the group, bringing its number to six.[94] The CCP appointed its own delegation consisting of Lin Biao, Lin Boqu, Ye Jianying, and Li Weihan, and indicated its willingness to begin talks in Beiping on April 1.[95] Within a week it became clear that the CCP would not show much flexibility, as its leaders laid new demands on the table, including sending PLA forces across the river to help reorganize the Nationalist military and the establishment of an interim provisional

[90] Tsung-jen Li, *Memoirs*, 497; "Debate over Delegates," *New York Times*, March 23, 1949; *FRUS, 1949*, vol. VIII, 185–86.
[91] He Yingqin, "Zuge yu huxian," 100; *HYQJJ*, II, 994.
[92] *FRUS, 1949*, vol. IX, 746, 753.   [93] Zhang Zhizhong, "He Yingqin zuge," 211.
[94] He Yingqin, "Zuge yu huxian," 100.
[95] "Communists Name China Peace Group; Talks Open April 1," *New York Times*, March 27, 1949.

government under Mao Zedong as chair with Li Zongren as one of two vice-chairs. The CCP also demanded punishment of members of the "Four Big Families," namely Chiang Kai-shek, his brothers-in-law Song Ziwen and Kong Xiangxi, and his longtime supporters Chen Lifu and Chen Guofu.[96] Addressing a group of thirty prominent members of the party at a meeting of the GMD Central Executive Committee in Guangzhou on April 7, He Yingqin gave a pessimistic report and expressed his view that little hope remained for a settlement. He reiterated his belief in the need to defend the laws of the state and the constitution, and predicted that the PLA would soon mount an attack across the Yangzi River.[97]

After a series of delays and informal talks, the CCP dropped all pretense of negotiation and presented the Nationalists with an ultimatum. On April 13, Nationalist delegate Huang Shaohong returned to Nanjing with a draft of a CCP peace agreement that included eight articles and twenty-four sections. Differing little from Mao's eight points of January 14, the draft called for the punishment of war criminals, the abrogation of the constitution and laws of the Republic of China, the reorganization of all "reactionary" military forces, systematic land reform, and the creation of a democratic coalition government to take overall authority of the Nanjing government. The CCP leaders gave Li Zongren and the Nationalist government until April 20 to accept the agreement, at which time the PLA would begin to cross the Yangzi River, either to implement the agreement or to attack Nationalist forces.[98] Top Nationalist leaders met at He Yingqin's residence to discuss the proposal and then conferred again at the Ministry of National Defense. On April 20, He Yingqin addressed the Legislative Yuan explaining that the CCP's "peace plan" amounted to a "document of surrender" even more harsh than that the Allied Powers had imposed on Japan at the end of the war of resistance. It placed all blame for the military conflict of the past three years, and all of the suffering and destruction that went along with it, squarely with the Nationalists. "How," he asked the members of the Legislative Yuan, "can we bear this heavy responsibility?" That evening, the government directed its delegates in Beiping to inform CCP representatives of its intention to reject the draft agreement. That night, PLA forces began crossing the Yangzi River.[99]

---

[96] Li-fu Chen, *The Storm Clouds Clear over China*, 216; "3 Key Issues Delay China Peace Talks," *New York Times*, April 12, 1949.
[97] He Yingqin, "Zuge yu huxian," 105; *FRUS, 1949*, vol. VIII, 234.
[98] *HYQJJ*, II, 1009; "Li Said to Reject Yangzi Crossing," *New York Times*, April 19, 1949.
[99] *HYQJJ*, II, 1010–13: Furuya, *Chiang Kai-shek*, 904.

The rejection of the CCP peace plan ushered in the final military phase of the civil war. Too divided to work together effectively, Nationalist commanders could not agree on a unified battle plan to defend the capital. For example, a month or two earlier, when the top military leaders met at the Ministry of National Defense to discuss how to deal with a CCP attack across the Yangzi River, Li Zongren, He Yingqin, Gu Zhutong, and Cai Wenzhi all agreed on a plan to defend the river with more troops at its narrowest points, where a CCP crossing would be easier, and to deploy fewer forces at the widest points. All agreed on the logic of this plan except Tang Enbo, commander of Nationalist forces along the Yangzi River, who refused to go along with it because Chiang preferred to defend Shanghai rather than Nanjing. When pressed on the matter, Tang rejected the plan and left the meeting.[100]

On April 22 Chiang summoned Li Zongren, He Yingqin, Bai Chongxi, and others to Hangzhou for a meeting to discuss the situation and how to proceed. With peace talks at an end and the CCP crossing the river to attack Nanjing, Chiang expressed a determination to fight to the end. Li asked Chiang to return to authority, but Chiang declined, promising to support Li in any way possible. The meeting concluded with an agreement to appoint He Yingqin to the position of minister of national defense and to give him unified command over all ground, air, and naval forces. Such a change had been under consideration for several days and He Yingqin had emerged as the logical candidate. The Nationalists' Acting Foreign Minister George Yeh told Lewis Clark of the American consulate in Guangzhou that the situation required a single leader who could unite the various factions of the military under the title of "supreme commander in chief." Yeh claimed that He Yingqin might be the one man who could do this and, though he had declined the position, Yeh believed he would eventually accept if no one else came forward. He Yingqin did just that at the meeting in Hangzhou but, while all agreed that the situation called for a unified command, the diverse factions within the Nationalist military made it impossible.[101]

He Yingqin returned to the capital the next day, where he heard artillery fire on the outskirts of the city, and immediately flew to Shanghai. There he announced that the government would move to Guangzhou. In a report two weeks later to the members of the Legislative Yuan, he

[100] Tsung-jen Li, *Memoirs*, 511–12. The date of this meeting is unclear. Li Zongren's memoir suggests that this incident took place in February 1949, but it might have been March. See Westad, *Decisive Encounters*, 242; Xiong Zongren, *He Yingqin: xuanwozhong de lishi*, II, 621–22; Li Zhongming, *He Yingqin dazhuan*, 322.
[101] *HYQJJ*, II, 1018–19; Tsung-jen Li, *Memoirs*, 514–15; Taylor, *Generalissimo*, 406; *FRUS, 1949*, vol. VIII, 254.

explained that the move had been necessary to avoid encirclement in the event that the CCP forces captured Hangzhou and attacked from the south as well. Moreover, after the defeats in Manchuria, Xuzhou, and Bengbu, Nationalist forces had suffered great losses and, though they had numerous replacement troops, they had not yet completed their training. The preservation of existing forces remained the first priority and required a withdrawal from Nanjing and Shanghai. He declined to provide any details on the military plan other than to call for a general strategy of protracted war.[102] From Shanghai He Yingqin flew to Guangzhou on April 25 where he would try to unify southern military and provincial officials to continue the war effort to defend the south.

In order to muster a defense of the south, He Yingqin needed to overcome two significant problems. First, he faced a divided military and government that did not agree on a single strategy and did not recognize him as unified commander of the military. As long as some officers and officials insisted on taking orders from Chiang Kai-shek alone, He Yingqin could not coordinate effective military operations. Second, the financial situation had grown so severe that the government teetered on the verge of collapse. Seeking an immediate injection of money and resources to address this latter problem, He Yingqin called on American chargé d'affaires in Guangzhou Lewis Clark to request emergency aid. Clark characterized their meeting on April 29 as a "chicken and egg" conversation in which He Yingqin insisted that successful resistance required American aid, and Clark pointed out that the US Congress would not likely grant this aid unless it first saw some sign of successful resistance. Moved by He Yingqin's appearance and demeanor, which Clark described as despondent, hopeless, and helpless, he promised to send forward a request for aid into his government.[103]

In his attempts to rally forces for a successful military defense of the south, He Yingqin found that his status as premier, minister of national defense, and supreme commander meant little, as officers loyal to Chiang refused to accept orders from anyone else. Two incidents from May 1949 clearly demonstrated He's lack of control over unit commanders. Hu Lian, commander of the Twelfth Group Army with 50,000 troops, ignored He's orders to take up positions in Jiangxi and submit to Bai Chongxi's command in central China. Instead, Hu acted on orders

---

[102] He Yingqin, "Yu zhonggong hetan polie jingguo ji zhengfu qiansui qingxing" [On the Failure of Peace Talks with the Communists and the Government's Move to Guangdong], in He Yingqin, ed., *Weibang bainian ji*, 673; *HYQJJ*, II, 1029.
[103] *FRUS, 1949*, vol. IX, 675–76.

from Chiang Kai-shek and moved his force east into Fujian, compromising Bai's position in central China and leaving Nanchang and Changsha vulnerable. Shortly thereafter, He Yingqin ordered Song Xilian, commander of the Hunan–Hubei border area pacification headquarters, to move his substantial force from Hubei into western Hunan as quickly as possible. Song refused with the now-common explanation that Chiang had ordered him to remain in Hubei. When He Yingqin pressed him, invoking his authority as premier and minister of national defense, Song simply remarked that he did not recognize He's authority and hung up the phone.[104]

In a final effort, He Yingqin called a series of meetings from May 16 to 20 in which he tried to coordinate armed forces and resources among the remaining southern generals and provincial officials. Attendees included Bai Chongxi, Zhang Qun, Zhang Fakui, Chen Jicheng, Xue Yue, Chen Cheng, Wang Longji, and Gu Zhenglun among others. They discussed military and financial issues but could not reach an agreement. Unable to direct effective military operations, to coordinate among provincial elites to combine resources, or to secure an emergency loan from the United States, He Yingqin concluded that he could not continue as premier and minister of national defense. He submitted his resignation to Li Zongren on May 21, but agreed to stay on until they found a successor. It took a couple of weeks, but eventually Yan Xishan, the old Shanxi warlord, agreed to form a new cabinet, which took effect on June 10. This brought He Yingqin's term as premier to an end less than three months after taking office. It also concluded his military and political career on the Chinese mainland. Weeks later, he flew to Taiwan, where he would spend the rest of his days.[105]

He Yingqin's resignation as premier and minister of national defense marked the end of his three decades and more in pursuit of a stable, unified, and militarily strong government on the Chinese mainland. Such a China did emerge, but under the CCP after its 1949 triumph in the civil war. In the years after the Sino-Japanese War, He Yingqin arrived at a greater understanding of the broad social, economic, and political policies the Nationalists needed to implement in order to address the problems that had made his goal elusive. Ironically, this realization came at a time when the window for making these changes was growing smaller. The period after the war with Japan also marked a change in his

---

[104] Li Zongren recounts both Hu Lian's and Song Xilian's refusal to follow orders. See Tsung-jen Li, *Memoirs*, 525–26.

[105] *HYQJJ*, II, 1030–31.

relationship with Chiang Kai-shek. After decades of close collaboration, He Yingqin concluded that Chiang's inability to let go of his military authority made it impossible to mount a successful defense against the CCP. On Taiwan, He Yingqin continued to hold high rank, but he no longer occupied the same position, as Chiang's "right-hand man," as he had since their days at the Whampoa Military Academy.

# Conclusion

He Yingqin turned sixty in the same year he withdrew to Taiwan, along with the remnants of the Nationalist government and army. He lived there for another thirty-eight years before his death in 1987, the same year the Guomindang lifted martial law on Taiwan and began a gradual process of democratization. Had He Yingqin had the opportunity to read his own obituary in the *New York Times*, he no doubt would have been disappointed, though not surprised. He understood that many American officials and observers took a dim view of his work as minister of military administration and Chiang Kai-shek's chief of staff, but he also knew that they did not see the full picture. Many described him as incompetent, yet his early education and training indicated otherwise. Others labeled him a "political general" who lacked genuine military skill as a commander, but he won a number of important victories in the NRA's early campaigns. Critics accused him of harboring pro-Japan sympathies and conceding Chinese sovereignty to the Japanese military in north China in the 1930s, but He Yingqin maintained that he had preserved control of Beiping (now Beijing) and Tianjin and held the Japanese at bay while the Nationalists continued to prepare for a larger conflict. Some claimed he wanted to kill Chiang at Xi'an in order to take his place, though he argued that military pressure would support negotiations and bring about Chiang's safe release. His detractors pointed to the problems in conscription during the Sino-Japanese War as evidence of his poor work as a military administrator, yet he saw it as the foundation of China's victory over Japan. American officials in particular decried his "obsession" with the communists and complained that he insisted on employing force alone, but He Yingqin actually advocated political, social, and economic policies for opposing the CCP, along with military force.

Collectively, these claims, complaints, and accusations surrounding He Yingqin reflect the dominant narrative of the Nationalist government and military as whole. Hans van de Ven is no doubt correct when he argues that the "Stilwell–White Paradigm" still exerts overwhelming influence over Western understanding of the Chinese Nationalist regime.

He lists the central tenets of this paradigm as "military incompetence, corruption, a debilitating obsession with the communists, authoritarianism, and a blind refusal to fight Japan."[1] With the possible exception of authoritarianism, this general description of the Nationalist regime as a whole perfectly matches descriptions of He Yingqin in the Western-language literature. This Western-centered perspective has its origins in American perceptions of problems with the Nationalist war effort, and does not adequately take into account the enormous challenges Chinese officials faced between 1925 and 1949. What began with American military officers, diplomats, journalists, and popular writers found support from academic historians who tended to confirm this paradigm rather than question it. Lloyd Eastman, one of the most influential and widely cited historians of the Nationalist period, attributed the defeat of the Nationalists in 1949 in large part to the "inherent structural infirmities" of the army and government including the "corruption and ineffectiveness of its administration." Eastman quoted Chiang Kai-shek himself as bemoaning the rampant "corruption and degeneracy manifested within our revolutionary army."[2] Western writings on the Nationalist period place He Yingqin firmly in this context, presenting him as representative of the corruption and incompetence that forced the Nationalists to yield the mainland to the CCP and withdraw to Taiwan. More than five decades later, scholars such as van de Ven, Rana Mitter, and Jay Taylor have contested these traditional assessments of the Nationalists, but He Yingqin's reputation remains unchanged.

This book began with a series of questions about He Yingqin, intended to challenge some of the central Western interpretations of his career and role in the Nationalist military. A careful analysis of his career allows for a number of conclusions that revise our understanding of He. First, there is no evidence to support claims of incompetence or corruption. Despite repeated assertions to this effect in the existing English- and some Chinese-language literature, a detailed examination of his career reveals this as a serious mischaracterization. To the contrary, his early career in particular reflects academic excellence, which won him admission and scholarships to some of the most prestigious military academies in China and Japan. He underwent rigorous training in Japan and served a brief term in the Japanese Imperial Army, which prepared him well for future combat operations. Once he returned to China, he acquired practical experience in running a military academy in Guizhou, which made him a particularly attractive candidate for work at the Whampoa Military Academy and brought him to the attention of Sun Yat-sen and Chiang

---

[1] Van de Ven, *War and Nationalism*, 7.    [2] Eastman, *Seeds of Destruction*, 225, 209.

Kai-shek. Perhaps the most important evidence of his skills as a military officer came with his successful performance as a regimental, brigade, division, corps, and ultimately route army commander in the Eastern and Northern Expeditions. Commanding elements of the NRA's First Corps, he won several important victories at critical moments in the revolution, usually in the face of superior numbers and firepower. His later work during the Central Plains War of 1930 and his counterattack on western Hunan in early 1945 also demonstrated his ability to direct successful military operations at critical moments. Clearly, his rise to the top ranks of the Nationalist military and his long career among the Nanjing elite came as a direct result of his own capabilities and successes. As for corruption, there is no evidence to support such claims. The documentary record reveals He Yingqin as a serious and sober officer, known for his Spartan habits and strong work ethic.

Second, while he occupies a small space in Western-language studies of the Nationalist period, it is clear that He Yingqin played a central role in most of the major military and diplomatic events of the time. Chiang Kai-shek consistently turned to He Yingqin as his most trusted and reliable subordinate when facing difficult challenges or pressing issues. From the earliest days of the Nationalist revolution, Chiang called upon He to lead the most loyal forces under Chiang's command, the loss of which would likely have spelled the end of both their careers. He Yingqin provided critical support for Chiang in the split with the Wuhan faction of the GMD and the CCP in 1927 and then played decisive roles in defeating regional commanders who revolted against Nanjing's authority between 1929 and in the Central Plains War of 1930. After the failure of the first encirclement campaign against the CCP base in Jiangxi, Chiang ordered He to organize the next two campaigns. When the Japanese military threatened Chinese positions in north China, Chiang dispatched He both to prepare for resistance and to negotiate a peaceful settlement. In fact, He Yingqin pushed a reluctant Chiang Kai-shek to accept the settlements of 1933 and 1935, which preserved Chinese control over Beiping and Tianjin and postponed a larger Sino-Japanese War. When Chiang's own generals kidnapped him in 1936, He Yingqin applied military pressure on Xi'an that helped create the context for successful negotiations and Chiang's safe return to Nanjing. As minister of military administration, he presided over the crucial task of recruiting and training endless Chinese soldiers, without which the final victory would have been impossible. Though he spent the early postwar years outside China, when the civil war took a serious turn for the worse in 1948, Chiang quickly called He back, hoping he might be able to help reverse the regime's fortunes. In the past, He's place in the existing Western historiography on

Nationalist China did not reflect this fact, but scholars must now acknowledge that He Yingqin played a central role in developing and implementing the most important military and diplomatic policies of the Nationalist period.

Third, He Yingqin and Chiang Kai-shek shared a close personal and professional relationship that served as one of the pillars of the Nationalist government and army. He Yingqin's rise through the ranks of the Nationalist regime came partly because of his professional capabilities, but there is no doubt that his relationship to Chiang Kai-shek paved the way for his rapid ascent. Rather than one of Chiang's cronies, one might best describe He as the man Chiang most often relied upon to get the job done. From their early days together at the Whampoa Military Academy, Chiang found He a reliable subordinate who shared his view of the military as the foundation of a new Chinese state and society. Chiang approved of He's attitude and work ethic at the academy, but only when he demonstrated his value as a combat commander with victories at Danshui, Mianhu, and Huizhou did Chiang begin to rely heavily on He as his right-hand man. An emotional man, Chiang had strong relationships with many of those he worked with and fought alongside over the course of his career. Within his inner circle of the Nanjing elite, He Yingqin stood out as the man to whom Chiang consistently turned when facing a critical challenge. Whether protecting the revolutionary base in eastern Guangdong, suppressing revolts within the Nationalist military, fending off the Japanese in north China, contending with American allies such as Joseph Stilwell, or defending southwest China during the Ichigo offensive, in each case Chiang turned to He. The bond between the two men grew strong, but it rested on the fact that Chiang Kai-shek trusted He Yingqin to achieve critical objectives.

Their relationship suffered strains along the way, as one might expect of two men who worked together closely under stressful conditions for more than two decades. Chiang felt deeply wounded when in 1927 He Yingqin failed to support him against Bai Chongxi's demand that he step down. He's subsequent cooperation with Bai and Li Zongren led Chiang to complain bitterly of He's treachery, but the two men quickly patched up their relationship and continued to pursue their common goal of a united country and strong military. Only at the end of their time on the mainland, as He Yingqin realized that Chiang would not agree to the necessary socioeconomic reforms or military preparations that might prevent defeat at the hands of the CCP, did He Yingqin finally break with Chiang and covertly seek to remove him from power. If one discounts these two incidents, no other officer worked as closely with Chiang Kai-shek over the course of the Nationalist period on the mainland. Even when American pressure forced Chiang to remove He as minister of military administration and later send him out of China as a representative to the UN Military Staff Committee, Chiang eventually called He back to take up important positions and once again support him in dealing with his most pressing problems. Chiang Kai-shek once angrily suggested that "without Chiang Kai-shek, there is no He Yingqin!" but one can also argue that the reverse is equally true. Without He's reliable support against internal and external opponents, Chiang might not have survived all the challenges he faced between 1924 and 1949. In short, without He Yingqin, the history of Nationalist China might have been quite different.

Finally, looking back on He Yingqin's career, the year 1930 stands out as a turning point. As minister of military administration from 1930 to 1944, his work changed, and he faced new and more complicated challenges. Most of his previous assignments had required leading troops in a decisive battle for a quick resolution. Beginning in 1930, he encountered a resilient and highly mobile CCP Red Army that enjoyed support from the local population. This force proved more difficult to defeat than the armies of old-style warlords such as Sun Chuanfang or rebellious Nationalist commanders such as Feng Yuxiang, Yan Xishan, and Li Zongren. Before long, he found himself in a difficult position in north China, charged with the complex task of preventing the Japanese military from making additional encroachments on Chinese territory without provoking a larger Sino-Japanese war for which the Chinese army had not sufficiently prepared. These challenges occupied him for the first several years of his tenure as minister of military administration, and he could not find quick or easy solutions, which rendered him vulnerable to criticism. His failures in the early encirclement campaigns against the Red Army in Jiangxi and his role in negotiations with the Japanese in 1933 and 1935 stood in stark contrast to his earlier military success in battles at Danshui, Mianhu, Huizhou, Yongding, Longtan, and elsewhere and gave rise to suggestions of incompetence, corruption, and even pro-Japan sympathies. His efforts to organize military pressure against Zhang Xueliang and Yang Hucheng in the 1936 Xi'an Incident planted the seeds of the myth that He Yingqin wanted to eliminate Chiang and take his place and led some to question his loyalty to Chiang and the Nanjing government. His inability to eliminate the abusive practices in the conscription system during the Sino-Japanese War and his contentious relationship with Joseph Stilwell made him a target of American critics who came to regard him as hopelessly reactionary and a major obstacle to reforming the Chinese army. The enormous challenges and limited or qualified accomplishments of his later career greatly overshadowed the decisive victories and clear successes of his early years. Few observers or writers have paid any attention to his early career, focusing instead on period of the 1930s and 1940s, a time when He Yingqin and the entire Nationalist military operated under extreme duress. This has greatly contributed to the tendency to identify He Yingqin with what many saw as the major characteristics of the Nationalist military establishment as a whole: corruption, incompetence, and cronyism.

That American writers and historians have misunderstood He Yingqin and his role in the Nationalist period is not necessarily an isolated event. In 1984, Paul Cohen published an influential book in which he reviewed trends in American historiography on China and found much of it West-centered. He urged scholars to avoid applying Western standards or values to evaluate historical events in China and advocated the practice of "China-centered history," which analyzes "Chinese problems set in a Chinese context."[3] Cohen's approach is essential in order to move beyond superficial and stereotypical characterizations of the Nationalists. In essence, this book is a "China-centered" analysis of He Yingqin, incorporating both Chinese and American source materials to arrive at a more accurate, nuanced, and even-handed assessment of this important Nationalist officer. Given his prominent role in the major military and diplomatic and events of the period, a better understanding of He Yingqin, his role in the Nationalist military, and his relationship with Chiang Kai-shek contributes to a better understanding of the Nationalist period in particular, and the history of twentieth-century China in general.

[3] Paul Cohen, *Discovering History in China: American Historical Writing on the Recent Chinese Past* (New York: Columbia University Press, 1984), 154.

# Bibliography

PERIODICALS

*Evening Observer*
*Los Angeles Times*
*New York Times*

CHINESE-LANGUAGE SOURCES

Cai Hailin. "Kangzhan shiqi guomin zhengfu bingyi zhidu yanjiu zongshu" [A Review of Studies on Nationalist Government Conscription During the Sino-Japanese War]. *Junshi lishi yanjiu*, 1 (2008): 182–88.

Chang Jui-te. "Kangzhan shiqi guojun de canmou renyuan" [General Staffs of the Nationalist Army During the Sino-Japanese War]. *Bulletin of the Institute of Modern History*, 24 (1995): 741–72.

Chang Jui-te. "Kangzhan shiqi lujun de renshi guanli" [Personnel in the Nationalist Army During the Sino-Japanese War]. *Bulletin of the Institute of Modern History*, 21 (1992): 643–86.

Chen Feng. *Wannan shibian shimo* [The New Fourth Army Incident from Beginning to End]. Hefei: Anhui renmin chubanshe, 1984.

Chen Jianxing and Qin Chengjie. "Lun xi'an shibian zhong He Yingqin de zhuzhan yitu" [On He Yingqin's Intentions in Advocating Military Action in the Xi'an Incident]. *Huanghe keji daxue xuebao*, 10, 1 (January 2008): 51–52, 66.

Chen Jiuru. "He Yingqin chubing xi'an de dongyin guanjian" [An Opinion on He Yingqin's Motives for Sending Troops Against Xi'an]. *Lishi jiaoxue wenti*, 1 (1999): 34–36.

Chen Ningsheng and Zhang Guangyu. *Jiang Jieshi he huangpu xi* [Chiang Kai-shek and the Whampoa Clique]. Zhengzhou: Henan renmin chubanshe, 1994.

Chen Sanpeng. "Beifa shiqi de min'ao bianzhanshi yu He Yingqin" [He Yingqin and the Fighting on the Fujian–Guangdong Border During the Northern Expedition]. *Hanshan shifan xueyuan xuebao*, 1 (March 1995): 36–42.

Chen Xianqiu. "Xinhai yihou ershinian jian guizhou junzheng gaishu" [A Summary of Guizhou Military and Political Affairs in the Twenty-Five Years After the 1911 Revolution]. *Guizhou wenshi ziliao xuanji*, 15 (n.d.): 115–21.

Chen Yanzhen. "Zai He Yingqin de canmou zongzhang bangongshi sannian" [Three Years in He Yingqin's Chief of Staff Office]. *Guiyang wenshi ziliao*, 3, (n.d.): 157–58.

Chen Yuquan. "He Yingqin yu huangpu junxiao" [He Yingqin and the Whampoa Military Academy], Part I. *Huangpu*, 6 (2010): 20–23.

Chen Yuquan. "He Yingqin yu huangpu junxiao" [He Yingqin and the Whampoa Military Academy], Part II. *Huangpu*, 1 (2011): 21–23.

Ding Yizhong. "Wosuo qinjian de Yuan Zuming he 'dingqinjun'" [What I Witnessed of Yuan Zuming and the "Guizhou Pacification Army"]. *Guizhou wenshi ziliao xuanji*, 1 (n.d.): 122–38.

Fang Qiuwei. "Kangzhan shiqi de 'Bingyi fa' he bingyi shu" [The Conscription Department and the "Conscription Law" During the War of Resistance]. *Minguo dang'an*, 1 (1996): 123–31.

Fang Yonggang. "Jiang Jieshi diaojiao He Yingqin" [Chiang Kai-shek Disciplines He Yingqin]. *Moulüe tiandi*, 6 (2008): 59–60.

Gong Xilin. "Kangzhan shiqi jiceng baojia zhengbing de zhidu yuexing yinsu tanxi" [An Analysis of the Facts Regarding the Grassroots-Level *Baojia* in the Conscription System During the War of Resistance]. *Lishi jiaoxue*, 16 (2011): 23.

Gu Yiping. "Wang Boling qiren qishi" [Wang Boling: The Man and His Work]. *Renwu chunqiu*, 3, 1 (2003): 12–14.

Gui Baizhu. "Liu Xianshi jituan neibu douzheng sanji" [Random Notes on the Internal Struggles of the Liu Xianshi Clique]. *Guizhou wenshi ziliao xuanji*, 1 (n.d.): 98–114.

Guizhou daxue lishixi. "Guizhou junfa Liu Xianshi fajiashi" [A History of the Rise of the Family of Guizhou Warlord Liu Xianshi]. *Guizhou wenshi ziliao xuanji*, 3 (n.d.): 186–200.

Guo Dafeng. "Chen Cheng: Jiang Jieshi zhengquan zhong de teshu renwu" [Chen Cheng: A Special Figure in Chiang Kai-shek's Regime]. *Hubei dang'an*, 1–2 (2001): 93–96.

Guo Tingyi. *Jindai zhongguo shigang* [An Outline of Modern Chinese History], 2 vols. Xianggang: Zhongwen daxue chubanshe, 1980.

Guo Tingyi and Jia Tingshi, eds. *Bai Chongxi xiansheng fangwen jilu* [A Record of Interviews with Bai Chongxi], 2 vols. Taipei: Zhongyang yanjiuyuan jindaishi yanjiusuo, 1984.

Guo Xuyin, ed. *Guomindang paixi douzhengshi* [A History of the Struggle Between Guomindang Factions]. Shanghai: Shanghai renmin chubanshe, 1992.

Guofangbu shizhengju. *Beifa zhanshi* [A History of the Northern Expedition], 5 vols. Taipei: Guofangbu shizhengju, 1967.

Guofangbu shizheng bianzeju. *Junzheng shiwu nian* [Fifteen Years in Military Administration]. Taipei: Guofangbu shizheng bianzeju, 1984.

Han Shengchao. "He Yingqin yu guangdong geming genjudi de gonggu" [He Yingqin and the Consolidation of the Guangdong Revolutionary Base]. *Shixue yuekan*, 8 (2008): 79–83.

Hasama Naoki. "'Sanda zhengce' yu huangpu junxiao" [The Three Great Policies and the Whampoa Military Academy]. *Lishi yanjiu*, 2 (1988): 131–44.

He Dehong. "He Yingqin zeng daibing zhu fugongci" [He Yingqin Led Troops to Stay at Fugongci]. *Wenshi yuekan*, 7 (2006): 57–59.

He Jiwu. *Guizhou zhengtan yiwang* [Recollections of Guizhou Politics]. Taipei: Zhongwai tushuguan chubanshe, 1982.

He Yingqin. "Dongzheng beifa dao tongyi" [Eastern and Northern Expeditions to Unification]. *Zhongwai zazhi*, 44, 2 (August 1988): 83–86.

He Yingqin. "Dui sichuan bingyi huiyi xunci" [Instructions to the Sichuan Conscription Conference]. *Bingyi yuekan*, 4, 3 (1942): 8–10.

He Yingqin. *He zongzhang Yingqin yan lun xuanji*. China: n.p., 1939.

He Yingqin. "Jiaomie chifei xu junzheng hezuo" [Destroying the Red Bandits Will Require Military and Political Cooperation]. *Zhongyang zhoubao*, 226 (1932): 32–33.

He Yingqin. "Mianhu zhanyi zhi huiyi" [Reminiscences of the Battle of Mianhu]. *Geming wenxian*, 11 (1977): 269–76.

He Yingqin. "Nianlai yizheng zhi qianzhan ji jinhou zhi gaijin" [A View of Conscription Policy and Future Improvements]. *Bingyi yuekan*, 2 (1941): 10–12.

He Yingqin. "Qiqi shibian yu banian kangzhan shilüe" [A Brief History of the Marco Polo Bridge Incident and the Eight-Year War of Resistance]. *Yiwenzhi*, 166 (July 1979): 24–27.

He Yingqin. *Weibang bainian ji* [A Century of Service to the State]. Taipei: Liming wenhua shiye gufen youxian gongsi, 1987.

He Yingqin. "Zhengbing zhengce zhi jiantao" [A Review of Conscription Policy]. *Bingyi yuekan*, 4, 7–8 (1942): 4–6.

He Yingqin. "Zhongguo bisheng" [China Will Be Victorious]. *Bingyi yuekan*, 4, 4 (1942): 5–7.

He Yingqin. "Zuge huxian huiyi" [Recollections on Organizing a Cabinet and Protecting the Constitution]. *Zhongwai zazhi*, 24, 3 (September 1978): 8–15.

He Yingqin shangjiang jiuwu shouyan congshu bianji weiyuanhui. *Beiping junfenhui sannian* [Three Years as Chair of the Beiping Branch of the Military Affairs Commission]. Taipei: Liming wenhua shiye youxian gongsi, 1984.

He Yingqin shangjiang jiuwu shouyan congshu bianji weiyuanhui. *Donglujun beifa zuozhan jishi* [Combat Record of the Eastern Route Army in the Northern Expedition]. Taipei: Liming wenhua shiye youxian gongsi, 1984.

He Yingqin shangjiang jiuwu shouyan congshu bianji weiyuanhui. *He Yingqin jiangjun jiangci xuanji* [General He Yingqin's Selected Speeches]. Taipei: Liming wenhua shiye youxian gongsi, 1984.

He Yingqin shangjiang jiuwu shouyan congshu bianji weiyuanhui. *He Yingqin jiangjun jiuwu jishi changbian* [A Record of General He Yingqin's Ninety-Five Years], 2 vols. Taipei: Liming wenhua shiye youxian gongsi, 1984.

He Yingqin shangjiang jiuwu shouyan congshu bianji weiyuanhui. *Rijun qinhua banian kangzhan shi* [A History of the Eight-Year War of Resistance Against the Japanese]. Taipei: Liming wenhua shiye youxian gongsi, 1984.

He Yingqin shangjiang jiuwu shouyan congshu bianji weiyuanhui. *Xi'an shibian de chuli yu shanhou* [The Handling and Aftermath of the Xi'an Incident]. Taipei: Liming wenhua shiye youxian gongsi, 1984.

He Zhihao. "He jingong dui bingyi zhidu zhi jianli" [Mr. He Yingqin and the Establishment of the Conscription System]. *Zhongguo yu riben*, 107 (March 1969), 13–20.

Hou Xiongfei. "Xi'an shibian heping jiejue yuanyin xintan" [A New Inquiry into the Reasons Behind the Peaceful Resolution of the Xi'an Incident]. *Lishi yanjiu*, 2 (1987): 16–30.

Huang Ming and Li Shicheng. "Huabei weiji yu guomin zhengfu duiri jiaoshe fangzheng: 1933–1935 nian zhongri tingzhan xieding bijiao yanjiu" [The North China Crisis and the Nationalist Government's Negotiations with the Japanese: A Comparison of Sino-Japanese Ceasefire Agreements of 1933–1935]. *Minguo dang'an*, 4 (1995): 85–95.

Jiang Junzhang. "Dongzheng beifa sida zhanyi" [Four Great Battles of the Eastern and Northern Expeditions], Part 1. *Zhongwai zazhi*, 25, 6 (June 1979): 22–27.

Jiang Junzhang, "Dongzheng beifa sida zhanyi" [Four Great Battles of the Eastern and Northern Expeditions], Part 3. *Zhongwai zazhi*, 26, 2 (August 1979): 78–83.

Jiang Zhiping, "He Yingqin milu" [A Secret Record of He Yingqin]. *Zhongwai zazhi*, 43, 6 (June 1988): 127–31.

Ke Huiling, "He Yingqin zai beifa chuqi de diwei yuqi gongxian" [He Yingqin's Status and Contribution in the Early Period of the Northern Expedition]. *Zhonghua junshi xuehui huikan*, 2 (May 1997): 63–76.

Keyun Liyang. "Jiang Jieshi qinzhan Cheng Zerun de zhenshi neimu" [The True Inside Story of How Chiang Kai-shek Personally Cut Down Cheng Zerun]. *Zhongshan fengyu*, 6 (2009): 51–52.

Li Baoming, *"Guojiahua" mingyixia de "sishuhua": Jiang Jieshi dui guomin gemingjun de kongzhi yanjiu* ["Privatization" in the Name of "Nationalization": A Study of Chiang Kai-shek's Control of the National Revolutionary Army]. Beijing: Shehui kexue wenxian chubanshe, 2010.

Li Qizhong. "Mianhu zhanyi zhong yilin banzhua" [Details of the Battle at Mianhu]. *Wenshi ziliao xuanji*, 77 (n.d.): 116–18.

Li Qizhong. "Tongyi guangdong geming genjudi de zhanzheng" [The War to Unify the Guangdong Revolutionary Base]. *Wenshi ziliao xuanji*, 2 (n.d.): 20–39.

Li Yuan. *Jiang Jieshi he He Yingqin* [Chiang Kai-shek and He Yingqin]. Changchun: Jilin wenshi chubanshe, 1996.

Li Zhonggong. "Wosuo zhidao de He Yingqin" [The He Yingqin I Knew]. *Wenshi ziliao xuanji*, 36 (n.d.): 203–21.

Li Zhongming. *He Yingqin dazhuan* [Biography of He Yingqin]. Beijing: Tuanjie chubanshe, 2008.

Li Zhongming. "He Yingqin yu xi'an shibian" [He Yingqin and the Xi'an Incident]. *Lishi jiaoxue*, 2 (1994): 8–11.

Li Zhongming. "JiuJiang haishi haiJiang? He Yingqin zai xi'an shibian zhong" [To Save Chiang or to Harm Chiang? He Yingqin in the Xi'an Incident]. *Wenshi jinghua*, 2 (1997): 12–18.

Li Zhongming. "Zhanhe paihuaizhong gensui Jiang Zhongzheng weiyuanzhang zou: qiqi shibian qianhou de He Yingqin" [Following Chairman Chiang Kai-shek in Wavering Between War and Peace: He Yingqin Before and After the Marco Polo Bridge Incident]. *Jindai zhongguo*, 1, 132 (August 1999): 41–52.

Lin Yuxian, "Guizhou 'minjiu shibian' qinliji" [A Personal Record of the Guizhou "Minjiu Incident"]. *Guizhou wenshi ziliao xuanji*, 1 (n.d.): 115–21.

Liu Bingcui, ed. *Gemingjun diyici dongzheng shizhanji fu: mianhu dajie wushi zhounian jinian tekan* [A Record of the Revolutionary Army's First Eastern Expedition with a Special Publication on the Fiftieth Anniversary of the Great Victory in the Battle at Mianhu]. Taipei: Wenhai chubanshe, 1981.

Liu Jianming. "Rijun yinsha He Yingqin de qianqian houhou" [The Whole Story of the Japanese Army's Secret Plan to Assassinate He Yingqin]. *Wenshi chunqiu*, 3 (2001): 66–67.

Liu Zhi. *Wode huiyi* [My Memoirs]. Taipei: Wenhai chubanshe, 1982.

Liu Zhiqiang, *et al.* "Baoding lujun junguan xuexiao lishi yange kao" [A History of Baoding Military Academy]. *Minguo dang'an*, 2 (2001): 106–08.

Long Yuezhou. "He Yingqin wei shouxiang daibiao neimu" [The Inside Story of He Yingqin's Role as Representative at the Surrender Ceremony]. *Wenshi tiandi*, 8 (2001): 46–49.

Lu Ping. *He Yingqin Jiangjun yinxiang ji* [A Record of Impressions of General He Yingqin]. Nanjing: Minben chuban gongsi, 1946.

Luo Yuming, Wen Bo and Zhang Zhiyong. "Huangpuxi jiangling yu xi'an shibian de heping jiejue" [The Whampoa Faction Leadership and the Peaceful Resolution of the Xi'an Incident]. *Jiangxi shehui kexue*, 7 (2001): 92–94.

Luo Yuming and Zhang Wangqing. "Xi'an shibian zhong de He Yingqin" [He Yingqin in the Xi'an Incident]. *Renwu zazhi*, 4 (1998): 112–15.

Ni Tuanjiu. *He Yingqin shangjiang zhuan* [Biography of General He Yingqin]. Taipei: Taibei yinhang, 1984.

Ni Tuanjiu. "Yunlong qihe shoujian qixun: He Yingqin zhuan zhi si" [A Perfect Occasion for Initial Outstanding Achievements: Biography of He Yingqin, Part IV]. *Zhongwai zazhi*, 43, 5 (May 1988): 62–67.

Qi Zhou. "Feng Yuxiang yu He Yingqin de maodun chongtu" [The Contradiction and Clash Between Feng Yuxiang and He Yingqin]. *Zonghuang*, 5 (1994): 29–32.

Qin Xiaoyi, ed. *Zhonghua minguo zhongyao shiliao chubian: duiri kangzhan shiqi* [Important Historical Materials of the Republic of China: The Period of the War of Resistance Against Japan], di'yi bian, *Xubian*, 3 vols. Taipei: Zhongguo guomindang zhongyang weiyuanhui dangshi weiyuanhui, 1981.

Qin Xiaoyi, ed. *Zhonghua minguo zhongyao shiliao chubian: duiri kangzhan shiqi* [Important Historical Materials of the Republic of China: The Period of the War of Resistance Against Japan], di'er bian, *Zuozhan jingguo*, 4 vols. Taipei: Zhongguo guomindang zhongyang weiyuanhui dangshi weiyuanhui, 1981.

Qin Xiaoyi, ed. *Zhonghua minguo zhongyao shiliao chubian: duiri kangzhan shiqi* [Important Historical Materials of the Republic of China: The Period of the War of Resistance Against Japan], di'wu bian, *Zhonggong huodongzhenxiang*, 4 vols. Taipei: Zhongguo guomindang zhongyang weiyuanhui dangshi weiyuanhui, 1981.

Qin Xiaoyi, ed. *Zhonghua minguo zhongyao shiliao chubian: duiri kangzhan shiqi* [Important Historical Materials of the Republic of China: The Period of the War of Resistance Against Japan], di'qi bian, *Zhanhou zhongguo*, 4 vols.

Taipei: Zhongguo guomindang zhongyang weiyuanhui dangshi weiyuanhui, 1981.

Qin Xiaoyi, ed. *Zongtong Jianggong dashi changbian chugao* [Preliminary Draft of President Chiang's Chronological Biography], 13 vols. Taipei: Caituan faren Zhongzheng wenjiao jijinhui, 1978.

Rao Donghui. "He Yingqin zaoqi zai guizhou de huodong" [He Yingqin's Early Activities in Guizhou]. *Huazhong shifan daxue xuebao*, S2 (1990): 53–58.

Sha Ping. "He Yingqin kunming yuci zhenxiang" [The True Story of the Attempt to Assassinate He Yingqin in Kunming]. *Wenshi bolan*, 8 (2007): 46–47.

Shao Minghuang. "Xiao Zhenying gongzuo: kangzhan chuqi riben yi He Yingqin wei duixiang de mouhe chujiao" [The Xiao Zhenying Work: Japanese Attempts to Use He Yingqin as a Counterpart for Secret Peace Talks in the Early Period of the Sino-Japanese War]. *Kangri zhanzheng yanjiu*, 3 (1998): 12–32.

Shen Yunlong, ed. *Riben lujun shiguan xuexiao zhonghua minguo liuxuesheng mingbu* [Foreign Students from the Republic of China at Japan's Rikugun Shikan Gakko]. Taipei: Wenhai chubanshe, 1977.

Song Xilian. *Yingquan jiangjun: Song Xilian zishu* [Lackey General: The Auto-biography of Song Xilian]. Beijing: Zhongguo wenshi chubanshe, 1986.

Tan Yizhi. "Huangpu jianjun" [The Founding of the Army at the Whampoa Military Academy]. *Wenshi ziliao xuanji*, 2 (n.d.): 1–19.

Tan Zhenqiang. "Li Zongren bi He Yingqin canyu longtan zuozhan de qianqian houhou" [The Whole Story of How Li Zongren Forced He Yingqin to Fight at the Battle of Longtan]. *Wenshi chunqiu*, 11 (2006): 12–13.

Tao Aiping. "Xi'an shibian zhong He Yingqin de zhuzhan yitu" [He Yingqin's Intention to Use Military Force in the Xi'an Incident]. *Anhui shixue*, 1 (1996): 81–82.

Tu Yueseng, ed. *Xingyi Liu, Wang, He sanda jiazu* [The Three Major Families of Xingyi County, Liu, Wang, and He]. Guizhou: Zhongguo wenshi chubanshe, 1990.

Wang Chengsheng. "He Yingqin Zhuanqi (yi)" [The Legend of He Yingqin (Part I)]. *Zhongwai zazhi*, 44, 1 (July 1988): 13–17.

Wang Chengsheng. "He Yingqin Zhuanqi (er)" [The Legend of He Yingqin (Part II)]. *Zhongwai zazhi*, 44, 2 (October 1988): 123–27.

Wang Dongmei. "Kangzhan shiqi guomindang bingyi fubai de yuanyin tanxi" [An Analysis of the Corruption in Guomindang Conscription During the War of Resistance Against the Japanese]. *Wenshi bolan (lilun)*, 10 (October 2010): 10–12.

Wang Huanpeng and Wang Runhu. "Xi'an shibian qijian He Yingqin 'wulitaofa' celue jianxi" [A Brief Analysis of He Yingqin's "Punitive Expedition" Strategy in the Xi'an Incident]. *Xibei di'er minzu xueyuan xuebao*, 5, 83 (2008): 84–89.

Wang Qiang. "Deng Yanda yu huangpu junxiao de chuangjian" [Deng Yanda and the Founding of the Whampoa Military Academy]. *Minguo dang'an*, 3 (1994): 81–85.

Wang Shouwen. "He Yingqin beici hou zhudong xiang chouren hejie yishi" [How He Yingqin Reconciled with His Enemies After the Assassination Attempt]. *Guiyang wenshi*, 2 (2002): 72–74.

Wang Xuezhen. "Dahoufang kangzhan wenxue de bingyi ticai" [The Theme of Conscription in Literature of the Rear Areas During the War of Resistance]. *Zhongguo xiandai wenxue yanjiu zongkan*, 7 (2011): 17.

Wang Yiquan and Yang Xuan. "Shilun xi'an shibian zhong de He Yingqin de zhuzhan" [On He Yingqin's Policy of Advocating Military Force in the Xi'an Incident]. *Guizhou wenshi zongkan*, 3 (2007): 61–64.

Wang Zhenhua, ed. *Jiang zhongzheng zongtong dang'an: shilüe gaoben* [The Chiang Kai-shek Collections: The Chronological Events], 81 vols. Taipei: Guoshiguan, 2011.

Wang Zhiping, ed. "He Yingqin (1889–1987)." *Zhongwai mingren zhuan*, 64, 10 (October 1997): 71–99.

Wu Jian. "Xu Yongchang zhi He Yingqin han yijian" [A Letter from Xu Yongchang to He Yingqin]. *Minguo dang'an*, 4 (1987): 53.

Wu Shufeng, ed. *Chen Cheng xiansheng huiyilu: beifa pingluan* [The Memoirs of Mr. Chen Cheng: The Northern Expedition]. Taipei xian xindian shi: Guoshiguan, 2005.

Wu Shufeng, ed. *Chen Cheng xiansheng huiyilu: guogong zhanzheng* [The Memoirs of Mr. Chen Cheng: The War Between the Nationalist and Communist Parties]. Taipei xian xindian shi: Guoshiguan, 2005.

Wu Shufeng, ed. *Chen Cheng xiansheng huiyilu: jangri zhanzheng* [The Memoirs of Mr. Chen Cheng: The War of Resistance Against Japan]. Taipei xian xindian shi: Guoshiguan, 2004.

Wu Tong. "Rijun mouci He Yingqin" [The Japanese Army's Plan to Assassinate He Yingqin]. *Chuban cankao*, 2 (2006): 23–25.

Wu Xiangxiang. "He Yingqin dajiang caineng fujiang mingyun" [General He Yingqin's Luck and Capability]. In *Minguo bairen zhuan*, vol. IV. Taipei: Zhuanji wenxue chubanshe, 1971.

Xia Jing. "Guomindang zhengfu bingyi zhidu yanjiu" [A Study of the Guomindang Government's Conscription System]. Master's thesis, Shandong shifan daxue, Jinan, Shandong, 2009.

Xia Lumei. "He Yingqin zai lujun zongbu" [He Yingqin as Commander of the Army]. In Tu Yueseng, ed., *Xingyi Wang, Liu, He sanda jiazu*, 194–95.

Xie Boyuan. "Wosuo liaojie de He Yingqin" [The He Yingqin I Knew]. In Tu Yueseng, ed., *Xingyi Liu, Wang, He sanda jiazu*, 136–51.

Xiong Zongren. *He Yingqin wannian* [He Yingqin's Later Years]. Hefei: Anhui renmin chubanshe, 1995.

Xiong Zongren. *He Yingqin: xuanwozhong de lishi* [He Yingqin: History in the Vortex], 2 vols. Guiyang: Guizhou renmin chubanshe, 2001.

Xiong Zongren. "He Yingqin yu Gangcun Yuci" [He Yingqin and Okamura Yasuji]. *Wenshi jinghua*, 2 (1999): 54–60.

Xiong Zongren. "He Yingqin yu Shidiwei" [He Yingqin and Joseph Stilwell]. *Wenshi jinghua*, 12 (1998): 34–39.

Xiong Zongren. "He Yingqin yu Wu Peifu de yiduan mishi" [A Secret History of He Yingqin and Wu Peifu]. *Wenshi tiandi*, 3 (1994): 24–26.

Xiong Zongren. *He Yingqin zhuan* [Biography of He Yingqin]. Taiyuan: Shanxi renmin chubanshe, 1993.

Xiong Zongren. "He Yingqin zonglun" [A Summary of He Yingqin's Life]. *Guizhou wenshi zongkan*, 2 (1989): 47–52.

Xiong Zongren. "Shilun He Yingqin yu Wang Tianpei zhi si" [On He Yingqin and the Death of Wang Tianpei]. *Guizhou shehui kexue,* 12 (1989): 33–40.

Xiong Zongren. *Wusi yundong zai guizhou* [The May Fourth Movement in Guizhou]. Guiyang: Guizhou renmin chubanshe, 1986.

Xiong Zongren. "Xi'an shibian fashenghou de He Yingqin" [He Yingqin After the Outbreak of the Xi'an Incident]. *Minguo chunqiu,* 2 (1995): 17–22.

Xiong Zongren. "Xi'an shibian yanjiu zhong de zhongda queshi: lun He Yingqin zhu 'taofa' zhi dongji ji 'qinripai' wenti" [An Important Missing Part in Research on the Xi'an Incident: On the Questions of He Yingqin's Motivations for Advocating "Punitive Action" and the "Pro-Japan Faction"]. *Guizhou shehui kexue,* 220, 4 (April 2008): 118–23.

Xiong Zongren. "Xi'an shibian zhong de He Yingqin zhuzhan dongji zhi bianxi: dui 'qujiang er daizhi' lun de zhiyi" [An Analysis of He Yingqin's Motives for Advocating Military Action During the Xi'an Incident: Calling into Question the Theory that He Sought to "Replace Chiang"]. *Junshi lishi,* 4 (1993): 38–43.

Xiong Zongren. "Yichang lanluan lishi zhenxiang de zhengchao: Xi'an shibian zhong de Song Meiling and He Yingqin" [The True History of a Chaotic Quarrel: Song Meiling and He Yingqin in the Xi'an Incident]. *Wenshi tiandi,* 2 (1994): 30–34.

Xu Ping. "Riben shiguan xuexiao he jiu zhongguo lujun 'shiguanxi'" [Japan's Shikan Gakko and the "Shikan Gakko Faction" in the Military of Old China], *Minguo chunqiu,* 4 (2001): 57–60.

Xu Tingdong. "Guizhou 'wusi' yundong de huiyi" [Recollections of the "May Fourth" Movement in Guizhou]. *Guizhou wenshi ziliao xuanji,* 3 (n.d.): 64–69.

Yang Chen. "He Yingqin yu huabei jiaoshe" [He Yingqin and the North China Negotiations]. *Kangri zhanzheng yanjiu,* 2 (1994): 73–88.

Yang Chenguang. "Beifa donglujun changjiang yinan zuozhan de zhanlue zhidao" [The Strategic Leadership of the Eastern Route Army South of the Yangzi River During the Northern Expedition]. *Zhonghua junshi xuehui huikan,* 12 (September 2007): 85–105.

Yang Huanpeng and Wang Runhu. "Xi'an shibian qijian He Yingqin 'wuli taofa' celue jianxi" [A Brief Analysis of He Yingqin's "Punitive Expedition" Strategy in the Xi'an Incident]. *Xibei di'er minzu xueyuan xuebao,* 5, 83 (2008): 84–89.

Yang Tianshi. *Jiangshi midang yu Jiang Jieshi zhenxiang* [The Truth About the Chiang Family Secret Archives and Chiang Kai-shek]. Beijing: Shehui kexuewenxian chubanshe, 2002.

Ye Yangbing. "Lun nanjing guomin zhengfu zai xi'an shibianzhong de duici" [The Nanjing Government's Countermeasures During the Xi'an Incident]. *Jianghai xuekan,* 2 (2004): 153–58.

Yin Fei. "Minguo yuanlao He Yingqin chenfulu" [A Record of the Rise and Fall of Republican Period Elder Statesman He Yingqin]. *Hubei wenshi ziliao,* 3 (1999): 115–34.

Yu Anzhu. "He Yingqin yu huangpu junxiao chuchuang" [He Yingqin and the Newly Established Whampoa Military Academy]. *Guiyang wenshi,* 3 (2004): 43–45.

Yu Xuezhong. "Wo shi zenyang bei rikou bichu huabei de" [How the Japanese Bandits Forced Me out of North China]. *Wenshi ziliao xuanji*, 14 (n.d.): 166–76.

Zeng Kuoqing. "Hemei xieding qian fuxingshe zai huabei de huodong" [Activities of the Fuxingshe in North China Prior to the He–Umezu Agreement]. *Wenshi ziliao xuanji*, 14 (n.d.): 131–46.

Zeng Kuoqing. "Huangpu tongxuehui shimo" [The Whole Story of the Whampoa Military Academy Alumni Association]. *Wenshi ziliao xuanji*, 19 (n.d.): 169–89.

Zeng Kuoqing. "Jiang Jieshi diyici xiaye yu fuzhi de jingguo" [The First Time Chiang Kai-shek Stepped Down and Then Returned to His Position]. *Wenshi ziliao xuanji*, 38 (n.d.): 45–50.

Zhai Chuanzhen. "'Xi'an shibian' zhong He Yingqin 'taofa zhengce' zhi wojian" [My View on He Yingqin's Policy of Using Military Force in the Xi'an Incident]. *Weifang jiaoyu xueyuan xuebao*, 4 (1997): 6–7.

Zhang Ming. "Xinhai geming qianhou de He Yingqin" [He Yingqin Before and After the 1911 Revolution]. *Dangdai guizhou*, 30 (October 2011): 65.

Zhang Pengnian. "Xinhai yilai sishi nianjian guizhou zhengju de yanbian" [The Evolution of Guizhou Politics in the Forty Years After the 1911 Revolution]. *Guizhou wenshi ziliao xuanji*, 2 (n.d.): 40–68.

Zhang Xianwen, ed. *Zhonghua minguo shigang* [An Outline History of the Republic of China]. Henan: Henan renmin chubanshe, 1985.

Zhang Xingzhi. "He Yingqin huixiang suoyi" [Some Comments on He Yingqin's Return to His Home Village]. *Wenshi tiandi*, 3 (1994): 27–28.

Zhang Xingzhi. "He Yingqin zai beiping fenhui" [He Yingqin at the Beiping Branch of the Military Affairs Commission]. In Tu Yueseng, ed., *Xingyi Lui, Wang, He sanda jiazu*, 180–93.

Zhang Zhizhong. "He Yingqin zuge" [He Yingqin Forms a Cabinet]. In Tu Yueseng, ed., *Xingyi Liu, Wang, He sanda jiazu*, 209–12.

Zhongguo di'er lishi dang'anguan. "Disanjie disanci minguo canzhenghui junshi xunwenan ji He Yingqin zhi dafu" [The Military Investigation of the Third Meeting of the Third Session of the People's Political Council and He Yingqin's Response]. *Minguo dang'an*, 3 (1997): 39–45.

Zhou Wenlin. "He Yingqin guanyu 'hemei xieding' dianwen sijian" [Four Telegrams from He Yingqin Relating to the "He–Umezu Agreement"]. *Minguo dang'an*, 2 (1988): 17–18.

Zhu Guangting. "He Yingqin zai Kunming beici jianwen" [An Account of the Shooting of He Yingqin in Kunming]. In Tu Yueseng, ed., *Xingyi Liu, Wang, He sanda jiazu*, 152–54.

Zhu Huilin, ed. *Yizheng shiliao* [Materials on Conscription], vol. I. Taipei: Guoshiguan, 1990.

Zhu Yan. "'Xiangbalao' jiangjun: He Yingqin" [The "Country Bumpkin" General: He Yingqin]. *Baike zhishi*, 3 (2006): 43–46.

Zuo Shuangwen. "'Tanggu xieding' hou Jiang Jieshi de duiri tuoxie waijiao" [Chiang Kai-shek's Foreign Policy of Compromise Toward Japan After the Tanggu Truce]. *Guangdong shehui kexue*, 6 (2010): 115–22.

Zuo Shuangwen. "Xi'an shibian hou de nanjing taofapai: yi Dai Jitao, He Yingqin wei zhongxin de zai tansuo" [The Nanjing "Punitive Faction" After the Xi'an

Incident: A Reexamination Centering on Dai Jitao and He Yingqin]. *Jindai zhongguo yanjiu*, 6 (2006): 58–69.

## ENGLISH-LANGUAGE SOURCES

Bedeski, Robert. "China's Wartime State." In Hsiung and Levine, eds., *China's Bitter Victory*, 33–49.

Bian, Morris. *The Making of State Enterprise System in Modern China: The Dynamics of Institutional Change*. Cambridge, MA: Harvard University Press, 2005.

Bjorge, Gary J. "Move the Enemy: Operational Art in the Chinese PLA's Huai Hai Campaign," Leavenworth Paper Number 22. Fort Leavenworth, KS: Combat Studies Institute Press, 2003.

Boorman, Howard. *Biographical Dictionary of Republican China*, 3 vols. New York: Columbia University Press, 1967–71.

*A Brief History of the Republic of China Armed Forces*. Microfilm, Scholarly Resources. Taipei: Office of Military History, 1971.

Buchman, Frank. *Remaking the World: The Speeches of Frank Buchman*. London: Blandford Press, 1961.

Bunker, Gerald. *The Peace Conspiracy: Wang Ching-wei and the China War, 1937–1941*. Cambridge, MA: Harvard University Press, 1972.

Carlson, Evans F. *The Chinese Army: Its Organization and Military Efficiency*. New York: Institute for Pacific Relations, 1940.

Ch'ien, Tuan-sheng. *The Government and Politics of China*. Cambridge, MA: Harvard University Press, 1950 (1961).

Chang, Jui-te. "Chiang Kai-shek's Coordination by Personal Directives." In Stephen B. MacKinnon, Diana Lary and Ezra F. Vogel, eds., *China at War: Regions of China, 1937–1945*, 65–87. Stanford: Stanford University Press, 2007.

Chang, Jui-te. "Nationalist Army Officers During the Sino-Japanese War, 1937–1945." *Modern Asian Studies*, 30, 4 (1996): 1033–56.

Chen, Leslie H. Dingyan. *Chen Jiongming and the Federalist Movement: Regional Leadership and Nation Building in Early Republican China*. Ann Arbor: Center for Chinese Studies, 1999.

Chen, Li. "The Chinese Army in the First Burma Campaign." *Journal of Chinese Military History* 2, 1 (2013): 43–73.

Chen, Li-fu. *The Storm Clouds Clear over China: The Memoir of Ch'en Li-fu, 1900–1993*. Edited and compiled with an Introduction and notes by Sidney H. Chang and Ramon H. Myers. Stanford: Stanford University Press, 1994.

Cherepanov, Alexander Ivanovich. *As Military Advisor in China*, translated by Sergei Sosinsky. Moscow: Progress Publishers, 1982.

Cherepanov, Alexander. *Notes of a Military Advisor in China*, translated by Alexandra O. Smith, edited by Harry H. Collier and Thomas M. Williamsen. Taipei: Office of Military History, 1970.

Ch'i, Hsi-sheng. *Nationalist China at War: Military Defeats and Political Collapse, 1937–1945*. Ann Arbor: University of Michigan Press, 1982.

Ch'i, Hsi-sheng. *Warlord Politics in China, 1916–1928*. Stanford: Stanford University Press, 1976.

Chiang, Mayling Soong. *Sian: A Coup d'Etat*. Shanghai: China Publishing Company, 1937.

Clubb, O. Edmund. *Twentieth-Century China*, 2nd edn. New York: Columbia University Press, 1972.

Coble, Parks. *Facing Japan: Chinese Politics and Japanese Imperialism, 1931–1937*. Cambridge, MA: Council on East Asian Studies, Harvard University Press, 1991.

Coble, Parks. *The Shanghai Capitalists and the National Government, 1927–1937*. Cambridge, MA: Council on East Asian Studies, Harvard University Press, 1980.

Cohen, Paul. *Discovering History in China: American Historical Writing on the Recent Chinese Past*. New York: Columbia University Press, 1984.

Collier, Harry H. and Paul Chin-chih Lai. *Organizational Changes in the Chinese Army, 1895–1950*. Taipei: Office of the Military Historian, 1969.

Cook, Theodore Failor. "The Japanese Officer Corps: The Making of a Military Elite, 1872–1945." Ph.D. dissertation, Princeton University, Princeton, NJ, 1987.

Dirlik, Arlif. "Mass Movements and the Kuomintang Left." *Modern China*, 1, 1 (January 1975): 46–74.

Dorn, Frank. *The Sino-Japanese War, 1937–1941: From Marco Polo Bridge to Pearl Harbor*. New York: Macmillan Press, 1974.

Dorn, Frank. *Walkout with Stilwell in Burma*. New York: Crowell, 1971.

Dreyer, Edward L. *China at War, 1901–1949*. New York: Longman, 1995.

Dryburgh, Marjorie. *North China and Japanese Expansion, 1933–1937: Regional Power and the National Interest*. Richmond, UK: Curzon, 2000.

Duara, Prasenjit. *Culture, Power, and the State: Rural North China, 1900–1942*. Stanford: Stanford University Press, 1988.

Eastman, Lloyd. *The Abortive Revolution: China Under Nationalist Rule, 1927–1937*. Cambridge, MA: Harvard University Press, 1974.

Eastman, Lloyd, ed. *Chiang Kai-shek's Secret Past: The Memoirs of His Second Wife, Ch'en Chieh-ju*. Boulder, CO: Westview Press, 1993.

Eastman, Lloyd. "Fascism in Kuomintang China: The Blue Shirts." *China Quarterly*, 49 (January–March 1972): 1–31.

Eastman, Lloyd. "Nationalist China During the Nanking Decade 1927–1937." In John K. Fairbank and Albert Feuerwerker, eds., *The Cambridge History of China*, vol. XIII, *Republican China 1912–1949, Part 2*, 116–67. Cambridge: Cambridge University Press, 1986.

Eastman, Lloyd. "Nationalist China During the Sino-Japanese War 1937–1945." In John K. Fairbank and Albert Feuerwerker, eds., *The Cambridge History of China*, vol. XIII, *Republican China 1912–1949, Part 2*, 547–608. Cambridge: Cambridge University Press, 1986.

Eastman, Lloyd. "Regional Politics and the Central Government: Yunnan and Chungking." In Sih, ed., *Nationalist China During the Sino-Japanese War*, 329–62.

Eastman, Lloyd. *Seeds of Destruction: Nationalist China in War and Revolution, 1937–1949*. Stanford: Stanford University Press, 1984.

Erickson, John. *The Soviet High Command: A Military and Political History 1918–1941*, 3rd edn. New York: Frank Cass, 2001.

Fenby, Jonathan. *Generalissimo: Chiang Kai-shek and the China He Lost*. London: Free Press, 2003.

Furuya, Keiji. *Chiang K'ai-shek: His Life and Times*, English edn. abridged by Chang Chun-ming. New York: St. Johns University Press, 1981.

Gallicchio, Marc. "The Other China Hands: US Army Officers and America's Failure in China, 1941–1950." *Journal of American–East Asian Relations*, 4, 1 (1995): 49–72.

Garver, John. "China's Wartime Diplomacy." In Hsiung and Levine, eds., *China's Bitter Victory*, 3–32.

Gibson, Michael Richard. "Chiang Kai-shek's Central Army, 1924–1938." Ph.D dissertation, George Washington University, Washington, DC, 1985.

Gillespie, Richard. "Whampoa and the Nanking Decade (1924–1936)." Ph.D. dissertation, American University, Washington, DC, 1971.

Gillin, Donald G. "Problems of Centralization in Republican China: The Case of Ch'en Ch'eng and the Kuomintang." *Journal of Asian Studies*, 29, 4 (August 1970): 835–50.

Gillin, Donald G. *Warlord: Yen His-shan in Shansi Province, 1911–1949*. Princeton: Princeton University Press, 1967.

Hara, Takeshi. "The Ichigo Offensive." In Peattie, Drea, and van de Ven, eds., *The Battle for China*, 392–402.

He, Yingqin. "Commemorating the July 7 Anniversary of the Outbreak of the War of Resistance Against Japan and Refuting for the Second Time the False Propaganda of the Chinese Communists." *Issues and Studies*, 8, 12 (1972): 23–33, and 9, 1 (1972): 54–61.

He, Yingqin. "The Disposition and Aftermath of the Xi'an Incident: Transfer of Forces of the Northeast Army." *Chinese Studies in History*, 22, 3 (1989): 77–79.

Herzog, James. "The Whampoa Military Academy." *US Naval Institute Proceedings*, 94, 4 (1968): 46–53.

Hsiung, James C. and Steven I. Levine, eds. *China's Bitter Victory: The War with Japan, 1937–1945*. Armonk, NY: M. E. Sharpe, 1992.

Huang, Ray. "Chiang Kai-shek and His Diary as a Historical Source." *Chinese Studies in History*, 29, 1–2 (Fall–Winter 1995–96): 3–176.

Jansen, Marius. *The Japanese and Sun Yat-sen*. Cambridge, MA: Harvard University Press, 1954.

Jordan, Donald. *China's Trial by Fire: The Shanghai War of 1932*. Ann Arbor: University of Michigan Press, 2001.

Jordan, Donald. *The Northern Expedition: China's National Revolution of 1926–1928*. Honolulu: University of Hawaii Press, 1976.

Kirby, William. *Germany and Republican China*. Stanford: Stanford University Press, 1984.

Kuo, Warren. "The Disbandment of the New Fourth Army." *Issues and Studies*, 6, 7 (1970): 66–79.

Landis, Richard. "Training and Indoctrination at the Whampoa Academy." In F. Gilbert Chan and Thomas Etzold, eds., *China in the 1920s: Nationalism and Revolution*, 73–93. New York: New Viewpoints, 1996.

Lary, Diana. *Region and Nation: The Kwangsi Clique in Chinese Politics, 1925–1937*. London: Cambridge University Press, 1974.

Lattimore, Owen. *China Memoirs: Chiang Kai-shek and the War Against Japan*, compiled by Fujiko Isono. Tokyo: University of Tokyo Press, 1990.

Li, Laura Tyson. *Madame Chiang Kai-shek: China's Eternal First Lady*. New York: Atlantic Monthly Press, 2006.

Li, Tsung-jen and Te-kong Tong, *The Memoirs of Li Tsung-jen*. Boulder, CO: Westview Press, 1979.

Liang, Chin-tung. *General Stilwell in China, 1942–1944: The Full Story*. New York: St. John's University Press, 1972.

Liu, F. F. *A Military History of Modern China, 1924–1949*. Princeton: Princeton University Press, 1956.

Liu, Hsiang-wang, "The Fall and Rise of the Nationalist Chinese: The Chinese Civil War from Huaihai to the Taiwan Strait, 1948–1950." Ph.D. dissertation, Pennsylvania State University, 1997.

Loh, Pichon P. Y. *The Early Chiang Kai-shek: A Study of His Personality and Politics, 1887–1924*. New York: Columbia University Press, 1971.

McCord, Edward. "Local Military Power and Elite Formation: The Liu Family of Xingyi, Guizhou." In Joseph Esherick and Mary Backus Rankin, eds., *Chinese Local Elites and Patterns of Dominance*, 162–88. Berkeley: University of California Press, 1990.

McLynn, Frank. *The Burma Campaign: Disaster into Triumph, 1942–1945*. New Haven: Yale University Press, 2011.

Mao, Tse-tung [Zedong]. *The Selected Works of Mao Tse-tung*, 4 vols. Beijing: Beijing Foreign Languages Press, 1961.

Mitter, Rana. *Forgotten Ally: China's World War II 1937–1945*. New York: Houghton Mifflin Harcourt, 2013.

O'Brien, Anita. "Military Academies in China, 1885–1915." In Joshua A. Fogel and William T. Rowe, eds., *Perspectives on a Changing China: Essays in Honor of Professor C. Martin Wilbur on the Occasion of His Retirement*, 157–81. Boulder, CO: Westview Press, 1979.

Paine, S. C. M. *The Wars for Asia 1911–1949*. Cambridge: Cambridge University Press, 2012.

Pakula, Hannah. *The Last Empress: Madame Chiang Kai-shek and the Birth of Modern China*. New York: Simon & Schuster, 2009.

Pantsov, Alexander V. with Steven Levine. *Mao: The Real Story*. New York: Simon & Schuster, 2012.

Peattie, Mark R., Edward J. Drea and Hans J. van de Ven, eds. *The Battle for China: Essays on the Military History of the Sino-Japanese War of 1937–1945*. Stanford: Stanford University Press, 2011.

Pepper, Suzanne. *Civil War in China: The Political Struggle, 1945–1949*, 2nd edn. Lanham, MD: Rowman & Littlefield, 1999.

Romanus, Charles F. and Riley Sunderland. *China-Burma-India Theater: Stilwell's Command Problems*. Washington, DC: Office of the Chief of Military History, 1955.

Romanus, Charles F. and Riley Sunderland. *China-Burma-India Theater: Time Runs Out in CBI*. Washington, DC: Office of the Chief of Military History, 1959.

Rowe, William. *Crimson Rain: Seven Centuries of Violence in a Chinese County*. Stanford: Stanford University Press, 2007.

Seagrave, Sterling. *The Soong Dynasty*. New York: Harper & Row, 1985.

Shai, Aron. *Zhang Xueliang: The General Who Never Fought*. New York: Palgrave Macmillan, 2012.

Sheridan, James. *Chinese Warlord: The Career of Feng Yü-Hsiang*. Stanford: Stanford University Press, 1966.

Sih, Paul K. T. "An Assessment of Nationalist China's Efforts During the War of Resistance of Japan, 1937–1945." *Issues and Studies*, 13, 5 (1977): 1–24.

Sih, Paul K. T., ed. *Nationalist China During the Sino-Japanese War, 1937–1945*. Hiscksville, NY: Exposition Press, 1977.

Smith, Steve A. *A Road Is Made: Communism in Shanghai 1920–1927*. Honolulu: University of Hawaii Press, 2000.

So, Chor Wai, "The Making of the Guomindang's Japan Policy, 1932–1937: The Roles of Chiang Kai-shek and Wang Jingwei." *Modern China*, 28, 2 (April 2002): 213–52.

Strauss, Julia. *Strong Institutions in Weak Politics: State Building in Republican China, 1927–1940*. Oxford, UK: Clarendon Press, 1998.

Sun, Youli. *China and the Origins of the Pacific War, 1931–1941*. New York: St. Martin's Press, 1993.

Sutton, Donald. "German Advice and Residual Warlordism in the Nanking Decade: Influences on Nationalist Military Training and Strategy." *China Quarterly*, 9, 91 (September 1982): 386–410.

Sutton, Donald. *Provincial Militarism and the Chinese Republic: The Yunnan Army, 1905–1925*. Ann Arbor: University of Michigan Press, 1980.

Tanner, Harold. *The Battle for Manchuria and the Fate of China*. Bloomington: Indiana University Press, 2013.

Tanner, Harold. "Guerrilla, Mobile, and Base Warfare in Communist Military Operations in Manchuria, 1945–1947." *Journal of Military History*, 67, 4 (October 2003): 1177–1222.

Taylor, Jay. *The Generalissimo: Chiang Kai-shek and the Struggle for Modern China*. Cambridge, MA: Harvard University Press, 2009.

Tien, Chen-ya. *Chinese Military Theory: Ancient and Modern*. Oakville, ON: Mosaic Press, 1992.

Tuchman, Barbara. *Stilwell and the American Experience in China, 1911–1945*. New York: Macmillan, 1971.

Yu, Maochun. *The Dragon's War: Allied Operations and the Fate of China, 1937–1947*. Annapolis, MD: Naval Institute Press, 2006.

United States Department of State. *Papers Relating to the Foreign Relations of the United States, 1930, Vol. II*. Washington, DC: Government Printing Office, 1945.

United States Department of State. *Papers Relating to the Foreign Relations of the United States, 1944, Vol. VI, Far East: China*. Washington, DC: Government Printing Office, 1967.

United States Department of State. *Papers Relating to the Foreign Relations of the United States, 1945, Vol. VII, The Far East: China*. Washington, DC: Government Printing Office, 1969.

United States Department of State. *Papers Relating to the Foreign Relations of the United States, 1946, Vols. IX, X, The Far East: China*. Washington, DC: Government Printing Office, 1972.

United States Department of State. *Papers Relating to the Foreign Relations of the United States, 1947, Vol. VII, The Far East: China.* Washington, DC: Government Printing Office, 1972.

United States Department of State. *Papers Relating to the Foreign Relations of the United States, 1948, Vols. VII, VIII, The Far East: China.* Washington, DC: Government Printing Office, 1973.

United States Department of State. *Papers Relating to the Foreign Relations of the United States, 1949, Vols. VII, VIII, IX, The Far East: China.* Washington, DC: Government Printing Office, 1974–78.

*US Military Intelligence Reports: China, 1911–1941.* Frederick, MD: University Publications of America, 1982.

Van de Ven, Hans. "The Sino-Japanese War in History." In Peattie, Drea, and van de Ven, eds., *The Battle for China,* 446–66.

Van de Ven, Hans. "Stilwell in the Stocks: The Chinese Nationalists and the Allied Powers in the Second World War." *Asian Affairs,* 34, 3 (November 2003): 243–59.

Van de Ven, Hans. *War and Nationalism in China, 1925–1945.* London: RoutledgeCurzon, 2003.

Wakeman, Frederic. *Spymaster: Dai Li and the Chinese Secret Service.* Berkeley: University of California Press, 2003.

Wang, Ke-wen. "Kuomintang in Transition: Ideology and Factionalism in the Nationalist Revolution, 1924–1932." Ph.D. dissertation, Stanford University, Stanford, CA, 1986.

Wang, Shizhen. "The Whampoa Military Academy and the Rise of Chiang Kai-shek." MA thesis, University of Texas at Austin, 1982.

Wedemeyer, Albert C. *Wedemeyer Reports!* New York: Henry Holt and Company, 1958.

Wei, William. *Counterrevolution in China: The Nationalists in Jiangxi During the Soviet Period.* Ann Arbor: University of Michigan Press, 1985.

Westad, Odd Arne. *Decisive Encounters: The Chinese Civil War, 1946–1950.* Stanford: Stanford University Press, 2003.

Wheeler, William G. "The United Nations Military Staff Committee: Relic or Revival?" Unpublished paper. National War College, Washington, DC, 1994.

White, Theodore, ed. *The Stilwell Papers: General Joseph Stilwell's Iconoclastic Account of America's Adventures in China.* New York: Schocken Books, 1972.

White, Theodore and Annalee Jacoby. *Thunder out of China.* New York: William Sloane Associates, 1946.

Whitson, William, Patrick Yang and Paul Lai, eds. *Military Campaigns in China: 1924–1950.* Taipei: Office of the Military Historian, 1966.

Wilbur, C. Martin. *The Nationalist Revolution in China, 1923–1928.* Cambridge: Cambridge University Press, 1983.

Wilbur, C. Martin and Julie Lien-ying How. *Missionaries of Revolution: Soviet Advisors and Nationalist China, 1920–1927.* Cambridge, MA: Harvard University Press, 1989.

Worthing, Peter. "Continuity and Change: Chinese Nationalist Army Tactics, 1925–1938." *Journal of Military History,* 78, 3 (July 2014): 995–1016.

Worthing, Peter. *Occupation and Revolution: China and the Vietnamese August Revolution of 1945*. Berkeley: University of California at Berkeley Center for Chinese Studies, 2001.

Worthing, Peter. "The Road Through Whampoa: The Early Career of He Yingqin." *Journal of Military History*, 69, 4 (October 2005): 953–86.

Worthing, Peter. "Toward the Minjiu Incident: Militarist Conflict in Guizhou, 1911–1921." *Modern China*, 33, 2 (April 2007): 258–83.

Wortzel, Larry M. "The Beiping–Tianjin Campaign of 1948–1949: The Strategic and Operational Thinking of the People's Liberation Army." In Mark A. Ryan, David M. Finkelstein, and Michael A. McDevitt, eds., *Chinese Warfighting: The PLA Experience Since 1949*, 56–72. Armonk, NY: M. E. Sharpe, 2003.

Wu, Hsiang-hsiang. "Total Strategy Used by China and Some Major Engagements in the Sino-Japanese War of 1937–1945." In Sih, ed., *Nationalist China During the Sino-Japanese War, 1937–1945*, 37–80.

Wu, Shouqi and Jing Wu. "Some Remarks on Joseph Stilwell's Relationship with Jiang Jieshi." *Republican China*, 14, 2 (1989): 37–55.

Wu, T'ien-wei. "Contending Political Forces During the War of Resistance." In Hsiung and Levine, eds., *China's Bitter Victory*, 51–78.

Wu, T'ien-wei. "New Materials on the Xi'an Incident: A Bibliographic Review." *Modern China*, 10, 1 (January 1984): 115–41.

Wu, Tien-wei. *The Sian Incident: A Pivotal Turning Point in Modern Chinese History*. Ann Arbor: Center for Chinese Studies, University of Michigan, 1976.

Yang, Tianshi. "Chiang Kai-shek and the Battles of Shanghai and Nanjing." In Peattie, Drea and van de Ven, eds., *The Battle for China*, 143–58.

Zhao, Suisheng. *Power by Design: Constitution-Making in Nationalist China*. Honolulu: University of Hawaii Press, 1996.

Zhong, Yang. *Local Government and Politics in China: Challenges from Below*. Armonk , NY: M. E. Sharpe, 2003.

# Index